FRIEDRICH HÖLDERLIN

POEMS AND FRAGMENTS

TRANSLATED BY MICHAEL HAMBURGER

BI-LINGUAL EDITION WITH A PREFACE
INTRODUCTION AND NOTES

ANN ARBOR

THE UNIVERSITY OF MICHIGAN PRESS

Translated from the German
HÖLDERLIN: SÄMTLICHE WERKE
Stuttgart 1961

English translation
Copyright © by Michael Hamburger 1967

Library of Congress Catalog Card Number 66-11083

Published in the United States of America by
The University of Michigan Press
and simultaneously in Toronto, Canada, by
Ambassador Books Limited

Printed in Great Britain

HÖLDERLIN · POEMS AND FRAGMENTS

CONTENTS

PREFACE   *page* ix

INTRODUCTION   1

BIBLIOGRAPHICAL NOTE   18

ODES AND EPIGRAMS (1797-1799)   21
    Five Epigrams (1797)   23
    To Diotima   25
    Diotima   27
    Bonaparte   29
    Empedocles   31
    To the Fates   33
    Diotima   35
    To her Genius   37
    Plea for Forgiveness   39
    Then and Now   41
    The Course of Life   43
    Brevity   45
    Human Applause   47
    Home   49
    Good Faith   51
    Her Recovery   53
    The Unpardonable   55
    To the Young Poets   57
    To the Germans   59
    The Sanctimonious Poets   61
    To the Sun-God   63
    Sunset   65
    Socrates and Alcibiades   67
    To our Great Poets   69
    Five Epigrams (1799)   71

THE LATER ODES (1798-1803)   *page* 72

    Vanini   73

    Man   75

    Hyperion's Song of Fate   79

    In my boyhood days . . .   81

    If to those warning ones . . .   85

    The Capricious   87

    The Spirit of the Age   89

    Evening Fantasy   91

    In the Morning   93

    The River Main   95

    My Possessions   99

    Palinode   103

    To a Princess of Dessau   105

    To Princess Augusta   109

    Though every day I follow . . .   113

    Go down, then, lovely sun . . .   115

    Peace   117

    To the Germans   123

    Rousseau   129

    Heidelberg   133

    The Gods   137

    The Neckar   139

    Home   143

    Love   145

    The Course of Life   149

    Her Recovery   151

    The Farewell   153

    Diotima   157

    Return to the Homeland   159

    Exhortation   161

    Nature and Art   165

    Sung beneath the Alps   169

    The Poet's Vocation   173

    Voice of the People   179

The Blind Singer   *page* 185
Chiron   189
Tears   193
To Hope   195
Vulcan   197
The Poet's Courage   201
Timidness   205
The Fettered River   207
Ganymede   209

HEXAMETERS AND ELEGIES (1800-1801)   211
    The Archipelago   213
    Menon's Lament for Diotima   233
    Bread and Wine   243
    Homecoming   255

THE DEATH OF EMPEDOCLES (1799-1800)   263
    Second Version   265
    Third Version   323

THE HYMNS (1799-1803)   367
    The Ages of Life   369
    The Middle of Life   371
    As on a holiday . . .   373
    For Mother Earth   379
    At the Source of the Danube   385
    The Journey   393
    Germania   401
    The Rhine   409
    Conciliator, you that no longer believed in . . .   423
    Celebration of Peace   433
    The Only One   447
    Patmos   463
    Remembrance   489
    The Ister   493
    Mnemosyne   499

vii

FRAGMENTS OF OTHER HYMNS (1800-1805?)   *page* 503

    German Song   505

    As slowly birds migrate . . .   509

    Home   511

    For when the grape-vine's sap . . .   513

    On fallow foliage . . .   515

    What is the life of men . . .   517

    To the Virgin Mary   519

    The Titans   531

    At one time I questioned the Muse . . .   537

    The Eagle   541

    Whatever is nearest   545

    And to feel with the lives . . .   551

    For from the abyss . . .   553

    . . . the Vatican . . .   557

    Greece   561

POEMS OF HIS MADNESS (1805-1843)   571

    If from the distance . . .   573

    The Walk   577

    When down from heaven . . .   579

    To Zimmer   583

    Conviction   585

    The world's agreeable things . . .   587

    To Zimmer   589

    Fame   591

    Summer   593

    Autumn   595

    Winter   597

    Spring   599

    In lovely blueness . . .   601

NOTES   607

INDEX OF FIRST LINES (ENGLISH)   615

INDEX OF FIRST LINES (GERMAN)   618

INDEX OF TITLES (ENGLISH)   621

INDEX OF TITLES (GERMAN)   623

PREFACE

Nearly twenty-five years have passed since these translations were begun. Now that I consider my work on them to be finished at last, it may be useful to retrace some of the stages of their growth and so to explain very briefly how they came to be what they are—a kind of verse translation by no means favoured in our time. To answer the related question of why I chose this particular poet, or was chosen by this particular poet, and devoted more time to him than to any other, would call for a chapter of autobiography. All that need be said here is that my repeated attempts to translate his work have to do with an attachment that has withstood all my changes of heart and mind over the best part of a quarter century, but also, increasingly, with 'the fascination of what's difficult'. Hölderlin is not only a difficult poet in himself, but a poet far removed from the main traditions and habits of English poetry. It was the very difficulty and remoteness of his best work that acted as a challenge to make it accessible, palpable, perhaps even tenantable, in English.

My earliest attempts to translate Hölderlin go back to my school and university years, and the first selection, *Poems of Hölderlin*, appeared in 1943. The Preface to that edition, written at the age of eighteen, contains the following statement: 'My aim, in these translations, was to reproduce the poems as literally as possible, and I was therefore at times obliged to sacrifice regularity of metre and also, perhaps, much of the musical quality of the originals, upon which their beauty and appeal largely depend. I consider these offences less unforgivable than an intrusion of the translator's idiosyncrasies into the author's work. Any substitution or grafting on of images, similes and thoughts by the translator seems to me like an act of trespass, and I have tried throughout to avoid these faults, at the risk of committing others.'

What disturbs me now in these words is a rather priggish dogmatism and rigour, the insistence on a general principle—and a moralistic principle at that—to justify tendencies which now seem to me to have been due as much to inexperience and lack of skill as to a genuine constraint imposed on me by a puritanical temper. My earliest renderings were metrically free because the classical metres of Hölderlin were still far from being second nature to me; but they could not be 'free verse', because such imagination and skill as I had were cramped by the constraint to be literally accurate. All that can be said for them is that they served their purpose, to provide a small, but representative, selection of poems by Hölderlin for English readers still ignorant of his work.

For the second edition, published in 1952, I added more poems and substituted new versions of those previously included. It had become clear to me in the meantime that no translation of Hölderlin's odes and elegies can be close to the originals without rendering their metres or at least their cadences, and conveying something of their peculiar dynamism, their peculiar stillness, brought about by the tension between a strict form and an impulse beating against it like Hölderlin's rivers against their banks. Again I quote from the Preface: 'Though the translator has adhered to his general principles, he has now attempted to combine literal fidelity with greater respect for the form of the originals. This has led to the occasional use of inversion, a poetic resort which, however objectionable in itself, is justified in this case by Hölderlin's own practice.'

I shall have more to say about Hölderlin's use and theoretical defence of inversion, which apply only to the later work included in my various selections. As for the general principles—which I should now prefer to call a general tendency—they have been modified in the course of those twenty-five years, and were substantially modified even between the first and the second attempt; but since they are not so much principles as rationalizations of a personal disposition, they are not wholly irrelevant even to my latest attempts. 'As you began, so you will remain,' Hölderlin declared in *The Rhine*, and though puritanism mellows in time, my approach to Hölderlin's poems has remained as constant in essentials as my admiration for his work and my desire to produce the best possible translation of a certain kind. Even my prose versions, published in the Penguin Poets series in 1961, did not stray very far from the dominant tendency, since they were based on verse renderings—many of which appear for the first time in the present edition—and I could not help insinuating some of the original verse cadences into what claimed and seemed to be paragraphs of 'plain prose'.

All my successive versions, then, have tended towards a kind of translation that is neither free imitation nor strict metaphrase—to use Dryden's still valid term—but something in between. Dryden called his middle way 'paraphrase', and many other writers on the subject agree in positing three distinct kinds of verse translation. Yet 'paraphrase', to modern ears, suggests a process more applicable to prose, just as the kind of imitation practised by English translators of Dryden's time rests on the assumption not only of the need to adapt foreign poets to the current modes and proprieties of English verse, but the assumption that what a poet said can be separated from the manner in which he said it. After my first attempt, with its pedantic insistence on metaphrase, the literal crib was ruled out as surely as the free imitation in Hölderlin's case, precisely because what he said is inseparable from his beautifully singular way of saying it.

In an age like ours, in which personal idiosyncrasy has replaced the general modes and proprieties of Dryden's—or any classical—age, free imitation has become something incomparably more free than the metrical transpositions which Dryden had in mind. The translations of Dryden's contemporaries and successors may have ironed out some of the individuality of their models, but they did so in the interest of a taste common to all their readers, not in order to impose the translator's individuality on that of his model; and no imitator in our time can avoid doing just that if he is a poet with a manner and sensibility of his own. Free imitation, in our time, has become a kind of occupational therapy for poets partly or temporarily disabled. I have no quarrel with it, and have enjoyed many of its products; but, as the imitators themselves insist, these products are to be judged as poems in their own right, preferably without reference to the original texts. In other words, they are not to be judged as translations at all, but as part of the opus of the imitators; and the crux of the difference between translation and imitation lies in the degree of appropriation involved in either process.

Even in my latest—and last—renderings I have stuck to my unfashionable habit of trying to get under the original poet's skin, rather than exhibiting the effects on my own skin of exposure to his work. I believe that this makes me roughly what Mr. Robert Lowell has called a 'taxidermist' translator; that is to say, I do not appropriate my text to the extent of transposing it into my own idiom, my own favourite verse forms and my own favourite imagery, but treat it as a phenomenon different in kind from anything I could ever produce. Though I will often adapt a passage where I feel that a literal rendering would create an effect different from that intended by the poet— for national, historical or other extraneous reasons—my overall purpose is to reproduce even those peculiarities of his diction, form and way of thinking and feeling which are alien both to myself and to English conventions obtaining either in his time or in ours. My assumption is that the reader who cannot cope with the original text does not want my personal response to it as much as he wants to get as close as possible to the text itself, for this is my first requirement in reading translations from languages which I do not know.

Apart from the risk of misinterpreting their texts without being able to claim, as the imitators frequently do, that they misinterpreted them on purpose, translators of my sort run the risk of being dismissed as pedestrian and pedantic. The imitators run other risks, and I am concerned not with the relative merits and shortcomings of the two procedures, but with their utterly different starting-points and destinations. Yet I believe that renderings of the kind I have attempted can work as poetry no less than free imitations do, if the reader approaches them with the right expectations; that is, if he reads them as poems necessarily different from any written in his own language, in his own time. Contrary to what the imitators assert, this adjustment is no more difficult than the adjustment required for the reading of any original work remote in space, time or 'ambiance'; it is part of the very business of reading, and imitations, too, demand it, though the adjustment they call for will be to the imitator's manner and vision, rather than to the original poet's.

I have mentioned the risk of misinterpretation. This is especially acute in the case of Hölderlin's later poems, which are unconventional to a degree scarcely equalled in his time, with the possible exception of William Blake. (Hölderlin's awareness of their originality is attested in his little preface to *The Celebration of Peace*, a poem never published until its discovery ten years ago; the preface, too, was addressed to deaf ears.) Above all, the structure and syntax of these late poems are deliberately designed to run counter to the structure and syntax of discursive statement. They are designed not only to convey meaning, but also to 'circumscribe' it, even at times to suspend or withhold it, so as to touch upon a strictly unutterable mystery. Ellipse and inversion of normal syntax are two of the principal devices deliberately adopted by Hölderlin to this end. His study of Greek poetry, especially the poetry of Pindar, led him to radical departures from prose logic on which he commented as follows: 'It is common practice to have inversions of word order within the period. But clearly much greater effects can be obtained by the inversion of the periods themselves. The logical order of periods, in which the basis (the basic period) is followed by its development, the development by its culmination, the culmination by its purpose, and subsidiary clauses are merely appended to the main clauses to which they primarily apply—all this can only rarely serve the poet's ends.' The choice of the word 'primarily' in this context points to Hölderlin's awareness of ambiguity as a distinguishing feature of poetic statement. In translating these late poems, therefore, I had to try not only to clarify certain passages so obscure as to have baffled and divided the scholarly commentators—simply because these passages could not be translated at all without such clarification—but also to refrain from interpreting other passages, so as to preserve their essential ambiguity. One instance occurs in the poem *The Only One*. In the lines

> Denn zu sehr
> O Christus! häng' ich an dir,
> Wiewohl Herakles Bruder

ellipse and lack of punctuation serve to create an equipoise between two possible meanings of the reference to Heracles. According to conventional grammar—and according to Professor Friedrich Beissner, the eminent Hölderlin scholar, editor and commentator—the poet is claiming Heracles as his own brother, not as the brother of Christ. Though I incline to the opposite view, and translated the lines accordingly in my earlier versions, it seemed best not to resolve the ambiguity, which is left intact here. How far Hölderlin was prepared to go in his inversion and contraction of normal syntax is most evident in the opening lines of the later version of *Patmos*. In this extraordinary period the subject, 'God', is not only suspended until the end, but also made to serve as the object of a second statement in the process.

The greatest difficulty confronting any translator of verse is that of evolving a diction and style not only consonant with his texts—and Hölderlin's mature poetry has so wide a range of diction and style as to anticipate possibilities developed more than a century later—but also consistent in themselves. Here the imitator would seem to enjoy a considerable advantage, for he is free to disregard historical 'ambiance' and turn Homeric heroes into gangsters or teddy-boys. Yet even the imitators fall into the most blatant inconsistencies of idiom. The characters in Ezra Pound's *Women of Trachis*, for instance, command a gamut of idioms that extends from the American vernacular to outmoded upper-class English slang and archaisms current in the verse of the 1890s. It is a powerful and a rich mixture, but whatever else it is, it is not consistent. Hölderlin's diction, though consistent in itself, evolved from the poetic diction of his eighteenth-century German masters, especially Klopstock and Schiller, towards a starkness and directness derived partly from Greek models, partly from Hölderlin's own intensely and radically original sensibility, which brought him close at times to what twentieth-century poets have done or tried to do. Except in his epigrams, modern slang had to be avoided throughout, because slang is a convention, and Hölderlin's diction gradually discarded every sort of convention—whether rhetorical and sublime or colloquial and worldly—so as to render a vision as pure as it was solitary. For the sake of what is timeless in Hölderlin I was willing to preserve much that is contrary to the twentieth-century mood—his apostrophes to Nature and other cosmic powers, for instance, though I have toned these down a little here and there—since the full effect of what is new in his diction could be conveyed only by juxtaposition with the more conventional elements.

The two dramatic fragments, *The Death of Empedocles*, are a case in point. These are the outcome of a singular fusion of a partly historical, partly mythical figure of the fifth century B.C. with the vision and aspirations of a German contemporary of Wordsworth. The form, structure and diction correspond to that singular fusion of ancient and modern elements. If my blank verse here has a tendency towards Miltonic involutions at times, towards a laconic bareness at others, this is a characteristic of Hölderlin's own manner (and, incidentally, even of Milton's in *Samson Agonistes*, one of the very few modern dramatic works with which Hölderlin's can be profitably compared),* not a resort on my part either to an archaic rhetoric or to a twentieth-century informality. Hölderlin applied his important principle of 'the modulation of tones' to his drama as well as to his poems; his plan for the third version includes specifications for the tone of each scene in terms of his own categories (as worked out in his essays *Über die verschiedenen Arten zu Dichten* and *Wechsel der Töne*). Another short prose piece by Hölderlin deals with the necessary combination and alternation of the tragic, epic and lyric modes in any poetic work, whatever its dominant kind; and it is no accident that Empedocles, in the third version of his play, praises Egyptian lyrical poetry for its modulations. In Hölderlin's hymns, too, the triadic structure derived from Pindar's odes is brought out not by metrical correspondence (except in his single experiment in strict Pindaric form, *Wie wenn am Feiertage* . . .), but by the alternation of modes or tones, heroic, elegiac and idyllic; and each of these modes or tones requires a diction of its own. A good example of the transition occurs towards the end of *Celebration of Peace*, with a striking modulation to

*See my essay *The Sublime Art* in *The Living Milton* (Ed. Frank Kermode, London, 1960), pp. 141-61.

shorter lines and an idyllic, naïve vocabulary in the tenth strophe, or fourth triad.

As for the metres of Hölderlin's odes and elegies, it has been generally assumed ever since the sixteenth century that these do not lend themselves to English adaptation. I say adaptation because of the vexed question of whether any modern use of metres originally quantitative can be more than an adaptation of those metres. That the classical hexameter can be adapted just as successfully in English as it has been in German was proved by Arthur Hugh Clough in his *Amours de Voyage*. It may well be that other English poets were put off these metres not only by the general prejudice against them but also by the notions of high seriousness and stilted sublimity that need never have attached to them. To Hölderlin, in any case, they became as natural and congenial a medium as rhymed iambics were to other poets, or to Hölderlin himself in his early years, when he was imitating Schiller, and again in his madness. In every case the medium was inseparable from his themes. The rhymed 'hymn' forms of his early twenties—no example of which is included here—represented a secularized, humanistic sequel to the poetry of religious enthusiasm; the brief rhymed poems of his madness a relapse into simple piety after the heroic and tragic exertions of his visionary 'colonization' of ancient Greece.

It is this colonization which the odes, elegies, hexameters and free-verse hymns both record and enact, in metres and rhythms exactly attuned to the successive stages of the undertaking, including the final homecoming and return to the 'source', origin and point of departure, as predicted in the early epigrammatic ode *The Course of Life*. Of the two ode forms preferred by Hölderlin, the Alcaic is the more suited to his lyrical or tragic modulations—he himself spoke of 'tragic odes'—the Asclepiadean the more suited to the exposition of an epigrammatic or dialectic theme. In a single instance, the Asclepiadean ode *Heidelberg*, it proved unsatisfactory to render Hölderlin's own metre; and a few of the other longer Asclepiadean odes proved recalcitrant in English. Though Hölderlin did succeed in making these odes flow on as lyrically as his alcaics, despite the awkward caesuras, many of his longer odes in this metre are continuations or developments of earlier epigrammatic odes, and it seems unlikely that he would have chosen the Asclepiadean metre but for this circumstance. It is the Alcaic form that invites naturalization in English—by which I do not mean self-conscious exercises in the grand manner like Tennyson's *Milton*—and more than one contemporary English poet has already shown that it is quite as amenable to English speech rhythms as the long-established, only too familiar, iambic.

For all I know, it may be a residual puritanism that has kept most of my later versions so close to the cadences and sense of the original poems. What I can be quite sure about is that every effort to improve my earlier versions has led to a still closer approximation to both—even in a free-verse fragment like *The Middle of Life*, which no amount of pedantry could have prevented me from rendering as freely as I pleased. Yet Hölderlin's rhythms were exactly right; the slightest change in cadence or word order might well upset the masterly balance of those few poignant images or blur some delicate modulation. The important thing, in the end, was to be guided not by an overall principle of literalness or invention, but by a spontaneous response to each poem's mood and quiddity, as well as by a sense of fitness no different from that which governs one's choice of words in any piece of writing. Other poets demand a greater measure of transposition, very often because they drew on stock devices and images that are interchangeable, as Hölderlin's hardly ever were after the apprentice work with which I was not concerned.

The present volume contains all the poetry of Hölderlin's mature years which I have been moved to translate. It includes by far the greater part of his odes in classical metres, the most characteristic of his later elegies, his long poem in classical hexameters *The Archipelago* and all his free-verse hymns, as well as many fragments of hymns and a representative selection from the poems of his madness. Of the three unfinished versions of his tragedy *The Death of Empedocles*, the second and third have been chosen, not only because they are shorter than the first but because they complement and illumine the lyrical poetry of the same critical years. Since the Introduction and notes had to be kept as short as possible, there was no space for extensive quotations from the novel *Hyperion*, the philosophical and critical essays or the letters. This gap will have to be filled by a companion volume of selections from Hölderlin's prose works; but the present volume omits little of the poetry written at the height of his creative power, in the six prolific years that preceded his mental collapse.

M.H.

September, 1964

INTRODUCTION

Johann Friedrich Hölderlin was born in the small Swabian town of Lauffen on the Neckar on March 20th, 1770. His father, the manager of estates belonging to the Lutheran Church, died soon after, in 1772. Two years later his mother remarried, and the family moved to Nürtingen, where her second husband was burgomaster. Hölderlin attended the local grammar school until 1784. His step-father had died in 1779, leaving Hölderlin·uncommonly dependent on his mother.* He remained deeply (if ambivalently) attached to her, as well as to his grandmother, his younger sister and his half-brother, Karl Gock. In 1784 Hölderlin entered the Lower Monastery School at Denkendorf, two years later the Upper Monastery School at Maulbronn. (Despite the name, both were Protestant institutions.)

From 1788 to 1793 he studied for his ordination at the Theological Seminary at Tübingen. There he founded a Poetry Association together with his friends Neuffer and Magenau, who shared his sympathy with the French Revolution, and formed friendships with two other fellow students who were to become eminent philosophers, Hegel and Schelling. As early as 1787 he became engaged to Luise Nast, the cousin of a school friend, but broke off the engagement in 1790. At Tübingen he fell in love with Elise Lebret, but by this time he knew that he would not take up the profession for which he was intended and might never be in a position to support a family. In the autumn of 1789 he had gone so far as to ask his mother's permission to leave the university, but was persuaded to stay on, wrote theses on the History of the Fine Arts in Greece and on the Parallels between the Proverbs of Solomon and Hesiod's *Works and Days*, as well as a great deal of poetry, obtained his degree of 'Magister' and passed·his final examinations in theology.

*His later schizophrenia has been traced to the emotional tensions of his childhood and youth by several biographers and psychologists, most recently in a Freudian study by Dr. Jean Laplanche, *Hölderlin et la Question du Père* (Paris, 1961).

1

Though Hölderlin was never to become a Lutheran minister, the kind of education he received is far from being irrelevant to his poetry. The harmonious blending of theological and classical studies that characterized Denkendorf, Maulbronn and Tübingen had a formative influence on his conception of poetry and of the poet's function. There may even be a vital connection between the peculiarities of Swabian theology, such as the millenarian and mystical doctrines of Bengel and Oetinger, and some of Hölderlin's chiliastic visions. Professor Robert Minder has written a brilliant summary of a theological tradition which he traces not only to Hölderlin but also to Hegel and Karl Marx.* Another critic has shown that Hölderlin's was the 'typical Renaissance view of the *poeta theologus* or *sacer vates*', relating it to that of poets from Tasso, Ronsard and Sidney to Milton and Klopstock.† The inner gate of the Tübingen Seminary bore the inscription *Aedes Deo et Musis Sacrae*, and it was Hölderlin's privilege and burden to dedicate himself to the same dual service when this Renaissance tradition was very close to extinction. The subject of the comparative study which Hölderlin wrote at Tübingen is significant. Because of his essential syncretism, it could be said of Hölderlin, as Hazlitt said of Milton, that 'he had his thoughts constantly fixed on the contemplation of Hebrew theocracy, and of a perfect commonwealth', even though it was the theocracy of an idealized Greece that Hölderlin much more frequently invoked in later years; and also that 'his religious zeal infused its character into his imagination, so that he devoted himself with the same sense of duty to the cultivation of his genius, as he did to the exercise of virtue, or the good of his country'. To these attributes of the *sacer vates*—complicated in Hölderlin's case by his fervent pantheism and his need, at one time, to come to terms with the latest trends in German philosophy—we must add the religious radicalism that prevented both Milton and Hölderlin from making a 'trade' of their religious vocation. Both were deterred by 'a conscience that would retch', as Milton put it, though their more specific reasons for

*'*Herrlichkeit*' chez Hegel, ou le Monde des Pères Souabes, in *Etudes Germaniques*, July-December 1951, pp. 225-90.
†L. S. Salzberger: *Hölderlin* (Cambridge, 1952), pp. 8-12.

2

preferring a 'blameless silence' were as different as the characters of the two men, their beliefs and their aspirations.

Even in his childhood Hölderlin had been moody, hypersensitive and subject to waves of extreme depression or elation. He was devoted to his friends—an enthusiastic and sentimental cult of friendship was common in late-eighteenth-century Germany—but found it hard to be sociable in a general way. His ode *Mein Vorsatz*, written when he was seventeen, shows how acutely aware he was at this early time that his poetic vocation and ambition set him apart even from his closest friends:

MY RESOLUTION

O friends, my friends, who love me so loyally,
   What is it that so troubles my lonely gaze?
     What makes my wretched heart seek refuge
       Here in this gloomy and deathly stillness?

I flee the tender clasp of your hands, avoid
   The soulful, happy touch of a brother's lips.
     O don't be angry, friends, forgive me!—
       Look at my innermost self, then judge me!—

Is it hot thirst for manly perfection, then?
   A quiet greed for fame and a hecatomb?
     A feeble urge to Pindar's flight? Or
       Strenuous striving for Klopstock's greatness?

Ah, friends, where can I hide, to what corner of
   The earth escape, and wrapped in perpetual night
     Weep there? For never I shall know the
       World-encompassing wings of genius.

And yet I will, I'll climb the steep path to fame!
   Climb on, climb on in ardent and reckless dreams
     Of reaching them; I will, though dying
       Faintly I mutter, forget me, children!

3

If we also take into account Hölderlin's increasing Hellenism and his political radicalism in these years it is not surprising that he preferred the humble drudgery, but relative independence, of a private tutor to the clerical duties for which he was qualified, and which he would do almost anything to avoid in later life. With the help of his friends and of Schiller, who remained Hölderlin's hero and patron for some years, he obtained the position of tutor to the son of Charlotte von Kalb, whose literary interests and connections made her a most congenial employer. In her home at Waltershausen, where he lived from the winter of 1793 to the following summer, Hölderlin worked at an early version of his novel *Hyperion*. In the autumn he took his pupil to Jena, attended Fichte's philosophical lectures, saw a good deal of Schiller and met several other prominent German writers, including Goethe. An early fragment of the novel was published by Schiller in his periodical *Thalia*.

Meanwhile Hölderlin's pupil proved intractable; Charlotte von Kalb sent them both to Weimar, then enabled Hölderlin to live independently at Jena and Nürtingen until the summer of 1795. He continued his work on *Hyperion*, on the philosophical 'hymns' of those years—rhymed poems very close to the manner of Schiller and dedicated to 'the ideals of humanity'—and on a translation from Ovid.

In December 1795 he was appointed tutor to the children of J. F. Gontard, a wealthy banker at Frankfurt, whose wife Susette became the 'Diotima' of Hölderlin's poems. Recent research has suggested that Hölderlin had entered into a liaison at Waltershausen with Wilhelmine Marianne Kirms, a young widow who acted as a companion to Charlotte von Kalb, and that he may have been the father of her daughter born in July 1795. (The child died of smallpox in the following year.) If so, he looked upon this affair as a mere lapse on his part. His love for Susette Gontard was of a different order, as all the Diotima poems and *Hyperion* show, though the most conclusive testimony to her influence is the change of style in the brief odes of 1797. After the wordiness and stock metaphors of the rhymed 'hymns', Hölderlin had found a living embodiment of his ideals. The diffuse diction of generalized enthusiasm began to crystallize.

In 1796 Susette, her four children, her mother-in-law and Hölderlin were forced to leave Frankfurt for Westphalia to escape the invading French Army. Gontard stayed behind in Frankfurt. At Kassel they were joined by Wilhelm Heinse, the author of *Ardinghello*, a novel that influenced Hölderlin's view of ancient Greece; it was to Heinse that he later addressed and dedicated the most Dionysian of his poems, the elegy *Brod und Wein*. In the following year, after their return to Frankfurt, Hegel also became a tutor there. Hölderlin met Goethe once more, at Schiller's recommendation, but the rather formal interview was not to Hölderlin's advantage, and Goethe remained unaware both of Hölderlin's gifts and of his best work. The first volume of *Hyperion* was published in 1797.

Hölderlin's novel *Hyperion* shares many of the peculiarities of his poems, but especially a tendency towards a cyclic progression that has been compared to the dialectic progression through thesis and anti-thesis to synthesis. This cyclic structure may have something to do with Hölderlin's vacillating moods and his complaint, 'if only one were not so periodical!' Yet in his tragic odes as in his novel Hölderlin's pantheism, his desire to be at one with the cosmos, continually comes up against his awareness not only of the essential differences between man and the rest of Nature but also of the isolation into which the individual man is precipitated by his consciousness. This awareness, confirmed by the philosophic preoccupations of Hölderlin's con-temporaries Fichte, Hegel and Schelling, accounts for those moments in *Hyperion* which shock the reader by their unexpected cynicism, their sharp dualism and almost nihilistic despair.

'Man is a god when he dreams, a beggar when he reflects,' Hyperion writes in the novel. Dreaming here means the state of mind that permits communion with Nature; reflection, the self-consciousness that cuts off the individual from the rest of creation. It is the alterna-tion of these states of mind, with characteristic variations or modula-tions and a gradual progression towards synthesis or reconciliation, that gives *Hyperion* a structure unlike that of any comparable novel. (Hölderlin chose an astronomical term, 'the eccentric orbit', to describe his mode of progression.) Hyperion's dualism is elaborated in another passage: 'There is an oblivion of all existence, a silencing of all individual being, in which it seems that we have found all things.

'There is a silencing, an oblivion of all existence, in which it seems that we have lost all things, a night of the soul in which not the faintest gleam of a star, not even the phosphorescence of rotten wood, can reach us.'

When Hyperion is plunged into this negative state of mind—and all his experiences as a fighter for the liberation of Greece from the Turks, and even as a lover and friend, are conducive to it—what had been 'all' before suddenly turns to nothing; he becomes like one of those persons whom he pities for being 'in the grip of that Nothing which rules over us, who are thoroughly aware that we are born for Nothing, believe in a Nothing, work ourselves to the bone for a Nothing, until we gradually dissolve into Nothing . . . .'

Hölderlin's love for his Diotima was religious because love itself is a unifying principle and power. As such it is celebrated not only in the poems to Diotima and in *Hyperion* but throughout his work and in poems with no personal context. Hölderlin's involuntary separation from Susette Gontard was bound to exacerbate his sense of isolation and division, to the point of undermining his already precarious idealism. Both his idealism and his humanism rested on the One and All of antiquity, rather than on the rationalism of modern progressive creeds. When his sense of isolation became extreme, Hölderlin's work entered a distinctly tragic phase.

It is of the utmost significance that his very definition of tragedy hinged on the same antithesis of union and separation. A lyric poem, Hölderlin wrote, is 'the continuous metaphor of a feeling'. A tragic poem, on the other hand, is 'the metaphor of an intellectual point of view', and this intellectual point of view 'can be none other than the awareness of being at one with all that lives'. The hero of Hölderlin's own unfinished tragedy, Empedocles, resembles his Hyperion in being a pantheist with a mission to inspire and unite a whole people; but in *The Death of Empedocles* the stress had to fall on the hero's total separation from all that he loves, not only from the Agrigentines and his favourite disciple but even from Nature and the gods, from the

6

very cosmos with which he had felt at one. After the play, Hölderlin's pantheism itself became modified by a sense of hubris, as though the downfall of his hero had taught Hölderlin himself that the mystery of Nature must remain unspoken, unrevealed. Here it is relevant to quote his later, profound and cryptic definition of the tragic (from his commentary on his translation of *Oedipus Rex*): 'The representation of the tragic is mainly based on this, that what is monstrous and terrible in the coupling of god and man, in the total fusion of the power of Nature with the innermost depth of man, so that they are one at the moment of wrath, shall be made intelligible by showing how this total fusion into one is purged by their total separation.'

It was in 1797 that Hölderlin began work on his tragedy *The Death of Empedocles*. An earlier dramatic project, *The Death of Socrates*, is mentioned in his correspondence, and several of his friends and contemporaries believed that he wrote a tragedy called *Agis*; not a line remains of either work. The first version of *The Death of Empedocles*, mainly written in 1798, comprises an almost complete first act and the greater part of a second act, though even this largest fragment shows *lacunae* and passages never intended to be definitive. (All three versions were conceived as a five-act tragedy.) The second version, mainly of 1799, differs both in plot and execution from the first. Unlike the earlier and later versions, it is written not in so-called iambic pentameters but in a shortened, predominantly iambic line that allows considerable rhythmic and metric variation—so much so that it is sometimes described as free verse. Professor Beissner believes that Hölderlin may have completed more of the second version than the extant fragments (which, thanks to Beissner's recent edition, now include part of a second act).

Hölderlin himself did not publish so much as an extract from any of the three versions. Hence the great difficulty of establishing an authentic text from the extant manuscripts. The plot, tone, style and conception of each version are wholly distinct. Between the second and third versions Hölderlin wrote his reflections on this dramatic project and on tragedy in general, *Grund zum Empedokles*. The essay helps us to understand why the basic conception of the third version was

7

totally different from that of the first and second. The planned introduction of a Chorus is only one instance of the much closer approximation in the last version to Hölderlin's Greek models, a shift that had begun in the second version, with its much greater stress, as compared with the first, on Empedocles' sin of hubris. As the essay confirms, in the process of writing the three successive versions Hölderlin became more and more aware of the dramatist's need to remain partly detached from his hero—to be objective, as he called it, and able to place himself at one remove from that 'deepest inwardness' which the tragic dramatic poem must convey even more dialectically than the tragic ode—Hölderlin's principal medium up to that time (apart from the novel, with its intimate and wholly 'subjective' self-identification).

Yet the main reason why Hölderlin finished no version of the play is undoubtedly that he remained too closely identified with Empedocles, at the very period of his life when his own view of the poet as philosopher, prophet and priest, and as tragic hero, was subject to perpetual crisis and re-examination. The special significance for Hölderlin of Empedocles' mode of death—involving, as it did, a physical fusion with the primal elements and a return to the very womb of Earth—is already evident in the short ode *Empedocles* (p. 31); but the increasing emphasis on his hero's guilt in the successive versions of the play also has its parallels in his later lyrical poetry—most nakedly and poignantly in the prose draft that abruptly cuts off his Pindaric hymn *As on a holiday* . . ., a poem contemporary with the last version of the play and almost identical with it in places. In the prose draft Hölderlin accuses himself of a hubris very much like that of which Manes accuses Empedocles. This is the prose draft in question:

when of

(a self-inflicted wound my heart is bleeding, and deeply lost
is peace of mind, and freely modest contentment,
And when unrest and deficiency drive me to
the superabundance of the banqueting table of gods,
when round about me . . .)

8

More remarkably still, Manes' characterization of the true saviour—as opposed to the hubristic pantheist, Empedocles—seems to point to that image of Christ which Hölderlin was to invoke in his elegies and hymns of the next years. Another way of putting it is that the play had to keep up with Hölderlin's own prodigious development in the years between 1797 and 1800, and that each version, therefore, ceased to be valid for him before it could be completed. It is even conceivable that, just as Empedocles had displaced Socrates in Hölderlin's sympathy and imagination, a still worthier hero had displaced Empedocles by the time that Hölderlin had mastered the laws of tragedy—and by then only a short respite remained for the writing of his last extraordinary hymns and fragments. But it is best to take up his biography again at this point.

After an unpleasant scene in the autumn of 1798 Hölderlin left the Gontard household and settled nearby at Homburg. He corresponded with Susette, and for a time they arranged secret meetings. At Homburg Hölderlin made the acquaintance of Isaak von Sinclair, the most helpful and loyal of his friends in later years. It was Sinclair who introduced Hölderlin to the Landgrave of Hessen-Homburg, whose daughter Princess Auguste appears to have been in love with Hölderlin, though the poet never knew it. Apart from the ode addressed to her she received the dedication of the very last work he prepared for publication before his total breakdown, his translations of the *Oedipus Rex* and *Antigone* of Sophocles. The Landgrave himself and Sinclair received the dedications of two of Hölderlin's greatest poems, *Patmos* and *The Rhine*.

1799 was a productive but critical year. For the first and last time Hölderlin did his utmost to establish himself as a self-supporting writer and to find the place which he thought was due to him in the intellectual and cultural life of Germany. He planned to edit a 'humanistic journal', *Iduna*, which would be devoted to 'the unification and reconciliation of the sciences with life, of art and good taste with genius, of the heart with the head, of the real with the ideal'—to the very ends, in fact, which were Hölderlin's deepest concern and which he believed to be crucial to the poet's religious and social

9

function. His choice of antinomies here related his personal conflicts to a dichotomy familiar enough to his age, after the revolutionary impact of Rousseau's thought, the cult of primitive genius in Herder and the literature of the *Sturm und Drang*, and the general tendency to posit an irreconcilable conflict between Nature and Art (or civilization). Schiller, too, was obsessed by it, and so were the foremost German philosophers of Hölderlin's time. Goethe alone could justly claim to have overcome it, though, in its own way, Hölderlin's poetry achieved a remarkable fusion of head and heart, of the real and the ideal, of 'Reason and Energy', as William Blake called two of his antinomies. The failure of Hölderlin's humanistic project, and of his appeal to Schiller to obtain an academic post for him, amounted to nothing less than his rejection by society. From now on Hölderlin felt himself to be a lonely outcast, like his hero Empedocles or the Rousseau of his ode, and as a prophet without honour in his own country. His poems of the next few years record the alienation, as do his letters and the three *Empedocles* fragments.

The second volume of *Hyperion* was published in 1799, and a number of Hölderlin's poems continued to appear in various periodicals and almanacs; but Hölderlin felt more and more isolated, more and more remote from the literature and culture of his time, which, in one of the last letters written before his madness, he described as 'childlike'. The last creative years before his madness show yet another transition—that from a tragic to a prophetic phase. The transition can be followed in several of his late odes, such as *Exhortation* or *Nature and Art*; and even the last version of *The Death of Empedocles* belongs more to his prophetic, than to his tragic phase, since the hero seems to have undergone a profound catharsis before the opening scene. It was as though in the year of extreme loneliness, frustration and self-doubt that followed his departure from Frankfurt —and one must not forget the humiliation inflicted on Hölderlin through his dismissal not only as an employee but also as a lover powerless to assert his claims—Hölderlin could preserve his faith only by renouncing all his own ambitions and attachments, to the point of giving up himself and becoming a disembodied voice crying out to 'future ages'. Hölderlin wrote to his half-brother in 1801 that he 'had struggled to the point of exhaustion to fix my faith and my vision upon that which is supreme in life; indeed I had struggled amid sufferings which—to judge by all the evidence that I know— were more overwhelming than anything that men are capable of enduring, though they exert their utmost strength. . . . At last, when my heart was already rent on more than one side, and yet held fast, I must also be induced to embroil my thoughts in those evil doubts, that question so easily answered if only one's eyes are clear, namely what is more important, the eternal fountainhead of all life or the temporal. . . . But I continued to struggle till I found out the truth. . . . There is only one quarrel in this world: which is more important, the whole or the individual part. And that quarrel, in every instance and application, is proved invalid in action, because the man who truly acts out of a sense of the whole is more dedicated to peace for that very reason, more disposed to honour every individual person and thing, because his sense of humanity, the very quality that distinguishes him, will sooner permit him to fall into egoism—or whatever you choose to call it—than into pure generality.

'*A Deo principium*. Whoever understands this, and lives up to it . . . . that man is free and strong and full of joy.'

This renewed faith sustained Hölderlin's prophetic, and increasingly impersonal, poetry, but it could not alleviate his personal solitude. Thanking his sister in 1800 for writing to remind him of their family bonds, he tells her that 'this sustains my heart, which in the end too often loses its own voice in a solitude all too complete, and withdraws from our very selves'. The voice of the heart—a phrase that also occurs in one of Hölderlin's odes—is more than a sentimental trope in a poet who believed that the capacity to feel determines human relations with the gods. Yet in another sense the quarrel between the whole and the part of which he speaks in the later letter was truly resolved in his poetry. If he had once been in acute danger of falling into 'pure generality', because his youthful idealism had shied away from particulars and had been jolted again and again by the modern dichotomy between subjective and objective

11

reality, the poetry of his prophetic phase became more and more physical, more and more sensuous, more and more concrete. Already in the various drafts of his ode *Des Morgens* (1799) we see how 'the leaves of the trees' becomes 'the poplar bends', then 'the birch-tree bends', finally 'the beech-tree bends'; but it is in the visionary landscapes of the hymns—whether drawn from direct experience or from imagination and literary sources, like the Greek landscapes he had never seen—that he succeeded best in honouring 'every individual person and thing', just because each is imbued with a 'sense of the whole'. His growing interest in history and local tradition was part of the same development.

At Homburg Hölderlin took up his Greek studies in a more critical and methodical manner than before, and began to formulate his own ideas about the differences between ancient and modern literature and the laws governing epic, dramatic and lyric poetry. In the spring of 1800 he went home to Nürtingen, then stayed at Stuttgart as the guest of his friend Landauer. He returned to Nürtingen for the rest of the year, and set out for Hauptwyl in Switzerland in January 1801, to take up another post as tutor. He was back at Nürtingen by April and spent the rest of that year at his mother's house or at Stuttgart.

In January 1802 he left for his last appointment as a private tutor, at Bordeaux. There, too, he spent only a few months, returning home in July in a state of acute mental illness. The circumstances and events of his last journey remain obscure. Susette Gontard had died on June 22nd, but Hölderlin can hardly have known of her death until after his return.

There is one letter written after his return from Bordeaux that conveys something of the strange state of mind in which he wrote the last of the hymns and fragments, and of the impact on him of his journey to France. It is the letter, or draft of a letter, to Casimir Ulrich Böhlendorff, written in the autumn of 1802:

> *Dear friend,*
>   *I have not written to you for a long time, and meanwhile have been in France and have seen the sad, lonely earth; the shepherds*

and shepherdesses of southern France and individual beauties, men and women, who grew up in the fear of political uncertainty and of hunger.

The mighty element, the fire of heaven and the silence of the people, their life in nature, their confinedness and their contentment, moved me continually, and as one says of heroes, I can well say of myself that Apollo has struck me.

In the regions bordering on the Vendée I was interested in a quality fiercely warlike, and purely male, to which the light of life becomes spontaneous, immediate in eye and limb, which experiences the sensation of death like a kind of virtuosity and satisfies its thirst for knowledge.

The athletic character of the southern peoples, in the ruins of the ancient spirit, made me more familiar with the true character of the Greeks; I came to understand their nature and their wisdom, their bodies, how they grew in their climate and the rule they used to preserve their exuberant genius from the violence of the element.

This determined their peculiarity as a people, their way of adopting foreign natures and of communicating with them, and it is from this that they derived their distinctive individuality which seems alive in so far as supreme understanding, to the Greeks, was the power to respond to reality; and this becomes comprehensible to us when we comprehend the heroic bodies of the Greeks; it is tenderness, like our own peculiarity as a people.

The contemplation of ancient statuary made an impression on me that brought me closer to an understanding not only of the Greeks, but of what is greatest in all art, which, even where movement is most intense, the conception most phenomenalized and the intention most serious, still preserves every detail intact and true to itself, so that assuredness, in this sense, is the supreme kind of representation.

After many shocks and disturbances of my mind it was necessary for me to settle down for a while, and for the time being I am living in my home town.

Nature in these parts moves me more powerfully, the more I study it. The thunderstorm, not only in its extreme manifestation, but precisely as a power and shape, among the other forms of the sky, light in its

13

workings, nationally and as a principle that fashions a mode of fate,
so that something is holy to us, its urgency in coming and going, what is
characteristic in forests and the convergence in one region of different
kinds of nature, so that all the holy places of the earth come together
around one place, and the philosophic light around my window—
these are now my joy; and may I bear in mind how I came here, as
far as this place!

Dear friend, I think that we shall not gloss the poets up to our time,
but that song altogether will assume a different character, and that
we cannot make ourselves heard because we, after the Greeks, are
beginning once more to sing nationally and naturally, that is, in a
truly original way.

Please write to me soon. I need pure tones. Psyche among friends,
the generation of thought in conversation and letters is necessary to
artists. . . . Otherwise we have no thought for ourselves; but it belongs
to the holy image which we are shaping. A sincere farewell.

Yours,

H.

Hölderlin recovered sufficiently to complete his translations of
Sophocles, which were published with Hölderlin's critical comments
in 1804, to continue his translation of Pindar's odes, and to write the
last—already partly disjointed and unintelligible—versions of his
hymns. In the autumn of 1802 Sinclair took him to Regensburg,
where Hölderlin came under the influence of the Landgrave of
Homburg, Sinclair's employer. It was at the Landgrave's suggestion
that Hölderlin wrote *Patmos;* and his changing attitudes are also
reflected in the dedication of the Sophocles versions to Princess
Auguste—'Apart from these, if time permits, I will sing the forefathers of our princes, their seats, and the angels of our holy country.'
This is part of Hölderlin's homecoming, his return to the source and
to his own origins. Yet to the very end he could not wholly renounce
ancient Greece or the Greek gods, and his last intense exertions before
his madness were directed towards a visionary reconciliation of the
two allegiances, even though this demanded an almost hopeless

attempt to syncretize a pantheistic or polytheistic system with a higher monotheism.

After his return to Nürtingen, so greatly improved in health that his mother believed Sinclair to have effected a complete cure, Hölderlin also prepared for publication the group of late short poems which he called *Nachtgesänge* (night songs) and these appeared in 1804. They included some of his odes, *Chiron, Tears, To Hope, Vulcan, Timidness* and *Ganymede*—but also fragments of free verse hymns, including *The Ages of Life* and *The Middle of Life*, which had originally been part of the draft of *As on a Holiday*. . . . By recognizing that this fragment could be published as a separate poem—and this in December 1803, when his illness was entering its last incurable phase—Hölderlin won a last victory over the taste of his own time. Nearly a century had to pass before this poem came into its own as one of the purest lyrical poems ever written, and one that anticipated both the Symbolist and the Imagist revolutions in poetry.

It is interesting, and disturbing, to reflect that it is in the poems and fragments written when his schizophrenia was passing into its final phase that Hölderlin strikes us as most 'modern'. Often the modernity lies in his reliance on particulars, the mere invocation of a person or thing, where more conventional poets would have felt (and still feel) obliged to present a sequence of arguments or metaphors. In the later versions of the hymns there are instances not only of inverted or deliberately ambiguous syntax but of a-syntactic one-word sentences that serve as a poetic shorthand. The poem proceeds by flashes of perception or allusion, true to the laws not of argument but of pre-articulate feeling and thought. In many cases it may well be that Hölderlin was only drafting poems which he was no longer capable of working out; yet even a sketch like the following seems to prefigure the kind of association practised by twentieth-century innovators, such as Mr. Ezra Pound in the *Cantos*:

So Mahommed *, Rinaldo,
Barbarossa, as a liberal spirit,

The Emperor Heinrich.
But we are mixing up
the periods
                    Demetrius Poliorcetes
Peter the Great
                    Heinrich's
crossing of the Alps, and that
with his own hand he gave the people food
and drink and his son Conrad died of poison
Example of one who changes an age
reformer
Conradin etc.
all as representative
of conditions.

* Hear the horn of the watchman by night
  After midnight it is, at the fifth hour.

The resemblances are partly fortuitous, mainly because Hölderlin's lines are only nuclei of an unwritten poem; but there is something about the quality of his historical imagination here that seems more characteristic of our time than of his. One thinks of his words in the letter to Böhlendorff about 'all the holy places of the earth coming together around one place', and the endeavour of a single imagination, a single consciousness, to embrace them all.

In July 1804 Sinclair took Hölderlin to Homburg, where he had previously obtained the appointment of Court Librarian for his friend, though it was Sinclair who paid the salary out of his own income. Despite Sinclair's care and protection, Hölderlin by now was not only incapable of doing a librarian's work but had to be removed to a Tübingen clinic in 1806. In the following year he was entrusted to a carpenter, Zimmer, at Tübingen, and spent the remaining thirty-six years of his life in the carpenter's house (or tower) on the Neckar embankment.

One of many reports of his madness must be quoted here because it sheds some light* on the genesis of the little poem *The lines of life* . . . (p. 589), and shows that Hölderlin remained capable of real affection and understanding (though he kept indifferent visitors at a distance by an excess of polite deference and forms of address such as 'Your Highness', or 'Your Majesty'). In one of his periodic letters to Hölderlin's mother the semi-literate carpenter informs her as follows of the writing of those lines: 'His poetic spirit still shows itself to be active, for instance in my house he saw a drawing of a temple. He told me to make one out of wood. I replied that I have to work for my living, that I am not fortunate enough to live in philosophic calm like him, immediately he replied, "Oh, I am a wretched creature" and in the same minute he wrote the following verses on a wooden board with his pencil:

> The lines of life are various; they diverge and cease
> Like footpaths and the mountains' utmost ends;
> What here we are, elsewhere a God amends
> With harmonies, eternal recompense and peace.

Like most of the extant poems of his madness, then, this was an occasional poem; but unlike many others, written at the request of casual visitors, it not only rose to the occasion, but outflew it. Though it is unlikely that all Hölderlin's visitors troubled to preserve the curios elicited from him, we have enough of them to know that his 'philosophic calm' remained productive to the end. These late verses have a serene, detached and ingenuous beauty of their own. What has gone out of them is not lucidity, but tension; they do not grapple with the world, but accept it as something ready-made. In *The Walk* this ready-made world itself is like an artifact, like the painted backcloth to a play. In other poems the use of abstract cliché creates a similar sense of unreality. Yet the lines to Zimmer are not the only ones in which there is a spark of self-awareness, and hence of an awareness of reality.

The little poem *Spring* (p. 599) is believed to have been written on Hölderlin's last birthday, in March 1843. He died suddenly of pulmonary congestion on June 7th of that year, at the age of seventy-three.

*For a fuller account, including a number of Hölderlin's letters to his mother written in those years, see the Introduction to the 1943 and 1952 editions of my translations.

17

The German texts reproduced here, and the translations, are based on Friedrich Beissner's edition, HÖLDERLIN: SÄMTLICHE WERKE (Grosse Stuttgarter Ausgabe, Stuttgart, 1943-61), with the single exception of the preliminary drafts for *Friedensfeier*, based on the reading by Wolfgang Binder and Alfred Kelletat in HÖLDERLINS FRIEDENSFEIER. *Lichtdruck der Reinschrift und ihrer Vorstufen* (Tübingen, 1959). Since the complete text of the successive drafts could not be included here—and their order remains controversial—I have taken the liberty of producing a conflation of my own in this case, so as to include those passages which seemed most fully realized or most essential to an understanding of the finished poem. I am also indebted to Professor Beissner's edition for much factual information and for variant readings.

Readers who wish to supplement the inevitably scanty material provided in the Introduction to this volume are referred to the following works on Hölderlin in English:

Marshall Montgomery: *Friedrich Hölderlin and the German Neo-Hellenic Movement*. Oxford, 1923
*E. M. Butler: *The Tyranny of Greece over Germany*. Cambridge, 1935
Ronald Peacock: *Hölderlin*. London, 1938
Agnes Stansfield: *Hölderlin*. Manchester, 1943
E. L. Stahl: *Hölderlin's Symbolism*. Oxford, 1945
*Edwin Muir: *Essays on Literature and Society*. London, 1949
L. S. Salzberger: *Hölderlin*. Cambridge, 1952
*C. M. Bowra: *Inspiration and Poetry*. London, 1955
*Michael Hamburger: *Reason and Energy*. London, 1957

*These books contain chapters on Hölderlin.

Quarterly Review of Literature (Annandale-on-Hudson, New York),
Hölderlin Issue, Vol. X, Nos. 1 & 2, 1959. (Contains essays by
Martin Heidegger, Norbert von Hellingrath, Erich Heller and
Anthony Thorlby; and excerpts from Hölderlin's *Hyperion*)

An English version, by Willard R. Trask, of Hölderlin's *Hyperion*
was published in 1965 in Signet Classics, New York and London.

These translations are dedicated to
the memory of
ARTHUR WALEY

ODES AND EPIGRAMS
(1797-1799)

GUTER RATH

Hast du Verstand und ein Herz, so zeige nur eines von beiden,
  Beides verdammen sie dir, zeigest du beides zugleich.

ADVOCATUS DIABOLI

Tief im Herzen haß ich den Troß der Despoten und Pfaffen
  Aber noch mehr das Genie, macht es gemein sich damit.

DIE VORTREFLICHEN

Lieben Brüder! versucht es nur nicht, vortreflich zu werden
  Ehrt das Schiksaal und tragts, Stümper auf Erden zu seyn
Denn ist Einmal der Kopf voran, so folget der Schweif auch
  Und die klassische Zeit deutscher Poëten ist aus.

DIE BESCHREIBENDE POËSIE

Wißt! Apoll ist der Gott der Zeitungsschreiber geworden
  Und sein Mann ist, wer ihm treulich das Factum erzählt.

FALSCHE POPULARITÄT

O der Menschenkenner! er stellt sich kindisch mit Kindern
  Aber der Baum und das Kind suchet, was über ihm ist.

EPIGRAMS (1797)

GOOD ADVICE

You've a head *and* a heart? Reveal only one of them, I say;
  If you reveal both at once, doubly they'll damn you, for both.

ADVOCATUS DIABOLI

Deep in my heart I abhor the nexus of rulers and clerics,
  Yet more deeply I loathe genius in league with that gang.

THE EXCELLENT

Dearest brothers, whatever you do, never try to be excellent writers;
  Honour fate, and accept that it's human to bungle your trade.
For if once the head ventures forth, the tail will certainly follow,
  And our classical age, Germans, is over for good.

DESCRIPTIVE POETRY

Latest news: Apollo's become the god of journalists, press men,
  And his blue-eyed boy he who reports all the facts.

FALSE POPULARITY

O the worldly wise man! With children his manner is childish;
  But the tree and the child seek what is higher than they.

23

AN DIOTIMA

Schönes Leben! du lebst, wie die zarten Blüthen im Winter,
  In der gealterten Welt blühst du verschlossen, allein.
Liebend strebst du hinaus, dich zu sonnen am Lichte des Frühlings,
  Zu erwarmen an ihr suchst du die Jugend der Welt.
Deine Sonne, die schönere Zeit, ist untergegangen
  Und in frostiger Nacht zanken Orkane sich nun.

TO DIOTIMA

Beautiful being, you live as do delicate blossoms in winter,
　　In a world that's grown old hidden you blossom, alone.
Lovingly outward you press to bask in the light of the springtime,
　　To be warmed by it still, look for the youth of the world.
But your sun, the lovelier world, has gone down now,
　　And the quarrelling gales rage in an icy bleak night.

DIOTIMA

Komm und besänftige mir, die du einst Elemente versöhntest
    Wonne der himmlischen Muse das Chaos der Zeit,
Ordne den tobenden Kampf mit Friedenstönen des Himmels
    Bis in der sterblichen Brust sich das entzweite vereint,
Bis der Menschen alte Natur die ruhige große,
    Aus der gährenden Zeit, mächtig und heiter sich hebt.
Kehr' in die dürftigen Herzen des Volks, lebendige Schönheit!
    Kehr an den gastlichen Tisch, kehr in die Tempel zurük!
Denn Diotima lebt, wie die zarten Blüthen im Winter,
    Reich an eigenem Geist sucht sie die Sonne doch auch.
Aber die Sonne des Geists, die schönere Welt ist hinunter
    Und in frostiger Nacht zanken Orkane sich nur.

DIOTIMA

Bliss of the heavenly Muse who on elements once imposed order,
　　Come, and for me now assuage the chaos come back in our time,
Temper the furious war with peace-giving, heavenly music
　　Till in the mortal heart all that's divided unites,
Till the former nature of men, the calm, the majestic,
　　From our turbulent age rises, restored to its prime.
Living beauty, return to the destitute hearts of the people,
　　To the banqueting table return, enter the temples once more!
For Diotima lives as do delicate blossoms in winter,
　　Blessed with a soul of her own, yet needing and seeking the sun.
But the lovelier world, the sun of the spirit is darkened,
　　Only quarrelling gales rage in an icy bleak night.

BUONAPARTE

Heilige Gefäße sind die Dichter,
   Worinn des Lebens Wein, der Geist
    Der Helden sich aufbewahrt,

Aber der Geist dieses Jünglings
   Der schnelle, müßt' er es nicht zersprengen
    Wo es ihn fassen wollte, das Gefäß?

Der Dichter laß ihn unberührt wie den Geist der Natur,
   An solchem Stoffe wird zum Knaben der Meister.

Er kann im Gedichte nicht leben und bleiben,
   Er lebt und bleibt in der Welt.

BONAPARTE

Poets are holy vessels
   In which the wine of life,
      The spirit of heroes is preserved;

But this young man's spirit,
   The quick—would it not burst
      Any vessel that tried to contain it?

Let the poet leave him untouched like the spirit of Nature,
   For both reduce to a bungling boy the masterly craftsman.

In the poem he cannot live and last;
   He lives and lasts in the world.

EMPEDOKLES

Das Leben suchst du, suchst, und es quillt und glänzt
  Ein göttlich Feuer tief aus der Erde dir,
    Und du in schauderndem Verlangen
      Wirfst dich hinab, in des Aetna Flammen.

So schmelzt' im Weine Perlen der Übermuth
  Der Königin; und mochte sie doch! hättst du
    Nur deinen Reichtum nicht, o Dichter
      Hin in den gährenden Kelch geopfert!

Doch heilig bist du mir, wie der Erde Macht,
  Die dich hinwegnahm, kühner Getödteter!
    Und folgen möcht' ich in die Tiefe,
      Hielte die Liebe mich nicht, dem Helden.

EMPEDOCLES

You look for life, you look and from deeps of Earth
  A fire, divinely gleaming wells up for you,
    And quick, aquiver with desire, you
      Hurl yourself down into Etna's furnace.

So did the Queen's exuberance once dissolve
  Rare pearls in wine, and why should she not? But you,
    If only you, O poet, had not
      Offered your wealth to the seething chalice!

Yet you are holy to me as is the power
  Of Earth that took you from us, the boldly killed!
    And gladly, did not love restrain me,
      Deep as the hero plunged down I'd follow.

AN DIE PARZEN

Nur Einen Sommer gönnt, ihr Gewaltigen!
  Und einen Herbst zu reifem Gesange mir,
    Daß williger mein Herz, vom süßen
      Spiele gesättiget, dann mir sterbe.

Die Seele, der im Leben ihr göttlich Recht
  Nicht ward, sie ruht auch drunten im Orkus nicht;
    Doch ist mir einst das Heil'ge, das am
      Herzen mir liegt, das Gedicht gelungen,

Willkommen dann, o Stille der Schattenwelt!
  Zufrieden bin ich, wenn auch mein Saitenspiel
    Mich nicht hinab geleitet; Einmal
      Lebt ich, wie Götter, und mehr bedarfs nicht.

TO THE FATES

One summer only grant me, you powerful Fates,
    And one more autumn only for mellow song,
      So that more willingly, replete with
        Music's late sweetness, my heart may die then.

The soul in life denied its god-given right
    Down there in Orcus also will find no peace;
      But when what's holy, dear to me, the
        Poem's accomplished, my art perfected,

Then welcome, silence, welcome cold world of shades!
    I'll be content, though here I must leave my lyre
      And songless travel down; for *once* I
        Lived like the gods, and no more is needed.

DIOTIMA

Du schweigst und duldest, und sie versteh'n dich nicht,
  Du heilig Leben! welkest hinweg und schweigst,
    Denn ach, vergebens bei Barbaren
      Suchst du die Deinen im Sonnenlichte,

Die zärtlichgroßen Seelen, die nimmer sind!
  Doch eilt die Zeit. Noch siehet mein sterblich Lied
    Den Tag, der, Diotima! nächst den
      Göttern mit Helden dich nennt, und dir gleicht.

DIOTIMA

You suffer and keep silent and, strange to them,
   You holy being, silently wilt away;
      For, ah, in vain among barbarians
         Here in the sunlight you seek your kindred,

The nobly tender spirits that are no more!
   Yet time speeds on. Though mortal, my song will live
      To see the day which next to gods, with
         Heroes will name you, itself be like you.

AN IHREN GENIUS

Send' ihr Blumen und Frücht' aus nieversiegender Fülle,
　　Send' ihr, freundlicher Geist, ewige Jugend herab!
Hüll' in deine Wonnen sie ein und laß sie die Zeit nicht
　　Sehn, wo einsam und fremd sie, die Athenerin, lebt,
Bis sie im Lande der Seeligen einst die fröhlichen Schwestern,
　　Die zu Phidias Zeit herrschten und liebten, umfängt.

TO HER GENIUS

Send her flowers and fruit from inexhaustible fulness,
    Send her, tutelar spirit, deathless youth from above!
Wrap her up in your joys and never let her experience
    Years when lonely, estranged, she, the Athenian, must live,
Till in the land of the blessed one day she fondly embraces
    Happy sisters who ruled, loved when Phidias was young.

ABBITTE

Heilig Wesen! gestört hab' ich die goldene
  Götterruhe dir oft, und der geheimeren,
    Tiefern Schmerzen des Lebens
      Hast du manche gelernt von mir.

O vergiß es, vergieb! gleich dem Gewölke dort
  Vor dem friedlichen Mond, geh' ich dahin, und du
    Ruhst und glänzest in deiner
      Schöne wieder, du süßes Licht!

PLEA FOR FORGIVENESS

Holy being, I know, often I've troubled your
   Golden, god-like repose, so that you learned from me
     Much that might have been spared you,
       Life's more hidden, obscurer griefs.

O forgive me, forget! Look, as the clouds up there
   Veil with black the slow moon, I drift away, while you
     Stay and shine in your beauty,
       Gentle light, as you shone before.

EHMALS UND JEZT

In jüngern Tagen war ich des Morgens froh,
  Des Abends weint' ich; jezt, da ich älter bin,
    Beginn ich zweifelnd meinen Tag, doch
      Heilig und heiter ist mir sein Ende.

THEN AND NOW

In younger days each morning I rose with joy,
To weep at nightfall; now, in my later years,
Though doubting I begin my day, yet
Always its end is serene and holy.

LEBENSLAUF

Hoch auf strebte mein Geist, aber die Liebe zog
    Schön ihn nieder; das Laid beugt ihn gewaltiger;
      So durchlauf ich des Lebens
        Bogen und kehre, woher ich kam.

THE COURSE OF LIFE

High my spirit aspired, truly, however, love
 Pulled it earthward; and grief lower still bows it down.
  So I follow the arc of
   Life and return to my starting-place.

DIE KÜRZE

»Warum bist du so kurz? liebst du, wie vormals, denn
　　»Nun nicht mehr den Gesang? fandst du, als Jüngling, doch,
　　　»In den Tagen der Hoffnung,
　　　　»Wenn du sangest, das Ende nie!

Wie mein Glük, ist mein Lied. —Willst du im Abendroth
　　Froh dich baden? hinweg ists! und die Erd' ist kalt,
　　　Und der Vogel der Nacht schwirrt
　　　　Unbequem vor das Auge dir.

BREVITY

'Why so brief now, so curt? Do you no longer, then,
    Love your art as you did? When in your younger days,
        Hopeful days, in your singing
            What you loathed was to make an end!'

Like my joy is my song.—Who in the sundown's red
    Glow would happily bathe? Gone it is, cold the earth,
        And the bird of the night whirs
            Down, so close that you shield your eyes.

MENSCHENBEIFALL

Ist nicht heilig mein Herz, schöneren Lebens voll,
   Seit ich liebe? warum achtetet ihr mich mehr,
     Da ich stolzer und wilder,
       Wortereicher und leerer war?

Ach! der Menge gefällt, was auf den Marktplaz taugt,
   Und es ehret der Knecht nur den Gewaltsamen;
     An das Göttliche glauben
      Die allein, die es selber sind.

HUMAN APPLAUSE

Has love not hallowed, filled with new life my heart,
   With lovelier life? Then why did you prize me more
     When I was proud and wild and frantic,
       Lavish of words, yet in substance empty?

The crowd likes best what sells in the market place,
   And loud-mouthed force alone wins a slave's respect.
     In gods and godhead only he can
      Truly believe who himself is godlike.

DIE HEIMATH

Froh kehrt der Schiffer heim an den stillen Strom
  Von fernen Inseln, wo er geerndtet hat;
    Wohl möcht' auch ich zur Heimath wieder;
      Aber was hab' ich, wie Laid, geerndtet? —

Ihr holden Ufer, die ihr mich auferzogt,
  Stillt ihr der Liebe Laiden? ach! gebt ihr mir,
    Ihr Wälder meiner Kindheit, wann ich
      Komme, die Ruhe noch Einmal wieder?

HOME

Content the boatman turns to the river's calm
  From distant isles, his harvest all gathered in;
    I too would gladly now turn homeward,
      Only, what harvest but pain have I reaped?

Kind river-banks that tended and brought me up,
  Can you allay love's sufferings, give me back,
    You forests of my childhood, should I
      Come to you now, the same peace as ever?

DER GUTE GLAUBE

Schönes Leben! du liegst krank, und das Herz ist mir
Müd vom Weinen und schon dämmert die Furcht in mir,
Doch, doch kann ich nicht glauben,
Daß du sterbest, so lang du liebst.

GOOD FAITH

Dearest one, you lie sick, so that with weeping my
   Heart is weary, and fear almost takes root in me;
     Yet I cannot believe that
       You could die when you still can love.

IHRE GENESUNG

Deine Freundin, Natur! leidet und schläft und du
  Allbelebende, säumst? ach! und ihr heilt sie nicht,
    Mächt'ge Lüfte des Aethers,
      Nicht ihr Quellen des Sonnenlichts?

Alle Blumen der Erd', alle die fröhlichen,
  Schönen Früchte des Hains, heitern sie alle nicht
    Dieses Leben, ihr Götter!
      Das ihr selber in Lieb' erzogt? —

Ach! schon athmet und tönt heilige Lebenslust
  Ihr im reizenden Wort wieder wie sonst und schon
    Glänzt das Auge des Lieblings
      Freundlichoffen, Natur! dich an.

HER RECOVERY

Nature, she who's your friend drowses and ails, and you
    Dally, giver of life? Cannot you heal her, then,
        Potent breezes of Aether,
            Sunlight's well-springs, will you not help?

All the flowers of the earth, all the good ripening
    Happy fruits of the grove, how can it be that all
        Fail to cheer this one life which,
            Gods, yourselves you raised up with love?

Ah, already restored, holy desire to live
    Breathes and sounds in her talk, charming as ever, and
        Fondly, Nature, your darling
            Open-eyed to your beam responds.

DAS UNVERZEIHLICHE

Wenn ihr Freunde vergeßt, wenn ihr den Künstler höhnt,
Und den tieferen Geist klein und gemein versteht,
  Gott vergiebt es, doch stört nur
  Nie den Frieden der Liebenden.

THE UNPARDONABLE

If you drop an old friend, laugh at the artist and
   Meanly, vulgarly judge, wronging the deeper mind,
     God forgives you; but never
       Break the quiet that lovers know.

AN DIE JUNGEN DICHTER

Lieben Brüder! es reift unsere Kunst vieleicht,
    Da, dem Jünglinge gleich, lange sie schon gegährt,
      Bald zur Stille der Schönheit;
        Seid nur fromm, wie der Grieche war!

Liebt die Götter und denkt freundlich der Sterblichen!
    Haßt den Rausch, wie den Frost! lehrt und beschreibet nicht!
      Wenn der Meister euch ängstigt,
        Fragt die große Natur um Rath.

TO THE YOUNG POETS

Quite soon, dear brothers, perhaps our art,
   So long in youth-like ferment, will now mature
      To beauty's plenitude, to stillness;
         Only be pious, like Grecian poets!

Of mortal men think kindly, but love the gods!
   Loathe drunkenness like frost! Don't describe or teach!
      And if you fear your master's bluntness,
         Go to great Nature, let her advise you!

AN DIE DEUTSCHEN

Spottet ja nicht des Kinds, wenn es mit Peitsch' und Sporn
  Auf dem Rosse von Holz muthig und groß sich dünkt,
    Denn, ihr Deutschen, auch ihr seyd
      Thatenarm und gedankenvoll.

Oder kömmt, wie der Stral aus dem Gewölke kömmt,
  Aus Gedanken die That? Leben die Bücher bald?
    O ihr Lieben, so nimmt mich,
      Daß ich büße die Lästerung.

TO THE GERMANS

Do not laugh at the child when with his whip and spurs
   Brave and mighty he feels up on his rocking-horse,
     For, you Germans, you too are
       Poor in deeds though you've thoughts enough!

Or, as lightning from clouds, out of mere thoughts will deeds,
   Potent, come leaping out? Books now begin to live?
     O, my dear ones, then seize me,
       Make me pay for my slanderous words.

DIE SCHEINHEILIGEN DICHTER

Ihr kalten Heuchler, sprecht von den Göttern nicht!
  Ihr habt Verstand! ihr glaubt nicht an Helios,
    Noch an den Donnerer und Meergott;
      Todt ist die Erde, wer mag ihr danken? —

Getrost ihr Götter! zieret ihr doch das Lied,
  Wenn schon aus euren Nahmen die Seele schwand,
    Und ist ein großes Wort vonnöthen,
      Mutter Natur! so gedenkt man deiner.

THE SANCTIMONIOUS POETS

Cold hypocrites, of gods do not dare to speak!
   You're rational! In Helios you don't believe,
      Nor in the Thunderer or the Sea-God;
         Dead is our Earth, so what fool would thank her?—

Take comfort, gods! For yet you adorn their verse
   Though now the soul's gone out of your pilfered names;
      And if some high-flown word is needed,
         You, Mother Nature, they still remember.

DEM SONNENGOTT

Wo bist du? trunken dämmert die Seele mir
   Von aller deiner Wonne; denn eben ists,
      Daß ich gesehn, wie, müde seiner
         Fahrt, der entzükende Götterjüngling

Die jungen Loken badet' im Goldgewölk';
   Und jezt noch blikt mein Auge von selbst nach ihm;
      Doch fern ist er zu frommen Völkern,
         Die ihn noch ehren, hinweggegangen.

Dich lieb' ich, Erde! trauerst du doch mit mir!
   Und unsre Trauer wandelt, wie Kinderschmerz,
      In Schlummer sich, und wie die Winde
         Flattern und flüstern im Saitenspiele,

Bis ihm des Meisters Finger den schönern Ton
   Entlokt, so spielen Nebel und Träum' um uns,
      Bis der Geliebte wiederkömt und
         Leben und Geist sich in uns entzündet.

TO THE SUN-GOD

Where are you? Dazzled, drunken my soul grows faint
    And dark with so much gladness; for only now
        It was 1 watched while weary with his
            Course, the enrapturing sun-god lingered

To bathe his youthful locks in the golden clouds;
    And, full of him, my eyes of themselves gaze on,
        Though far from here, to pious nations
            Who still revere him, by now he's journeyed.

You, Earth, I love who join me in mourning him,
    And like the griefs of children our mourning turns
        To sleep and, much as in the lyre-strings
            Fluttering winds will run wild and whisper

Until the master's finger lures forth a tone
    More pure, so dreams and mist all around us play
        Until the loved one comes again and
            Kindles new life in our minds, new vigour.

SONNENUNTERGANG

Wo bist du? trunken dämmert die Seele mir
Von aller deiner Wonne; denn eben ist's,
  Daß ich gelauscht, wie, goldner Töne
    Voll, der entzükende Sonnenjüngling

Sein Abendlied auf himmlischer Leyer spielt';
Es tönten rings die Wälder und Hügel nach.
  Doch fern ist er zu frommen Völkern,
    Die ihn noch ehren, hinweggegangen.

SUNSET

Where are you? Dazzled, drunken my soul grows faint
  And dark with so much gladness; for even now
    I listened while, too rich in golden
      Sounds, the enrapturing youth, the sun-god

Intoned his evening hymn on a heavenly lyre;
  All round the hills and forests re-echoed it,
    Though far from here—to pious nations
      Who still revere him—by now he's journeyed.

SOKRATES UND ALCIBIADES

»Warum huldigest du, heiliger Sokrates,
  »Diesem Jünglinge stets? kennest du Größers nicht?
    »Warum siehet mit Liebe,
      »Wie auf Götter, dein Aug' auf ihn?

Wer das Tiefste gedacht, liebt das Lebendigste,
  Hohe Jugend versteht, wer in die Welt geblikt
    Und es neigen die Weisen
      Oft am Ende zu Schönem sich.

SOCRATES AND ALCIBIADES

'Holy Socrates, why always with deference
  Do you treat this young man? Don't you know greater things?
    Why so lovingly, raptly,
      As on gods, do you gaze on him?'

Who the deepest has thought loves what is most alive,
  Wide experience may well turn to what's best in youth,
    And the wise in the end will
      Often bow to the beautiful.

AN UNSRE GROSSEN DICHTER

Des Ganges Ufer hörten des Freudengotts
   Triumph, als alleroberend vom Indus her
      Der junge Bacchus kam, mit heilgem
         Weine vom Schlafe die Völker wekend.

O wekt, ihr Dichter! wekt sie vom Schlummer auch,
   Die jezt noch schlafen, gebt die Geseze, gebt
      Uns Leben, siegt, Heroën! ihr nur
         Habt der Eroberung Recht, wie Bacchus.

TO OUR GREAT POETS

The banks of Ganges heard how the god of joy
    Was hailed when conquering all from far Indus came
       The youthful Bacchus, and with holy
          Wine from their drowsiness woke the peoples.

You also, poets, rouse them, awaken those
    Who still are sleepy, give us the laws, and give
       Us life! Make known your triumph! Only
          You, like that god, have the right to conquer.

ΠΡΟΣ ΕΑΥΤΟΝ

Lern im Leben die Kunst, im Kunstwerk lerne das Leben,
  Siehst du das Eine recht, siehst du das andere auch.

SOPHOKLES

Viele versuchten umsonst das Freudigste freudig zu sagen
  Hier spricht endlich es mir, hier in der Trauer sich aus.

DER ZÜRNENDE DICHTER

Fürchtet den Dichter nicht, wenn er edel zürnet, sein Buchstab
  Tödtet, aber es macht Geister lebendig der Geist.

DIE SCHERZHAFTEN

Immer spielt ihr und scherzt? ihr müßt! o Freunde! mir geht diß
  In die Seele, denn diß müssen Verzweifelte nur.

WURZEL ALLES ÜBELS

Einig zu seyn, ist göttlich und gut; woher ist die Sucht denn
  Unter den Menschen, daß nur Einer und Eines nur sei?

EPIGRAMS (1799)

ΠΡΟΣ ΕΑΥΤΟΝ
(TO HIMSELF)

Living, in life, learn your art, in art works learn about living;
  If the one you see clearly, aright, likewise the other you'll see.

SOPHOCLES

Many have tried, but in vain, with joy to express the most joyful;
  Here at last, in grave sadness, wholly I find it expressed.

THE ANGRY POET

Never fear the poet when nobly he rages; his letter
  Kills, but his spirit to spirits gives new vigour, new life.

THE JOKERS

Always you trifle and joke? You have to? O friends, how my very
  Soul responds to your plight: No one has to but those in despair.

THE ROOT OF ALL EVIL

Being at one is god-like and good, but human, too human, the mania
  Which insists there is only the One, one country, one truth and one way.

THE LATER ODES

(1798-1803)

VANINI

Den Gottverächter schalten sie dich? mit Fluch
   Beschwerten sie dein Herz dir und banden dich
     Und übergaben dich den Flammen,
       Heiliger Mann! o warum nicht kamst du

Vom Himmel her in Flammen zurük, das Haupt
   Der Lästerer zu treffen und riefst dem Sturm;
     Daß er die Asche der Barbaren
       Fort aus der Erd', aus der Heimath werfe!

Doch die du lebend liebtest, die dich empfieng,
   Den Sterbenden, die heil'ge Natur vergißt
     Der Menschen Thun und deine Feinde
       Kehrten, wie du, in den alten Frieden.

VANINI

God's enemy, despiser, they called you, heaped
   Their curses on your heart and then bound you fast
     And left you to the flames, you holy
       Man! O but why did you not come back then

In flames from Heaven, blazing, to strike the heads
   Of those blasphemers, call on the gales to sweep
     The ashes of those cold barbarians
       Out of this earth, of the sullied homeland!

Yet she who had your love while you lived, received
   You dying—holy Nature, I know, forgets
     Our human acts and, as to you, gave
       Back the old peace to your persecutors.

DER MENSCH

Kaum sproßten aus den Wassern, o Erde, dir
  Der jungen Berge Gipfel und dufteten
    Lustathmend, immergrüner Haine
      Voll, in des Oceans grauer Wildniß

Die ersten holden Inseln; und freudig sah
  Des Sonnengottes Auge die Neulinge
    Die Pflanzen, seiner ew'gen Jugend
      Lächelnde Kinder, aus dir geboren.

Da auf der Inseln schönster, wo immerhin
  Den Hain in zarter Ruhe die Luft umfloß,
    Lag unter Trauben einst, nach lauer
      Nacht, in der dämmernden Morgenstunde

Geboren, Mutter Erde! dein schönstes Kind; —
  Und auf zum Vater Helios sieht bekannt
    Der Knab', und wacht und wählt die süßen
      Beere versuchend, die heil'ge Rebe

Zur Amme sich; und bald ist er groß; ihn scheun
  Die Thiere, denn ein anderer ist, wie sie
    Der Mensch; nicht dir und nicht dem Vater
      Gleicht er, denn kühn ist in ihm und einzig

Des Vaters hohe Seele mit deiner Lust,
  O Erd'! und deiner Trauer von je vereint;
    Der Göttermutter, der Natur, der
      Allesumfassenden möcht' er gleichen!

MAN

When scarcely from the waters, O Earth, for you
   Young mountain peaks had sprouted and, breathing joy,
     The first delightful islands, full of
       Evergreen copses, gave out their fragrance

Amid the sea's grey desert; and glad of them
   The Sun-God's eye looked down at the newly raised,
     The plants, the smiling children of his
       Weariless youth, and of you, their mother—

Then on the loveliest island where delicate
   And calm the air flowed ceaselessly round the copse,
     One morning, born in early halflight
       After a temperate night, and bedded

Beneath the clustered grapes, lay your loveliest child;—
   And up to Father Helios now the boy
     Turns eyes that know him, wakes and, tasting
       Berries for sweetness, as nurse he chooses

The holy vine; and soon is grown up. He's shunned
   By animals, for different from them is Man.
     Not you, his mother, nor his father
       Does he resemble, for in him, boldly

Uniquely blended, live both his father's soul
   And, Earth, your joy, your sadness, inveterate;
     He longs to be like her, like Nature,
       Mother of gods and the all-embracing!

Ach! darum treibt ihn, Erde! vom Herzen dir
  Sein Übermuth, und deine Geschenke sind
    Umsonst und deine zarten Bande;
      Sucht er ein Besseres doch, der Wilde!

Von seines Ufers duftender Wiese muß
  Ins blüthenlose Wasser hinaus der Mensch,
    Und glänzt auch, wie die Sternenacht, von
      Goldenen Früchten sein Hain, doch gräbt er

Sich Höhlen in den Bergen und späht im Schacht
  Von seines Vaters heiterem Lichte fern,
    Dem Sonnengott auch ungetreu, der
      Knechte nicht liebt und der Sorge spottet.

Denn freier athmen Vögel des Walds, wenn schon
  Des Menschen Brust sich herrlicher hebt, und der
    Die dunkle Zukunft sieht, er muß auch
      Sehen den Tod und allein ihn fürchten.

Und Waffen wider alle, die athmen, trägt
  In ewigbangem Stolze der Mensch; im Zwist
    Verzehrt er sich und seines Friedens
      Blume, die zärtliche, blüht nicht lange.

Ist er von allen Lebensgenossen nicht
  Der seeligste? Doch tiefer und reißender
    Ergreift das Schiksaal, allausgleichend,
      Auch die entzündbare Brust dem Starken.

O that is why his arrogance drives him far
  From your safe-keeping, Earth, and in vain are all
    Your gifts and all your gentle fetters—
      Little to him, who wants more, the wild one!

Beyond his fragrant river-side meadows, out
  Into the flowerless water is Man impelled
    And though with golden fruit his orchard
      Gleams like the star-jewelled night, yet caves for

Himself he digs in mountains and scans the shaft,
  Remote from his great father's untroubled light,
    Disloyal also to the Sun-God,
      Scorner of cares never fond of drudges.

For woodland birds more freely draw breath, and though
  Man's breast more grandly, proudly expands, his gaze
    Can penetrate the future's darkness,
      Death he sees too and alone must fear it.

And arms against all creatures that live and stir
  In pride for ever anxious he bears; consumes
    Himself in discord; and not long the
      Delicate bloom of his peace contents him.

Is Man not blessed, not blissful compared to all
  His fellow creatures? Yet with a tighter hold,
    More deeply Fate, all-levelling, grips the
      Strong one's inflammable heart to wrench it.

HYPERIONS SCHIKSAALSLIED

Ihr wandelt droben im Licht
   Auf weichem Boden, seelige Genien!
  Glänzende Götterlüfte
  Rühren euch leicht,
    Wie die Finger der Künstlerin
   Heilige Saiten.

Schiksaallos, wie der schlafende
   Säugling, athmen die Himmlischen;
  Keusch bewahrt
  In bescheidener Knospe,
  Blühet ewig
   Ihnen der Geist,
    Und die seeligen Augen
   Bliken in stiller
    Ewiger Klarheit.

Doch uns ist gegeben,
  Auf keiner Stätte zu ruhn,
  Es schwinden, es fallen
   Die leidenden Menschen
   Blindlings von einer
   Stunde zur andern,
    Wie Wasser von Klippe
   Zu Klippe geworfen,
    Jahr lang ins Ungewisse hinab.

HYPERION'S SONG OF FATE

You walk above in the light,
　Weightless tread a soft floor, blessed genii!
　　Radiant the gods' mild breezes
　　　Gently play on you
　　　　As the girl artist's fingers
　　　　　On holy strings.

Fateless the Heavenly breathe
　　Like an unweaned infant asleep;
　　　Chastely preserved
　　　　In modest bud
　　　　　For ever their minds
　　　　　　Are in flower
　　　　　　　And their blissful eyes
　　　　　　　　Eternally tranquil gaze,
　　　　　　　　Eternally clear.

But we are fated
　To find no foothold, no rest,
　　And suffering mortals
　　　Dwindle and fall
　　　　Headlong from one
　　　　　Hour to the next,
　　　　　　Hurled like water
　　　　　　　From ledge to ledge
　　　　　　　　Downward for years to the vague abyss.

DA ICH EIN KNABE WAR...

Da ich ein Knabe war,
  Rettet' ein Gott mich oft
    Vom Geschrei und der Ruthe der Menschen,
    Da spielt' ich sicher und gut
    Mit den Blumen des Hains,
      Und die Lüftchen des Himmels
      Spielten mit mir.

Und wie du das Herz
Der Pflanzen erfreust,
Wenn sie entgegen dir
Die zarten Arme streken,

So hast du mein Herz erfreut
Vater Helios! und, wie Endymion,
War ich dein Liebling,
Heilige Luna!

O all ihr treuen
Freundlichen Götter!
Daß ihr wüßtet,
Wie euch meine Seele geliebt!

Zwar damals rieff ich noch nicht
Euch mit Nahmen, auch ihr
Nanntet mich nie, wie die Menschen sich nennen
Als kennten sie sich.

Doch kannt' ich euch besser,
Als ich je die Menschen gekannt,

IN MY BOYHOOD DAYS...

In my boyhood days
   Often a god would save me
      From the shouts and the rod of men;
     Safe and good then I played
       With the orchard flowers
        And the breezes of heaven
       Played with me.

And as you make glad
The hearts of the plants
When toward you they stretch
Their delicate arms,

So you made glad my heart,
Father Helios, and like Endymion
I was your darling,
Holy Luna.

O all you loyal,
Kindly gods!
Would that you knew how
My soul loved you then.

True, at that time I did not
Evoke you by name yet, and you
Never named me, as men use names,
As though they knew one another.

Yet I knew you better
Than ever I have known men,

Ich verstand die Stille des Aethers
Der Menschen Worte verstand ich nie.

Mich erzog der Wohllaut
Des säuselnden Hains
Und lieben lernt' ich
Unter den Blumen.

Im Arme der Götter wuchs ich groß.

I understood the silence of Aether,
But human words I've never understood.

I was reared by the euphony
Of the rustling copse
And learned to love
Amid the flowers.

I grew up in the arms of the gods.

HÖRT' ICH DIE WARNENDEN IZT...

Hört' ich die Warnenden izt, sie lächelten meiner und dächten,
  Früher anheim uns fiel, weil er uns scheute, der Thor.
Und sie achtetens keinen Gewinn,

Singt, o singet mir nur, unglükweissagend, ihr Furchtbarn
  Schiksaalsgötter das Lied immer und immer ums Ohr
Euer bin ich zulezt, ich weiß es, doch will zuvor ich
  Mir gehören und mir Leben erbeuten und Ruhm.

IF TO THOSE WARNING ONES . . .

If to those warning ones now I listened, they'd smile at me, thinking,
    Sooner we got him because always he shunned us, the fool;
Yet they'd count it no gain,

Sing then, sing your old song foretelling my doom, and repeat it,
    Terrible Gods of Fate, ceaselessly drone in my ears.
Yours I shall be in the end, I know, but first I'll belong to
    None but myself and secure life for myself and a name.

DIE LAUNISCHEN

Hör' ich ferne nur her, wenn ich für mich geklagt,
    Saitenspiel und Gesang, schweigt mir das Herz doch gleich;
        Bald auch bin ich verwandelt,
           Blinkst du, purpurner Wein! mich an

Unter Schatten des Walds, wo die gewaltige
    Mittagssonne mir sanft über dem Laube glänzt;
        Ruhig siz' ich daselbst, wenn
           Zürnend schwerer Belaidigung

Ich im Felde geirrt — Zürnen zu gerne doch
    Deine Dichter, Natur! trauern und weinen leicht,
        Die Beglükten; wie Kinder,
           Die zu zärtlich die Mutter hält,

Sind sie mürrisch und voll herrischen Eigensinns;
    Wandeln still sie des Wegs, irret Geringes doch
        Bald sie wieder; sie reißen
           Aus dem Gleise sich sträubend dir.

Doch du rührest sie kaum, Liebende! freundlich an,
    Sind sie friedlich und fromm; fröhlich gehorchen sie;
        Du lenkst, Meisterinn! sie mit
           Weichem Zügel, wohin du willst.

THE CAPRICIOUS

From afar let me hear music of strings or song
 When alone I've complained—peace fills my heart at once;
  Likewise soon I'm transformed when,
   Purple vine, you appear to me

In the shade of the wood where the strong noonday sun
 Mildly gleams up above, gilding the summer leaves;
  Quiet there I will sit, though
   Until then I had roamed the fields

Angry, grievously wronged—that's how your poets are,
 Nature, too prone to rage, ready to mourn and weep,
  Pampered fellows; like children
   Spoilt by mothers too lax, too fond,

Always moody they are, stubborn and arrogant;
 If contented they walk, yet will some little thing
  Soon confuse them; and wildly
   From your path they will rush, astray,

Scarcely touched, though, by you, fond one, with tenderness,
 Now they're docile and good, gladly obey your word;
  You, their goddess, can lead them
   Where you choose with your gentle reins.

DER ZEITGEIST

Zu lang schon waltest über dem Haupte mir
   Du in der dunkeln Wolke, du Gott der Zeit!
     Zu wild, zu bang ist's ringsum, und es
        Trümmert und wankt ja, wohin ich blike.

Ach! wie ein Knabe, seh' ich zu Boden oft,
   Such' in der Höhle Rettung von dir, und möcht'
     Ich Blöder, eine Stelle finden,
        Alleserschütt'rer! wo du nicht wärest.

Lass' endlich, Vater! offenen Aug's mich dir
   Begegnen! hast denn du nicht zuerst den Geist
     Mit deinem Stral aus mir gewekt? mich
        Herrlich an's Leben gebracht, o Vater! —

Wohl keimt aus jungen Reben uns heil'ge Kraft;
   In milder Luft begegnet den Sterblichen,
     Und wenn sie still im Haine wandeln,
        Heiternd ein Gott; doch allmächt'ger wekst du

Die reine Seele Jünglingen auf, und lehrst
   Die Alten weise Künste; der Schlimme nur
     Wird schlimmer, daß er bälder ende,
        Wenn du, Erschütterer! ihn ergreiffest.

THE SPIRIT OF THE AGE

Too long above my head you have governed there,
  Wrapped in the thunder cloud, you the God of Time!
    Too desolate and awed the land lies,
      All that I look at breaks up and totters.

O like a boy at times I cast down my eyes,
  Seek refuge from you in some deep cave, and search,
    Poor craven, for a single place where
      You, the all-shattering, might be absent.

But, Father, open-eyed let me meet at last
  Your face! Was it not you with your beam who first
    Drew out the mind in me, awakened,
      Gloriously brought me to life, O Father?—

True, from young vines we gather a holy strength;
  In mild spring air, or when they are wandering
    In orchards calmly, men will meet a
      Brightening god; yet with powers more far-flung

You rouse the souls of youths, and to older men
  Impart wise arts; the bad man alone grows worse,
    So that his end will come the sooner,
      When with your world-shaking might you seize him.

ABENDPHANTASIE

Vor seiner Hütte ruhig im Schatten sizt
   Der Pflüger, dem Genügsamen raucht sein Heerd.
     Gastfreundlich tönt dem Wanderer im
       Friedlichen Dorfe die Abendgloke.

Wohl kehren izt die Schiffer zum Hafen auch,
   In fernen Städten, fröhlich verrauscht des Markts
     Geschäfft'ger Lärm; in stiller Laube
       Glänzt das gesellige Mahl den Freunden.

Wohin denn ich? Es leben die Sterblichen
   Von Lohn und Arbeit; wechselnd in Müh' und Ruh'
     Ist alles freudig; warum schläft denn
       Nimmer nur mir in der Brust der Stachel?

Am Abendhimmel blühet ein Frühling auf;
   Unzählig blühn die Rosen und ruhig scheint
     Die goldne Welt; o dorthin nimmt mich
       Purpurne Wolken! und möge droben

In Licht und Luft zerrinnen mir Lieb' und Laid! —
   Doch, wie verscheucht von thöriger Bitte, flieht
     Der Zauber; dunkel wirds und einsam
       Unter dem Himmel, wie immer, bin ich —

Komm du nun, sanfter Schlummer! zu viel begehrt
   Das Herz; doch endlich, Jugend! verglühst du ja,
     Du ruhelose, träumerische!
       Friedlich und heiter ist dann das Alter.

EVENING FANTASY

At peace the ploughman sits in the shade outside
   His cottage; smoke curls up from his modest hearth.
     A traveller hears the bell for vespers
       Welcome him in to a quiet village.

Now too the boatmen make for the harbour pool,
   In distant towns the market's gay noise and throng
     Subside; a glittering meal awaits the
       Friends in the garden's most hidden arbour.

But where shall I go? Does not a mortal live
   By work and wages? Balancing toil with rest
     All makes him glad. Must I alone then
       Find no relief from the thorn that goads me?

A springtime buds high up in the evening sky,
   There countless roses bloom, and the golden world
     Seems calm, fulfilled; O there now take me,
       Crimson odged clouds, and up there at last let

My love and sorrow melt into light and air!—
   As if that foolish plea had dispersed it, though,
     The spell breaks; darkness falls, and lonely
       Under the heavens I stand as always.—

Now you come, gentle sleep! For the heart demands
   Too much; but youth at last, you the dreamy, wild,
     Unquiet, will burn out, and leave me
       All my late years for serene contentment.

DES MORGENS

Vom Thaue glänzt der Rasen; beweglicher
   Eilt schon die wache Quelle; die Buche neigt
      Ihr schwankes Haupt und im Geblätter
         Rauscht es und schimmert; und um die grauen

Gewölke streifen röthliche Flammen dort,
   Verkündende, sie wallen geräuschlos auf;
      Wie Fluthen am Gestade, woogen
         Höher und höher die Wandelbaren.

Komm nun, o komm, und eile mir nicht zu schnell,
   Du goldner Tag, zum Gipfel des Himmels fort!
      Denn offner fliegt, vertrauter dir mein
         Auge, du Freudiger! zu, so lang du

In deiner Schöne jugendlich blikst und noch
   Zu herrlich nicht, zu stolz mir geworden bist;
      Du möchtest immer eilen, könnt ich,
         Göttlicher Wandrer, mit dir! – doch lächelst

Des frohen Übermüthigen du, daß er
   Dir gleichen möchte; seegne mir lieber dann
      Mein sterblich Thun und heitre wieder
         Gütiger! heute den stillen Pfad mir.

IN THE MORNING

With dew the lawn is glistening; more nimbly now,
  Awake, the stream speeds onward; the beech inclines
    Her limber head and in the leaves a
      Rustle, a glitter begins; and round the

Grey cloud-banks there a flicker of reddish flames,
  Prophetic ones, flares up and in silence plays;
    Like breakers by the shore they billow
      Higher and higher, the ever-changing.

Now come, O come, and not too impatiently,
  You golden day, speed on to the peaks of heaven!
    For more familiar and more open,
      Glad one, my vision flies up towards you

While youthful in your beauty you gaze and have
  Not grown too glorious, dazzling and proud for me;
    Speed as you will, I'd say, if only
      I could go with you, divinely ranging!

But at my happy arrogance now you smile,
   That would be like you; rather, then, rambler, bless
    My mortal acts, and this day also,
      Kindly one, brighten my quiet pathway.

DER MAIN

Wohl manches Land der lebenden Erde möcht'
  Ich sehn, und öfters über die Berg' enteilt
    Das Herz mir, und die Wünsche wandern
      Über das Meer, zu den Ufern, die mir

Vor andern, so ich kenne, gepriesen sind;
  Doch lieb ist in der Ferne nicht Eines mir,
    Wie jenes, wo die Göttersöhne
      Schlafen, das trauernde Land der Griechen.

Ach! einmal dort an Suniums Küste möcht'
  Ich landen, deine Säulen, Olympion!
    Erfragen, dort, noch eh der Nordsturm
      Hin in den Schutt der Athenertempel

Und ihrer Götterbilder auch dich begräbt;
  Denn lang schon einsam stehst du, o Stolz der Welt,
    Die nicht mehr ist! — und o ihr schönen
      Inseln Ioniens, wo die Lüfte

Vom Meere kühl an warme Gestade wehn,
  Wenn unter kräft'ger Sonne die Traube reift,
    Ach! wo ein goldner Herbst dem armen
      Volk in Gesänge die Seufzer wandelt,

Wenn die Betrübten izt ihr Limonenwald
  Und ihr Granatbaum, purpurner Äpfel voll
    Und süßer Wein und Pauk' und Zithar
      Zum labyrintischen Tanze ladet —

THE RIVER MAIN

True, on this living earth there are many lands
  I long to see, and over the hills at times
    My heart runs off, my wishes wander
      Seaward, and on to those shores which more than

All others that I know have been glorified;
  But far away not one is as dear to me
    As that where now the sons of gods lie
      Sleeping, the mournful, the Hellenes' country.

O once I long to land there, on Sunium's coast,
  Once ask my way to your columns, Olympion,
    And soon, before the northern gale can
      Bury you too in the scattered rubble

Of temples Athens raised, and their imaged gods;
  For long now desolate you have stood, O pride
    Of worlds that are no more! And O you
      Lovely Ionian isles, where breezes

Waft coolness to warm shores from the open sea
  While under potent sunbeams the grape matures,
    And, oh, where still a golden autumn
      Turns into songs the poor people's sighing,

Now that their lemon grove, their pomegranate tree
  That bends with purple fruit, and sweet wine and drum
    And zither to the labyrinthine
      Dance have allured them, however troubled—

Zu euch vieleicht, ihr Inseln! geräth noch einst
   Ein heimathloser Sänger; denn wandern muß
     Von Fremden er zu Fremden, und die
       Erde, die freie, sie muß ja leider!

Statt Vaterlands ihm dienen, so lang er lebt,
   Und wenn er stirbt — doch nimmer vergeß ich dich,
     So fern ich wandre, schöner Main! und
       Deine Gestade, die vielbeglükten.

Gastfreundlich nahmst du Stolzer! bei dir mich auf
   Und heitertest das Auge dem Fremdlinge,
     Und still hingleitende Gesänge
       Lehrtest du mich und geräuschlos Leben.

O ruhig mit den Sternen, du Glüklicher!
   Wallst du von deinem Morgen zum Abend fort,
     Dem Bruder zu, dem Rhein; und dann mit
       Ihm in den Ocean freudig nieder!

To you, perhaps, you islands, yet one day shall
  A homeless singer come; for he's driven on
    From stranger still to stranger, and the
      Earth, the unbounded, alas, must serve him

In place of home and nation his whole life long,
  And when he dies—but never, delightful Main,
    Shall I forget you or your banks, the
      Variously blessed, on my farthest travels.

Hospitably, though proud, you admitted me,
  And, smoothly flowing, brightened the stranger's eye
    And taught me gently gliding songs, and
      Taught me the strength that's alive in silence.

O calmly as the stars move, you happy one,
  You travel from your morning to evening,
    Towards your brother, Rhine; then, with him,
      Joyfully down to the greater ocean.

MEIN EIGENTUM

In seiner Fülle ruhet der Herbsttag nun,
   Geläutert ist die Traub und der Hain ist roth
     Vom Obst, wenn schon der holden Blüthen
       Manche der Erde zum Danke fielen.

Und rings im Felde, wo ich den Pfad hinaus
   Den stillen wandle, ist den Zufriedenen
     Ihr Gut gereift und viel der frohen
       Mühe gewähret der Reichtum ihnen.

Vom Himmel bliket zu den Geschäfftigen
   Durch ihre Bäume milde das Licht herab,
     Die Freude theilend, denn es wuchs durch
       Hände der Menschen allein die Frucht nicht.

Und leuchtest du, o Goldnes, auch mir, und wehst
   Auch du mir wieder, Lüftchen, als seegnetest
     Du eine Freude mir, wie einst, und
       Irrst, wie um Glükliche, mir am Busen?

Einst war ichs, doch wie Rosen, vergänglich war
   Das fromme Leben, ach! und es mahnen noch,
     Die blühend mir geblieben sind, die
       Holden Gestirne zu oft mich dessen.

Beglükt, wer, ruhig liebend ein frommes Weib,
   Am eignen Heerd in rühmlicher Heimath lebt,
     Es leuchtet über vestem Boden
       Schöner dem sicheren Mann sein Himmel.

MY POSSESSIONS

At rest in fulness, calm lies the autumn day,
   The mellow grape is clear and the orchard red
      With fruit, though many treasured blossoms
         Long ago fell to the Earth in tribute.

And all around where now by the quiet path
   I cross the field, for satisfied men their crops
      Have ripened, and their riches grant them
         Hour after hour of rewarding labour.

From heaven through leafy boughs on the busy ones
   A light subdued and temperate glances down
      To share their pleasure; for not human
         Hands by themselves made the cornfield prosper.

And, golden light, for me will you also shine,
   And, breeze, once more for me will you waft, as though
      To bless a joy, and still around me
         Flutter and play, as for happy mortals?

I too was one, but brief as the full-blown rose
   My good life passed, and they that alone are left
      In flower for me, the constellations,
         Often, too often, remind me of it.

Blessed he who calmly loving a gentle wife
   Can call a worthy homeland and hearth his own;
      Above firm ground more brightly to the
         Settled, secure man his heaven glitters.

Denn, wie die Pflanze, wurzelt auf eignem Grund
Sie nicht, verglüht die Seele des Sterblichen,
  Der mit dem Tageslichte nur, ein
    Armer, auf heiliger Erde wandelt.

Zu mächtig ach! ihr himmlischen Höhen zieht
Ihr mich empor, bei Stürmen, am heitern Tag
  Fühl ich verzehrend euch im Busen
    Wechseln, ihr wandelnden Götterkräfte.

Doch heute laß mich stille den trauten Pfad
Zum Haine gehn, dem golden die Wipfel schmükt
  Sein sterbend Laub, und kränzt auch mir die
    Stirne, ihr holden Erinnerungen!

Und daß mir auch zu retten mein sterblich Herz,
Wie andern eine bleibende Stätte sei,
  Und heimathlos die Seele mir nicht
    Über das Leben hinweg sich sehne,

Sei du, Gesang, mein freundlich Asyl! sei du
Beglükender! mit sorgender Liebe mir
  Gepflegt, der Garten, wo ich, wandelnd
    Unter den Blüthen, den immerjungen,

In sichrer Einfalt wohne, wenn draußen mir
Mit ihren Wellen allen die mächtge Zeit
  Die Wandelbare fern rauscht und die
    Stillere Sonne mein Wirken fördert.

Ihr seegnet gütig über den Sterblichen
Ihr Himmelskräfte! jedem sein Eigentum,
  O seegnet meines auch und daß zu
    Frühe die Parze den Traum nicht ende.

For like the plant that fails to take root within
  Its native ground, the soul of that mortal wilts
    Who with the daylight only roams, a
      Pauper astray on our Earth, the hallowed.

Too strongly always, heavenly heights, you pull
  Me upward; gales that rage on a sunny day
    Bring home to me your clashing powers,
      Mutable gods, and they rend, destroy me.

Today, though, let me walk the familiar path
  In silence to the copse that is crowned with gold
    Of dying leaves; and my brow also
      Garland with gold now, dear recollections!

And that my mortal heart nonetheless may last,
  A quiet, sure retreat, as are other men's,
    And that my soul may not outfly this
      Life in its longing, for ever homeless,

You be my gracious refuge now, song, and you,
  Joy-giver, now be tended with loving care,
    The garden where intently walking
      Under the blossoms that do not wither,

I live in safe ingenuousness while outside
  With all its waves the changeable, mighty Time,
    Roars far away, and to my labours
      Only the quieter sun contributes.

Above us mortals, heavenly powers, you bless
  Each man's possessions, kindly disposed to all;
    O bless mine also, lest too soon the
      Fate put an end to my earthly dreaming.

PALINODIE

Was dämmert um mich, Erde! dein freundlich Grün?
  Was wehst du wieder, Lüftchen, wie einst, mich an?
    In allen Wipfeln rauschts,

Was wekt ihr mir die Seele? was regt ihr mir
  Vergangnes auf, ihr Guten! o schonet mein
    Und laßt sie ruhn, die Asche meiner
      Freuden, ihr spottetet nur! o wandelt,

Ihr schiksaallosen Götter, vorbei und blüht
  In eurer Jugend über den Alternden
    Und wollt ihr zu den Sterblichen euch
      Gerne gesellen, so blühn der Jungfraun

Euch viel, der jungen Helden, und schöner spielt
  Der Morgen um die Wange der Glüklichen.
    Denn um ein trübes Aug' und lieblich
      Tönen die Sänge der Mühelosen.

Ach! vormals rauschte leicht des Gesanges Quell
  Auch mir vom Busen, da noch die Freude mir
    Die himmlische vom Auge glänzte

Versöhnung o Versöhnung, ihr gütigen
  Ihr immergleichen Götter und haltet ein
    Weil ihr die reinen Quellen liebt

PALINODE

Why, Earth, around me glimmer your friendly leaves?
　　Why, little wind, as once do you breathe on me?
　　　　In all the tree-tops there's a rustling,

Why do you rouse my soul and stir up the past .
　　In me, you kindly ones? O be kinder still
　　　　And let them be, the embers of my
　　　　　　Joys! You were mocking me! Travel on, then,

You fateless gods, pass by, while high up you flower
　　In ever-youthful prime, this decrepit man,
　　　　And if you seek the company of
　　　　　　Mortals, young virgins enough like blossoms

Await you, and young heroes, and morning plays
　　More sweetly on the cheeks of the fortunate
　　　　Than on an eye that's dim, and pleasing
　　　　　　Sound all the songs of the blithely carefree.

Ah, easy once the wellspring of song flowed out
　　Of my breast also, purling, when still pure joy,
　　　　The heavenly, glittered in my eyes and

Be merciful, make peace, you benevolent,
　　You never-changing gods, and desist, desist,
　　　　Because you love pure sources

AN EINE FÜRSTIN VON DESSAU

Aus stillem Hauße senden die Götter oft
  Auf kurze Zeit zu Fremden die Lieblinge
    Damit, erinnert, sich am edlen
      Bilde der Sterblichen Herz erfreue.

So kommst du aus Luisiums Hainen auch
  Aus heilger Schwelle dort, wo geräuschlos rings
    Die Lüfte sind und friedlich um dein
      Dach die geselligen Bäume spielen,

Aus deines Tempels Freuden, o Priesterin!
  Zu uns, wenn schon die Wolke das Haupt uns beugt
    Und längst ein göttlich Ungewitter
      über dem Haupt uns wandelt.

O theuer warst du, Priesterin! da du dort
  Im Stillen göttlich Feuer behütetest,
    Doch theurer heute, da du Zeiten
      Unter den Zeitlichen seegnend feierst.

Denn wo die Reinen wandeln, vernehmlicher
  Ist da der Geist, und offen und heiter blühn
    Des Lebens dämmernde Gestalten
      Da, wo ein sicheres Licht erscheinet.

Und wie auf dunkler Wolke der schweigende
  Der schöne Bogen blühet, ein Zeichen ist
    Er künftger Zeit, ein Angedenken
      Seeliger Tage, die einst gewesen,

TO A PRINCESS OF DESSAU

The gods will often send from a quiet house
   To strangers briefly those whom their love prefers,
      So that, reminded, by that noble
         Image the hearts of us men are gladdened.

So from Luisium's groves now you too have come
   Across a holy threshold where breezes play
      In silence, peacefully around your
         Gables the sociable fruit trees whisper,

To us, O priestess, out of your temple's joys,
   Although the cloud hangs heavy above our heads
      And long a God-sent thunderstorm has
         Drifted towards us, remotely rumbling.

How dear to us you were when in silence there
   You, priestess, lived and guarded the sacred flame,
      Yet dearer now, amid the time-bound
         Blessing the times by your celebration.

For where the pure are present, more palpable
   The spirit is, and, flower-like, more open, clear
      The dimly glimmering shapes of life grow
         Where they are lit by a steady radiance,

And as on dark clouds blossoms the beautiful,
   The silent rainbow, gleaming to signify
      A future time or else recall the
         Happier days of a former season,

So ist dein Leben, heilige Fremdlingin!
Wenn du Vergangnes über Italiens
   Zerbrochnen Säulen, wenn du neues
      Grünen aus stürmischer Zeit betrachtest.

So *your* life, holy foreigner, must appear
    When over broken pillars in Italy
        You contemplate things past, or else new
            Leaves on the trees which today's gale lashes.

DER PRINZESSIN AUGUSTE
VON HOMBURG

DEN 28TEN NOV. 1799

Noch freundlichzögernd scheidet vom Auge dir
  Das Jahr, und in hesperischer Milde glänzt
    Der Winterhimmel über deinen
      Gärten, den dichtrischen, immergrünen.

Und da ich deines Festes gedacht' und sann,
  Was ich dir dankend reichte, da weilten noch
    Am Pfade Blumen, daß sie dir zur
      Blühenden Krone, du Edle, würden.

Doch Andres beut dir, Größeres, hoher Geist!
  Die festlichere Zeit, denn es hallt hinab
    Am Berge das Gewitter, sieh! und
      Klar, wie die ruhigen Sterne, gehen

Aus langem Zweifel reine Gestalten auf;
  So dünkt es mir; und einsam, o Fürstin! ist
    Das Herz der Freigebornen wohl nicht
      Länger im eigenen Glük; denn würdig

Gesellt im Lorbeer ihm der Heroë sich,
  Der schöngereifte, ächte; die Weisen auch,
    Die Unsern sind es werth; sie bliken
      Still aus der Höhe des Lebens, die ernsten Alten.

Geringe dünkt der träumende Sänger sich,
  Und Kindern gleich am müßigen Saitenspiel,

TO PRINCESS AUGUSTA OF HOMBURG

NOVEMBER 28th, 1799

Still kindly lingering the year from your eye departs,
   And in hesperian mildness now faintly gleams
      The winter sky above your gardens,
         Evergreen arbours, poetic orchards.

And as I pondered here on your birthday, thought
   What, thankful, I might offer, there still remained
      Late flowers beside the pathway, fit to
         Make you a crown that's alive, Augusta.

Yet, lofty spirit, other and greater things
   A time more festive yields you; the thunder rolls
      Away down mountain-sides and, look, as
         Tranquil and clear as the constellations

Pure shapes, pure signs arise from protracted doubt;
   So now it seems to me; and no longer shall
      The hearts of free-born men be lonely
         In their own triumph, Princess; for worthy,

The hero in his laurel consorts with them,
   The well-matured, the true one; and wise men too,
      Our own, deserve to join them; calmly
         Down from life's summit they gaze, those grave ones

How small the dreaming singer must think himself,
   How like a child who randomly plucks the strings,

Wenn ihn der Edlen Glük, wenn ihn die
  That und der Ernst der Gewalt'gen aufwekt.

Doch herrlicht mir dein Nahme das Lied; dein Fest
  Augusta! durft' ich feiern; Beruf ist mirs,
    Zu rühmen Höhers, darum gab die
      Sprache der Gott und den Dank ins Herz mir.

O daß von diesem freudigen Tage mir
  Auch meine Zeit beginne, daß endlich auch
    Mir ein Gesang in deinen Hainen,
      Edle! gedeihe, der deiner werth sei.

When roused by triumph of the noble,
　　Deeds, and decisions of mighty rulers.

Yet by your name my song is enhanced for me;
　Allowed to mark your day, my own call I serve,
　　To praise what's higher: for this the
　　　God gave me speech and a heart that's grateful.

O that this joyful day would initiate
　For me a new time also, one song of mine
　　Within your groves at last would prosper,
　　　Noble as you are and worthy of you.

WOHL GEH' ICH TÄGLICH...

Wohl geh' ich täglich andere Pfade, bald
  Ins grüne Laub im Walde, zur Quelle bald,
    Zum Felsen, wo die Rosen blühen,
      Blike vom Hügel ins Land, doch nirgend

Du Holde, nirgend find ich im Lichte dich
  Und in die Lüfte schwinden die Worte mir
    Die frommen, die bei dir ich ehmals

Ja, ferne bist du, seeliges Angesicht!
  Und deines Lebens Wohllaut verhallt von mir
    Nicht mehr belauscht, und ach! wo seid ihr
      Zaubergesänge, die einst das Herz mir

Besänftiget mit Ruhe der Himmlischen?
  Wie lang ist's! o wie lange! der Jüngling ist
    Gealtert, selbst die Erde, die mir
      Damals gelächelt, ist anders worden.

Leb immer wohl! es scheidet und kehrt zu dir
  Die Seele jeden Tag, und es weint um dich
    Das Auge, daß es helle wieder
      Dort wo du säumest, hinüberblike.

THOUGH EVERY DAY I FOLLOW...

Though every day I follow a different path,
  Now deep into green leaves in the wood, and now
    Towards the spring, the rock where roses
      Bloom, from the hilltop look out, yet nowhere

I can find you, my love, in the light of day,
  And into air dissolve all the words I learned,
    Devout ones, when with you I

Yes, you are far indeed from me, blessèd face,
  And now the euphony of your life is lost
    To me, your listener, and where are you,
      Magical songs that would once make gentle

My heart with quiet known to the Heavenly?
  How long ago, how long! That young man has aged,
    And Earth, the very Earth that seemed to
      Smile on me then, now is changed and shrunken.

Farewell, then, always. Daily the soul takes leave
  Of you, returns to you, and the eye will weep
    For you each day, to look more keenly
      Into the distance where you are staying.

GEH UNTER, SCHÖNE SONNE...

Geh unter, schöne Sonne, sie achteten
   Nur wenig dein, sie kannten dich, Heilge, nicht,
      Denn mühelos und stille bist du
        Über den mühsamen aufgegangen.

Mir gehst du freundlich unter und auf, o Licht!
   Und wohl erkennt mein Auge dich, herrliches!
      Denn göttlich stille ehren lernt' ich
        Da Diotima den Sinn mir heilte.

O du des Himmels Botin! wie lauscht ich dir!
   Dir, Diotima! Liebe! wie sah von dir
      Zum goldnen Tage dieses Auge
        Glänzend und dankend empor. Da rauschten

Lebendiger die Quellen, es athmeten
   Der dunkeln Erde Blüthen mich liebend an,
      Und lächelnd über Silberwolken
        Neigte sich seegnend herab der Aether.

GO DOWN, THEN, LOVELY SUN ...

Go down, then, lovely sun, for but little they
   Regarded you, nor, holy one, knew your worth,
      Since without toil you rose, and quiet,
         Over a people for ever toiling.

To me, however, kindly you rise and set,
   O glorious light, and brightly my eyes respond,
      For godly, silent reverence I
         Learned when Diótima soothed my frenzy.

O how I listened, Heaven's own messenger,
   To you, my teacher! Love! How to the golden day
      These eyes transfused with thanks looked up from
         Gazing at you. And at once more living

The brooks began to murmur, more lovingly
   The blossoms of dark Earth breathed their scent at me
      And through the silver clouds a smiling
         Aether bowed down to bestow his blessing.

DER FRIEDEN

Wie wenn die alten Wasser, die
        in andern Zorn
   In schröklichern verwandelt wieder
    Kämen, zu reinigen, da es noth war,

So gählt und wuchs und woogte von Jahr zu Jahr
   Rastlos und überschwemmte das bange Land
   Die unerhörte Schlacht, daß weit hüllt
    Dunkel und Blässe das Haupt der Menschen.

Die Heldenkräfte flogen, wie Wellen, auf
   Und schwanden weg, du kürztest o Rächerin!
   Den Dienern oft die Arbeit schnell und
    Brachtest in Ruhe sie heim, die Streiter.

O du die unerbittlich und unbesiegt
   Den Feigern und den Übergewaltgen trift,
    Daß bis ins lezte Glied hinab vom
    Schlage sein armes Geschlecht erzittert,

Die du geheim den Stachel und Zügel hältst
   Zu hemmen und zu fördern, o Nemesis,
    Strafst du die Todten noch, es schliefen
    Unter Italiens Lorbeergärten

Sonst ungestört die alten Eroberer.
   Und schonst du auch des müßigen Hirten nicht,
    Und haben endlich wohl genug den
    Üppigen Schlummer gebüßt die Völker?

PEACE

As though the old flood waters, which
                                  wilder still,
    Whipped up to new, more dreadful fury,
       Now were returning, to cleanse, as needed,

So grew and swelled and billowed from year to year
    This battle like no other and overflowed
       The awe-struck land, till far and wide in
          Darkness and pallor men's heads were shrouded.

The strength of heroes rose like the wind-lashed waves
    And then died down, Avenger, for often you
       Cut short your servants' work and quickly
          Brought them back home to their rest, those fighters.

O you the unrelenting, unvanquished, who
    Strike both the coward and the too violent
       That down to the last limb his wretched
          Lineage will feel the reverberation,

Who, hidden, hold the spur and the rein as well,
    To further and restrain us, O Nemesis,
       The very dead you punish—under
          Italy's laurel-dark gardens nothing

Disturbed the ancient conquerors where they slept.
    And now the idle shepherds you do not spare?
       And still have not the nations done you
          Penance enough for luxurious slumber?

Wer hub es an? wer brachte den Fluch? von heut
  Ists nicht und nicht von gestern, und die zuerst
    Das Maas verloren, unsre Väter
      Wußten es nicht, und es trieb ihr Geist sie.

Zu lang, zu lang schon treten die Sterblichen
  Sich gern aufs Haupt, und zanken um Herrschaft sich,
    Den Nachbar fürchtend, und es hat auf
      Eigenem Boden der Mann nicht Seegen.

Und unstät wehn und irren, dem Chaos gleich,
  Dem gährenden Geschlechte die Wünsche noch
    Umher und wild ist und verzagt und kalt von
      Sorgen das Leben der Armen immer.

Du aber wandelst ruhig die sichre Bahn
  O Mutter Erd im Lichte. Dein Frühling blüht,
    Melodischwechselnd gehn dir hin die
      Wachsenden Zeiten, du Lebensreiche!

Komm du nun, du der heiligen Musen all,
  Und der Gestirne Liebling, verjüngender
    Ersehnter Friede, komm und gieb ein
      Bleiben im Leben, ein Herz uns wieder.

Unschuldiger! sind klüger die Kinder doch
  Beinahe, denn wir Alten; es irrt der Zwist
    Den Guten nicht den Sinn, und klar und
      Freudig ist ihnen ihr Auge blieben.

Und wie mit andern Schauenden lächelnd ernst
  Der Richter auf der Jünglinge Rennbahn sieht,
    Wo glühender die Kämpfenden die
      Wagen in stäubende Wolken treiben,

Who started it? Who brought us the curse? Not from
    Today, nor yesterday does it spring, and those
        Who first transgressed the bounds, our forbears,
            Did it unknowing, their daemons drove them.

Too long, too long now mortals have liked to tread
    On others' heads, and bickered for mastery,
        In fear of neighbours, and no man on
            Soil that's his own ever finds contentment.

And chaos-like, inconstant, the wishes of
    This race in ferment waver and flutter still,
        And always wild and awed and cold with
            Care is the life of these wretched beings.

But you, O Mother Earth, in the light pursue
    Your steady course. Your springtime as ever flowers,
        Melodious in their modulations,
            Seasons go by but leave you more living.

Now come, best loved by all the nine Muses and
    The circling constellations, you long desired
        Rejuvenator, Peace, and give us
            Back a firm foothold in life, a centre.

You innocent! But almost, it seems, a child
    Is wiser than we old ones; no conflict tears
        His mind or heart, and still untroubled,
            Joyful and clear are the eyes of children.

And as the umpire, smilingly earnest, looks
    Upon the young men's racecourse with other guests
        And sees the combatants more hotly
            Drive into clouds their dust-whirling chariots,

So steht und lächelt Helios über uns
Und einsam ist der Göttliche, Frohe nie,
Denn ewig wohnen sie, des Aethers
Blühende Sterne, die Heiligfreien.

So up above us Helios stands and smiles,
   The glad, divine, and never is lonely there,
      For without end they dwell there, Aether's
         Blossoming stars, in their holy freedom.

AN DIE DEUTSCHEN

Spottet nimmer des Kinds, wenn noch das alberne
  Auf dem Rosse von Holz herrlich und viel sich dünkt,
    O ihr Guten! auch wir sind
      Thatenarm und gedankenvoll!

Aber kommt, wie der Stral aus dem Gewölke kommt,
  Aus Gedanken vieleicht, geistig und reif die That?
    Folgt die Frucht, wie des Haines
      Dunklem Blatte, der stillen Schrift?

Und das Schweigen im Volk, ist es die Feier schon
  Vor dem Feste? die Furcht, welche den Gott ansagt?
    O dann nimmt mich, ihr Lieben!
      Daß ich büße die Lästerung.

Schon zu lange, zu lang irr ich, dem Laien gleich,
  In des bildenden Geists werdender Werkstatt hier,
    Nur was blühet, erkenn ich,
      Was er sinnet, erkenn ich nicht.

Und zu ahnen ist süß, aber ein Leiden auch,
  Und schon Jahre genug leb' ich in sterblicher
    Unverständiger Liebe
      Zweifelnd, immer bewegt vor ihm,

Der das stetige Werk immer aus liebender
  Seele näher mir bringt, lächelnd dem Sterblichen
    Wo ich zage, des Lebens
      Reine Tiefe zu Reife bringt.

TO THE GERMANS

Never laugh at the child, seeing the silly one
  Feel important and great up on his rocking-horse;
    O my brothers, we too are
      Poor in deeds though we've thoughts enough!

But as lightning from clouds, out of mere thoughts perhaps
  Will the deed in the end, lucid, mature, leap out?
    As from dark orchard leaves, from
      Quiet scripts does the fruit issue?

And this hush in the crowd, is it the joy before
  Joy's occasion? The awe marking the god's approach?
    O then seize me, my dear ones,
      Make me pay for my slanderous words.

Far too long now, too long like a poor layman I
  In the shaping Spirit's workshop have roamed perplexed;
    Things half-grown I can see there,
      What he schemes I can not make out.

Sweet it is to divine, but an affliction too,
  And enough years I've spent loving as mortals do,
    Doubting, uncomprehending,
      Ever moved in his presence who

Ever closer to me out of his loving soul
  Brings the constant great work, smiles at the mortal man
    Where I falter, and to its
      Ripeness brings the pure depth of life.

Schöpferischer, o wann, Genius unsers Volks,
Wann erscheinest du ganz, Seele des Vaterlands,
Daß ich tiefer mich beuge,
Daß die leiseste Saite selbst

Mir verstumme vor dir, daß ich beschämt
Eine Blume der Nacht, himmlischer Tag, vor dir
Enden möge mit Freuden,
Wenn sie alle, mit denen ich

Vormals trauerte, wenn unsere Städte nun
Hell und offen und wach, reineren Feuers voll
Und die Berge des deutschen
Landes Berge der Musen sind,

Wie die herrlichen einst, Pindos und Helikon,
Und Parnassos, und rings unter des Vaterlands
Goldnem Himmel die freie,
Klare, geistige Freude glänzt.

Wohl ist enge begränzt unsere Lebenszeit,
Unserer Jahre Zahl sehen und zählen wir,
Doch die Jahre der Völker,
Sah ein sterbliches Auge sie?

Wenn die Seele dir auch über die eigne Zeit
Sich die sehnende schwingt, trauernd verweilest du
Dann am kalten Gestade
Bei den Deinen und kennst sie nie,

Und die Künftigen auch, sie, die Verheißenen
Wo, wo siehest du sie, daß du an Freundeshand
Einmal wieder erwarmest,
Einer Seele vernehmlich seist?

O creative one, when, genius innate in us,
    Wholly will you appear, soul of our fatherland?
        So that lower I bow then,
            Of my strings the most muted then

Dare not sound, and ashamed, dumb before you I droop
    Like a flower of the night, heavenly day, and long
        But to wither with gladness,
            When all those in whose midst I could

Only mourn—when our towns, brightened now, are awake,
    Open and communal, full of a purer fire,
        And the mountains of German
            Lands are mountains the Muses haunt

Like those glorious ones then, Pindos and Helicon
    And Parnassus, and here under the fatherland's
        Golden sky the pellucid,
            Free and enlightened gladness gleams.

True, the span of our lives briefly extends, we can
    See and count the few years granted to us on earth,
        But the years of the peoples,
            These what mortal man's eye has seen?

Though your soul roams away, winged with its yearning soars
    Far beyond your own time, mournful you linger here,
        Cold on desolate shores, with
            Your own kind, but estranged from them;

And those others to come, those for whose advent we wait,
    Where, O where can you see them, that once more you'll be
        Warmed by one hand that's friendly,
            Audible to one living soul?

Klanglos,   ists in der Halle längst,
　　Armer Seher! bei dir, sehnend verlischt dein Aug
　　Und du schlummerst hinunter
　　　Ohne Namen und unbeweint.

Without resonance, long empty for you it's been
  In your hall, poor seer, now; yearning your eye grows dim,
    And you drowse away, vanish
      Never noticed, unnamed, unwept.

ROUSSEAU

Wie eng begränzt ist unsere Tageszeit.
  Du warst und sahst und stauntest, schon Abend ists,
    Nun schlafe, wo unendlich ferne
      Ziehen vorüber der Völker Jahre.

Und mancher siehet über die eigne Zeit
  Ihm zeigt ein Gott ins Freie, doch sehnend stehst
    Am Ufer du, ein Ärgerniß den
      Deinen, ein Schatten, und liebst sie nimmer,

Und jene, die du nennst, die Verheißenen,
  Wo sind die Neuen, daß du an Freundeshand
    Erwarmst, wo nahn sie, daß du einmal
      Einsame Rede, vernehmlich seiest?

Klanglos ists, armer Mann, in der Halle dir,
  Und gleich den Unbegrabenen, irrest du
    Unstät und suchest Ruh und niemand
      Weiß den beschiedenen Weg zu weisen.

Sei denn zufrieden!   der Baum entwächst
  Dem heimatlichen Boden, aber es sinken ihm
    Die liebenden, die jugendlichen
      Arme, und trauernd neigt er sein Haupt.

Des Lebens Überfluß, das Unendliche,
  Das um ihn   und dämmert, er faßt es nie.
    Doch lebts in ihm und gegenwärtig,
      Wärmend und wirkend, die Frucht entquillt ihm.

ROUSSEAU

How narrowly confined is our day-time here.
   You were and saw and wondered, and darkness falls;
     Now sleep, where infinitely far the
       Years of the peoples go drifting past you.

And some there are whose vision outflies their time;
   Abroad a god directs them, but, yearning, you
     Must haunt the shore, a shade, an outcast
       Cursed by your kin, and no longer love them,

And those you name, whose coming is promised us,
   Where are those new ones, that by a friendly hand
     You may be warmed, where drawing near, that
       Audibly, you, lonely speech, may sound then?

The hall yields no response to your voice, poor man;
   And like the unburied dead you must roam about
     Unquiet, seeking rest, and no one
       To the allotted way can direct you.

So be content!   the tree outgrows
   His native soil, but soon will his branching arms
     The loving, youthful, then begin to
       Droop, and his head he will bow in sadness.

Life's superfluity, the immensely rich
   That teems and glimmers round him, he'll never grasp.
     And yet it lives in him, and present,
       Warming, effective, his fruit contains it.

Du hast gelebt!   auch dir, auch dir
   Erfreuet die ferne Sonne dein Haupt,
      Und Stralen aus der schönern Zeit. Es
         Haben die Boten dein Herz gefunden.

Vernommen hast du sie, verstanden die Sprache der Fremdlinge,
   Gedeutet ihre Seele! Dem Sehnenden war
      Der Wink genug, und Winke sind
         Von Alters her die Sprache der Götter.

Und wunderbar, als hätte von Anbeginn
   Des Menschen Geist das Werden und Wirken all,
      Des Lebens Weise schon erfahren

Kennt er im ersten Zeichen Vollendetes schon,
   Und fliegt, der kühne Geist, wie Adler den
      Gewittern, weissagend seinen
         Kommenden Göttern voraus,

You lived! and *your* crest too, though but once, yours too
　　Is gladdened by the light of a distant sun,
　　　　The radiance of a better age. The
　　　　　　Heralds who looked for your heart have found it.

You've heard and comprehended the strangers' tongue,
　　Interpreted their soul! For the yearning man
　　　　The hint sufficed, because in hints from
　　　　　　Time immemorial the gods have spoken.

And marvellous, as though from the very first
　　The human mind had known all that grows and moves,
　　　　Foreknown life's melody and rhythm,

In seed grains he can measure the full-grown plant;
　　And flies, bold spirit, flies as the eagles do
　　　　Ahead of thunderstorms, preceding
　　　　　　Gods, his own gods, to announce their coming.

HEIDELBERG

Lange lieb' ich dich schon, möchte dich, mir zur Lust,
  Mutter nennen, und dir schenken ein kunstlos Lied,
    Du, der Vaterlandsstädte
      Ländlichschönste, so viel ich sah.

Wie der Vogel des Walds über die Gipfel fliegt,
  Schwingt sich über den Strom, wo er vorbei dir glänzt,
    Leicht und kräftig die Brüke,
      Die von Wagen und Menschen tönt.

Wie von Göttern gesandt, fesselt' ein Zauber einst
  Auf die Brüke mich an, da ich vorüber gieng,
    Und herein in die Berge
      Mir die reizende Ferne schien,

Und der Jüngling, der Strom, fort in die Ebne zog,
  Traurigfroh, wie das Herz, wenn es, sich selbst zu schön,
    Liebend unterzugehen,
      In die Fluthen der Zeit sich wirft.

Quellen hattest du ihm, hattest dem Flüchtigen
  Kühle Schatten geschenkt, und die Gestade sahn
    All' ihm nach, und es bebte
      Aus den Wellen ihr lieblich Bild.

Aber schwer in das Thal hieng die gigantische,
  Schiksaalskundige Burg nieder bis auf den Grund,
    Von den Wettern zerrissen;
      Doch die ewige Sonne goß

HEIDELBERG

Long I have loved you and wish, for my own delight,
  I could call you Mother and give you an artless song,
    You of my native land's cities
      Known to me, the most rurally beautiful.

As the bird of the forest does over mountain peaks—
  Over the river, where gleaming it passes your site
    Lightly and strongly the bridge vaults,
      Noisy with coaches and men.

As though sent by gods, once an enchantment transfixed
  Me upon that bridge as I was walking by,
    And the alluring distance
      Shone for me into the hills,

And that youth, the river, travelled on to the plain,
  Sadly glad, like the heart when, too full of itself,
    To perish lovingly
      It casts itself into the currents of time.

To that fugitive one you had given sources,
  Had given him cool shadows, and all the banks
    Gazed after him, from the wavelets
      Their charming image, tremulous, rose.

But heavily into the valley hung the gigantic
  Castle acquainted with fate, to its very foundations
    Blasted and torn by all weathers;
      Yet the eternal sun poured down

Ihr verjüngendes Licht über das alternde
   Riesenbild, und umher grünte lebendiger
     Epheu; freundliche Wälder
      Rauschten über die Burg herab.

Sträuche blühten herab, bis wo im heitern Thal,
   An den Hügel gelehnt, oder dem Ufer hold,
     Deine fröhlichen Gassen
      Unter duftenden Gärten ruhn.

His rejuvenating light, even over the aging
   Giant hulk, and round about it living ivy
      Greenly grew; benevolent copses
         Rustled down to the castle walls,

Shrubs came blossoming down to where in the bright, calm valley,
   Leaning against the hill or loving the river bank,
      Your cheerful streets and pathways
         Under fragrant gardens repose.

DIE GÖTTER

Du stiller Aether! immer bewahrst du schön
   Die Seele mir im Schmerz, und es adelt sich
     Zur Tapferkeit vor deinen Stralen,
       Helios! oft die empörte Brust mir.

Ihr guten Götter! arm ist, wer euch nicht kennt,
   Im rohen Busen ruhet der Zwist ihm nie,
     Und Nacht ist ihm die Welt und keine
       Freude gedeihet und kein Gesang ihm.

Nur ihr, mit eurer ewigen Jugend, nährt
   In Herzen die euch lieben, den Kindersinn,
     Und laßt in Sorgen und in Irren
       Nimmer den Genius sich vertrauern.

THE GODS

You silent Aether, always in pain or grief
   You keep my soul untouched, and when, hurt, I rage,
      Yet often I take heart, ennobled,
         Helios, in face of your nobler brightness.

You kindly gods, not knowing you men are poor,
   Their coarse hearts rent by war that will not abate;
      The world is night to them, no pleasure
         Prospers for them and no song grows mellow.

But you alone can feed with your deathless youth,
   In those that truly love you, the childlike mind,
      And never, when they stray or suffer,
         Wholly let sadness becloud their genius.

DER NEKAR

In deinen Thälern wachte mein Herz mir auf
Zum Leben, deine Wellen umspielten mich,
Und all der holden Hügel, die dich
Wanderer! kennen, ist keiner fremd mir.

Auf ihren Gipfeln löste des Himmels Luft
Mir oft der Knechtschaft Schmerzen; und aus dem Thal,
Wie Leben aus dem Freudebecher,
Glänzte die bläuliche Silberwelle.

Der Berge Quellen eilten hinab zu dir,
Mit ihnen auch mein Herz und du nahmst uns mit,
Zum stillerhabnen Rhein, zu seinen
Städten hinunter und lustgen Inseln.

Noch dünkt die Welt mir schön, und das Aug entflieht
Verlangend nach den Reizen der Erde mir,
Zum goldenen Paktol, zu Smirnas
Ufer, zu Ilions Wald. Auch möcht ich

Bei Sunium oft landen, den stummen Pfad
Nach deinen Säulen fragen, Olympion!
Noch eh der Sturmwind und das Alter
Hin in den Schutt der Athenertempel

Und ihrer Gottesbilder auch dich begräbt,
Denn lang schon einsam stehst du, o Stolz der Welt,
Die nicht mehr ist. Und o ihr schönen
Inseln Ioniens! wo die Meerluft

THE NECKAR

Your banks and dells awakened my heart to life,
    Your wavelets played, their rippling my music then;
      Of all the lovely hills that know you,
        Rambler, not one is unknown to me there.

Up on their tops quite often the heavens' air
    Allayed the pangs of servitude; from the vale,
      As from the wine-cup life and gladness,
        Glittered the bluish and silver wavelet.

The mountain brooks came hurrying down to you,
    And with them came my heart, and you carried us
      To calm, exalted Rhine, conveyed us
        Down to his cities and pleasant islets.

The world seems lovely still, and my vision flees
    From me, allured by Earth and her various charms,
      To golden Pactolus, to Smyrna's
        Coast or to Ilium's woods. And often

I long to land at Sunium and ask the path,
    The dumb, where are your pillars, Olympion,
      And soon, before the gales and age can
        Bury you too in the scattered rubble

Of temples Athens raised, and her imaged gods,
    For long now desolate you have stood, O pride
      Of worlds that are no more. And O you
        Lovely Ionian isles where the sea breeze

Die heißen Ufer kühlt und den Lorbeerwald
  Durchsäuselt, wenn die Sonne den Weinstok wärmt,
    Ach! wo ein goldner Herbst dem armen
      Volk in Gesänge die Seufzer wandelt,

Wenn sein Granatbaum reift, wenn aus grüner Nacht
  Die Pomeranze blinkt, und der Mastyxbaum
    Von Harze träuft und Pauk und Cymbel
      Zum labyrintischen Tanze klingen.

Zu euch, ihr Inseln! bringt mich vielleicht, zu euch
  Mein Schuzgott einst; doch weicht mir aus treuem Sinn
    Auch da mein Nekar nicht mit seinen
      Lieblichen Wiesen und Uferweiden.

Wafts coolness on hot shores and runs rustling through
 The laurel wood, when sunbeams caress the vine,
  And oh, where still a golden autumn
   Turns into songs the poor people's sighing,

When their pomegranate ripens, the orange glints
 In a green night and richly the resin drips
  From mastic trees and drum and cymbal
   Beat to the wild labyrinthine dances.

To you, perhaps, you islands, my guardian god
 One day will take me; yet even then I should
  Recall my Neckar, loyal to his
   Amiable meadows and bankside willows.

DIE HEIMATH

Froh kehrt der Schiffer heim an den stillen Strom,
  Von Inseln fernher, wenn er geerndtet hat;
    So käm' auch ich zur Heimath, hätt' ich
      Güter so viele, wie Laid, geerndtet.

Ihr theuern Ufer, die mich erzogen einst,
  Stillt ihr der Liebe Leiden, versprecht ihr mir,
    Ihr Wälder meiner Jugend, wenn ich
      Komme, die Ruhe noch einmal wieder?

Am kühlen Bache, wo ich der Wellen Spiel,
  Am Strome, wo ich gleiten die Schiffe sah,
    Dort bin ich bald; euch traute Berge,
      Die mich behüteten einst, der Heimath

Verehrte sichre Grenzen, der Mutter Haus
  Und liebender Geschwister Umarmungen
    Begrüß' ich bald und ihr umschließt mich,
      Daß, wie in Banden, das Herz mir heile,

Ihr treugebliebnen! aber ich weiß, ich weiß,
  Der Liebe Laid, diß heilet so bald mir nicht,
    Diß singt kein Wiegensang, den tröstend
      Sterbliche singen, mir aus dem Busen.

Denn sie, die uns das himmlische Feuer leihn,
  Die Götter schenken heiliges Laid uns auch,
    Drum bleibe diß. Ein Sohn der Erde
      Schein' ich; zu lieben gemacht, zu leiden.

HOME

Content the boatman turns to the river's calm
    From distant isles, his harvest all gathered in;
        So too would I go home now, had I
            Reaped as much wealth as I've gathered sorrow.

Dear river-banks that reared me and taught me once,
    Do you allay love's sufferings, promise me,
        You forests of my childhood, should I
            Come to you now, the same peace as ever?

Where by the stream, the cool, I saw wavelets play
    And on the river's meadow watched boats glide past,
        There soon I'll be; you long-loved mountains,
            Once my protectors, and still the homeland's

Revered and certain frontiers, my mother's house,
    Embrace of loving brother and sister there
        I'll welcome soon, and you'll enclose me,
            Healing my heart like a gentle bandage,

You ever loyal ones; but I know, I know,
    This grief, the grief of love, will be slow to heal,
        Of this no lullaby that mortals
            Chant to give comfort will now relieve me.

For they who lend us heavenly light and fire,
    The gods, with holy sorrow endow us too.
        So be it, then. A son of Earth I
            Seem; and was fashioned to love, to suffer.

DIE LIEBE

Wenn ihr Freunde vergeßt, wenn ihr die Euern all,
　O ihr Dankbaren, sie, euere Dichter schmäht,
　　Gott vergeb' es, doch ehret
　　　Nur die Seele der Liebenden.

Denn o saget, wo lebt menschliches Leben sonst,
　Da die knechtische jezt alles, die Sorge zwingt?
　　Darum wandelt der Gott auch
　　　Sorglos über dem Haupt uns längst.

Doch, wie immer das Jahr kalt und gesanglos ist
　Zur beschiedenen Zeit, aber aus weißem Feld
　　Grüne Halme doch sprossen,
　　　Oft ein einsamer Vogel singt,

Wenn sich mälig der Wald dehnet, der Strom sich regt,
　Schon die mildere Luft leise von Mittag weht
　　Zur erlesenen Stunde,
　　　So ein Zeichen der schönern Zeit,

Die wir glauben, erwächst einziggenügsam noch,
　Einzig edel und fromm über dem ehernen,
　　Wilden Boden die Liebe,
　　　Gottes Tochter, von ihm allein.

Sei geseegnet, o sei, himmlische Pflanze, mir
　Mit Gesange gepflegt, wenn des ätherischen
　　Nektars Kräfte dich nähren,
　　　Und der schöpfrische Stral dich reift.

LOVE

If you drop an old friend, if, O you grateful ones,
    Your own poets you slight, slander and cheapen, may
        God forgive you, but always
            Honour lovers, respect their soul.

For, I ask you, where else humanly do men live
    Now that slavish one, Care, rules and compels us all?
        Therefore too has the God long
            Moved uncaring above our heads.

Yet no matter how cold, songless the year may be,
    When the season is due still from the field all white
        New green blades will be sprouting,
            Often one lonely small bird will sing,

When the woods all expand, slowly, the river stirs
    Milder breezes at last tenderly blow from the south,
        At the hour pre-elected,
            So, a sign of the better age

We believe in, unique thanks to her self-content,
    Noble, pious, above soil hard as brass and waste
        Love, the daughter of God, comes,
            Only his and from him alone.

You, then, heavenly plant, now let me bless, and be
    Ever tended with song, when the aetherial
        Nectar's energies feed you,
            Ripened by the creative ray.

Wachs und werde zum Wald! eine beseeltere,
Vollentblühende Welt! Sprache der Liebenden
Sei die Sprache des Landes,
Ihre Seele der Laut des Volks!

Grow and be a whole wood! Be a more soul-inspired,
  Fully blossoming world! Language of lovers now
    Be the language our land speaks,
      And their soul be the people's lilt!

LEBENSLAUF

Größers wolltest auch du, aber die Liebe zwingt
  All uns nieder, das Laid beuget gewaltiger,
    Doch es kehret umsonst nicht
      Unser Bogen, woher er kommt.

Aufwärts oder hinab! herrschet in heil'ger Nacht,
  Wo die stumme Natur werdende Tage sinnt,
    Herrscht im schiefesten Orkus
      Nicht ein Grades, ein Recht noch auch?

Diß erfuhr ich. Denn nie, sterblichen Meistern gleich,
  Habt ihr Himmlischen, ihr Alleserhaltenden,
    Daß ich wüßte, mit Vorsicht
      Mich des ebenen Pfads geführt.

Alles prüfe der Mensch, sagen die Himmlischen,
  Daß er, kräftig genährt, danken für Alles lern',
    Und verstehe die Freiheit,
      Aufzubrechen, wohin er will.

THE COURSE OF LIFE

More you also desired, but every one of us
   Love draws earthward, and grief bends with still greater power;
     Yet our arc not for nothing
       Brings us back to our starting-place.

Whether upward or down—does not in holy night
   Where mute Nature thinks out days that are still to come,
     Though in crookedest Orcus,
       Yet a straightness, a law prevail?

This I learned. For not once, as mortal masters do,
   Did you heavenly ones, wise preservers of all,
     To my knowledge, with caution
       Lead me on by a level path.

All a man shall try out, thus say the heavenly,
   So that strongly sustained he shall give thanks for all,
     Learn to grasp his own freedom
       To be gone where he's moved to go.

IHRE GENESUNG

Sieh! dein Liebstes, Natur, leidet und schläft und du
  Allesheilende, säumst? oder ihr seids nicht mehr,
    Zarte Lüfte des Aethers,
      Und ihr Quellen des Morgenlichts?

Alle Blumen der Erd, alle die goldenen
  Frohen Früchte des Hains, alle sie heilen nicht
    Dieses Leben, ihr Götter,
      Das ihr selber doch euch erzogt?

Ach! schon athmet und tönt heilige Lebenslust
  Ihr im reizenden Wort wieder, wie sonst und schon
    Glänzt in zärtlicher Jugend
      Deine Blume, wie sonst, dich an,

Heilge Natur, o du, welche zu oft, zu oft,
  Wenn ich trauernd versank, lächelnd das zweifelnde
    Haupt mit Gaaben umkränzte,
      Jugendliche, nun auch, wie sonst!

Wenn ich altre dereinst, siehe so geb ich dir,
  Die mich täglich verjüngt, Allesverwandelnde,
    Deiner Flamme die Schlaken,
      Und ein anderer leb ich auf.

HER RECOVERY

Nature, look, your most loved drowses and ails, and you
Dally, healer of all? Have you grown weak, then, tired,
Gentle breezes of Aether,
Limpid sources of morning light?

All the flowers of the earth, all the deep golden-hued
Happy fruits of the grove, how can it be that all
Fail to cure this one life which,
Gods, you raised for your own delight?

Ah, already restored, holy desire to live
Breathes and sounds in her talk, charming as ever, and
Tenderly youthful your flower
Gleams at you as she did before,

Holy Nature, the same who all too often when
Sadness made me sink down, smiling would garland my
Head with gifts, with your riches,
Youthful Nature, now too restored!

Look, one day when I'm old, you that transmute all things,
And now daily renew youth in me, I will give
To your flame the dead cinders
And revive as a different man.

DER ABSCHIED

Zweite Fassung

Trennen wollten wir uns? wähnten es gut und klug?
  Da wirs thaten, warum schrökte, wie Mord, die That?
    Ach! wir kennen uns wenig,
      Denn es waltet ein Gott in uns.

Den verrathen? ach ihn, welcher uns alles erst,
  Sinn und Leben erschuff, ihn, den beseelenden
    Schuzgott unserer Liebe,
      Diß, diß Eine vermag ich nicht.

Aber anderen Fehl denket der Weltsinn sich,
  Andern ehernen Dienst übt er und anders Recht,
    Und es listet die Seele
      Tag für Tag der Gebrauch uns ab.

Wohl! ich wußt' es zuvor. Seit die gewurzelte
  Ungestalte die Furcht Götter und Menschen trennt,
    Muß, mit Blut sie zu sühnen,
      Muß der Liebenden Herz vergehn.

Laß mich schweigen! o laß nimmer von nun an mich
  Dieses Tödtliche sehn, daß ich im Frieden doch
    Hin ins Einsame ziehe,
      Und noch unser der Abschied sei!

Reich die Schaale mir selbst, daß ich des rettenden
  Heilgen Giftes genug, daß ich des Lethetranks
    Mit dir trinke, daß alles
      Haß und Liebe vergessen sei!

THE FAREWELL

Second Version

So we wanted to part? Thought it both good and wise?
Why, then, why did the act shock us as murder would?
Ah, ourselves we know little,
For within us a god commands.

Wrong that god? And betray him who created for us
Meaning, life, all we had, him who inspired and moved,
Who protected our loving,
This, this one thing I cannot do.

But a different wrong, different slavery
Now the world's mind invents, threatens with other laws,
And, by cunning, convention
Day by day steals away our souls.

Oh, I knew it before. Ever since deep-rooted Fear,
Ugly, crippled, estranged mortals from heaven's gods
To appease them with bloodshed
Lovers' hearts must be sacrificed.

Silent now let me be! Never henceforth let me know
This, my deadly disgrace, so that in peace I may
Hide myself where it's lonely
And the parting at least be ours.

Pass the cup, then, yourself, that of the rescuing,
Holy poison enough, that of the lethal draught
I may drink with you, all things,
Hate and love be forgotten then.

Hingehn will ich. Vieleicht seh' ich in langer Zeit
   Diotima! dich hier. Aber verblutet ist
     Dann das Wünschen und friedlich
       Gleich den Seeligen, fremde gehn

Wir umher, ein Gespräch führet uns ab und auf,
   Sinnend, zögernd, doch izt mahnt die Vergessenen
     Hier die Stelle des Abschieds,
       Es erwarmet ein Herz in uns,

Staunend seh' ich dich an, Stimmen und süßen Sang,
   Wie aus voriger Zeit hör' ich und Saitenspiel,
     Und die Lilie duftet
       Golden über dem Bach uns auf.

To be gone is my wish. Later perhaps one day,
  Diotima, we'll meet—here, but desire by then
    Will have bled away, peaceful
      Like the blessed, and like strangers we'll

Walk about, as our talk leads us now here, now there,
  Musing, hesitant, but then the oblivious ones
    See the place where they parted,
      And a heart newly warms in us,

Wondering I look at you, voices and lovely song
  As from distant times, music of strings, I hear
    And the lily unfolds her
      Fragrance, golden above the brook.

DIOTIMA

Du schweigst und duldest, denn sie verstehn dich nicht,
  Du edles Leben! siehest zur Erd' und schweigst
    Am schönen Tag, denn ach! umsonst nur
      Suchst du die Deinen im Sonnenlichte,

Die Königlichen, welche, wie Brüder doch,
  Wie eines Hains gesellige Gipfel sonst
    Der Lieb' und Heimath sich und ihres
      Immerumfangenden Himmels freuten,

Des Ursprungs noch in tönender Brust gedenk;
  Die Dankbarn, sie, sie mein' ich, die einzigtreu
    Bis in den Tartarus hinab die Freude
      Brachten, die Freien, die Göttermenschen,

Die zärtlichgroßen Seelen, die nimmer sind;
  Denn sie beweint, so lange das Trauerjahr
    Schon dauert, von den vor'gen Sternen
      Täglich gemahnet, das Herz noch immer

Und diese Todtenklage, sie ruht nicht aus.
  Die Zeit doch heilt. Die Himmlischen sind jezt stark,
    Sind schnell. Nimmt denn nicht schon ihr altes
      Freudiges Recht die Natur sich wieder?

Sieh! eh noch unser Hügel, o Liebe, sinkt,
  Geschiehts, und ja! noch siehet mein sterblich Lied
    Den Tag, der, Diotima! nächst den
      Göttern mit Helden dich nennt, und dir gleicht.

DIOTIMA

You suffer and keep silent, unknown to them,
  You noble being, silently earthward gaze
    At brightest noon, for it's in vain that
      Here in the sunlight you seek your kindred,

Those regal ones who truly like brothers once,
  Like crests of one companionable grove were glad
    Of love and of their homeland and the
      Heaven that ever enfolded, blessed them,

Their tuneful bosoms true to their origin;
  Those grateful ones, I mean, who unmatched in faith
    As far as deepest Tartarus proffered
      Gladness, untrammelled as gods, though human,

Those tender noble spirits that are no more;
  For these, though long already our time of loss
    Has lasted, by the former planets
      Daily reminded, the heart still weeps, and

This keening for the dead does not flag or rest.
  Yet time heals all. The Heavenly now are strong,
    Are quick. Already does not Nature
      Claim her old joy-giving rights, reclaim them?

Look, Diotima, dear one, before our mound
  Subsides that age will come, and my mortal song
    Yet see the day which next to gods, with
      Heroes will name you, itself be like you.

RÜKKEHR IN DIE HEIMATH

Ihr milden Lüfte! Boten Italiens!
  Und du mit deinen Pappeln, geliebter Strom!
    Ihr woogenden Gebirg! o all ihr
      Sonnigen Gipfel, so seid ihrs wieder?

Du stiller Ort! in Träumen erschienst du fern
  Nach hoffnungslosem Tage dem Sehnenden,
    Und du mein Haus, und ihr Gespielen,
      Bäume des Hügels, ihr wohlbekannten!

Wie lang ists, o wie lange! des Kindes Ruh
  Ist hin, und hin ist Jugend und Lieb' und Lust;
    Doch du, mein Vaterland! du heilig-
      Duldendes! siehe, du bist geblieben.

Und darum, daß sie dulden mit dir, mit dir
  Sich freun, erziehst du, theures! die Deinen auch
    Und mahnst in Träumen, wenn sie ferne
      Schweifen und irren, die Ungetreuen.

Und wenn im heißen Busen dem Jünglinge
  Die eigenmächt'gen Wünsche besänftiget
    Und stille vor dem Schiksaal sind, dann
      Giebt der Geläuterte dir sich lieber.

Lebt wohl dann, Jugendtage, du Rosenpfad
  Der Lieb', und all' ihr Pfade des Wanderers,
    Lebt wohl! und nimm und seegne du mein
      Leben, o Himmel der Heimath, wieder!

RETURN TO THE HOMELAND

You gentle breezes, heralds of Italy,
  And you with all your poplars, dear river banks,
    You billowing mountain range, and sunny
      Peaks—can it be, is it really you, then?

You quiet place, in dreams after hopeless days
  You taunted me, the homesick, but stayed remote,
    And you, my house, and you, my playmates,
      Trees of the hillside, my old companions!

How long ago, how long! Now the child's calm trust
  Is gone, and gone are youth and delight and love;
    But you, the suffering, the holy,
      Look, you alone have remained, my homeland.

And it's for that, to suffer with you, with you
  To share their joys that, dear one, you raise your sons,
    And when, unfaithful, far from you they
      Wander astray, in their dreams remind them.

And when at last the youth in his fervid heart
  Feels autocratic wishes abate, grow still
    In face of destiny, to you more
      Readily too will the mellowed yield then.

Good-bye, then, days of youth, and you rose-lined path
  Of love, and all you paths of the roaming man,
    Good-bye! And you, my homeland's heaven,
      Take back this life that was yours, and bless it.

ERMUNTERUNG

Zweite Fassung

Echo des Himmels! heiliges Herz! warum,
　Warum verstummst du unter den Lebenden,
　　Schläfst, freies! von den Götterlosen
　　　Ewig hinab in die Nacht verwiesen?

Wacht denn, wie vormals, nimmer des Aethers Licht?
　Und blüht die alte Mutter, die Erde nicht?
　　Und übt der Geist nicht da und dort, nicht
　　　Lächelnd die Liebe das Recht noch immer?

Nur du nicht mehr! doch mahnen die Himmlischen,
　Und stillebildend weht, wie ein kahl Gefild,
　　Der Othem der Natur dich an, der
　　　Alleserheiternde, seelenvolle.

O Hoffnung! bald, bald singen die Haine nicht
　Des Lebens Lob allein, denn es ist die Zeit,
　　Daß aus der Menschen Munde sie, die
　　　Schönere Seele sich neuverkündet,

Dann liebender im Bunde mit Sterblichen
　Das Element sich bildet, und dann erst reich,
　　Bei frommer Kinder Dank, der Erde
　　　Brust, die unendliche, sich entfaltet

Und unsre Tage wieder, wie Blumen, sind,
　Wo sie, des Himmels Sonne sich ausgetheilt
　　Im stillen Wechsel sieht und wieder
　　　Froh in den Frohen das Licht sich findet,

EXHORTATION

Second Version

Echo of Heaven, heart that are hallowed, why,
    Why do you now fall silent, though living still,
        And sleep, you free one, by the godless
            Banished for ever to Night's deep dungeons?

Does not the light of Aether, as always, wake?
    And Earth, our ancient mother, still thrive and flower?
        And here and there does not the spirit,
            Love with a smile wield her laws as ever?

You only fail! Yet heavenly powers exhort,
    And silently at work, like a stubble field,
        The breath of Nature blows upon you,
            She the all-brightening, soul-inspiring.

O hope, now soon, now soon not the groves alone
    Shall sing life's praise, for almost the time is come
        When through the mouths of mortals, this, the
            Lovelier soul will make known her coming,

Allied with men more lovingly then once more
    The element will form, and not rich or full
        But when her pious children thank her,
            Endless the breast of our Earth unfold then,

And once again like blossoms our days will be
    Where heavenly Helios sees his own light shared out
        In quiet alternation, finding
            Joy in the joy of those mortal mirrors,

Und er, der sprachlos waltet und unbekannt
Zukünftiges bereitet, der Gott, der Geist
   Im Menschenwort, am schönen Tage
      Kommenden Jahren, wie einst, sich ausspricht.

And he who silent rules and in secret plans
   Things yet to come, the Godhead, the Spirit housed
    In human words, once more, at noontide,
      Clearly will speak to the future ages.

NATUR UND KUNST

ODER

SATURN UND JUPITER

Du waltest hoch am Tag' und es blühet dein
    Gesez, du hältst die Waage, Saturnus Sohn!
        Und theilst die Loos' und ruhest froh im
           Ruhm der unsterblichen Herrscherkünste.

Doch in den Abgrund, sagen die Sänger sich,
    Habst du den heil'gen Vater, den eignen, einst
        Verwiesen und es jammre drunten,
           Da, wo die Wilden vor dir mit Recht sind,

Schuldlos der Gott der goldenen Zeit schon längst:
    Einst mühelos, und größer, wie du, wenn schon
        Er kein Gebot aussprach und ihn der
           Sterblichen keiner mit Nahmen nannte.

Herab denn! oder schäme des Danks dich nicht!
    Und willst du bleiben, diene dem Älteren,
        Und gönn' es ihm, daß ihn vor Allen,
           Göttern und Menschen, der Sänger nenne!

Denn, wie aus dem Gewölke dein Bliz, so kömmt
    Von ihm, was dein ist, siehe! so zeugt von ihm,
        Was du gebeutst, und aus Saturnus
           Frieden ist jegliche Macht erwachsen.

Und hab' ich erst am Herzen Lebendiges
    Gefühlt und dämmert, was du gestaltetest,

NATURE AND ART

OR

SATURN AND JUPITER

High up in day you govern, your law prevails,
  You hold the scales of judgement, O Saturn's son,
    Hand out our lots and well-contented
      Rest on the fame of immortal kingship.

Yet, singers know it, down the abyss you hurled
  The holy father once, your own parent, who
    Long now has lain lamenting where the
      Wild ones before you more justly languish,

Quite guiltless he, the god of the golden age:
  Once effortless and greater than you, although
    He uttered no commandment, and no
      Mortal on earth ever named his presence.

So down with you! Or cease to withhold your thanks!
  And if you'll stay, defer to the older god
    And grant him that above all others,
      Gods and great mortals, the singer name him!

For as from clouds your lightning, from him has come
  What you call yours. And, look, the commands you speak
    To him bear witness, and from Saturn's
      Primitive peace every power developed.

And once my heart can feel and contain that life
  Most living, his, and things that you shaped grow dim,

Und war in ihrer Wiege mir in
　　Wonne die wechselnde Zeit entschlummert:

Dann kenn' ich dich, Kronion! dann hör' ich dich,
　Den weisen Meister, welcher, wie wir, ein Sohn
　　Der Zeit, Geseze giebt und, was die
　　　Heilige Dämmerung birgt, verkündet.

And in his cradle changing Time has
  Fallen asleep and sweet quiet lulls me—

I'll know you then, Kronion, and hear you then,
  The one wise master who, like ourselves, a son
  Of Time, gives laws to us, uncovers
    That which lies hidden in holy twilight.

UNTER DEN ALPEN GESUNGEN

Heilige Unschuld, du der Menschen und der
Götter liebste vertrauteste! du magst im
Haußse oder draußen ihnen zu Füßen
        Sizen, den Alten,

Immerzufriedner Weisheit voll; denn manches
Gute kennet der Mann, doch staunet er, dem
Wild gleich, oft zum Himmel, aber wie rein ist
        Reine, dir alles!

Siehe! das rauhe Thier des Feldes, gerne
Dient und trauet es dir, der stumme Wald spricht
Wie vor Alters, seine Sprüche zu dir, es
        Lehren die Berge

Heil'ge Geseze dich, und was noch jezt uns
Vielerfahrenen offenbar der große
Vater werden heißt, du darfst es allein uns
        Helle verkünden.

So mit den Himmlischen allein zu seyn, und
Geht vorüber das Licht, und Strom und Wind, und
Zeit eilt hin zum Ort, vor ihnen ein stetes
        Auge zu haben,

Seeliger weiß und wünsch' ich nichts, so lange
Nicht auch mich, wie die Weide, fort die Fluth nimmt,
Daß wohl aufgehoben, schlafend dahin ich
        Muß in den Woogen;

SUNG BENEATH THE ALPS

Innocence, you the holy, dearest and nearest
Both to men and to gods! In the house or
Out of doors alike to sit at the ancients'
    Feet it behoves you,

Ever contented wisdom yours; for men know
Much that's good, yet like animals often
Scan the heavens perplexed; to you, though, how pure are
    All things, you pure one!

Look, the rough grassland beast is glad to serve and
Trust you; mute though it be, yet the forest
Now as ever yields its oracles up, the
    Mountains still teach you

God-hallowed laws, and that which even now the
Mighty Father desires to make known to
Us the much experienced, you, and you only
    Clearly may tell us.

Being alone with heavenly powers, and when the
Light begins to pass by, and swiftly river,
Wind and time seek out the place, with a constant
    Eye then to face them—

Nothing more blessed I know, nor want, as long as
Not like willows me too the flood sweeps on, and
Well looked after, sleeping, down I must travel,
    Waves for my bedding;

169

Aber es bleibt daheim gern, wer in treuem
Busen Göttliches hält, und frei will ich, so
Lang ich darf, euch all', ihr Sprachen des Himmels!
                     Deuten und singen.

Gladly, though, he will stay at home who harbours
Things divine in his heart; and you, all Heaven's
Languages, freely, as long as I may, I'll
                Sing and interpret.

DICHTERBERUF

Des Ganges Ufer hörten des Freudengotts
   Triumph, als allerobernd vom Indus her
      Der junge Bacchus kam, mit heilgem
         Weine vom Schlafe die Völker wekend.

Und du, des Tages Engel! erwekst sie nicht,
   Die jezt noch schlafen? gieb die Geseze, gieb
      Uns Leben, siege, Meister, du nur
         Hast der Eroberung Recht, wie Bacchus.

Nicht, was wohl sonst des Menschen Geschik und Sorg’
   Im Haus und unter offenem Himmel ist,
      Wenn edler, denn das Wild, der Mann sich
         Wehret und nährt! denn es gilt ein anders,

Zu Sorg’ und Dienst den Dichtenden anvertraut!
   Der Höchste, der ists, dem wir geeignet sind,
      Daß näher, immerneu besungen
         Ihn die befreundete Brust vernehme.

Und dennoch, o ihr Himmlischen all, und all
   Ihr Quellen und ihr Ufer und Hain’ und Höhn,
      Wo wunderbar zuerst, als du die
         Loken ergriffen, und unvergeßlich

Der unverhoffte Genius über uns
   Der schöpferische, göttliche kam, daß stumm
      Der Sinn uns ward und, wie vom
         Strale gerührt das Gebein erbebte,

THE POET'S VOCATION

The banks of Ganges heard how the god of joy
    Was hailed when conquering all from far Indus came
        The youthful Bacchus, and with holy
            Wine from their drowsiness woke the peoples.

And you, our own day's angel, do not awake
    Those drowsing still? O give us the laws, and give
        Us life. You, Master, triumph! Only
            You, like that god, have the right to conquer.

Not that which else is human kind's care and skill
    Both in the house and under the open sky
        When, nobler than wild beasts, men work to
            Fend, to provide for themselves—to poets

A different task and calling have been assigned.
    The Highest, he it is whom alone we serve,
        So that more closely, ever newly
            Sung, he will meet with a friendly echo.

And yet, you heavenly powers, you all, and all
    You fountains, all you banks and you groves and peaks
        Where marvellous at first when by the
            Forelock you seized us, and unforeseen the

Divine, creative Genius came over us,
    Dumbfounding mind and sense, unforgettably,
        And left us as though struck by lightning
            Down to our bones that were still aquiver,

173

Ihr ruhelosen Thaten in weiter Welt!
   Ihr Schiksaalstag', ihr reißenden, wenn der Gott
     Stillsinnend lenkt, wohin zorntrunken
       Ihn die gigantischen Rosse bringen,

Euch sollten wir verschweigen, und wenn in uns
   Vom stetigstillen Jahre der Wohllaut tönt,
     So sollt' es klingen, gleich als hätte
       Muthig und müßig ein Kind des Meisters

Geweihte, reine Saiten im Scherz gerührt?
   Und darum hast du, Dichter! des Orients
     Propheten und den Griechensang und
       Neulich die Donner gehört, damit du

Den Geist zu Diensten brauchst und die Gegenwart
   Des Guten übereilest, in Spott, und den Albernen
     Verläugnest, herzlos, und zum Spiele
       Feil, wie gefangenes Wild, ihn treibest?

Bis aufgereizt vom Stachel im Grimme der
   Des Ursprungs sich erinnert und ruft, daß selbst
     Der Meister kommt, dann unter heißen
       Todesgeschossen entseelt dich lässet.

Zu lang ist alles Göttliche dienstbar schon
   Und alle Himmelskräfte verscherzt, verbraucht
     Die Gütigen, zur Lust, danklos, ein
       Schlaues Geschlecht und zu kennen wähnt es,

Wenn ihnen der Erhabne den Aker baut,
   Das Tagslicht und den Donnerer, und es späht
     Das Sehrohr wohl sie all und zählt und
       Nennet mit Nahmen des Himmels Sterne.

You restless deeds at large in a boundless world!
  You fateful days, you sweeping ones, when the God
    Drives calmly pondering where, drunk with
      Rage, the gigantic horses take him—

Of you should we keep silent, and when in us
  Euphonious peals the constant, the quiet year,
    Then should it sound as though capricious,
      Curious, a child had been idly twanging

The Master's lyre, the hallowed, the pure, in jest?
  And for that only, poet, you heard the East's
    Great prophets, heard Greek song, and lately
      Heard divine thunder ring out—to make a

Vile trade of it, exploiting the Spirit, presume
  On his kind presence, mocking him, heartlessly
    Deny the simple one and drive him
      Round like a captured wild beast for pennies?

Till by that prodding roused in fierce anger he
  Recalls his origin and cries out, so that
    The Master comes himself, to leave you
      Lifeless and seared by his lethal missiles.

Too long now things divine have been cheaply used
  And all the powers of heaven, the kindly, spent
    In trifling waste by cold and cunning
      Men without thanks, who when he, the Highest,

In person tills their field for them, think they know
  The daylight and the Thunderer, and indeed
    Their telescope may find them all, may
      Count and may name every star of heaven,

Der Vater aber deket mit heilger Nacht,
  Damit wir bleiben mögen, die Augen zu.
    Nicht liebt er Wildes! Doch es zwinget
      Nimmer die weite Gewalt den Himmel.

Noch ists auch gut, zu weise zu seyn. Ihn kennt
  Der Dank. Doch nicht behält er es leicht allein,
    Und gern gesellt, damit verstehn sie
      Helfen, zu anderen sich ein Dichter.

Furchtlos bleibt aber, so er es muß, der Mann
  Einsam vor Gott, es schüzet die Einfalt ihn,
    Und keiner Waffen brauchts und keiner
      Listen, so lange, bis Gottes Fehl hilft.

Yet will the Father cover with holy night,
　　That we may last on earth, our too knowing eyes.
　　　　He loves no Titan! Never will our
　　　　　　Free-ranging power coerce his heaven.

Nor is it good to be all too wise. Our thanks
　　Know God. Yet never gladly the poet keeps
　　　　His lore unshared, but likes to join with
　　　　　　Others who help him to understand it.

But, if he must, undaunted the man remains
　　Alone with God—ingenuousness keeps him safe—
　　　　And needs no weapon and no wile till
　　　　　　God's being missed in the end will help him.

STIMME DES VOLKS

Zweite Fassung

Du seiest Gottes Stimme, so glaubt' ich sonst
  In heil'ger Jugend; ja, und ich sag' es noch!
    Um unsre Weisheit unbekümmert
      Rauschen die Ströme doch auch, und dennoch,

Wer liebt sie nicht? und immer bewegen sie
  Das Herz mir, hör' ich ferne die Schwindenden,
    Die Ahnungsvollen meine Bahn nicht,
      Aber gewisser ins Meer hin eilen.

Denn selbstvergessen, allzubereit den Wunsch
  Der Götter zu erfüllen, ergreift zu gern
    Was sterblich ist, wenn offnen Augs auf
      Eigenen Pfaden es einmal wandelt,

Ins All zurük die kürzeste Bahn; so stürzt
  Der Strom hinab, er suchet die Ruh, es reißt,
    Es ziehet wider Willen ihn, von
      Klippe zu Klippe den Steuerlosen

Das wunderbare Sehnen dem Abgrund zu;
  Das Ungebundne reizet und Völker auch
    Ergreifft die Todeslust und kühne
      Städte, nachdem sie versucht das Beste,

Von Jahr zu Jahr forttreibend das Werk, sie hat
  Ein heilig Ende troffen; die Erde grünt
    Und stille vor den Sternen liegt, den
      Betenden gleich, in den Sand geworfen

VOICE OF THE PEOPLE

Second Version

The voice of God I called you and thought you once,
  In holy youth; and still I do not recant!
    No less indifferent to our wisdom
      Likewise the rivers rush on, but who does

Not love them? Always too my own heart is moved
  When far away I hear those foreknowing ones,
    The fleeting, by a route not mine but
      Surer than mine, and more swift, roar seaward,

For once they travel down their allotted paths
  With open eyes, self-oblivious, too ready to
    Comply with what the gods have wished them,
      Only too gladly will mortal beings

Speed back into the All by the shortest way;
  So rivers plunge—not movement, but rest they seek—
    Drawn on, pulled down against their will from
      Boulder to boulder—abandoned, helmless—

By that mysterious yearning toward the chasm;
  Chaotic deeps attract, and whole peoples too
    May come to long for death, and valiant
      Towns that have striven to do the best thing,

Year in, year out pursuing their task—these too
  A holy end has stricken; the earth grows green,
    And there beneath the stars, like mortals
      Deep in their prayers, quite still, prostrated

Freiwillig überwunden die lange Kunst
   Vor jenen Unnachahmbaren da; er selbst,
      Der Mensch, mit eigner Hand zerbrach, die
         Hohen zu ehren, sein Werk der Künstler.

Doch minder nicht sind jene den Menschen hold,
   Sie lieben wieder, so wie geliebt sie sind,
      Und hemmen öfters, daß er lang im
         Lichte sich freue, die Bahn des Menschen.

Und, nicht des Adlers Jungen allein, sie wirft
   Der Vater aus dem Neste, damit sie nicht
      Zu lang' ihm bleiben, uns auch treibt mit
         Richtigem Stachel hinaus der Herrscher.

Wohl jenen, die zur Ruhe gegangen sind,
   Und vor der Zeit gefallen, auch die, auch die
      Geopfert, gleich den Erstlingen der
         Erndte, sie haben ein Theil gefunden.

Am Xanthos lag, in griechischer Zeit, die Stadt,
   Jezt aber, gleich den größeren die dort ruhn
      Ist durch ein Schiksaal sie dem heilgen
         Lichte des Tages hinweggekommen.

Sie kamen aber nicht in der offnen Schlacht
   Durch eigne Hand um. Fürchterlich ist davon,
      Was dort geschehn, die wunderbare
         Sage von Osten zu uns gelanget.

Es reizte sie die Güte von Brutus. Denn
   Als Feuer ausgegangen, so bot er sich
      Zu helfen ihnen, ob er gleich, als Feldherr,
         Stand in Belagerung vor den Thoren.

On sand, outgrown, and willingly, lies long art
  Flung down before the Matchless; and he himself,
    The man, the artist with his own two
      Hands broke his work for their sake, in homage.

Yet they, the Heavenly, to men remain well-disposed,
  As we love them so they will return our love
    And lest too briefly he enjoy the
      Light, will obstruct a man's course to ruin.

And not the eagle's fledgelings alone their sire
  Throws out of eyries, knowing that else too long
    They'd idle—us the Ruler also
      Goads into flight with a prong that's fitting.

Those men I praise who early lay down to rest,
  Who fell before their time, and those also, those
    Like firstfruits of the harvest offered
      Up—they were granted a part, a portion.

By Xanthos once, in Grecian times, there stood
  The town, but now, like greater ones resting there,
    Because a destiny ordained it
      Xanthos is lost to our holy daylight.

But not in open battle, by their own hands
  Her people perished. Dreadful and marvellous
    The legend of that town's destruction,
      Travelling on from the East, has reached us.

The kindliness of Brutus provoked them. For
  When fire broke out, most nobly he offered them
    His help, although he led those troops which
      Stood at their gates to besiege the township.

Doch von den Mauern warfen die Diener sie
  Die er gesandt. Lebendiger ward darauf
    Das Feuer und sie freuten sich und ihnen
      Streket' entgegen die Hände Brutus

Und alle waren außer sich selbst. Geschrei
  Entstand und Jauchzen. Drauf in die Flamme warf
    Sich Mann und Weib, von Knaben stürzt' auch
      Der von dem Dach, in der Väter Schwerdt der.

Nicht räthlich ist es, Helden zu trozen. Längst
  Wars aber vorbereitet. Die Väter auch
    Da sie ergriffen waren, einst, und
      Heftig die persischen Feinde drängten,

Entzündeten, ergreiffend des Stromes Rohr,
  Daß sie das Freie fänden, die Stadt. Und Haus
    Und Tempel nahm, zum heilgen Aether
      Fliegend, und Menschen hinweg die Flamme.

So hatten es die Kinder gehört, und wohl
  Sind gut die Sagen, denn ein Gedächtniß sind
    Dem Höchsten sie, doch auch bedarf es
      Eines, die heiligen auszulegen.

Yet from the walls they threw all the servants down
  Whom he had sent. Much livelier then at once
    The fire flared up, and they rejoiced, and
      Brutus extended his arms towards them,

All were beside themselves. And great crying there,
  Great jubilation sounded. Then into flames
    Leapt man and woman; boys came hurtling
      Down from the roofs or their fathers stabbed them.

It is not wise to fight against heroes. But
  Events long past prepared it. Their ancestors
    When they were quite encircled once and
      Strongly the Persian forces pressed them,

Took rushes from the rivers and, that their foes
  Might find a desert there, set ablaze their town;
    And house and temple—breathed to holy
      Aether—and men did the flame carry off there.

So their descendants heard, and no doubt such lore
  Is good, because it serves to remind us of
    The Highest; yet there's also need of
      One to interpret these holy legends.

DER BLINDE SÄNGER

Ελυσεν αινον αχος απ' ομματων Αρης

Sophokles

Wo bist du, Jugendliches! das immer mich
　Zur Stunde wekt des Morgens, wo bist du, Licht!
　　Das Herz ist wach, doch bannt und hält in
　　　Heiligem Zauber die Nacht mich immer.

Sonst lauscht' ich um die Dämmerung gern, sonst harrt'
　Ich gerne dein am Hügel, und nie umsonst!
　　Nie täuschten mich, du Holdes, deine
　　　Boten, die Lüfte, denn immer kamst du,

Kamst allbeseeligend den gewohnten Pfad
　Herein in deiner Schöne, wo bist du, Licht!
　　Das Herz ist wieder wach, doch bannt und
　　　Hemmt die unendliche Nacht mich immer.

Mir grünten sonst die Lauben; es leuchteten
　Die Blumen, wie die eigenen Augen, mir;
　　Nicht ferne war das Angesicht der
　　　Meinen und leuchtete mir und droben

Und um die Wälder sah ich die Fittige
　Des Himmels wandern, da ich ein Jüngling war;
　　Nun siz ich still allein, von einer
　　　Stunde zur anderen und Gestalten

Aus Lieb und Laid der helleren Tage schafft
　Zur eignen Freude nun mein Gedanke sich,
　　Und ferne lausch' ich hin, ob nicht ein
　　　Freundlicher Retter vieleicht mir komme.

THE BLIND SINGER

Ελυσεν αινον αχος απ' ομματων Αρης

Sophocles

Where are you, youthful herald who always once
  Would waken me at daybreak, where are you, light?
    The heart's awake, but always Night now
      Holds me and binds me with holy magic.

Once towards dawn I'd listen, was glad to wait
  For you upon your hillside, and never in vain!
    Nor ever did your messengers, the
      Breezes, deceive me, for always, dear one,

You came, delighting all, in your loveliness,
  Came down the usual pathway; where are you, light?
    The heart's awake once more, but always
      Infinite Night now constricts me, binds me.

Once green the bowers would beckon to me; the flowers
  Would shine for me, would gleam like my own two eyes;
    Not distant from me were my loved ones'
      Faces and shone for me, up above me

And round the woods I saw, as they travelled on,
  The wings of heaven—then, in the time of youth;
    Now here I sit alone in silence
      Hour after hour and for cheer, for comfort

My mind devises shapes for itself, made up
  Of love and grief remembered from brighter days,
    And far I strain my hearing lest a
      Kindly deliverer perhaps is coming.

185

Dann hör ich oft die Stimme des Donnerers
Am Mittag, wenn der eherne nahe kommt,
Wenn ihm das Haus bebt und der Boden
Unter ihm dröhnt und der Berg es nachhallt.

Den Retter hör' ich dann in der Nacht, ich hör'
Ihn tödtend, den Befreier, belebend ihn,
Den Donnerer vom Untergang zum
Orient eilen und ihm nach tönt ihr,

Ihm nach, ihr meine Saiten! es lebt mit ihm
Mein Lied und wie die Quelle dem Strome folgt,
Wohin er denkt, so muß ich fort und
Folge dem Sicheren auf der Irrbahn.

Wohin? wohin? ich höre dich da und dort
Du Herrlicher! und rings um die Erde tönts.
Wo endest du? und was, was ist es
Über den Wolken und o wie wird mir?

Tag! Tag! du über stürzenden Wolken! sei
Willkommen mir! es blühet mein Auge dir.
O Jugendlicht! o Glük! das alte
Wieder! doch geistiger rinnst du nieder

Du goldner Quell aus heiligem Kelch! und du,
Du grüner Boden, friedliche Wieg'! und du,
Haus meiner Väter! und ihr Lieben,
Die mir begegneten einst, o nahet,

O kommt, daß euer, euer die Freude sei,
Ihr alle, daß euch seegne der Sehende!
O nimmt, daß ichs ertrage, mir das
Leben, das Göttliche mir vom Herzen.

Then often I can hear the great Thunderer's voice,
  At noon when he, the brazen one, draws most near,
    When his own house quakes, the foundations
      Under him boom and the hill repeats it.

The saviour then I hear in the night, I hear
  Him kill, the liberator, and give new life,
    From West to East I hear the Thunderer
      Quickly sweep on, and it's him you echo,

My strings! With him, with him does my poem live,
  And as the stream must follow the river's course,
    Where his thought goes I'm drawn, impelled to
      Follow the sure one through devious orbits.

Where to? where to? I hear you now here now there,
  You glorious one! And all round the earth it sounds.
    Where do you end? And what, what is it
      Lurks above clouds there, and what befalls me?

Day! Day! Above the tottering clouds, it's you
  I welcome back! My eyes are in flower for you.
    O light of youth! And joy, the same as
      Once! Yet more spiritual now you pour from

A holy chalice, pure golden source! And you,
  You verdant earth, our cradle of peace, and you,
    Ancestral house, and all you dear ones
      Met in the past, O draw near, assemble,

O come that yours, that yours be the joy, return
  And all receive the seeing man's blessing now!
    O take, that I may bear it, take this
      Life, the divine, from my heart too burdened.

187

CHIRON

Wo bist du, Nachdenkliches! das immer muß
Zur Seite gehn, zu Zeiten, wo bist du, Licht?
Wohl ist das Herz wach, doch mir zürnt, mich
Hemmt die erstaunende Nacht nun immer.

Sonst nemlich folgt' ich Kräutern des Walds und lauscht'
Ein waiches Wild am Hügel; und nie umsonst.
Nie täuschten, auch nicht einmal deine
Vögel; denn allzubereit fast kamst du,

So Füllen oder Garten dir labend ward,
Rathschlagend, Herzens wegen; wo bist du, Licht?
Das Herz ist wieder wach, doch herzlos
Zieht die gewaltige Nacht mich immer.

Ich war's wohl. Und von Krokus und Thymian
Und Korn gab mir die Erde den ersten Straus.
Und bei der Sterne Kühle lernt' ich,
Aber das Nennbare nur. Und bei mir

Das wilde Feld entzaubernd, das traur'ge, zog
Der Halbgott, Zevs Knecht, ein, der gerade Mann;
Nun siz' ich still allein, von einer
Stunde zur anderen, und Gestalten

Aus frischer Erd' und Wolken der Liebe schafft,
Weil Gift ist zwischen uns, mein Gedanke nun;
Und ferne lausch' ich hin, ob nicht ein
Freundlicher Retter vieleicht mir komme.

CHIRON

Where are you, thought-infusing, which at this time
    Must always move beside me, where are you, light?
        Indeed the heart's awake, but, wrathful,
            Always astonishing Night constricts me.

For then I'd look for herbs of the wood, and on
    The hillside hear soft game; and never in vain.
        And never once your birds deceived me,
            Never; but almost too promptly then you

Would come, when foal or garden contented you,
    Advising, for the heart's sake; where are you, light?
        The heart's awake once more, but, heartless,
            Always most powerful Night allures me.

That once was I, it seems. And of crocus, thyme
    And corn then Earth would pick the first bunch for me.
        And in the cool of stars I learned, but
            Only the namable. Disenchanting

That wild, sad open meadow the demigod,
    Zeus' servant came, the straight man, to lodge with me;
        Now here I sit alone in silence
            Hour after hour, and my mind devises

Shapes for itself—since poison divides us now—
    Made up of love's new earth and the clouds of love;
        And far I strain my hearing lest a
            Kindly deliverer perhaps is coming.

Dann hör' ich oft den Wagen des Donnerers
   Am Mittag, wenn er naht, der bekannteste,
      Wenn ihm das Haus bebt und der Boden
         Reiniget sich, und die Quaal Echo wird.

Den Retter hör' ich dann in der Nacht, ich hör'
   Ihn tödtend, den Befreier, und drunten voll
      Von üpp'gem Kraut, als in Gesichten
         Schau ich die Erd', ein gewaltig Feuer;

Die Tage aber wechseln, wenn einer dann
   Zusiehet denen, lieblich und bös', ein Schmerz,
      Wenn einer zweigestalt ist, und es
         Kennet kein einziger nicht das Beste;

Das aber ist der Stachel des Gottes; nie
   Kann einer lieben göttliches Unrecht sonst.
      Einheimisch aber ist der Gott dann
         Angesichts da, und die Erd' ist anders.

Tag! Tag! Nun wieder athmet ihr recht; nun trinkt,
   Ihr meiner Bäche Weiden! ein Augenlicht,
      Und rechte Stapfen gehn, und als ein
         Herrscher, mit Sporen, und bei dir selber

Örtlich, Irrstern des Tages, erscheinest du,
   Du auch, o Erde, friedliche Wieg', und du,
      Haus meiner Väter, die unstädtisch
         Sind, in den Wolken des Wilds, gegangen.

Nimm nun ein Roß, und harnische dich und nimm
   Den leichten Speer, o Knabe! Die Wahrsagung
      Zerreißt nicht, und umsonst nicht wartet,
         Bis sie erscheinet, Herakles Rükkehr.

Then often I can hear the great Thunderer's voice
    At noon when he, the best-known of all, draws near,
        When his own house quakes, the foundations,
            Shaken, are cleansed and my torment echoes.

The Saviour then I hear in the night, I hear
    Him kill, the liberator, and down below,
        As if in visions, full of luscious
            Weeds I see Earth, a tremendous fire;

But days go by, both lovely and bad, when one
    Observes their changes, suffering pain because
        Of twofold nature, and when none can
            Ever be sure what is best and fittest;

But that's the very sting of the god; and else
    Divine injustice never could claim men's love.
        But native then, at home, the god is
            Visibly present, and Earth is different.

Day! Day! Once more you can breathe, now drink,
    You willows of my streams, an illumined sight,
        And sure, true footsteps go, and as a
            Ruler, with spurs, and located in your

Own orbit you, the planet of day, appear,
    And you, O Earth, our cradle of peace, and you,
        House of my forbears who unurban
            Travelled in clouds with the woodland creatures.

Now take a horse and armour and lastly, boy,
    Take up the slender spear! For the prophecy
        Will not be torn, and not for nothing
            Heracles' promised return awaits it.

THRÄNEN

Himmlische Liebe! zärtliche! wenn ich dein
   Vergäße, wenn ich, o ihr geschiklichen,
     Ihr feur'gen, die voll Asche sind und
       Wüst und vereinsamet ohnediß schon,

Ihr lieben Inseln, Augen der Wunderwelt!
   Ihr nemlich geht nun einzig allein mich an,
     Ihr Ufer, wo die abgöttische
       Büßet, doch Himmlischen nur, die Liebe.

Denn allzudankbar haben die Heiligen
   Gedienet dort in Tagen der Schönheit und
     Die zorn'gen Helden; und viel Bäume
       Sind, und die Städte daselbst gestanden,

Sichtbar, gleich einem sinnigen Mann; izt sind
   Die Helden todt, die Inseln der Liebe sind
     Entstellt fast. So muß übervortheilt,
       Albern doch überall seyn die Liebe.

Ihr waichen Thränen, löschet das Augenlicht
   Mir aber nicht ganz aus; ein Gedächtniß doch,
     Damit ich edel sterbe, laßt ihr
       Trügrischen, Diebischen, mir nachleben.

TEARS

O heavenly love, the tender, if you I should
   Forget, if you, the site that a fate has marked,
      The fiery that are full of ash and
         Even before that were wild, deserted,

Dear islands, you, the eyes of the wondrous world!
   Since only you concern me and matter now,
      You banks where the idolatrous, where
         Love, but to heaven alone, does penance.

For too devoutly almost, too gratefully
   In days of beauty there did the holy serve,
      And furious heroes; and no lack of
         Trees, and the cities at one time stood there,

Visible, like a pondering man; now dead
   Those heroes are, the islands of love defaced,
      Disfigured nearly. So for ever
         Love is outwitted, for ever silly

And yet, soft tears, not utterly now put out
   For me the light of vision; a memory,
      To make my dying noble, still, you
         Thievish, deceitful ones, let outlast me.

AN DIE HOFNUNG

O Hofnung! holde! gütiggeschäfftige!
  Die du das Haus der Trauernden nicht verschmähst,
    Und gerne dienend, Edle! zwischen
      Sterblichen waltest und Himmelsmächten,

Wo bist du? wenig lebt' ich; doch athmet kalt
  Mein Abend schon. Und stille, den Schatten gleich,
    Bin ich schon hier; und schon gesanglos
      Schlummert das schaudernde Herz im Busen.

Im grünen Thale, dort, wo der frische Quell
  Vom Berge täglich rauscht, und die liebliche
    Zeitlose mir am Herbsttag aufblüht,
      Dort, in der Stille, du Holde, will ich

Dich suchen, oder wenn in der Mitternacht
  Das unsichtbare Leben im Haine wallt,
    Und über mir die immerfrohen
      Blumen, die blühenden Sterne, glänzen,

O du des Aethers Tochter! erscheine dann
  Aus deines Vaters Gärten, und darfst du nicht
    Ein Geist der Erde, kommen, schrök', o
      Schröke mit anderem nur das Herz mir.

TO HOPE

O hope, benignly active one, dear to men,
  Who do not scorn the house of the sorrowing
    And, noble, love to serve, to fashion
      Links between mortals and heavenly powers,

Where are you? Little yet I have lived; but cold
  My evening breathes. And silent already, like
    The shades, I walk here while within me
      Songless my shuddering heart is drowsing.

That vale so green where down from the mountain purls
  The spring's cool water daily, and now for me
    The lovely autumn crocus opens,
      There in the stillness I'll wait and, dear one,

Look out for you, or when in the rustling grove
  At midnight wild, invisible creatures teem
    And when, above, the ever-joyful
      Blossoms, the flowering stars, are gleaming,

Then come, O Aether's daughter, appear to me
  Out of your father's gardens; and if you may
    Not wear the shape of earthly spirits,
      Frighten my heart with a different aspect.

VULKAN

Jezt komm und hülle, freundlicher Feuergeist,
  Den zarten Sinn der Frauen in Wolken ein,
    In goldne Träum' und schüze sie, die
      Blühende Ruhe der Immerguten.

Dem Manne laß sein Sinnen, und sein Geschäfft,
  Und seiner Kerze Schein, und den künftgen Tag
    Gefallen, laß des Unmuths ihm, der
      Häßlichen Sorge zu viel nicht werden,

Wenn jezt der immerzürnende Boreas,
  Mein Erbfeind, über Nacht mit dem Frost das Land
    Befällt, und spät, zur Schlummerstunde,
      Spottend der Menschen, sein schröklich Lied singt,

Und unsrer Städte Mauren und unsern Zaun,
  Den fleißig wir gesezt, und den stillen Hain
    Zerreißt, und selber im Gesang die
      Seele mir störet, der Allverderber,

Und rastlos tobend über den sanften Strom
  Sein schwarz Gewölk ausschüttet, daß weit umher
    Das Thal gährt, und, wie fallend Laub, vom
      Berstenden Hügel herab der Fels fällt.

Wohl frömmer ist, denn andre Lebendige,
  Der Mensch; doch zürnt es draußen, gehöret der
    Auch eigner sich, und sinnt und ruht in
      Sicherer Hütte, der Freigeborne.

VULCAN

You come now, friendly spirit of fire, and wrap
   The women's delicate minds in a veil of clouds,
      In golden dreams, and there keep safe the
         Blossoming peace of the ever-kindly.

The man leave still content with his pondering,
   His work, his candle's gleam and the day to come,
      And not too many vexing tangles,
         Ugly small cares let impose upon him

When now the ever-raging one, Boreas,
   My enemy from birth, overnight assails
      The land with frost, and late, past midnight,
         Jeering at men, sings his dreadful war-song,

And blasts our city walls and tears down the fence
   That in long toil we built, and the quiet grove,
      And even interrupts my soul in
         Making its music, for all provokes him,

And wild with fury over the gentle stream
   Pours out his black cloud-bundles, till far and wide
      The valley seethes, like falling foliage
         Down come great rocks from the bursting hillside.

More godly, true, than all that shares life with him
   Is Man. Yet, faced with fury outside, he too
      Is more himself and rests and ponders
         Safe in his cottage, the free-born mortal.

Und immer wohnt der freundlichen Genien
Noch Einer gerne seegnend mit ihm, und wenn
Sie zürnten all', die ungelehrgen
Geniuskräfte, doch liebt die Liebe.

And one at least, one spirit friendly to Man,
 Still, blessing, gladly dwells with him there, and though
  All others, fierce untutored spirit
   Powers, were to rage, yet will Love be loving.

DICHTERMUTH

Erste Fassung

Sind denn dir nicht verwandt alle Lebendigen?
   Nährt zum Dienste denn nicht selber die Parze dich?
     Drum! so wandle nur wehrlos
       Fort durch's Leben und sorge nicht!

Was geschiehet, es sei alles geseegnet dir,
   Sei zur Freude gewandt! oder was könnte denn
     Dich belaidigen, Herz! was
       Da begegnen, wohin du sollst?

Denn, wie still am Gestad, oder in silberner
   Fernhintönender Fluth, oder auf schweigenden
     Wassertiefen der leichte
       Schwimmer wandelt, so sind auch wir,

Wir, die Dichter des Volks, gerne, wo Lebendes
   Um uns athmet und wallt, freudig, und jedem hold,
     Jedem trauend; wie sängen
       Sonst wir jedem den eignen Gott?

Wenn die Wooge denn auch einen der Muthigen,
   Wo er treulich getraut, schmeichlend hinunterzieht,
     Und die Stimme des Sängers
       Nun in blauender Halle schweigt;

Freudig starb er und noch klagen die Einsamen,
   Seine Haine, den Fall ihres Geliebtesten;
     Öfters tönet der Jungfrau
       Vom Gezweige sein freundlich Lied.

THE POET'S COURAGE

First Version

Is not all that's alive close and akin to you,
    Does the Fate not herself keep you to serve her ends?
        Well, then, travel defenceless
           On through life, and fear nothing there!

All that happens there be welcome, be blessed to you,
    Be an adept in joy, or is there anything
        That could harm you there, heart, that
           Could offend you, where you must go?

For, as quiet near shores, or in the silvery
    Flood resounding afar, or over silent deep
        Water travels the flimsy
           Swimmer, likewise we love to be

Where around us there breathe, teem those alive, our kin,
    We, their poets; and glad, friendly to every man,
        Trusting all. And how else for
           Each of them could we sing his god?

Though the wave will at times, flattering, drag below
    One such brave man where, true, trusting he makes his way,
        And the voice of that singer
           Now falls mute as the hall turns blue;

Glad he died there, and still lonely his groves lament
    Him whom most they had loved, lost, though with joy he drowned;
        Often a virgin will hear his
           Kindly song in the distant boughs.

Wenn des Abends vorbei Einer der Unsern kömmt,
Wo der Bruder ihm sank, denket er manches wohl
 An der warnenden Stelle,
  Schweigt und gehet gerüsteter.

When at nightfall a man like him, of our kind, comes
    Past the place where he sank, many a thought he'll give
      To the site and the warning,
        Then in silence, more armed, walk on.

BLÖDIGKEIT

Sind denn dir nicht bekannt viele Lebendigen?
  Geht auf Wahrem dein Fuß nicht, wie auf Teppichen?
    Drum, mein Genius! tritt nur
      Baar in's Leben, und sorge nicht!

Was geschiehet, es sei alles gelegen dir!
  Sei zur Freude gereimt, oder was könnte denn
    Dich belaidigen, Herz, was
      Da begegnen, wohin du sollst?

Denn, seit Himmlischen gleich Menschen, ein einsam Wild
  Und die Himmlischen selbst führet, der Einkehr zu,
    Der Gesang und der Fürsten
      Chor, nach Arten, so waren auch

Wir, die Zungen des Volks, gerne bei Lebenden,
  Wo sich vieles gesellt, freudig und jedem gleich,
    Jedem offen, so ist ja
      Unser Vater, des Himmels Gott,

Der den denkenden Tag Armen und Reichen gönnt,
  Der, zur Wende der Zeit, uns die Entschlafenden
    Aufgerichtet an goldnen
      Gängelbanden, wie Kinder, hält.

Gut auch sind und geschikt einem zu etwas wir,
  Wenn wir kommen, mit Kunst, und von den Himmlischen
    Einen bringen. Doch selber
      Bringen schikliche Hände wir.

TIMIDNESS

Of the living are not many well-known to you?
   On the truth don't your feet walk as they would on rugs?
     Boldly, therefore, my genius,
       Step right into the thick of life!

All that happens there be welcome, a boon to you!
   Be disposed to feel joy, or is there anything
     That could harm you there, heart, that
       Could affront you, where you must go?

For since gods grew like men, lonely as woodland beasts,
   And since, each in its way, song and the princely choir
     Brought the Heavenly in person
       Back to earth, so we too, the tongues

Of the people, have liked living men's company,
   Where all kinds are conjoined, equal and open to
     Everyone, full of joy—for
       So our Father is, Heaven's God,

Who to rich men and poor offers the thinking day,
   At the turning of Time hold us, the sleepy ones,
     Upright still with his golden
       Leading-strings, as one holds a child.

Someone, some way, we too serve, are of use, are sent
   When we come, with our art, and of the heavenly powers
     Bring one with us. But fitting,
       Skilful hands we ourselves provide.

DER GEFESSELTE STROM

Was schläfst und träumst du, Jüngling, gehüllt in dich,
  Und säumst am kalten Ufer, Geduldiger,
    Und achtest nicht des Ursprungs, du, des
      Oceans Sohn, des Titanenfreundes!

Die Liebesboten, welche der Vater schikt,
  Kennst du die lebenathmenden Lüfte nicht?
    Und trift das Wort dich nicht, das hell von
      Oben der wachende Gott dir sendet?

Schon tönt, schon tönt es ihm in der Brust, es quillt,
  Wie, da er noch im Schoose der Felsen spielt',
    Ihm auf, und nun gedenkt er seiner
      Kraft, der Gewaltige, nun, nun eilt er,

Der Zauderer, er spottet der Fesseln nun,
  Und nimmt und bricht und wirft die Zerbrochenen
    Im Zorne, spielend, da und dort zum
      Schallenden Ufer und an der Stimme

Des Göttersohns erwachen die Berge rings,
  Es regen sich die Wälder, es hört die Kluft
    Den Herold fern und schaudernd regt im
      Busen der Erde sich Freude wieder.

Der Frühling kommt; es dämmert das neue Grün;
  Er aber wandelt hin zu Unsterblichen;
    Denn nirgend darf er bleiben, als wo
      Ihn in die Arme der Vater aufnimmt.

THE FETTERED RIVER

Why do you sleep and dream, in yourself wrapped up,
   And by the cold bank linger, too patient youth,
      And do not heed your origin, you
         Son of great Ocean, the friend of Titans!

Those messengers of love whom your father sends,
   Do you not know those winds breathing life at you?
      Does not that word strike home which, bright, the
         Vigilant god from above dispatches?

Yet now, already now it resounds in him,
   Wells up for him as when in the lap of rocks
      He played, and he recalls his strength, the
         Power of his youth now, and now he hurries,

The loiterer, and laughs at his fetters now
   And takes and tears and throws the torn fetters down
      In fury, playing, here and there on
         Banks that re-echo, and at the voice of

That son of gods the mountains all round awake,
   The woods begin to stir, the ravine can hear
      The distant herald, roused within the
         Bosom of Earth with a shudder joy stirs.

Spring comes; new verdure glistens, a dawn of leaves;
   But he far off departs, to immortal kin;
      For nowhere he may rest, but where the
         Arms of his father once more receive him.

GANYMED

Was schläfst du, Bergsohn, liegest in Unmuth, schief,
  Und frierst am kahlen Ufer, Gedultiger!
    Denkst nicht der Gnade du, wenn's an den
      Tischen die Himmlischen sonst gedürstet?

Kennst drunten du vom Vater die Boten nicht,
  Nicht in der Kluft der Lüfte geschärfter Spiel?
    Trift nicht das Wort dich, das voll alten
      Geists ein gewanderter Mann dir sendet?

Schon tönet's aber ihm in der Brust. Tief quillt's,
  Wie damals, als hoch oben im Fels er schlief,
    Ihm auf. Im Zorne reinigt aber
      Sich der Gefesselte nun, nun eilt er

Der Linkische; der spottet der Schlaken nun,
  Und nimmt und bricht und wirft die Zerbrochenen
    Zorntrunken, spielend, dort und da zum
      Schauenden Ufer und bei des Fremdlings

Besondrer Stimme stehen die Heerden auf,
  Es regen sich die Wälder, es hört tief Land
    Den Stromgeist fern, und schaudernd regt im
      Nabel der Erde der Geist sich wieder.

Der Frühling kömmt. Und jedes, in seiner Art,
  Blüht. Der ist aber ferne; nicht mehr dabei.
    Irr gieng er nun; denn allzugut sind
      Genien; himmlisch Gespräch ist sein nun.

GANYMEDE

Why do you sleep, lie crooked, ill-humoured here,
And freeze on banks all bare, you the mountains' son?
Too patient, do not think of grace, when
Once there was thirst at the heavenly tables?

Nor know your father's messengers now, down there,
In the ravine the breezes' more whetted play?
Does not that word strike home which now a
Travelled man sends you, its ancient meaning?

But now it sounds in him, as deeply wells up
As when before high up on the rock he slept.
And in his anger now the fettered
Cleanses himself, and now he hurries,

The clumsy one; he laughs at his fetters now,
And takes and tears and throws the torn fetters down,
Wrath-drunken, playing, here and there on
Banks that observe him, and at the stranger's

Peculiar voice, the herds that were resting rise,
The woods awake, far down all the land can hear
The river-god, and roused within the
Navel of Earth now the spirit shivers.

Spring comes. And everything, in its way and kind,
Blossoms. But he's far off; is no longer there.
Has gone astray; for all too good are
Genii; heavenly talk is his now.

HEXAMETERS AND ELEGIES

(1800-1801)

DER ARCHIPELAGUS

Kehren die Kraniche wieder zu dir, und suchen zu deinen
Ufern wieder die Schiffe den Lauf? umathmen erwünschte
Lüfte dir die beruhigte Fluth, und sonnet der Delphin,
Aus der Tiefe gelokt, am neuen Lichte den Rüken?
Blüht Ionien? ists die Zeit? denn immer im Frühling,
Wenn den Lebenden sich das Herz erneut und die erste
Liebe den Menschen erwacht und goldner Zeiten Erinnrung,
Komm' ich zu dir und grüß' in deiner Stille dich, Alter!

Immer, Gewaltiger! lebst du noch und ruhest im Schatten
Deiner Berge, wie sonst; mit Jünglingsarmen umfängst du
Noch dein liebliches Land, und deiner Töchter, o Vater!
Deiner Inseln ist noch, der blühenden, keine verloren.
Kreta steht und Salamis grünt, umdämmert von Lorbeern,
Rings von Stralen umblüht, erhebt zur Stunde des Aufgangs
Delos ihr begeistertes Haupt, und Tenos und Chios
Haben der purpurnen Früchte genug, von trunkenen Hügeln
Quillt der Cypriertrank, und von Kalauria fallen
Silberne Bäche, wie einst, in die alten Wasser des Vaters.
Alle leben sie noch, die Heroënmütter, die Inseln,
Blühend von Jahr zu Jahr, und wenn zu Zeiten, vom Abgrund
Losgelassen, die Flamme der Nacht, das untre Gewitter,
Eine der holden ergriff, und die Sterbende dir in den Schoos sank,
Göttlicher! du, du dauertest aus, denn über den dunkeln
Tiefen ist manches schon dir auf und untergegangen.

Auch die Himmlischen, sie, die Kräfte der Höhe, die stillen,
Die den heiteren Tag und süßen Schlummer und Ahnung
Fernher bringen über das Haupt der fühlenden Menschen

THE ARCHIPELAGO

Are the cranes returning to you, and the mercantile vessels
Making again for your shores? Do breezes longed for and prayed for
Blow for you round the quieter flood and, lured from beneath it,
Does the dolphin now warm his back in a new year's gathering radiance?
Is Ionia in flower? Is it the season? For always in springtime
When the hearts of the living renew themselves, the first love of
Human kind, reawakened, stirs and the golden age is remembered,
You, old Sea-God, I visit and you I greet in your stillness.

Even now you live on and, mighty as ever, untroubled
Rest in the shade of your mountains; with arms ever youthful
Still embrace your beautiful land, and still of your daughters, O Father,
Of your islands, the flowering, not one has been taken.
Crete remains, and Salamis lies in a dark-green twilight of laurels,
In a ring of blossoming beams even now at the hour of sunrise
Delos lifts her ecstatic head, and Tenos and Chios
Still have plenty of purple fruit, and the Cyprian liquor
Gushes from drunken hillsides while from Calauria the silver
Brooks cascade, as before, into the Father's old vastness.
Every one of them lives, those mothers of heroes, the islands,
Flowering year after year, and if at times the subterranean
Thunder, the flame of Night, let loose from the primal abysses,
Seized on one of the dear isles and, dying, she sank in your waters,
You, divine one, endured, for much already has risen,
Much gone down for you here above your deeper foundations.

And the heavenly, too, the powers up above us, the silent,
Who from afar bring the cloudless day, delicious sleep and forebodings
Down to the heads of sentient mortals, bestowing

Aus der Fülle der Macht, auch sie, die alten Gespielen,
Wohnen, wie einst, mit dir, und oft am dämmernden Abend,
Wenn von Asiens Bergen herein das heilige Mondlicht
Kömmt und die Sterne sich in deiner Wooge begegnen,
Leuchtest du von himmlischem Glanz, und so, wie sie wandeln,
Wechseln die Wasser dir, es tönt die Weise der Brüder
Droben, ihr Nachtgesang, im liebenden Busen dir wieder.
Wenn die allverklärende dann, die Sonne des Tages,
Sie, des Orients Kind, die Wunderthätige, da ist,
Dann die Lebenden all' im goldenen Traume beginnen,
Den die Dichtende stets des Morgens ihnen bereitet,
Dir, dem trauernden Gott, dir sendet sie froheren Zauber,
Und ihr eigen freundliches Licht ist selber so schön nicht
Denn das Liebeszeichen, der Kranz, den immer, wie vormals,
Deiner gedenk, doch sie um die graue Loke dir windet.
Und umfängt der Aether dich nicht, und kehren die Wolken,
Deine Boten, von ihm mit dem Göttergeschenke, dem Strale
Aus der Höhe dir nicht? dann sendest du über das Land sie,
Daß am heißen Gestad die gewittertrunkenen Wälder
Rauschen und woogen mit dir, daß bald, dem wandernden Sohn gleich,
Wenn der Vater ihn ruft, mit den tausend Bächen Mäander
Seinen Irren enteilt und aus der Ebne Kayster
Dir entgegenfrohlokt, und der Erstgeborne, der Alte,
Der zu lange sich barg, dein majestätischer Nil izt
Hochherschreitend aus fernem Gebirg, wie im Klange der Waffen,
Siegreich kömmt, und die offenen Arme der sehnende reichet.

Dennoch einsam dünkest du dir; in schweigender Nacht hört
Deine Weheklage der Fels, und öfters entflieht dir
Zürnend von Sterblichen weg die geflügelte Wooge zum Himmel.
Denn es leben mit dir die edlen Lieblinge nimmer,
Die dich geehrt, die einst mit den schönen Tempeln und Städten
Deine Gestade bekränzt, und immer suchen und missen,
Immer bedürfen ja, wie Heroën den Kranz, die geweihten
Elemente zum Ruhme das Herz der fühlenden Menschen.

Gifts in their fullness and might, they too, your playmates as ever,
Dwell with you as before, and often in evening's glimmer
When from Asia's mountains the holy moonlight comes drifting
In and the stars commingle and meet in your billows,
With a heavenly brightness you shine, and just as they circle
So do your waters turn, and the theme of your brothers, their night song
Vibrant up there, re-echoes lovingly here in your bosom.
When the all-transfiguring, then, she, the child of the Orient,
Miracle-worker, the sun of our day-time, is present,
All that's alive in a golden dream recommences,
Golden dream the poetic one grants us anew every morning,
Then to you, the sorrowing god, she will send a still gladder enchantment,
And her own beneficent light is not equal in beauty
To the token of love, the wreath, which even now and as ever
Mindful of you, she winds round your locks that are greying.
Does not Aether enfold you, too, and your heralds, the clouds, do
They not return to you with his gift, the divine, with the rays that
Come from above? And then you scatter them over the country
So that drunken with thunderstorms woods on the sweltering coastline
Heave and roar as you do, and soon like a boy playing truant,
Hearing his father call out, with his thousand sources Meander
Hurries back from his wanderings and from his lowlands Kayster
Cheering rushes towards you, and even the first-born, that old one
Who too long lay hidden, your Nile, the imperious, majestic,
Haughtily striding down from the distant peaks, as though armed with
Clanging weapons, victorious arrives, and longs to enfold you.

Yet you think yourself lonely; at night in the silence the rock hears
Your repeated lament, and often, winged in their anger,
Up to heaven away from mortals your waves will escape you.
For no longer they live beside you, these noble beloved ones
Who revered you, who once with beautiful temples and cities
Wreathed your shores; and always they seek it and miss it,
Always, as heroes need garlands, the hallowed elements likewise
Need the hearts of us men to feel and to mirror their glory.

Sage, wo ist Athen? ist über den Urnen der Meister
Deine Stadt, die geliebteste dir, an den heiligen Ufern,
Trauernder Gott! dir ganz in Asche zusammengesunken,
Oder ist noch ein Zeichen von ihr, daß etwa der Schiffer,
Wenn er vorüberkommt, sie nenn' und ihrer gedenke?
Stiegen dort die Säulen empor und leuchteten dort nicht
Sonst vom Dache der Burg herab die Göttergestalten?
Rauschte dort die Stimme des Volks, die stürmischbewegte,
Aus der Agora nicht her, und eilten aus freudigen Pforten
Dort die Gassen dir nicht zu geseegnetem Hafen herunter?
Siehe! da löste sein Schiff der fernhinsinnende Kaufmann,
Froh, denn es wehet' auch ihm die beflügelnde Luft und die Götter
Liebten so, wie den Dichter, auch ihn, dieweil er die guten
Gaaben der Erd' ausglich und Fernes Nahem vereinte.
Fern nach Cypros ziehet er hin und ferne nach Tyros,
Strebt nach Kolchis hinauf und hinab zum alten Aegyptos,
Daß er Purpur und Wein und Korn und Vließe gewinne
Für die eigene Stadt, und öfters über des kühnen
Herkules Säulen hinaus, zu neuen seeligen Inseln
Tragen die Hoffnungen ihn und des Schiffes Flügel, indessen
Anders bewegt, am Gestade der Stadt ein einsamer Jüngling
·Weilt und die Wooge belauscht, und Großes ahndet der Ernste,
Wenn er zu Füßen so des erderschütternden Meisters
Lauschet und sizt, und nicht umsonst erzog ihn der Meergott.

Denn des Genius Feind, der vielgebietende Perse,
Jahrlang zählt' er sie schon, der Waffen Menge, der Knechte,
Spottend des griechischen Lands und seiner wenigen Inseln,
Und sie deuchten dem Herrscher ein Spiel, und noch, wie ein Traum, war
Ihm das innige Volk, vom Göttergeiste gerüstet.
Leicht aus spricht er das Wort und schnell, wie der flammende Bergquell,
Wenn er furchtbar umher vom gährenden Aetna gegossen,
Städte begräbt in der purpurnen Fluth und blühende Gärten,
Bis der brennende Strom im heiligen Meere sich kühlet,

Tell me, where now is Athens? Over the urns of the masters
Here, on your shores, on the holy, sorrowing god, has your city
Dearest of all to you perished, utterly crumbled to ashes,
Or does a token, a trace remain, just so much that a sailor
Passing by will mention her name, will notice the site and recall her?
There did not columns rise high, and there on the citadel roof-top
Did not shining figures of gods once gaze down at the people?
And the voice of the people, did it not roar like a wind-lashed
Forest from the Agora, and there, to a prosperous harbour
From the joyful gates did the streets not come hurrying down to meet you?
Look, the distantly scheming merchant unmoored his good ship there,
Glad, since the winged breeze blew for his sake no less and him also,
Like their poets, the gods could love for his service in sharing
Out the good gifts of Earth and linking far countries to near ones.
Far away to Cyprus he sails and still farther to Tyros,
Makes his way up to Colchis and down to the ancient Aegyptos,
Bringing the purple dye and the wine and the corn and the fleeces
Back to his native town and even at times well beyond the
Pillars of daring Hercules, to the new, to the fortunate islands
Widely ranging hope and his vessel's taut wings will convey him,
While, quite differently moved, a lonely young man on the shore will
Long sit listening, and much that's great from the waves he will gather
Sitting there at the feet of him, the world-battering master,
Listening to waves; and not in vain was he reared by the Sea-God

For the foe of genius, the vastly, far-governing Persian,
Now for years has been counting the strength of his weapons and soldiers,
Laughing at Greece, full of scorn at her handful of minuscule islands,
Less than a trifle to him, and still like a dream to that ruler
Seemed the fervent people of Greece, the divinely defended.
Lightly he speaks the command and fast as the flames of the torrent
Horribly spurted and poured from Etna's ebullient crater
Buries towns in its purple flood, and blossoming gardens,
Till the glowing effusion cools in the holy sea's waters—

So mit dem Könige nun, versengend, städteverwüstend,
Stürzt von Ekbatana daher sein prächtig Getümmel;
Weh! und Athene, die herrliche, fällt; wohl schauen und ringen
Vom Gebirg, wo das Wild ihr Geschrei hört, fliehende Greise
Nach den Wohnungen dort zurük und den rauchenden Tempeln;
Aber es wekt der Söhne Gebet die heilige Asche
Nun nicht mehr, im Thal ist der Tod, und die Wolke des Brandes
Schwindet am Himmel dahin, und weiter im Lande zu erndten,
Zieht, vom Frevel erhizt, mit der Beute der Perse vorüber.

Aber an Salamis Ufern, o Tag an Salamis Ufern!
Harrend des Endes stehn die Athenerinnen, die Jungfraun,
Stehn die Mütter, wiegend im Arm das gerettete Söhnlein,
Aber den Horchenden schallt von Tiefen die Stimme des Meergotts
Heilweissagend herauf, es schauen die Götter des Himmels
Wägend und richtend herab, denn dort an den bebenden Ufern
Wankt seit Tagesbeginn, wie langsamwandelnd Gewitter,
Dort auf schäumenden Wassern die Schlacht, und es glühet der Mittag,
Unbemerket im Zorn, schon über dem Haupte den Kämpfern.
Aber die Männer des Volks, die Heroënenkel, sie walten
Helleren Auges jezt, die Götterlieblinge denken
Des beschiedenen Glüks, es zähmen die Kinder Athenes
Ihren Genius, ihn, den todverachtenden, jezt nicht.
Denn wie aus rauchendem Blut das Wild der Wüste noch einmal
Sich zulezt verwandelt erhebt, der edleren Kraft gleich,
Und den Jäger erschrökt; kehrt jezt im Glanze der Waffen,
Bei der Herrscher Gebot, furchtbargesammelt den Wilden,
Mitten im Untergang die ermattete Seele noch einmal.
Und entbrandter beginnts; wie Paare ringender Männer
Fassen die Schiffe sich an, in die Wooge taumelt das Steuer,
Unter den Streitern bricht der Boden, und Schiffer und Schiff sinkt.

Aber in schwindelnden Traum vom Liede des Tages gesungen,
Rollt der König den Blik; irrlächelnd über den Ausgang

So with that King now: a fire destroying, devouring the cities,
Down from Ekbatana his gaudily flashing wild hordes rush;
Oh, and glorious Athene falls; though high up in their mountain
Refuge where animals hear their outcry, old men do their utmost
Even now to press back to their dwellings and smouldering temples,
Yet no prayer of their sons will awaken those ashes, the holy,
Now that death is let loose in the valley, the cloud of destruction
Drifts away in the sky, and whetted by one crime the Persian
Passes by with his booty and on to more plentiful harvest.

   But by the shores of Salamis—O day by the shores of Salamis!—
Waiting there for the end, the Athenian virgins and mothers
Stand and rock in their arms small daughters and sons who were rescued;
As they strain their ears, from the depths now the voice of the Sea-God
Rises, predicting salvation; weighing and judging, the eyes of
Heaven's gods now gaze down, for there by the shores which repeated
Tremors rock, on the waves all foaming, like slow-moving thunder
Ever since dawn a battle has hung in the balance, and noon now
Glows on the combatants' heads, unnoticed by them in their fury.
But the Grecian men, the grandsons of heroes, with brighter
Eyes give battle now; beloved of the gods, they grow mindful
Of the triumph allotted to them; and no longer Athene's
Children suppress their genius, the reckless and death-deprecating.
As, in the end, from its steaming blood the wild beast of the desert
Rises once more, transformed, restored to his prowess, his pride, and
Startling the huntsman, turns; so now, with their weapons aglitter,
At their rulers' command, to the terribly straining, ferocious,
In the midst of defeat their once flagging spirit returns now.
And the battle flares up, like pairs of interlocked wrestlers
Triremes engage and grapple, the rudder's ripped off and adrift the
Floating battlefield cracks, and down go both triremes and sailors.

   Yet lulled off into dizzying dream by the song which that day crooned,
Now the King rolls his eyes; and, smiling askew at the outcome,

Droht er, und fleht, und frohlokt, und sendet, wie Blize, die Boten.
Doch er sendet umsonst, es kehret keiner ihm wieder.
Blutige Boten, Erschlagne des Heers, und berstende Schiffe,
Wirft die Rächerin ihm zahllos, die donnernde Wooge,
Vor den Thron, wo er sizt am bebenden Ufer, der Arme,
Schauend die Flucht, und fort in die fliehende Menge gerissen,
Eilt er, ihn treibt der Gott, es treibt sein irrend Geschwader
Über die Fluthen der Gott, der spottend sein eitel Geschmeid ihm
Endlich zerschlug und den Schwachen erreicht' in der drohenden Rüstung.

   Aber liebend zurük zum einsamharrenden Strome
Kommt der Athener Volk und von den Bergen der Heimath
Woogen, freudig gemischt, die glänzenden Schaaren herunter
Ins verlassene Thal, ach! gleich der gealterten Mutter,
Wenn nach Jahren das Kind, das verlorengeachtete, wieder
Lebend ihr an die Brüste kehrt, ein erwachsener Jüngling,
Aber im Gram ist ihr die Seele gewelkt und die Freude
Kommt der hoffnungsmüden zu spät und mühsam vernimmt sie,
Was der liebende Sohn in seinem Danke geredet;
So erscheint den Kommenden dort der Boden der Heimath.
Denn es fragen umsonst nach ihren Hainen die Frommen,
Und die Sieger empfängt die freundliche Pforte nicht wieder,
Wie den Wanderer sonst sie empfieng, wenn er froh von den Inseln
Wiederkehrt' und die seelige Burg der Mutter Athene
Über sehnendem Haupt ihm fernherglänzend heraufgieng.
Aber wohl sind ihnen bekannt die verödeten Gassen
Und die trauernden Gärten umher und auf der Agora,
Wo des Portikus Säulen gestürzt und die göttlichen Bilder
Liegen, da reicht in der Seele bewegt, und der Treue sich freund,
Jezt das liebende Volk zum Bunde die Hände sich wieder.
Bald auch suchet und sieht den Ort des eigenen Haußes
Unter dem Schutt der Mann; ihm weint am Halse, der trauten
Schlummerstäte gedenk, sein Weib, es fragen die Kindlein
Nach dem Tische, wo sonst in lieblicher Reihe sie saßen,

Threatens, beseeches, exults and sends away runners like lightning.
But he sends them in vain: not one will return with a message.
Runners all covered in blood, and corpses of soldiers and wrecks of
Ships that have split, the thundering wave, the avenger,
Hurls at the poor man's throne where quaking he sits on the shore and
Watches his hordes in retreat; till, himself swept up by the fleeing,
Off he hurries, spurred on by the god, his squadrons all scattered
Driven to sea by the god, who, laughing at last at the weakling,
Smashed his vain baubles and reached him under his threatening armour.

   But now lovingly back to the river that, lonely, awaits them
Come the Athenians, and down from their homeland's neighbourly mountains,
Joyfully mingled, they surge, a colourful, shining procession
Into the desolate valley—but oh, like a time-ravaged mother
When the child long ago given up for lost after years comes
Back alive to her breast, no child but a fully grown youth now,
But with grieving her soul has withered, and joy comes too late for
Her, exhausted with hoping, and hardly she hears and can follow
What her loving son in gratitude hastens to tell her;
So to the people come back now seemed the old soil of their homeland.
For in vain after grove and garden the pious enquire now
And no friendly old door is waiting to welcome the victors
As it used to do once when, happy, a man voyaged homeward
From the islands and, blessed, the fortress of Mother Athene,
Distantly gleaming, appeared to eyes uplifted in longing.
Yet familiar enough, though stripped and deserted, the streets are,
All the gardens that mourn within and beyond the Agora,
Where the portico's pillars and limbs of the gods lie in pieces,
There, stirred up in their souls and rejoicing in faith, now the people
Lovingly link their hands in token of newly pledged union.
Soon the man, too, will seek and find the old site of his dwelling
Under the rubble; his wife, recalling the look of their bedroom,
Weeps and embraces him; the children excitedly ask him
For the table at which they'd sit in a circle at mealtimes

Von den Vätern gesehn, den lächelnden Göttern des Haußes.
Aber Gezelte bauet das Volk, es schließen die alten
Nachbarn wieder sich an, und nach des Herzens Gewohnheit
Ordnen die luftigen Wohnungen sich umher an den Hügeln.
So indessen wohnen sie nun, wie die Freien, die Alten,
Die, der Stärke gewiß und dem kommenden Tage vertrauend,
Wandernden Vögeln gleich, mit Gesange von Berge zu Berg' einst
Zogen, die Fürsten des Forsts und des weitumirrenden Stromes.
Doch umfängt noch, wie sonst, die Muttererde, die treue,
Wieder ihr edel Volk, und unter heiligem Himmel
Ruhen sie sanft, wenn milde, wie sonst, die Lüfte der Jugend
Um die Schlafenden wehn, und aus Platanen Ilissus
Ihnen herüberrauscht, und neue Tage verkündend,
Lokend zu neuen Thaten, bei Nacht die Wooge des Meergotts
Fernher tönt und fröhliche Träume den Lieblingen sendet.
Schon auch sprossen und blühn die Blumen mälig, die goldnen,
Auf zertretenem Feld, von frommen Händen gewartet,
Grünet der Ölbaum auf, und auf Kolonos Gefilden
Nähren friedlich, wie sonst, die Athenischen Rosse sich wieder.

    Aber der Muttererd' und dem Gott der Wooge zu Ehren
Blühet die Stadt izt auf, ein herrlich Gebild, dem Gestirn gleich
Sichergegründet, des Genius Werk, denn Fesseln der Liebe
Schafft er gerne sich so, so hält in großen Gestalten,
Die er selbst sich erbaut, der immerrege sich bleibend.
Sieh! und dem Schaffenden dienet der Wald, ihm reicht mit den andern
Bergen nahe zur Hand der Pentele Marmor und Erze,
Aber lebend, wie er, und froh und herrlich entquillt es
Seinen Händen, und leicht, wie der Sonne, gedeiht das Geschäfft ihm.
Brunnen steigen empor und über die Hügel in reinen
Bahnen gelenkt, ereilt der Quell das glänzende Beken;
Und umher an ihnen erglänzt, gleich festlichen Helden
Am gemeinsamen Kelch, die Reihe der Wohnungen, hoch ragt
Der Prytanen Gemach, es stehn Gymnasien offen,

Watched by ancestors, by benevolent gods of the household.
But the people raise tents, and neighbours renew their old friendships,
Choosing familiar sites, and true to the heart and its habits
Airy new habitations fall into place on the hillsides.
Meanwhile, however, they live as did their forefathers, the free ones,
Who, assured of their strength and trusting the day and its morrow
As do migrant birds, from mountain to mountain once travelled
Singing, the princes of woods and of far-meandering rivers.
Yet their maternal earth, the faithful, as ever enfolds her
Noble people once more, and under a heaven still holy
Gently they sleep, while mild as ever the breezes of youth blow
Over each sleeping head, and out of the plane trees Ilissus,
Murmuring, makes himself known and nightly the wave of the Sea-God,
Which, predicting new days, to new deeds lures them on and inspires them,
Sounds from afar and grants enlivening dreams to his loved ones.
And already their crops, the golden, spring up and burst into flower
In the trampled fields, and piously, patiently tended,
Olive trees are in leaf, and once again at Colonus
In their old pasture, at peace, Athenian horses are grazing.

   But to please the maternal earth and honour the god of the waters
Now the city revives, a glorious artifice, firmly
Founded as galaxies, wrought by genius that readily thus will
Make himself fetters of love, and thus in majestic constructions,
Raised for his restless self, maintains a durable dwelling.
Look, and the forest serves that creator; Pentele, like other
Mountains near by, provides rich ores and offers him marble,
But alive as he is, and glad and splendid it seems to
Leap from his hands, and his work seems easily done, like the sun's work.
Fountains rise from the ground, and over the hills in pure conduits
Quickly the spring is conveyed and rushes to fill the bright basin;
Round about them, bright, as heroes dressed up for a banquet
Gleam round the communal cup, a circle of houses; above it
Looms the Prytanean hall, and now the gymnasia are open.

Göttertempel entstehn, ein heiligkühner Gedanke
Steigt, Unsterblichen nah, das Olympion auf in den Aether
Aus dem seeligen Hain; noch manche der himmlischen Hallen!
Mutter Athene, dir auch, dir wuchs dein herrlicher Hügel
Stolzer aus der Trauer empor und blühte noch lange,
Gott der Woogen und dir, und deine Lieblinge sangen
Frohversammelt noch oft am Vorgebirge den Dank dir.

O die Kinder des Glüks, die frommen! wandeln sie fern nun
Bei den Vätern daheim, und der Schiksaalstage vergessen,
Drüben am Lethestrom, und bringt kein Sehnen sie wieder?
Sieht mein Auge sie nie? ach! findet über den tausend
Pfaden der grünenden Erd', ihr göttergleichen Gestalten!
Euch das Suchende nie, und vernahm ich darum die Sprache,
Darum die Sage von euch, daß immertrauernd die Seele
Vor der Zeit mir hinab zu euern Schatten entfliehe?
Aber näher zu euch, wo eure Haine noch wachsen,
Wo sein einsames Haupt in Wolken der heilige Berg hüllt,
Zum Parnassos will ich, und wenn im Dunkel der Eiche
Schimmernd, mir Irrenden dort Kastalias Quelle begegnet,
Will ich, mit Thränen gemischt, aus blüthenumdufteter Schaale
Dort, auf keimendes Grün, das Wasser gießen, damit doch,
O ihr Schlafenden all! ein Todtenopfer euch werde.
Dort im schweigenden Thal, an Tempes hangenden Felsen,
Will ich wohnen mit euch, dort oft, ihr herrlichen Nahmen!
Her euch rufen bei Nacht, und wenn ihr zürnend erscheinet,
Weil der Pflug die Gräber entweiht, mit der Stimme des Herzens
Will ich, mit frommem Gesang euch sühnen, heilige Schatten!
Bis zu leben mit euch, sich ganz die Seele gewöhnet.
Fragen wird der Geweihtere dann euch manches, ihr Todten!
Euch, ihr Lebenden auch, ihr hohen Kräfte des Himmels,
Wenn ihr über dem Schutt mit euren Jahren vorbeigeht,
Ihr in der sicheren Bahn! denn oft ergreiffet das Irrsaal
Unter den Sternen mir, wie schaurige Lüfte, den Busen,

Temples are built for the gods and, near to immortals, a thought as
Holy as it is bold, the Olympion rises to Aether
From the sacred grove; still many a heavenly hall rose,
Mother Athene, for you; and prouder your glorious hill rose
From its affliction, and long it flourished there, also for your sake,
God of the waters, yours too, and happily gathered your loved ones
Often yet would intone their paean to you on the foothills.

O the children of bliss, the godly, far off are they walking
With their ancestors now, at home, on the far side of Lethe,
Fate's own days quite forgotten? And never will yearning recall them?
Shall my eyes never see them? Nor yet, though he tries all the thousand
Paths of the greening earth, the seeker his life long discover
You, most godlike of men? And was it for this that I heard your
Language, your legend, that now for ever saddened my soul should
Flee me before it is time, drawn down to your shadowy regions?
Yet more close to you rather, where still your orchards are growing,
Where the holy mountain's lone head lies cloud-veiled as ever,
To Parnassus I'll go, and when there in the darkness of oak-trees,
Gleaming, Castalia's spring appears to me, aimlessly roving,
Then, mixed with tears, from the cup that blossoms make fragrant
Water I'll pour on a site all green again now and all budding,
One libation at least for you sleepers who will not awaken.
There in the valley now hushed, where Tempe's great rocks hang suspended,
I will live with you all and often invoke you, the glorious
Names of the dead, in the night, and if then you appear, but in anger
Since your graves are profaned by the plough, with the voice of the heart, with
Pious song I'll appease you all, holy shades, till my soul is
Wholly accustomed and fit to live with you, heroes and wise men.
Many a question, you dead, then the more hallowed will ask you,
You, the living, no less, exalted and heavenly powers,
When with your years you pass by above the Grecian rubble,
You of the certain course! For often, like shivery breezes
Wild confusion grips me till lost I wander in starlight,

Daß ich spähe nach Rath, und lang schon reden sie nimmer
Trost den Bedürftigen zu, die prophetischen Haine Dodonas,
Stumm ist der delphische Gott, und einsam liegen und öde
Längst die Pfade, wo einst, von Hoffnungen leise geleitet,
Fragend der Mann zur Stadt des redlichen Sehers heraufstieg.
Aber droben das Licht, es spricht noch heute zu Menschen,
Schöner Deutungen voll und des großen Donnerers Stimme
Ruft es: denket ihr mein? und die trauernde Wooge des Meergotts
Hallt es wieder: gedenkt ihr nimmer meiner, wie vormals?
Denn es ruhn die Himmlischen gern am fühlenden Herzen;
Immer, wie sonst, geleiten sie noch, die begeisternden Kräfte,
Gerne den strebenden Mann und über Bergen der Heimath
Ruht und waltet und lebt allgegenwärtig der Aether,
Daß ein liebendes Volk in des Vaters Armen gesammelt,
Menschlich freudig, wie sonst, und Ein Geist allen gemein sei.
Aber weh! es wandelt in Nacht, es wohnt, wie im Orkus,
Ohne Göttliches unser Geschlecht. Ans eigene Treiben
Sind sie geschmiedet allein, und sich in der tosenden Werkstatt
Höret jeglicher nur und viel arbeiten die Wilden
Mit gewaltigem Arm, rastlos, doch immer und immer
Unfruchtbar, wie die Furien, bleibt die Mühe der Armen.
Bis, erwacht vom ängstigen Traum, die Seele den Menschen
Aufgeht, jugendlich froh, und der Liebe seegnender Othem
Wieder, wie vormals oft, bei Hellas blühenden Kindern,
Wehet in neuer Zeit und über freierer Stirne
Uns der Geist der Natur, der fernherwandelnde, wieder
Stilleweilend der Gott in goldnen Wolken erscheinet.
Ach! und säumest du noch? und jene, die göttlichgebornen,
Wohnen immer, o Tag! noch als in Tiefen der Erde
Einsam unten, indeß ein immerlebender Frühling
Unbesungen über dem Haupt den Schlafenden dämmert?
Aber länger nicht mehr! schon hör' ich ferne des Festtags
Chorgesang auf grünem Gebirg' und das Echo der Haine,
Wo der Jünglinge Brust sich hebt, wo die Seele des Volks sich

Looking for guidance, advice, and long now they've ceased to speak words of
Comfort to men in such need, the prophetic groves of Dodona,
Mute is the Delphian god, and desolate, long now deserted
Lie the pathways where once, while hopes would gently escort him,
Up walked the questioning man to the town of the truth-loving seer.
But the light above speaks kindly to mortals as ever,
Full of promises, hints, and the great Thunderer's voice, it
Cries: do you think of me? and the sorrowing wave of the Sea-God
Echoes it back: do you never think of me now, as you once did?
For the Heavenly like to repose on a human heart that can feel them;
Still the enrapturing powers, as ever, are glad to escort a
Man who seeks and aspires, and still does ubiquitous Aether
Rest and govern and live above the old hills of their homeland,
So that a loving people conjoined in the arms of the Father
Shall be humanly glad, *one* spirit be common to all men.
Ah, but our kind walks in darkness, it dwells as in Orcus,
Severed from all that's divine. To his own industry only
Each man is forged, and can hear only himself in the workshop's
Deafening noise; and much the savages toil there, for ever
Moving their powerful arms, they labour, yet always and always
Vain, like the Furies, unfruitful the wretches' exertions remain there.
Till the nightmare ends, and the human spirit, awakened,
Burgeons, youthfully glad, and love like a gentle warm breath blows
Over this new age as often once it would blow over Hellas,
Blessing her children in flower, and over our brows less constricted
Nature's spirit that comes to men from far-distant places,
Calmly abiding, in clouds all golden the god reappears now.
What, and you hesitate still? And they, though their birth was divine, still
Live as they did before, O day, as though lonely, confined in
Gloomy depths of the earth, while a springtime eternally living
Glimmers away unsung above the heads of those sleepers?
Not a moment longer! Already I hear on far foothills
Choric song, the feast day's, and hear the green groves all re-echo,
Where the young men more deeply breathe, where the soul of the people

Stillvereint im freieren Lied, zur Ehre des Gottes,
Dem die Höhe gebührt, doch auch die Thale sind heilig;
Denn, wo fröhlich der Strom in wachsender Jugend hinauseilt,
Unter Blumen des Lands, und wo auf sonnigen Ebnen
Edles Korn und der Obstwald reift, da kränzen am Feste
Gerne die Frommen sich auch, und auf dem Hügel der Stadt glänzt,
Menschlicher Wohnung gleich, die himmlische Halle der Freude.
Denn voll göttlichen Sinns ist alles Leben geworden,
Und vollendend, wie sonst, erscheinst du wieder den Kindern
Überall, o Natur! und, wie vom Quellengebirg, rinnt
Seegen von da und dort in die keimende Seele dem Volke.
Dann, dann, o ihr Freuden Athens! ihr Thaten in Sparta!
Köstliche Frühlingszeit im Griechenlande! wenn unser
Herbst kömmt, wenn ihr gereift, ihr Geister alle der Vorwelt!
Wiederkehret und siehe! des Jahrs Vollendung ist nahe!
Dann erhalte das Fest auch euch, vergangene Tage!
Hin nach Hellas schaue das Volk, und weinend und dankend
Sänftige sich in Erinnerungen der stolze Triumphtag!

Aber blühet indeß, bis unsre Früchte beginnen,
Blüht, ihr Gärten Ioniens! nur, und die an Athens Schutt
Grünen, ihr Holden! verbergt dem schauenden Tage die Trauer!
Kränzt mit ewigem Laub, ihr Lorbeerwälder! die Hügel
Eurer Todten umher, bei Marathon dort, wo die Knaben
Siegend starben, ach! dort auf Chäroneas Gefilden,
Wo mit den Waffen ins Blut die lezten Athener enteilten,
Fliehend vor dem Tage der Schmach, dort, dort von den Bergen
Klagt ins Schlachtthal täglich herab, dort singet von Oetas
Gipfeln das Schiksaalslied, ihr wandelnden Wasser, herunter!
Aber du, unsterblich, wenn auch der Griechengesang schon
Dich nicht feiert, wie sonst, aus deinen Woogen, o Meergott!
Töne mir in die Seele noch oft, daß über den Wassern
Furchtlosrege der Geist, dem Schwimmer gleich, in der Starken
Frischem Glüke sich üb', und die Göttersprache, das Wechseln

Quietly gathers in freer singing in praise of that god whose
Realm is the mountain heights, but the valleys also are holy;
For where youthful and growing the river lightheartedly hurries
Out amid flowers of the land, and where on sun-flooded plains the
Noble corn and the orchards mature, there too on the feast-day
Pious folk like to wear bright garlands, and up in the town gleams,
Not unlike human homes, the heavenly hall of pure gladness.
For the gods have restored to all life their spirit, their meaning,
And perfecting, as once you did, you appear to your children
Everywhere, Nature, once more, and as from the brook-threaded mountains
Blessings from this place and that transfuse the new soul of the people.
Then, O then, you joys of Athens, you deeds done at Sparta,
You delicious springtime in Grecian lands! When our autumn
Comes, when you all, grown mature, you genii known in the ancient
World return—and, look, the year's consummation approaches—
Then may the feast-day preserve you also, great era long ended,
May the people look towards Hellas and thanksgiving, weeping,
Making the proud day of their triumph gentle with solemn remembrance!

   Meanwhile, however, flower, till our fruition commences,
Flower, Ionian gardens, no less, and you others, you dear ones
Green behind Athens' rubble, hide her, lest day see her sadness!
And with evergreen leaves, you laurel woods, garland the gravemounds
Of your dead there at Marathon, where in the act of winning
Boys fell dead, and oh, there too, on the plains of Charonea
Where the last Athenians rushed into blood with their weapons,
Fleeing the day of disgrace, and there, over there, from the mountains
Daily down to the battlefield sound your lament, from Oeta's
Peaks give voice to your hymn of destiny, wandering waters!
You, however, immortal although the great hymns of the Grecians
Now do not praise you, may you, O God of the Sea, from your breakers
Often yet with your music infuse my soul, so that on your
Waters fearlessly nimble my mind like a swimmer may practise
Joy which the strong know, fresh joy, and master the language of gods, of

Und das Werden versteh', und wenn die reißende Zeit mir
Zu gewaltig das Haupt ergreifft und die Noth und das Irrsaal
Unter Sterblichen mir mein sterblich Leben erschüttert,
Laß der Stille mich dann in deiner Tiefe gedenken.

All that changes and grows; and if Time, as it rushes on ruthless
Seizes my head too firmly, and need, and this walking bewildered,
Lost, among mortals at last should shatter my mortal existence,
Then in your deeps the calm, the quietness let me remember.

MENONS KLAGEN UM DIOTIMA

1

Täglich geh' ich heraus, und such' ein Anderes immer,
  Habe längst sie befragt alle die Pfade des Lands;
Droben die kühlenden Höhn, die Schatten alle besuch' ich,
  Und die Quellen; hinauf irret der Geist und hinab,
Ruh' erbittend; so flieht das getroffene Wild in die Wälder,
  Wo es um Mittag sonst sicher im Dunkel geruht;
Aber nimmer erquikt sein grünes Lager das Herz ihm,
  Jammernd und schlummerlos treibt es der Stachel umher.
Nicht die Wärme des Lichts, und nicht die Kühle der Nacht hilft,
  Und in Woogen des Stroms taucht es die Wunden umsonst.
Und wie ihm vergebens die Erd' ihr fröhliches Heilkraut
  Reicht, und das gährende Blut keiner der Zephyre stillt,
So, ihr Lieben! auch mir, so will es scheinen, und niemand
  Kann von der Stirne mir nehmen den traurigen Traum?

2

Ja! es frommet auch nicht, ihr Todesgötter! wenn einmal
  Ihr ihn haltet, und fest habt den bezwungenen Mann,
Wenn ihr Bösen hinab in die schaurige Nacht ihn genommen,
  Dann zu suchen, zu flehn, oder zu zürnen mit euch,
Oder geduldig auch wohl im furchtsamen Banne zu wohnen,
  Und mit Lächeln von euch hören das nüchterne Lied.
Soll es seyn, so vergiß dein Heil, und schlummere klanglos!
  Aber doch quillt ein Laut hoffend im Busen dir auf,
Immer kannst du noch nicht, o meine Seele! noch kannst du's
  Nicht gewohnen, und träumst mitten im eisernen Schlaf!
Festzeit hab' ich nicht, doch möcht' ich die Loke bekränzen;
  Bin ich allein denn nicht? aber ein Freundliches muß

MENON'S LAMENT FOR DIOTIMA

1

Daily I search, now here, now there my wandering takes me
  Countless times I have probed every highway and path;
Coolness I seek on those hilltops, all the shades I revisit,
  Then the wellsprings again; up my mind roves and down
Begging for rest; so a wounded deer will flee to the forests
  Where he used to lie low, safe in the dark towards noon;
Yet his green lair no longer now can refresh him or soothe him,
  Crying and sleepless he roams, cruelly pricked by the thorn,
Neither the warmth of the daylight nor the cool darkness of night helps,
  In the river's waves too vainly he washes his wounds.
And as vainly to him now Earth offers herbs that might heal them,
  Cheer him, and none of the winds quiets his feverish blood,
So, beloved ones, it seems, with me it is too, and can no one
  Lift this dead weight from my brow, break the all-saddening dream?

2

And indeed, gods of death, when once you have utterly caught him
  Seized and fettered the man, so that he cringes, subdued,
When you evil ones down into horrible night have conveyed him
  Useless it is to implore, then to be angry with you,
Useless even to bear that grim coercion with patience,
  Smiling to hear you each day chant him the sobering song.
If you must, then forget your welfare and drowse away tuneless!
  Yet in your heart even now, hoping, a sound rises up,
Still, my soul, even now you cling to your habit of music
  Will not give in yet, and dream deep in the lead of dull sleep!
Cause I have none to be festive, but long to put on a green garland;
  Am I not quite alone? Yet something kind now must be

Fernher nahe mir seyn, und lächeln muß ich und staunen,
Wie so seelig doch auch mitten im Leide mir ist.

3

Licht der Liebe! scheinest du denn auch Todten, du goldnes!
Bilder aus hellerer Zeit leuchtet ihr mir in die Nacht?
Liebliche Gärten seid, ihr abendröthlichen Berge,
Seid willkommen und ihr, schweigende Pfade des Hains,
Zeugen himmlischen Glüks, und ihr, hochschauende Sterne,
Die mir damals so oft seegnende Blike gegönnt!
Euch, ihr Liebenden auch, ihr schönen Kinder des Maitags,
Stille Rosen und euch, Lilien, nenn' ich noch oft!
Wohl gehn Frühlinge fort, ein Jahr verdränget das andre,
Wechselnd und streitend, so tost droben vorüber die Zeit
Über sterblichem Haupt, doch nicht vor seeligen Augen,
Und den Liebenden ist anderes Leben geschenkt.
Denn sie alle die Tag' und Jahre der Sterne, sie waren
Diotima! um uns innig und ewig vereint;

4

Aber wir, zufrieden gesellt, wie die liebenden Schwäne,
Wenn sie ruhen am See, oder, auf Wellen gewiegt,
Niedersehn in die Wasser, wo silberne Wolken sich spiegeln,
Und ätherisches Blau unter den Schiffenden wallt,
So auf Erden wandelten wir. Und drohte der Nord auch,
Er, der Liebenden Feind, klagenbereitend, und fiel
Von den Ästen das Laub, und flog im Winde der Reegen,
Ruhig lächelten wir, fühlten den eigenen Gott
Unter trautem Gespräch; in Einem Seelengesange,
Ganz in Frieden mit uns kindlich und freudig allein.
Aber das Haus ist öde mir nun, und sie haben mein Auge
Mir genommen, auch mich hab' ich verloren mit ihr.
Darum irr' ich umher, und wohl, wie die Schatten, so muß ich
Leben, und sinnlos dünkt lange das Übrige mir.

Close to me from afar, so that I smile as I wonder
　　How in the midst of my grief I can feel happy and blessed.

3

Golden light of love, for dead men, for shades, do you shine then?
　　Radiant visions recalled, even this night, then, you pierce?
Pleasant gardens, and mountains tinged with crimson at sunset,
　　Welcome I call you, and you, murmurless path of the grove,
Witness to heavenly joy, and stars more loftily gazing,
　　Who so freely would grant looks that were blessings to me!
And you lovers, you too, the May-day's beautiful children,
　　Quiet roses, and you, lilies, I often invoke!
Springs, it is true, go by, one year still supplanting the other,
　　Changing and warring, so Time over us mortal men's heads
Rushes past up above, but not in the eyes of the blessed ones,
　　Nor of lovers, to whom different life is vouchsafed.
For all these, all the days and years of the heavenly planets,
　　Diotima, round us closely, for ever, conjoined;

4

Meanwhile we—like the mated swans in their summer contentment
　　When by the lake they rest or on the waves, lightly rocked,
Down they look, at the water, and silvery clouds through that mirror
　　Drift, and ethereal blue flows where the voyagers pass—
Moved and dwelled on this earth. And though the North Wind was threatening
　　Hostile to lovers, he, gathering sorrows, and down
Came dead leaves from the boughs, and rain filled the spluttering storm-gusts
　　Calmly we smiled, aware, sure of the tutelar god
Present in talk only ours, one song that our two souls were singing,
　　Wholly at peace with ourselves, childishly, wraptly alone.
Desolate now is my house, and not only her they have taken,
　　No, but my own two eyes, myself I have lost, losing her.
That is why, astray, like wandering phantoms I live now
　　Must live, I fear, and the rest long has seemed senseless to me.

5

Feiern möcht' ich; aber wofür? und singen mit Andern,
  Aber so einsam fehlt jegliches Göttliche mir.
Diß ist's, diß mein Gebrechen, ich weiß, es lähmet ein Fluch mir
  Darum die Sehnen, und wirft, wo ich beginne, mich hin,
Daß ich fühllos size den Tag, und stumm wie die Kinder,
  Nur vom Auge mir kalt öfters die Thräne noch schleicht,
Und die Pflanze des Felds, und der Vögel Singen mich trüb macht,
  Weil mit Freuden auch sie Boten des Himmlischen sind,
Aber mir in schaudernder Brust die beseelende Sonne,
  Kühl und fruchtlos mir dämmert, wie Stralen der Nacht,
Ach! und nichtig und leer, wie Gefängnißwände, der Himmel
  Eine beugende Last über dem Haupte mir hängt!

Sonst mir anders bekannt! o Jugend, und bringen Gebete
  Dich nicht wieder, dich nie? führet kein Pfad mich zurük?
Soll es werden auch mir, wie den Götterlosen, die vormals
  Glänzenden Auges doch auch saßen an seeligem Tisch',
Aber übersättiget bald, die schwärmenden Gäste,
  Nun verstummet, und nun, unter der Lüfte Gesang,
Unter blühender Erd' entschlafen sind, bis dereinst sie
  Eines Wunders Gewalt sie, die Versunkenen, zwingt,
Wiederzukehren, und neu auf grünendem Boden zu wandeln. —
  Heiliger Othem durchströmt göttlich die lichte Gestalt,
Wenn das Fest sich beseelt, und Fluthen der Liebe sich regen,
  Und vom Himmel getränkt, rauscht der lebendige Strom,
Wenn es drunten ertönt, und ihre Schäze die Nacht zollt,
  Und aus Bächen herauf glänzt das begrabene Gold. —

Aber o du, die schon am Scheidewege mir damals,
  Da ich versank vor dir, tröstend ein Schöneres wies,
Du, die Großes zu sehn, und froher die Götter zu singen,

Celebrate—yes, but what? And gladly with others I'd sing now,
    Yet alone as I am nothing that's godlike rings true,
This, I know, is it, my failing, a curse maims my sinews
    Only because of this, making me flag from the start,
So that numb all day long I sit like a child that is moping
    Dumb, though at times a tear coldly creeps out of my eyes,
And the flowers of the field, the singing of birds make me sad now,
    Being heralds of heaven, bearers of heavenly joy,
But to me, in my heart's dank vault, now the soul-giving sun dawns
    Cool, infertile, in vain, feeble as rays of the night,
Oh, and futile and empty, walls of a prison, the heavens
    Press, a smothering load heaped on my head from above!

Once, how different it was! O youth, will no prayer bring you back, then,
    Never again? And no path ever again lead me back?
Shall it be my fate, as once it was that of the godless,
    Bright-eyed to sit for a time feasting at heavenly boards
But to be cloyed with that food, all those fantastical guests now
    Fallen silent, and now, deaf to the music of winds,
Under the flowering earth asleep, till a miracle's power shall
    Force them one day to return, deep though they lie now, at rest,
Force them to walk anew the soil that is sprouting new verdure—
    Holy breath, then, divine, through their bright bodies will flow
While the feast is inspired and love like great flood waters gathers,
    Fed by the heavens themselves, on sweeps the river, alive,
When the deep places boom, Night pays her tribute of riches
    And from the beds of streams up glitters gold long submerged.—

You, though, who even then, already then at the crossroads
    When I fell at your feet, comforting showed me the way,
Taught me to see what is great, to sing with a beauty more mellow,

Schweigend, wie sie, mich einst stille begeisternd gelehrt;
Götterkind! erscheinest du mir, und grüßest, wie einst, mich,
   Redest wieder, wie einst, höhere Dinge mir zu?
Siehe! weinen vor dir, und klagen muß ich, wenn schon noch,
   Denkend edlerer Zeit, dessen die Seele sich schämt.
Denn so lange, so lang auf matten Pfaden der Erde
   Hab' ich, deiner gewohnt, dich in der Irre gesucht,
Freudiger Schuzgeist! aber umsonst, und Jahre zerrannen,
   Seit wir ahnend um uns glänzen die Abende sahn.

8

Dich nur, dich erhält dein Licht, o Heldinn! im Lichte,
   Und dein Dulden erhält liebend, o Gütige, dich;
Und nicht einmal bist du allein; Gespielen genug sind,
   Wo du blühest und ruhst unter den Rosen des Jahrs;
Und der Vater, er selbst, durch sanftumathmende Musen
   Sendet die zärtlichen Wiegengesänge dir zu.
Ja! noch ist sie es ganz! noch schwebt vom Haupte zur Sohle,
   Stillherwandelnd, wie sonst, mir die Athenerinn vor.
Und wie, freundlicher Geist! von heitersinnender Stirne
   Seegnend und sicher dein Stral unter die Sterblichen fällt;
So bezeugest du mir's, und sagst mir's, daß ich es andern
   Wiedersage, denn auch Andere glauben es nicht,
Daß unsterblicher doch, denn Sorg' und Zürnen, die Freude
   Und ein goldener Tag täglich am Ende noch ist.

9

So will ich, ihr Himmlischen! denn auch danken, und endlich
   Athmet aus leichter Brust wieder des Sängers Gebet.
Und wie, wenn ich mit ihr, auf sonniger Höhe mit ihr stand,
   Spricht belebend ein Gott innen vom Tempel mich an.
Leben will ich denn auch! schon grünt's! wie von heiliger Leier
   Ruft es von silbernen Bergen Apollons voran!
Komm! es war wie ein Traum! Die blutenden Fittige sind ja

Joy more serene, the gods, silent as gods are yourself,
  Child of the gods, will you appear to me, greet me once more now,
    Quietly raising me up, speak to me now of those things?
Look, in your presence I weep, lament, though remembering always
    Worthier times that are past, deep in my soul I feel shame.
For so very long on weary paths of the earth now,
    Still accustomed to you, you I have sought in the wilds,
Tutelar spirit, but all in vain, and whole years have gone by since
    Late in the evenings we walked, bathed in that ominous glow.

                    8

You, only you, your own light, O heroine, keeps in the light still,
    And your patience still keeps you both loving and kind;
Nor indeed are you lonely; playmates enough are provided
    Where amid roses you bloom, rest with the flowers of the year;
And the Father himself by means of the balm-breathing Muses
    Sends you those cradle-songs warm as a southerly breeze.
Yes, she is quite the same! From her head to her heels the Athenian,
    Quiet and poised as before hovers in front of my eyes.
And as blessing and sure your radiance falls upon mortals,
    Tender soul, from your brow wrapt in deep thought, yet serene.
So you prove it to me, and tell me, that also to others
    Then I may pass it on, others who doubt as I doubt,
That more enduring than care and anger is holy rejoicing
    And that golden the day daily still shines in the end.

                    9

Thanks, once more, then, I'll give to you up in heaven; once more now
    Freely at last can my prayer rise from a heart unoppressed.
And, as before, when with her I stood on a sun-gilded hilltop,
    Quickening, to me now a god speaks from the temple within.
I will live, then! New verdure! As though from a lyre that is hallowed
    Onward! from silvery peaks, Apollo's mountains ring out.
Come, it was all like a dream, the wounds in your wings have already

                    239

Schon genesen, verjüngt leben die Hoffnungen all.
Großes zu finden, ist viel, ist viel noch übrig, und wer so
    Liebte, gehet, er muß, gehet zu Göttern die Bahn.
Und geleitet ihr uns, ihr Weihestunden! ihr ernsten,
    Jugendlichen! o bleibt, heilige Ahnungen, ihr
Fromme Bitten! und ihr Begeisterungen und all ihr
    Guten Genien, die gerne bei Liebenden sind;
Bleibt so lange mit uns, bis wir auf gemeinsamem Boden
    Dort, wo die Seeligen all niederzukehren bereit,
Dort, wo die Adler sind, die Gestirne, die Boten des Vaters,
    Dort, wo die Musen, woher Helden und Liebende sind,
Dort uns, oder auch hier, auf thauender Insel begegnen,
    Wo die Unsrigen erst, blühend in Gärten gesellt,
Wo die Gesänge wahr, und länger die Frühlinge schön sind,
    Und von neuem ein Jahr unserer Seele beginnt.

Healed, and restored to youth all your old hopes leap alive.
Knowledge of greatness is much, yet much still remains to be done, and
    One who loved as you loved only to gods can move on.
You conduct us, then, you solemn ones, Hours of Communion,
    Youthful ones, stay with us, holy Presentiments also,
Pious prayers, and you, Inspirations, and all of you kindly
    Spirits who like to attend lovers, to be where they are.
Stay with us two until on communal ground, reunited
    Where, when their coming is due, all the blessed souls will return,
Where the eagles are, the planets, the Father's own heralds,
    Where the Muses are still, heroes and lovers began,
There we shall meet again, or here, on a dew-covered island
    Where what is ours for once, blooms that a garden conjoins,
All our poems are true and springs remain beautiful longer
    And another, a new year of our souls can begin.

BROD UND WEIN

AN HEINZE

1

Rings um ruhet die Stadt; still wird die erleuchtete Gasse,
　　Und, mit Fakeln geschmükt, rauschen die Wagen hinweg.
Satt gehn heim von Freuden des Tags zu ruhen die Menschen,
　　Und Gewinn und Verlust wäget ein sinniges Haupt
Wohlzufrieden zu Haus; leer steht von Trauben und Blumen,
　　Und von Werken der Hand ruht der geschäfftige Markt.
Aber das Saitenspiel tönt fern aus Gärten; vieleicht, daß
　　Dort ein Liebendes spielt oder ein einsamer Mann
Ferner Freunde gedenkt und der Jugendzeit; und die Brunnen
　　Immerquillend und frisch rauschen an duftendem Beet.
Still in dämmriger Luft ertönen geläutete Gloken,
　　Und der Stunden gedenk rufet ein Wächter die Zahl.
Jezt auch kommet ein Wehn und regt die Gipfel des Hains auf,
　　Sieh! und das Schattenbild unserer Erde, der Mond
Kommet geheim nun auch; die Schwärmerische, die Nacht kommt,
　　Voll mit Sternen und wohl wenig bekümmert um uns,
Glänzt die Erstaunende dort, die Fremdlingin unter den Menschen
　　Über Gebirgeshöhn traurig und prächtig herauf.

2

Wunderbar ist die Gunst der Hocherhabnen und niemand
　　Weiß von wannen und was einem geschiehet von ihr.
So bewegt sie die Welt und die hoffende Seele der Menschen,
　　Selbst kein Weiser versteht, was sie bereitet, denn so
Will es der oberste Gott, der sehr dich liebet, und darum
　　Ist noch lieber, wie sie, dir der besonnene Tag.
Aber zuweilen liebt auch klares Auge den Schatten
　　Und versuchet zu Lust, eh' es die Noth ist, den Schlaf,

BREAD AND WINE

TO HEINSE

1

Round us the town is at rest; the street, in pale lamplight, grows quiet
  And, their torches ablaze, coaches rush through and away.
People go home to rest, replete with the day and its pleasures,
  There to weigh up in their heads, pensive, the gain and the loss,
Finding the balance good; stripped bare now of grapes and of flowers,
  As of their hand-made goods, quiet the market stalls lie.
But faint music of strings comes drifting from gardens; it could be
  Someone in love who plays there, could be a man all alone
Thinking of distant friends, the days of his youth; and the fountains,.
  Ever welling and new, plash amid fragrance from beds.
Church-bells ring; every stroke hangs still in the quivering half-light
  And the watchman calls out, mindful, no less, of the hour.
Now a breeze rises too and ruffles the crests of the coppice,
  Look, and in secret our globe's shadowy image, the moon,
Slowly is rising too; and Night, the fantastical, comes now
  Full of stars and, I think, little concerned about us,
Night, the astonishing, there, the stranger to all that is human,
  Over the mountain-tops mournful and gleaming draws on.

2

Marvellous is her favour, Night's, the exalted, and no one
  Knows what it is or whence comes all she does and bestows.
So she works on the world and works on our souls ever hoping,
  Not even wise men can tell what is her purpose, for so
God, the Highest, has willed, who very much loves you, and therefore
  Dearer even than Night reasoning Day is to you.
Nonetheless there are times when clear eyes too love the shadows,
  Tasting sleep uncompelled, trying the pleasure it gives,

Oder es blikt auch gern ein treuer Mann in die Nacht hin,
  Ja, es ziemet sich ihr Kränze zu weihn und Gesang,
Weil den Irrenden sie geheiliget ist und den Todten,
  Selber aber besteht, ewig, in freiestem Geist.
Aber sie muß uns auch, daß in der zaudernden Weile,
  Daß im Finstern für uns einiges Haltbare sei,
Uns die Vergessenheit und das Heiligtrunkene gönnen,
  Gönnen das strömende Wort, das, wie die Liebenden, sei,
Schlummerlos und vollern Pokal und kühneres Leben,
  Heilig Gedächtniß auch, wachend zu bleiben bei Nacht.

3

Auch verbergen umsonst das Herz im Busen, umsonst nur
  Halten den Muth noch wir, Meister und Knaben, denn wer
Möcht' es hindern und wer möcht' uns die Freude verbieten?
  Göttliches Feuer auch treibet, bei Tag und bei Nacht,
Aufzubrechen. So komm! daß wir das Offene schauen,
  Daß ein Eigenes wir suchen, so weit es auch ist.
Fest bleibt Eins; es sei um Mittag oder es gehe
  Bis in die Mitternacht, immer bestehet ein Maas,
Allen gemein, doch jeglichem auch ist eignes beschieden,
  Dahin gehet und kommt jeder, wohin er es kann.
Drum! und spotten des Spotts mag gern frohlokkender Wahnsinn,
  Wenn er in heiliger Nacht plözlich die Sänger ergreift.
Drum an den Isthmos komm! dorthin, wo das offene Meer rauscht
  Am Parnaß und der Schnee delphische Felsen umglänzt,
Dort ins Land des Olymps, dort auf die Höhe Cithärons,
  Unter die Fichten dort, unter die Trauben, von wo
Thebe drunten und Ismenos rauscht im Lande des Kadmos,
  Dorther kommt und zurük deutet der kommende Gott.

4

Seeliges Griechenland! du Haus der Himmlischen alle,
  Also ist wahr, was einst wir in der Jugend gehört?

Or a loyal man too will gaze into Night and enjoy it,
  Yes, and rightly to her garlands we dedicate, hymns,
Since to all those astray, the mad and the dead she is sacred,
  Yet herself remains firm, always, her spirit most free.
But to us in her turn, so that in the wavering moment,
  Deep in the dark there shall be something at least that endures,
Holy drunkenness she must grant and frenzied oblivion,
  Grant the on-rushing word, sleepless as lovers are too,
And a wine-cup more full, a life more intense and more daring,
  Holy remembrance too, keeping us wakeful at night.

                                3

And in vain we conceal our hearts deep within us, in vain we,
  Master and novice alike, still keep our courage in check.
For who now would stop us, who would forbid us rejoicing?
  Day-long, night-long we're urged on by a fire that's divine.
Urged to be gone. Let us go, then! Off to see open spaces,
  Where we may seek what is ours, distant, remote though it be!
One thing is sure even now: at noon or just before midnight,
  Whether it's early or late, always a measure exists,
Common to all, though his own to each one is also allotted,
  Each of us makes for the place, reaches the place that he can.
Well, then, may jubilant madness laugh at those who deride it,
  When in hallowed Night poets are seized by its power;
Off to the Isthmus, then! To land where wide open the sea roars
  Near Parnassus and snow glistens on Delphian rocks;
Off to Olympian regions, up to the heights of Cithaeron,
  Up to the pine-trees there, up to the grapes, from which rush
Thebe down there and Ismenos, loud in the country of Cadmus:
  Thence has come and back there points the god who's to come.

                                4

Happy land of the Greeks, you house of them all, of the Heavenly,
  So it is true what we heard then, in the days of our youth?

Festlicher Saal! der Boden ist Meer! und Tische die Berge,
  Wahrlich zu einzigem Brauche vor Alters gebaut!
Aber die Thronen, wo? die Tempel, und wo die Gefäße,
  Wo mit Nectar gefüllt, Göttern zu Lust der Gesang?
Wo, wo leuchten sie denn, die fernhintreffenden Sprüche?
  Delphi schlummert und wo tönet das große Geschik?
Wo ist das schnelle? wo brichts, allgegenwärtigen Glüks voll
  Donnernd aus heiterer Luft über die Augen herein?
Vater Aether! so riefs und flog von Zunge zu Zunge
  Tausendfach, es ertrug keiner das Leben allein;
Ausgetheilet erfreut solch Gut und getauschet, mit Fremden,
  Wirds ein Jubel, es wächst schlafend des Wortes Gewalt
Vater! heiter! und hallt, so weit es gehet, das uralt
  Zeichen, von Eltern geerbt, treffend und schaffend hinab.
Denn so kehren die Himmlischen ein, tiefschütternd gelangt so
Aus den Schatten herab unter die Menschen ihr Tag.

5

Unempfunden kommen sie erst, es streben entgegen
  Ihnen die Kinder, zu hell kommet, zu blendend das Glük,
Und es scheut sie der Mensch, kaum weiß zu sagen ein Halbgott,
  Wer mit Nahmen sie sind, die mit den Gaaben ihm nahn.
Aber der Muth von ihnen ist groß, es füllen das Herz ihm
  Ihre Freuden und kaum weiß er zu brauchen das Gut,
Schafft, verschwendet und fast ward ihm Unheiliges heilig,
  Das er mit seegnender Hand thörig und gütig berührt.
Möglichst dulden die Himmlischen diß; dann aber in Wahrheit
  Kommen sie selbst und gewohnt werden die Menschen des Glüks
Und des Tags und zu schaun die Offenbaren, das Antliz
  Derer, welche, schon längst Eines und Alles genannt,
Tief die verschwiegene Brust mit freier Genüge gefüllet,
  Und zuerst und allein alles Verlangen beglükt;
So ist der Mensch; wenn da ist das Gut, und es sorget mit Gaaben
  Selber ein Gott für ihn, kennet und sieht er es nicht.

Festive hall, whose floor is ocean, whose tables are mountains,
  Truly, in time out of mind built for a purpose unique!
But the thrones, where are they? Where are the temples, the vessels,
  Where, to delight the gods, brim-full with nectar, the songs?
Where, then, where do they shine, the oracles winged for far targets?
  Delphi's asleep, and where now is great fate to be heard?
Where is the swift? And full of joy omnipresent, where does it
  Flash upon dazzled eyes, thundering fall from clear skies?
Father Aether! one cried, and tongue after tongue took it up then,
  Thousands, no man could bear life so intense on his own;
Shared, such wealth gives delight and later, when bartered with strangers,
  Turns to rapture; the word gathers new strength when asleep:
Father! Clear light! and long resounding it travels, the ancient
  Sign handed down, and far, striking, creating, rings out.
So do the Heavenly enter, shaking the deepest foundations,
  Only so from the gloom down to mankind comes their Day.

5

Unperceived at first they come, and only the children
  Surge towards them, too bright, dazzling, this joy enters in,
So that men are afraid, a demigod hardly can tell yet
  Who they are, and name those who approach him with gifts.
Yet their courage is great, his heart soon is full of their gladness
  And he hardly knows what's to be done with such wealth,
Busily runs and wastes it, almost regarding as sacred
  Trash which his blessing hand foolishly, kindly has touched.
This, while they can, the Heavenly bear with; but then they appear in
  Truth, in person, and now men grow accustomed to joy,
And to Day, and the sight of godhead revealed, and their faces—
  One and All long ago, once and for all, they were named—
Who with free self-content had deeply suffused silent bosoms,
  From the first and alone satisfied every desire.
Such is man; when the wealth is there, and no less than a god in
  Person tends him with gifts, blind he remains, unaware.

Tragen muß er, zuvor; nun aber nennt er sein Liebstes,
   Nun, nun müssen dafür Worte, wie Blumen, entstehn.

6

Und nun denkt er zu ehren in Ernst die seeligen Götter,
   Wirklich und wahrhaft muß alles verkünden ihr Lob.
Nichts darf schauen das Licht, was nicht den Hohen gefället,
   Vor den Aether gebührt müßigversuchendes nicht.
Drum in der Gegenwart der Himmlischen würdig zu stehen,
   Richten in herrlichen Ordnungen Völker sich auf
Untereinander und baun die schönen Tempel und Städte
   Vest und edel, sie gehn über Gestaden empor —
Aber wo sind sie? wo blühn die Bekannten, die Kronen des Festes?
   Thebe welkt und Athen; rauschen die Waffen nicht mehr
In Olympia, nicht die goldnen Wagen des Kampfspiels,
   Und bekränzen sich denn nimmer die Schiffe Korinths?
Warum schweigen auch sie, die alten heilgen Theater?
   Warum freuet sich denn nicht der geweihete Tanz?
Warum zeichnet, wie sonst, die Stirne des Mannes ein Gott nicht,
   Drükt den Stempel, wie sonst, nicht dem Getroffenen auf?
Oder er kam auch selbst und nahm des Menschen Gestalt an
   Und vollendet' und schloß tröstend das himmlische Fest.

7

Aber Freund! wir kommen zu spät. Zwar leben die Götter,
   Aber über dem Haupt droben in anderer Welt.
Endlos wirken sie da und scheinens wenig zu achten,
   Ob wir leben, so sehr schonen die Himmlischen uns.
Denn nicht immer vermag ein schwaches Gefäß sie zu fassen,
   Nur zu Zeiten erträgt göttliche Fülle der Mensch.
Traum von ihnen ist drauf das Leben. Aber das Irrsaal
   Hilft, wie Schlummer und stark machet die Noth und die Nacht,
Biß daß Helden genug in der ehernen Wiege gewachsen,
   Herzen an Kraft, wie sonst, ähnlich den Himmlischen sind.

First he must suffer; but now he names his most treasured possession,
    Now for it words like flowers leaping alive he must find.

6

Now in earnest he means to honour the gods who have blessed him,
    Now in truth and in deed all must re-echo their praise.
Nothing must see the light but what to those high ones is pleasing,
    Idle and bungled work never for Aether was fit.
So, to be worthy and stand unashamed in the heavenly presence,
    Nations rise up and soon, gloriously ordered, compete
One with the other in building beautiful temples and cities,
    Noble and firm they tower high above river and sea—
Only, where are they? Where thrive those famed ones, the festival's garlands?
    Athens is withered, and Thebes; now do no weapons ring out
In Olympia, nor now those chariots, all golden, in games there,
    And no longer are wreaths hung on Corinthian ships?
Why are they silent too, the theatres, ancient and hallowed?
    Why not now does the dance celebrate, consecrate joy?
Why no more does a god imprint on the brow of a mortal
    Struck, as by lightning, the mark, brand him, as once he would do?
Else he would come himself, assuming a shape that was human,
    And, consoling the guests, crowned and concluded the feast.

7

But, my friend, we have come too late. Though the gods are living,
    Over our heads they live, up in a different world.
Endlessly there they act and, such is their kind wish to spare us,
    Little they seem to care whether we live or do not.
For not always a frail, a delicate vessel can hold them,
    Only at times can our kind bear the full impact of gods.
Ever after our life is dream about them. But frenzy,
    Wandering, helps, like sleep; Night and distress make us strong
Till in that cradle of steel heroes enough have been fostered,
    Hearts in strength can match heavenly strength as before.

249

Donnernd kommen sie drauf. Indessen dünket mir öfters
    Besser zu schlafen, wie so ohne Genossen zu seyn,
So zu harren und was zu thun indeß und zu sagen,
    Weiß ich nicht und wozu Dichter in dürftiger Zeit?
Aber sie sind, sagst du, wie des Weingotts heilige Priester,
    Welche von Lande zu Land zogen in heiliger Nacht.

8

Nemlich, als vor einiger Zeit, uns dünket sie lange,
    Aufwärts stiegen sie all, welche das Leben beglükt,
Als der Vater gewandt sein Angesicht von den Menschen,
    Und das Trauern mit Recht über der Erde begann,
Als erschienen zu lezt ein stiller Genius, himmlisch
    Tröstend, welcher des Tags Ende verkündet' und schwand,
Ließ zum Zeichen, daß einst er da gewesen und wieder
    Käme, der himmlische Chor einige Gaaben zurük,
Derer menschlich, wie sonst, wir uns zu freuen vermöchten,
    Denn zur Freude, mit Geist, wurde das Größre zu groß
Unter den Menschen und noch, noch fehlen die Starken zu höchsten
    Freuden, aber es lebt stille noch einiger Dank.
Brod ist der Erde Frucht, doch ists vom Lichte geseegnet,
    Und vom donnernden Gott kommet die Freude des Weins.
Darum denken wir auch dabei der Himmlischen, die sonst
    Da gewesen und die kehren in richtiger Zeit,
Darum singen sie auch mit Ernst die Sänger den Weingott
    Und nicht eitel erdacht tönet dem Alten das Lob.

9

Ja! sie sagen mit Recht, er söhne den Tag mit der Nacht aus,
    Führe des Himmels Gestirn ewig hinunter, hinauf,
Allzeit froh, wie das Laub der immergrünenden Fichte,
    Das er liebt, und der Kranz, den er von Epheu gewählt,
Weil er bleibet und selbst die Spur der entflohenen Götter
    Götterlosen hinab unter das Finstere bringt.

Thundering then they come. But meanwhile too often I think it's
   Better to sleep than to be friendless as we are, alone,
Always waiting, and what to do or to say in the meantime
   I don't know, and who wants poets at all in lean years?
But they are, you say, like those holy ones, priests of the wine-god
   Who in holy Night roamed from one place to the next.

8

For, when some time ago now—to us it seems ages—
   Up rose all those by whom life had been brightened, made glad,
When the Father had turned his face from the sight of us mortals
   And all over the earth, rightly, they started to mourn,
Lastly a Genius had come, dispensing heavenly comfort,
   He who proclaimed the Day's end, then himself went away,
Then, as a token that once they had been down here and once more would
   Come, the heavenly choir left a few presents behind,
Gifts in which now as ever humanly men might take pleasure,
   Since for spiritual joy great things had now grown too great
Here, among men, and even now there's a lack of those strong for
   Joy's extremity, but silent some thanks do live on.
Bread is a fruit of Earth, yet touched by the blessing of sunlight,
   From the thundering god issues the gladness of wine.
Therefore in tasting them we think of the Heavenly who once were
   Here and shall come again, come when their advent is due;
Therefore also the poets in serious hymns to the wine-god,
   Never idly devised, sound that most ancient one's praise.

9

Yes, and rightly they say he reconciles Day with our Night-time,
   Leads the stars of the sky upward and down without end,
Always glad, like the living boughs of the evergreen pine-tree
   Which he loves, and the wreath wound out of ivy for choice
Since it lasts and conveys the trace of the gods now departed
   Down to the godless below, into the midst of their gloom.

251

Was der Alten Gesang von Kindern Gottes geweissagt,
  Siehe! wir sind es, wir; Frucht von Hesperien ists!
Wunderbar und genau ists als an Menschen erfüllet,
  Glaube, wer es geprüft! aber so vieles geschieht,
Keines wirket, denn wir sind herzlos, Schatten, bis unser
  Vater Aether erkannt jeden und allen gehört.
Aber indessen kommt als Fakelschwinger des Höchsten
  Sohn, der Syrier, unter die Schatten herab.
Seelige Weise sehns; ein Lächeln aus der gefangnen
  Seele leuchtet, dem Licht thauet ihr Auge noch auf.
Sanfter träumet und schläft in Armen der Erde der Titan,
  Selbst der neidische, selbst Cerberus trinket und schläft.

What of the children of God was foretold in the songs of the ancients,
    Look, we are it, ourselves; fruit of Hesperia it is!
Strictly it has come true, fulfilled as in men by a marvel,
    Let those who have seen it believe! Much, however, occurs,
Nothing succeeds, because we are heartless, mere shadows until our
    Father Aether, made known, recognized, fathers us all.
Meanwhile, though, to us shadows comes the Son of the Highest,
    Comes the Syrian and down into our gloom bears his torch.
Blissful, the wise men see it; in souls that were captive there gleams a
    Smile, and their eyes shall yet thaw in response to the light.
Dreams more gentle and sleep in the arms of Earth lull the Titan,
    Even that envious one, Cerberus, drinks and lies down.

HEIMKUNFT

AN DIE VERWANDTEN

1

Drinn in den Alpen ists noch helle Nacht und die Wolke,
   Freudiges dichtend, sie dekt drinnen das gähnende Thal.
Dahin, dorthin toset und stürzt die scherzende Bergluft,
   Schroff durch Tannen herab glänzet und schwindet ein Stral.
Langsam eilt und kämpft das freudigschauernde Chaos,
   Jung an Gestalt, doch stark, feiert es liebenden Streit
Unter den Felsen, es gährt und wankt in den ewigen Schranken,
   Denn bacchantischer zieht drinnen der Morgen herauf.
Denn es wächst unendlicher dort das Jahr und die heilgen
   Stunden, die Tage, sie sind kühner geordnet, gemischt.
Dennoch merket die Zeit der Gewittervogel und zwischen
   Bergen, hoch in der Luft weilt er und rufet den Tag.
Jezt auch wachet und schaut in der Tiefe drinnen das Dörflein
   Furchtlos, Hohem vertraut, unter den Gipfeln hinauf.
Wachstum ahnend, denn schon, wie Blize, fallen die alten
   Wasserquellen, der Grund unter den Stürzenden dampft,
Echo tönet umher, und die unermeßliche Werkstatt
   Reget bei Tag und Nacht, Gaaben versendend, den Arm.

2

Ruhig glänzen indeß die silbernen Höhen darüber,
   Voll mit Rosen ist schon droben der leuchtende Schnee.
Und noch höher hinauf wohnt über dem Lichte der reine
   Seelige Gott vom Spiel heiliger Stralen erfreut.
Stille wohnt er allein und hell erscheinet sein Antliz,
   Der ätherische scheint Leben zu geben geneigt,
Freude zu schaffen, mit uns, wie oft, wenn, kundig des Maases,
   Kundig der Athmenden auch zögernd und schonend der Gott

HOMECOMING

TO HIS RELATIVES

1

There in the Alps a gleaming night still delays and, composing
  Portents of gladness, the cloud covers a valley agape.
This way, that way roars and rushes the breeze of the mountains,
  Teasing, sheer through the firs falls a bright beam, and is lost.
Slowly it hurries and wars, this Chaos trembling with pleasure,
  Young in appearance, but strong, celebrates here amid rocks
Loving discord, and seethes, shakes in its bounds that are timeless,
  For more bacchantically now morning approaches within.
For more endlessly there the year expands, and the holy
  Hours and the days in there more boldly are ordered and mixed.
Yet the bird of thunder marks and observes the time, and
  High in the air, between peaks, hangs and calls out a new day.
Now, deep inside, the small village also awakens and fearless
  Looks at the summits around, long now familiar with height;
Growth it foreknows, for already ancient torrents like lightning
  Crash, and the ground below steams with the spray of their fall.
Echo sounds all around and, measureless, tireless the workshop,
  Sending out gifts, is astir, active by day and by night.

2

Quiet, meanwhile, above, the silvery peaks lie aglitter,
  Full of roses up there, flushed with dawn's rays, lies the snow.
Even higher, beyond the light, does the pure, never clouded
  God have his dwelling, whom beams, holy, make glad with their play.
Silent, alone he dwells, and bright his countenance shines now,
  He, the aethereal one, seems kindly, disposed to give life,
Generate joys, with us men, as often when, knowing the measure,
  Knowing those who draw breath, hesitant, sparing the God

255

Wohlgediegenes Glük den Städten und Häußern und milde
  Reegen, zu öffnen das Land, brütende Wolken, und euch,
Trauteste Lüfte dann, euch, sanfte Frühlinge, sendet,
  Und mit langsamer Hand Traurige wieder erfreut,
Wenn er die Zeiten erneut, der Schöpferische, die stillen
  Herzen der alternden Menschen erfrischt und ergreifft,
Und hinab in die Tiefe wirkt, und öffnet und aufhellt,
  Wie ers liebet, und jezt wieder ein Leben beginnt,
Anmuth blühet, wie einst, und gegenwärtiger Geist kömmt,
  Und ein freudiger Muth wieder die Fittige schwellt.

3

Vieles sprach ich zu ihm, denn, was auch Dichtende sinnen
  Oder singen, es gilt meistens den Engeln und ihm;
Vieles bat ich, zu lieb dem Vaterlande, damit nicht
  Ungebeten uns einst plözlich befiele der Geist;
Vieles für euch auch, die im Vaterlande besorgt sind,
  Denen der heilige Dank lächelnd die Flüchtlinge bringt,
Landesleute! für euch, indessen wiegte der See mich,
  Und der Ruderer saß ruhig und lobte die Fahrt.
Weit in des Sees Ebene wars Ein freudiges Wallen
  Unter den Seegeln und jezt blühet und hellet die Stadt
Dort in der Frühe sich auf, wohl her von schattigen Alpen
  Kommt geleitet und ruht nun in dem Hafen das Schiff.
Warm ist das Ufer hier und freundlich offene Thale,
  Schön von Pfaden erhellt grünen und schimmern mich an.
Gärten stehen gesellt und die glänzende Knospe beginnt schon,
  Und des Vogels Gesang ladet den Wanderer ein.
Alles scheinet vertraut, der vorübereilende Gruß auch
  Scheint von Freunden, es scheint jegliche Miene verwandt.

4

Freilich wohl! das Geburtsland ists, der Boden der Heimath,
  Was du suchest, es ist nahe, begegnet dir schon.

Sends well-allotted fortune both to the cities and houses,
    Showers to open the land, gentle, and you, brooding clouds,
You, then, most dearly loved breezes, followed by temperate springtime,
    And with a slow hand once more gladdens us mortals grown sad,
When he renews the seasons, he, the creative, and quickens,
    Moves once again those hearts weary and numb with old age,
Works on the lowest depths to open them up and to brighten
    All, as he loves to do; so now does life bud anew,
Beauty abounds, as before, and spirit is present, returned now,
    And a joyful zest urges furled wings to unfold.

                            3

Much I said to him; for whatever the poets may ponder,
    Sing, it mostly concerns either the angels or him.
Much I besought, on my country's behalf, lest unbidden one day the
    Spirit should suddenly come, take us by storm unprepared;
Much, too, for your sake to whom, though troubled now in our country,
    Holy gratitude brings fugitives back with a smile,
Fellow Germans, for your sake! Meanwhile the lake gently rocked me,
    Calmly the boatman sat, praising the weather, the breeze.
Out on the level lake one impulse of joy had enlivened
    All the sails, and at last, there in a new day's first hour
Brightening, the town unfurls, and safely conveyed from the shadows
    Cast by the Alps, now the boat glides to its mooring and rests.
Warm the shore is here, and valleys open in welcome,
    Pleasantly lit by paths, greenly allure me and gleam.
Gardens, forgathered, lie here and already the dew-laden bud breaks
    And a bird's early song welcomes the traveller home.
All seems familiar; even the word or the nod caught in passing
    Seems like a friend's, every face looks like a relative's face.

                            4

And no wonder! Your native country and soil you are walking,
    What you seek, it is near, now comes to meet you half-way.

                            257

Und umsonst nicht steht, wie ein Sohn, am wellenumrauschten
     Thor' und siehet und sucht liebende Nahmen für dich,
Mit Gesang ein wandernder Mann, glükseeliges Lindau!
     Eine der gastlichen Pforten des Landes ist diß,
Reizend hinauszugehn in die vielversprechende Ferne,
     Dort, wo die Wunder sind, dort, wo das göttliche Wild
Hoch in die Ebnen herab der Rhein die verwegene Bahn bricht,
     Und aus Felsen hervor ziehet das jauchzende Thal,
Dort hinein, durchs helle Gebirg, nach Komo zu wandern,
     Oder hinab, wie der Tag wandelt, den offenen See;
Aber reizender mir bist du, geweihete Pforte!
     Heimzugehn, wo bekannt blühende Wege mir sind,
Dort zu besuchen das Land und die schönen Thale des Nekars,
     Und die Wälder, das Grün heiliger Bäume, wo gern
Sich die Eiche gesellt mit stillen Birken und Buchen,
     Und in Bergen ein Ort freundlich gefangen mich nimmt.

5

Dort empfangen sie mich. O Stimme der Stadt, der Mutter!
     O du triffest, du regst Langegelerntes mir auf!
Dennoch sind sie es noch! noch blühet die Sonn' und die Freud' euch,
     O ihr Liebsten! und fast heller im Auge, wie sonst.
Ja! das Alte noch ists! Es gedeihet und reifet, doch keines
     Was da lebet und liebt, lässet die Treue zurük.
Aber das Beste, der Fund, der unter des heiligen Friedens
     Bogen lieget, er ist Jungen und Alten gespart.
Thörig red ich. Es ist die Freude. Doch morgen und künftig
     Wenn wir gehen und schaun draußen das lebende Feld
Unter den Blüthen des Baums, in den Feiertagen des Frühlings
     Red' und hoff' ich mit euch vieles, ihr Lieben! davon.
Vieles hab' ich gehört vom großen Vater und habe
     Lange geschwiegen von ihm, welcher die wandernde Zeit
Droben in Höhen erfrischt, und waltet über Gebirgen
     Der gewähret uns bald himmlische Gaaben und ruft

Nor by mere chance like a son a wandering man now stands gazing
  Here by the wavelet-loud gate, looking for names to convey
Love to you in his poem, Lindau, the favoured and happy!
  Not the least of our land's many hospitable doors,
Urging men to go out allured by the promise of distance,
  Go where the wonders are, go where that god-like wild beast,
High up the Rhine blasts his reckless way to the plains of the lowlands,
  Where out of rocks at last bursts the lush valley's delight,
Wander in there, through the sunlit mountain range, making for Como,
  Or, as the day drifts on, drift on the wide open lake;
Yet, you door that are hallowed, me much more strongly you urge to
  Make for home where I know blossoming pathways and lanes,
There to visit the fields and the Neckar's beautiful valleys,
  And the woods, green leaves holy to me, where the oak
Does not disdain to consort with quiet birches and beeches,
  Where amid mountains one place holds me, a captive content.

                                   5

There they too receive me. Voice of my town, of my mother!
  How to your sound respond things that I learned long ago!
Yet they are still themselves! More radiantly, almost, than ever,
  Dearest ones, in your eyes joy and the sun are alight.
Yes, it's all what it was. It thrives and grows ripe, but no creature
  Living and loving there ever abandons its faith.
But the best thing of all, the find to be made underneath the
  Holy rainbow of peace, waits for the young and the old.
Like a fool I speak. In my joy. But tomorrow and later
  When we go outside, look at the living green field
Under the trees in blossom, on holidays due in the springtime,
  Much of those things with you, dear ones, I'll speak and I'll hope.
Much in the meantime I've heard of him, the great Father, and long now
  I have kept silent about him who on summits renews
Wandering Time up above and governs the high mountain ranges,
  Him who soon now will grant heavenly gifts and calls forth

                          /

Hellern Gesang und schikt viel gute Geister. O säumt nicht,
    Kommt, Erhaltenden ihr! Engel des Jahres! und ihr,

6

Engel des Haußes, kommt! in die Adern alle des Lebens,
    Alle freuend zugleich, theile das Himmlische sich!
Adle! verjünge! damit nichts Menschlichgutes, damit nicht
    Eine Stunde des Tags ohne die Frohen und auch
Solche Freude, wie jezt, wenn Liebende wieder sich finden,
    Wie es gehört für sie, schiklich geheiliget sei.
Wenn wir seegnen das Mahl, wen darf ich nennen und wenn wir
    Ruhn vom Leben des Tags, saget, wie bring' ich den Dank?
Nenn' ich den Hohen dabei? Unschikliches liebet ein Gott nicht,
    Ihn zu fassen, ist fast unsere Freude zu klein.
Schweigen müssen wir oft; es fehlen heilige Nahmen,
    Herzen schlagen und doch bleibet die Rede zurük?
Aber ein Saitenspiel leiht jeder Stunde die Töne,
    Und erfreuet vieleicht Himmlische, welche sich nahn.
Das bereitet und so ist auch beinahe die Sorge
    Schon befriediget, die unter das Freudige kam.
Sorgen, wie diese, muß, gern oder nicht, in der Seele
    Tragen ein Sänger und oft, aber die anderen nicht.

Song more effulgent, and sends us many good spirits. No longer
    Wait now, preservers, the year's angels, O come now, and you,

6

Angels, too, of our house, re-enter the veins of all life now,
    Gladdening all at once, let what is heavenly be shared!
Make us noble and new! Till nothing that's humanly good, no
    Hour of the day without them, them the most joyful, or such
Joy as now too is known when lovers return to each other,
    Passes, not fitting for them, hallowed as angels demand.
When we bless the meal, whose name may I speak, and when late we
    Rest from the life of each day, tell me, to whom give my thanks?
Him, the most High, should I name then? A god does not love what's unseemly,
    Him to embrace and to hold our joy is too small.
Silence often behoves us: deficient in names that are holy,
    Hearts may beat high, while the lips hesitate, wary of speech?
Yet a lyre to each hour lends the right mode, the right music,
    And, it may be, delights heavenly ones who draw near.
This make ready, and almost nothing remains of the care that
    Darkened our festive day, troubled the promise of joy.
Whether he likes it or not, and often, a singer must harbour
    Cares like these in his soul; not, though, the wrong sort of cares.

THE DEATH OF EMPEDOCLES

FRAGMENTS OF A TRAGEDY

IN

FIVE ACTS

PERSONEN

EMPEDOKLES

PAUSANIAS

PANTHEA

DELIA

HERMOKRATES

MEKADES

AMPHARES

DEMOKLES | Agrigentiner

HYLAS

Der Schauplaz ist theils in Agrigent, theils am Aetna.

CHARACTERS

EMPEDOCLES

PAUSANIAS

PANTHEA

DELIA

HERMOCRATES

MECADES

AMPHARES ⎫

DEMODES ⎬ Citizens of Agrigentum

IIYLAS ⎭

The action takes place partly at Agrigentum, partly at the foot of Etna.

ERSTER ACT

ERSTER AUFTRITT

CHOR DER AGRIGENTINER in der Ferne

MEKADES. HERMOKRATES

MEKADES

Hörst du das trunkne Volk?

HERMOKRATES

Sie suchen ihn.

MEKADES

Der Geist des Manns
Ist mächtig unter ihnen.

HERMOKRATES

Ich weiß, wie dürres Gras
Entzünden sich die Menschen.

MEKADES

Daß Einer so die Menge bewegt, mir ists,
Als wie wenn Jovis Bliz den Wald
Ergreift, und furchtbarer.

HERMOKRATES

Drum binden wir den Menschen auch
Das Band ums Auge, daß sie nicht
Zu kräftig sich am Lichte nähren.
Nicht gegenwärtig werden
Darf Göttliches vor ihnen.
Es darf ihr Herz
Lebendiges nicht finden.

ACT ONE

SCENE ONE

CHORUS OF AGRIGENTINES in the distance

MECADES. HERMOCRATES

MECADES

Do you hear the frenzied crowd?

HERMOCRATES

They're looking for him.

MECADES

The spirit of that man
Persuades, pervades them.

HERMOCRATES

I know, like withered grass
The minds of men catch fire.

MECADES

That any man should have such power to move
The mob, to me is like Jove's lightning
Loose in a forest, and more terrible.

HERMOCRATES

And that is why we wrap that band
Around men's eyes, lest all too richly
They feed upon the light.
Never what is divine
Must be quite present to them,
Nor may their hearts
Take hold of what's alive.

267

Kennst du die Alten nicht,
Die Lieblinge des Himmels man nennt?
Sie nährten die Brust
An Kräften der Welt
Und den Hellaufblikenden war
Unsterbliches nahe,
Drum beugten die Stolzen
Das Haupt auch nicht
Und vor den Gewaltigen konnt'
Ein Anderes nicht bestehn,
Es ward verwandelt vor ihnen.

MEKADES

Und er?

HERMOKRATES

Das hat zu mächtig ihn
Gemacht, daß er vertraut
Mit Göttern worden ist.
Es tönt sein Wort dem Volk',
Als käm es vom Olymp;
Sie dankens ihm,
Daß er vom Himmel raubt
Die Lebensflamm' und sie
Verräth den Sterblichen.

MEKADES

Sie wissen nichts, denn ihn,
Er soll ihr Gott,
Er soll ihr König seyn.
Sie sagen, es hab' Apoll
Die Stadt gebaut den Trojern,
Doch besser sei, es helf'
Ein hoher Mann durchs Leben.
Noch sprechen sie viel Unverständiges

Think of those ancients
Known as the darlings, favourites of Heaven:
They nourished their minds
With the world's own powers
And to their bright, up-gazing eyes
Things immortal were near.
That's why those proud ones
Never would bow their heads
And, wilful, could not leave
Intact what was other than they;
Their very looking transformed it.

MECADES

And he?

HERMOCRATES

What's made him overreach
Himself, is that he's grown
Familiar with the gods.
To them, to the people, his word
Rings out as from Olympus.
They give him thanks
For stealing from very Heaven
The fire of life, and so
Betraying it to mortals.

MECADES

They've ears for none but him.
In him they see
Their god, their king.
They say, Apollo built
The Trojans their great city,
But better still to be helped
And led through life by a man exalted.
And other things as foolish

Von ihm und achten kein Gesez
Und keine Noth und keine Sitte.
Ein Irrgestirn ist unser Volk
Geworden und ich fürcht',
Es deute dieses Zeichen
Zukünft'ges noch, das er
Im stillen Sinne brütet.

HERMOKRATES

Sei ruhig, Mekades!
Er wird nicht.

MEKADES

Bist du denn mächtiger?

HERMOKRATES

Der sie versteht,
Ist stärker, denn die Starken.
Und wohlbekannt ist dieser Seltne mir.
Zu glüklich wuchs er auf;
Ihm ist von Anbeginn
Der eigne Sinn verwöhnt, daß ihn
Geringes irrt; er wird es büßen
Daß er zu sehr geliebt die Sterblichen.

MEKADES

Mir ahndet selbst,
Es wird mit ihm nicht lange dauern,
Doch ist es lang genug,
So er erst fällt, wenn ihms gelungen ist.

HERMOKRATES

Und schon ist er gefallen.

MEKADES

Was sagst du?

They say about him, and respect
No law, no custom, no necessity.
Our people has turned
Into a dizzy comet;
The sign, I fear, portends
Much more to come which now
In silence he is hatching.

HERMOCRATES

Never fear, Mecades.
He will not.

MECADES

Are you more powerful, then?

HERMOCRATES

Stronger than strong men
Are those who understand them,
And this egregious one is known to me.
Too happily he grew up;
From the beginning
His will was pampered, so
That little things confuse him; he will pay
For having loved mere mortal men too well.

MECADES

I too have felt
That he will not last long,
Yet it is long enough
If by the time he falls he's won his game.

HERMOCRATES

Already he has fallen.

MECADES

What are you saying?

Siehst du denn nicht? es haben
Den. hohen Geist die Geistesarmen
Geirrt, die Blinden den Verführer.
Die Seele warf er vor das Volk, verrieth
Der Götter Gunst gutmüthig den Gemeinen,
Doch rächend äffte leeren Wiederhalls
Genug denn auch aus todter Brust den Thoren.
Und eine Zeit ertrug ers, grämte sich
Geduldig, wußte nicht,
Wo es gebrach; indessen wuchs
Die Trunkenheit dem Volke; schaudernd
Vernahmen sie's, wenn ihm vom eignen Wort
Der Busen bebt', und sprachen:
So hören wir nicht die Götter!
Und Nahmen, so ich dir nicht nenne, gaben
Die Knechte dann dem stolzen Trauernden.
Und endlich nimmt der Durstige das Gift,
Der Arme, der mit seinem Sinne nicht
Zu bleiben weiß und Ähnliches nicht findet,
Er tröstet mit der rasenden
Anbetung sich, verblindet, wird, wie sie,
Die seelenlosen Aberglaubigen;
Die Kraft ist ihm entwichen,
Er geht in einer Nacht, und weiß sich nicht
Herauszuhelfen und wir helfen ihm.

MEKADES

Deß bist du so gewiß?

HERMOKRATES

Ich kenn' ihn.

MEKADES

Ein übermüthiges Gerede fällt
Mir bei, das er gemacht, da er zulezt

HERMOCRATES

Oh, can't you see it? That noble mind
Has been confounded by the feeble-minded,
That one-eyed king misguided by the blind.
His very soul he cast before the people,
Good-naturedly betrayed to vulgar men
The grace of gods; but amply was repaid
With hollow echoes from their own dead hearts,
The fool. And bore it for a time, and grieved,
But patiently, not knowing
Where lay the fault; meanwhile
The people's frenzy grew; and shuddering
They listened when with his own word
His breast reverberated, saying:
It is not thus we listen to gods!
And, servile as they are, went on to call
The proudly sorrowing by names I will not repeat,
And in the end the thirsty man drinks the poison,
That wretch who neither can contain his mind
Nor yet find other minds, akin to it,
And with their raving adoration
Consoles himself, goes blind, becomes like them,
That superstitious rabble with no soul;
His power has ebbed away.
He walks in his own night and cannot find
His own way out—so we shall help him.

MECADES

Are you so sure of that?

HERMOCRATES

I know him.

MECADES

A piece of arrogant talk occurs to me
That issued from the babbler's lips when last

273

Auf der Agora war. Ich weiß es nicht,
Was ihm das Volk zuvor gesagt; ich kam
Nur eben, stand von fern; ihr ehret mich,
Antwortet' er, und thuet recht daran;
Denn stum ist die Natur,
Es leben Sonn und Luft und Erd' und ihre Kinder
Fremd umeinander,
Die Einsamen, als gehörten sie sich nicht.
Wohl wandeln immerkräftig
Im Göttergeiste die freien
Unsterblichen Mächte der Welt
Rings um der andern
Vergänglich Leben,
Doch wilde Pflanzen
Auf wilden Grund
Sind in den Schoos der Götter
Die Sterblichen alle gesäet
Die Kärglichgenährten und todt
Erschiene der Boden wenn Einer nicht
Deß wartete, lebenerwekend,
Und mein ist das Feld. Mir tauschen
Die Kraft und Seele zu Einem,
Die Sterblichen und die Götter.
Und wärmer umfangen die ewigen Mächte
Das strebende Herz und kräftger gedeihn
Vom Geiste der Freien die fühlenden Menschen,
Und wach ists! Denn ich
Geselle das Fremde,
Das Unbekannte nennet mein Wort,
Und die Liebe der Lebenden trag'
Ich auf und nieder; was Einem gebricht,
Ich bring es vom andern, und binde
Beseelend, und wandle
Verjüngend die zögernde Welt

He came to the Agora. I did not catch
What spokesmen of the mob had said to him;
Newly arrived, and far from him, I heard
These words: You honour me, and rightly so,
For inarticulate is Nature,
For Sun and Air and Earth and all her children
Like strangers live together,
And lonely, as though no bond connected them.
True, ever strong, by virtue
Of spirit that is divine,
The free, immortal powers of the world
Revolve around those others'
Ephemeral lives,
But wildflowers growing
On soil as wild
We mortals on to the lap of the gods
Have all been sown,
But scantily nourished, and dead
That soil would appear, did not someone
Attend to it, raising up life,
And mine is that field. My strength and
My soul are fused into one,
By mortals and by the gods.
And more warmly immortal powers embrace
The aspiring heart and, infused with
The freedom of their spirit, feeling mortals more richly thrive,
And all's awake! For I
Conjoin the estranged,
My word can name the unknown,
And the love of the living I carry
Now up, now down; what one of them lacks
I bring to him from another
And, soul-inspiring, connect,
Rejuvenating, transform
This hesitant world,

Und gleiche keinem und Allen.
So sprach der Übermüthige.

HERMOKRATES

Das ist noch wenig. Aergers schläft in ihm.
Ich kenn' ihn, kenne sie, die überglüklichen
Verwöhnten Söhne des Himmels,
Die anders nicht, denn ihre Seele, fühlen.
Stört einmal sie der Augenblik heraus –
Und leichtzerstörbar sind die Zärtlichen –
Dann stillet nichts sie wieder, brennend
Treibt eine Wunde sie, unheilbar gährt
Die Brust. Auch er! so still er scheint,
So glüht ihm doch, seit ihm das Volk mißfällt,
Im Busen die tyrannische Begierde,
Er oder wir! Und Schaden ist es nicht,
So wir ihn opfern. Untergehen muß
Er doch!

MEKADES

O reiz ihn nicht! schaff ihr nicht Raum und laß
Sie sich erstiken, die verschloßne Flamme!
Laß ihn! gieb ihm nicht Anstoß! findet den
Zu frecher That der Übermüthge nicht,
Und kann er nur im Worte sündigen,
So stirbt er, als ein Thor, und schadet uns
Nicht viel. Ein kräftger Gegner macht ihn furchtbar.
Sieh nur, dann erst, dann fühlt er seine Macht.

HERMOKRATES

Du fürchtest ihn und alles, armer Mann!

MEKADES

Ich mag die Reue nur mir gerne sparen,
Mag gerne schonen, was zu schonen ist.
Das braucht der Priester nicht, der alles weiß,
Der Heilge der sich alles heiliget.

And resemble no one and all.
Those were his arrogant words.

HERMOCRATES

That's very little. Worse lies dormant in him.
I know him, know his kind, the all too happy,
Heaven's own spoilt and darling sons
Aware of nothing else than their own souls.
If once the moment shakes them out of themselves—
And those too tender ones are easily shaken—
Then nothing calms or comforts them, they're driven
This way and that way by a burning wound,
Their hearts incurably seething. And he too,
Calm though he seems; disgusted with the people,
Deep down he glows now with despotic lust.
His rule or ours! And we shall do no wrong
In sacrificing him. His ruin is sure
In any case.

MECADES

Do not provoke him, though. Do not let loose,
But let it starve and choke, the pent-up flame!
Leave him alone! Give him no cause to act!
If he, the arrogant, himself finds none
For insolent deeds, and only in words can sin,
He dies a fool and does us little harm.
Day-dreaming let him walk on clouds, or fly!
A strong opponent makes him dangerous,
And only then, you see, he'll feel his power.

HERMOCRATES

You fear him, and fear all things, my poor friend.

MECADES

No, but I wish to spare myself remorse,
And like to spare whatever can be spared.
Different in that from the omniscient priest
Who, holy, hallows all his ends and means.

277

HERMOKRATES

Begreife mich, Unmündiger! eh du
Mich lästerst. Fallen muß der Mann; ich sag'
Es dir und glaube mir, wär' er zu schonen,
Ich würd' es mehr, wie du. Denn näher ist
Er mir, wie dir. Doch lerne diß:
Verderblicher denn Schwerd und Feuer ist
Der Menschengeist, der götterähnliche,
Wenn er nicht schweigen kan, und sein Geheimniß
Unaufgedekt bewahren. Bleibt er still
In seiner Tiefe ruhn, und giebt, was noth ist,
Wohlthätig ist er dann, ein fressend Feuer,
Wenn er aus seiner Fessel bricht.
Hinweg mit ihm, der seine Seele blos
Und ihre Götter giebt, verwegen
Aussprechen will Unauszusprechendes
Und sein gefährlich Gut, als wär es Wasser,
Verschüttet und vergeudet, schlimmer ists
Wie Mord, und du, du redest für diesen?
Bescheide dich! Sein Schiksaal ists. Er hat
Es sich gemacht und leben soll,
Wie er, und vergehn wie er, in Weh und Thorheit jeder,
Der Göttliches verräth, und allverkehrend
Verborgenherrschendes
In Menschenhände liefert!
Er muß hinab!

MEKADES

So theuer büßen muß er, der sein Bestes
Aus voller Seele Sterblichen vertraut?

HERMOKRATES

Er mag es, doch es bleibt die Nemesis nicht aus,
Mag große Worte sagen, mag

HERMOCRATES

First understand me, novice that you are,
Before insulting me. The man must fall,
I tell you. If he could be spared, be sure
I'd spare him more than you would, being closer
To him than you are. But take note of this:
More ruinous than sword or raging fire
Is human spirit, though akin to gods,
If it can not keep silent and contain
Its secret unexposed. If in its depth
It lies at rest and proffers what is needed,
Wholesome it is; a wild, devouring flame
As soon as from its fetters it breaks loose.
Away with that man who lays bare his soul
And, with it, his soul's gods, recklessly seeks
To utter the unutterable, wasting
His dangerous wealth like water lightly spilt.
That folly is worse than murder; and can you,
Can you, of all men, plead on his behalf?
Accept the inevitable! *His* fate it is,
He made it for himself, and like him
Shall all those live, all perish in pain and folly
Who have betrayed the divine and, all-perverting,
Delivered up into human hands
That which rules us in secret!
He shall not live!

MECADES

So dear, then, must he pay who of his soul's
Most treasured wealth entrusts the best to mortals?

HERMOCRATES

Let him, but Nemesis will surely come.
Let him mouth mighty words, and let him

Entwürdigen das keuschverschwiegne Leben,
Ans Tageslicht das Gold der Tiefe ziehn.
Er mag es brauchen, was zum Brauche nicht
Den Sterblichen gegeben ist, ihn wirds
Zuerst zu Grunde richten – hat es ihm
Den Sinn nicht schon verwirrt, ist ihm
Bei seinem Volke denn die volle Seele
Die Zärtliche, wie ist sie nun verwildert?
Wie ist denn nun ein Eigenmächtiger
Geworden dieser Allmittheilende?
Der gütge Mann! wie ist er so verwandelt
Zum Frechen, der wie seiner Hände Spiel
Die Götter und die Menschen achtet.

MEKADES

Du redest schröklich, Priester, und es dünkt
Dein dunkel Wort mir wahr. Es sei!
Du hast zum Werke mich. Nur weiß ich nicht,
Wo er zu fassen ist. Es sei der Mann
So groß er will, zu richten ist nicht schwer.
Doch mächtig seyn des Übermächtigen,
Der, wie ein Zauberer, die Menge leitet,
Es dünkt ein anders mir, Hermokrates.

HERMOKRATES

Gebrechlich ist sein Zauber, Kind, und leichter,
Denn nötig ist, hat er es uns bereitet.
Es wandte zur gelegnen Stunde sich
Sein Unmuth um, der stolze stillempörte Sinn
Befeindet izt sich selber, hätt' er auch
Die Macht, er achtets nicht, er trauert nur,
Und siehet seinen Fall, er sucht
Rükkehrend das verlorne Leben,
Den Gott, den er aus sich
Hinweggeschwäzt.

Dishonour life that should be chastely veiled,
Drag into daylight the deeply hidden gold.
Let him make use of that which was not given
To mortals for their use, but he will be
The first to perish. Has it not confused
His mind already? Is his entire soul
Vested, as he pretends, in his dear people?
That tender soul, how it has run to waste!
And how self-willed, tyrannical he has grown
Whose one desire was to communicate all,
Kind as he is! How utterly he's turned
Into an insolent man who looks upon
Both gods and men as playthings for his hands.

MECADES

Of dreadful things you speak; and, Priest, it seems
To me that your dark words are true. So be it!
I'll serve your cause. My only doubt is how
To lay our hands on him. However great
A man may be, to try him is not hard;
To overpower a man supremely powerful, though,
Who like a skilled magician rules the mob,
This is another thing, Hermocrates.

HERMOCRATES

Frail is his magic, child, and he has made
Our business easier than he need have done.
For at a moment opportune to us
His anger turned; his proud, indignant mood
Turns in upon itself, and though he had
The power, he would not heed it, only grieves
And broods upon his downfall,
Retracing, looks for his lost life,
The god whom by his prattling
He's driven out of himself.

Versammle mir das Volk; ich klag' ihn an,
Ruf über ihn den Fluch, erschreken sollen sie
Vor ihrem Abgott, sollen ihn
Hinaus verstoßen in die Wildniß
Und nimmer wiederkehrend soll er dort
Mirs büßen, daß er mehr, wie sich gebührt,
Verkündiget den Sterblichen.

MEKADES

Doch weß beschuldigest du ihn?

HERMOKRATES

Die Worte, so du mir genannt,
Sie sind genug.

MEKADES

        Mit dieser schwachen Klage
Willst du das Volk ihm von der Seele ziehn?

HERMOKRATES

Zu rechter Zeit hat jede Klage Kraft
Und nicht gering ist diese.

MEKADES

Und klagtest du des Mords ihn an vor ihnen,
Es wirkte nichts.

HERMOKRATES

Diß eben ists! die offenbare That
Vergeben sie, die Aberglaubigen,
Unsichtbar Aergerniß für sie
Unheimlich muß es seyn! ins Auge muß es
Sie treffen, das bewegt die Blöden.

MEKADES

Es hängt ihr Herz an ihm, das bändigest,
Das lenkst du nicht so leicht! Sie lieben ihn!

The people now assemble; I will charge him,
Pronounce the curse on him, make them recoil
In horror from their idol
And cast him out into the wilderness,
And, never more returning, there he shall pay
For making manifest to mortals more
Than they are fit to hear.

MECADES

But of what crime will you accuse him?

HERMOCRATES

Those words of his you cited,
They'll do.

MECADES

And with that feeble charge alone
You hope to wean them from their sustenance?

HERMOCRATES

At the right time, friend, any charge will work,
And this one is not slight.

MECADES

I say that if you charged that man with murder
In front of them, they would not flinch.

HERMOCRATES

Quite true! The flagrant act they will forgive,
That superstitious mob! Mysterious
The offence must be for them,
Occult, uncanny; hit them in the eye,
And blind them—then the timid herd will run.

MECADES

Their hearts are bound to him, and these you will
Not easily tame or guide; they love the man!

283

HERMOKRATES

Sie lieben ihn? ja wohl! so lang er blüht'
Und glänzt'

                     naschen sie.
Was sollen sie mit ihm, nun er
Verdüstert ist, verödet? Da ist nichts
Was nüzen könnt, und ihre lange Zeit
Verkürzen, abgeerndtet ist das Feld.
Verlassen liegts, und nach Gefallen gehn
Der Sturm und unsre Pfade drüber hin.

MEKADES

Empör' ihn nur! empör' ihn! siehe zu!

HERMOKRATES

Ich hoffe, Mekades! er ist geduldig.

MEKADES

So wird sie der geduldige gewinnen!

HERMOKRATES

Nichts weniger!

MEKADES

Du achtest nichts, wirst dich
Und mich und ihn und alles verderben.

HERMOKRATES

Das Träumen und das Schäumen
Der Sterblichen, ich acht' es wahrlich nicht!
Sie möchten Götter seyn, und huldigen
Wie Göttern sich, und eine Weile dauerts!
Sorgst du, es möchte sie der Leidende
Gewinnen, der Geduldige?
Empören wird er gegen sich die Thoren,
An seinem Laide werden sie den theuern
Betrug erkennen, werden unbarmherzig

HERMOCRATES

They love him? Certainly, as long as he
Is glorious, prospers
                              they will nibble.
Much good he'll do them, though,
Now that he's darkened, desolate! There's nothing
Here they could use with which to while away
The tedious hours; that field has been picked bare,
It lies forsaken now, and over it
The gales may freely run now—and our paths.

MECADES

Provoke him, then, provoke him! But take care!

HERMOCRATES

I hope, Mecades, that he's a patient man.

MECADES

The patient man, in that case, will persuade them.

HERMOCRATES

Never!

MECADES

You've no respect for anything, and so will
Ruin yourself and me and him and all things.

HERMOCRATES

The dreaming and the scheming
Of mortals—no, I never will respect it.
Gods they would like to be, and as to gods
Do homage to each other—for a while!
Are you afraid the suffering man will sway them,
The patient win them over?
Not so! To fury he will rouse the fools,
And by his suffering they'll recognize
The dearly paid imposture, brutally

285

Ihms danken, daß der Angebetete
Doch auch ein Schwacher ist, und ihm
Geschiehet recht, warum bemengt er sich
Mit ihnen,

MEKADES

Ich wollt', ich wär aus dieser Sache, Priester!

HERMOKRATES

Vertraue mir und scheue nicht, was noth ist.

MEKADES

Dort kömt er. Suche nur dich selbst,
Du irrer Geist! indeß verlierst du alles.

HERMOKRATES

Laß ihn! hinweg!

ZWEITER AUFTRITT

EMPEDOKLES
(allein)

In meine Stille kamst du leise wandelnd,
Fandst drinnen in der Halle Dunkel mich aus,
Du Freundlicher! du kamst nicht unverhoft
Und fernher, wirkend über der Erde vernahm
Ich wohl dein Wiederkehren, schöner Tag
Und meine Vertrauten euch, ihr schnellgeschäftgen
Kräfte der Höh! – und nahe seid auch ihr
Mir wieder, seid wie sonst ihr Glüklichen
Ihr irrelosen Bäume meines Hains!
Ihr ruhetet und wuchs't und täglich tränkte
Des Himmels Quelle die Bescheidenen

Exacting retribution from their idol
For being weak as they are; and it serves
Him right, I say. He should have had no truck
With them.

I wish I were well out of this business, Priest.

HERMOCRATES

Rely on me, and do not shirk what must be.

MECADES

Look, there he comes. Go on, then, seek yourself,
You poor crazed mind! And meanwhile you lose all.

HERMOCRATES

Leave him! Away!

SCENE TWO

EMPEDOCLES
(alone)

Your movement hushed, you came into my stillness,
Deep in the gloomy hall you sought me out,
You kindly light; and not unhoped for came,
But from afar, at work above the earth,
Well I could hear you come again, bright Day!
And my familiars, you, the quick and busy
Powers of the heights—now you are close to me
Once more, as once you were, the joyous,
Trees of my grove that neither stray nor falter!
You rested there and grew there well-contented
Since daily Heaven's own wellsprings watered you

Mit Licht und Lebensfunken säte
Befruchtend auf die Blühenden der Aether. –
O innige Natur! ich habe dich
Vor Augen, kennest du den Freund noch
Den Hochgeliebten kennest du mich nimmer?
Den Priester, der lebendigen Gesang,
Wie frohvergoßnes Opferblut, dir brachte?

O bei den heilgen Brunnen,
Wo Wasser aus Adern der Erde
Sich sammeln und
Am heißen Tag
Die Dürstenden erquiken! in mir
In mir, ihr Quellen des Lebens, strömtet
Aus Tiefen der Welt ihr einst
Zusammen und es kamen
Die Dürstenden zu mir – wie ists denn nun?
Vertrauert? bin ich ganz allein?
Und ist es Nacht hier außen auch am Tage?
Der höhers, denn ein sterblich Auge, sah
Der Blindgeschlagene tastet nun umher –
Wo seid ihr, meine Götter?
Weh! laßt ihr nun
Wie einen Bettler mich
Und diese Brust
Die liebend euch geahndet,
Was stoßt ihr sie hinab
Und schließt sie mir in schmählichenge Bande
Die Freigeborene, die aus sich
Und keines andern ist? und wandeln soll
Er nun so fort, der Langverwöhnte,
Der seelig oft mit allen Lebenden
Ihr Leben, ach, in heiligschöner Zeit
Sie, wie das Herz gefühlt von einer Welt,

With light, and Aether on the flowering scattered
Sparks of pure life that fertilized their bloom.
O intimate Nature, close again to my eyes,
Do you still know your friend, the fondly loved,
Or never again will you acknowledge me,
The priest who brought you gifts of living song,
Offered it up like life-blood gladly shed?

O by the holy wells
Where waters from veins of Earth
Collect, and on
A summer day
Refresh the thirsty man! In me,
In me, you wellsprings of life, you flowed
Together once from depths of the world, and
The thirsty came to me—how is it now?
All saddened? Am I quite alone?
And is it night out here in daytime too?
He who saw higher things than ever did mortal eye,
Now struck with blindness faltering picks his way—
Where are you now, my gods?
O will you now
Leave me a beggar,
And why do you cast off
This heart that once
By loving you divined you,
And into shamefully narrow bonds confine it,
A heart born free, that to itself
And no one else belonged? And is he now
To drag his days out thus who long was pampered,
Who often, one with all the living, felt
Their life, in holy, lovely times was blessed
To feel them as the heart of a whole world

289

Und ihren königlichen Götterkräften,
Verdammt in seiner Seele soll er so
Da hingehn, ausgestoßen? freundlos er,
Der Götterfreund? an seinem Nichts
Und seiner Nacht sich waiden immerdar
Unduldbares duldend gleich den Schwächlingen, die
Ans Tagewerk im scheuen Tartarus
Geschmiedet sind. Was daherab
Gekommen? um nichts? ha! Eines
Eins mußtet ihr mir lassen! Thor! bist du
Derselbe doch und träumst, als wärest du
Ein Schwacher. Einmal noch! noch Einmal
Soll mirs lebendig werden, und ich wills!
Fluch oder Seegen! täusche nun die Kraft
Demüthiger! dir nimmer aus dem Busen!
Weit will ichs um mich machen, tagen solls
Von eigner Flamme mir! Du sollst
Zufrieden werden, armer Geist,
Gefangener! sollst frei und groß und reich
In eigner Welt dich fühlen –
Und wieder einsam, weh! und wieder einsam?

Weh! einsam! einsam! einsam!
Und nimmer find ich
Euch, meine Götter,
Und nimmer kehr ich
Zu deinem Leben, Natur!
Dein Geächteter! – weh! hab ich doch auch
Dein nicht geachtet, dein
Mich überhoben, hast du
Umfangend doch mit den warmen Fittigen einst
Du Zärtliche! mich vom Schlafe gerettet?
Den Thörigen ihn, den Nahrungsscheuen,
Mitleidig schmeichelnd zu deinem Nectar

And of that world's divinely regal powers?
Damned in his very soul, shall he now perish
An outcast? And without a single friend,
Who was the friend of gods? For ever feed
Upon his nothingness, upon his night,
Bear the unbearable like those weaklings who
Are welded to their daily drudgery
In cringing Tartarus? Reduced to that?
For no good reason? Ah, but one thing,
One thing you had to leave me. Fool, for still
You are the man you were, and only dream
That you are feeble. Once again, once more
All shall become alive for me; I will it!
Blessing or curse, no longer, humble man,
Disarm the strength in you by self-deception!
I will have space around me! My own flame
Shall make a new day dawn! Poor mind immured,
You shall be satisfied again,
Shall feel in your own world—
And yet be lonely now, for ever lonely?

Ah, lonely, lonely, lonely!
And nevermore
I shall find you,
My gods, and nevermore,
Nature, return to your life!
Your outcast! And, oh, it's true, I paid
No heed to you then, but thought
Myself superior to you, although,
Enfolding me tenderly once with your warm wings,
You saved me from sleep,
And in your compassion, flattering, lured
The fool to your nectar,

Gelokt, damit er trank und wuchs
Und blüht', und mächtig geworden und trunken,
Dir ins Angesicht höhnt' – o Geist,
Geist, der mich groß genährt, du hast
Dir deinen Herrn, hast, alter Saturn,
Dir einen neuen Jupiter
Gezogen, einen schwächern nur und frechern.
Denn schmähen kann die böse Zunge dich nur,
Ist nirgend ein Rächer, und muß ich denn allein
Den Hohn und Fluch in meine Seele sagen?
Muß einsam seyn auch so?

DRITTER AUFTRITT

PAUSANIAS. EMPEDOKLES

EMPEDOKLES

Ich fühle nur des Tages Neige, Freund!
Und dunkel will es werden mir und kalt!
Es gehet rükwärts, lieber! nicht zur Ruh,
Wie wenn der beutefrohe Vogel sich
Das Haupt verhüllt zu frischer erwachendem
Zufriednem Schlummer, anders ists mit mir!
Erspare mir die Klage! laß es mir!

PAUSANIAS

Sehr fremde bist du mir geworden,
Mein Empedokles! kennest du mich nicht?

So that, drinking of it, he would grow
And thrive, and then, grown mighty and drunken,
Would mock you to your face—O spirit,
Spirit that raised me to manhood,
You've raised your master, old Saturn,
A second Jupiter you've raised
For yourself, only weaker, more insolent,
For this malicious tongue can only revile you.
With no avenger anywhere, must I myself
Heap all the scorn and curses on my soul?
Even in that be lonely?

SCENE THREE

PAUSANIAS, EMPEDOCLES

EMPEDOCLES

I feel the day declining now, my friend,
And all is growing dark for me, and cold.
Backward I go, dear friend, but not to rest
As when provided, satisfied with booty
A bird will swathe his head for pleasant sleep
And fresher wakening—different it is with me.
But spare me the complaint. Ask no more questions.

PAUSANIAS

How very strange to me you have become,
Empedocles. Do you not know me now?

Und kenn' ich nimmer dich, du Herrlicher? –
Du konntst dich so verwandeln, konntest so
Zum Räthsel werden, edel Angesicht,
Und so zur Erde beugen darf der Gram
Die Lieblinge des Himmels? bist du denn
Es nicht? und sieh! wie danken dir es all',
Und so in goldner Freude mächtig war
Kein anderer, wie du, in seinem Volke.

EMPEDOKLES

Sie ehren mich? o sag es ihnen doch,
Sie sollens lassen – Übel steht
Der Schmuk mir an und welkt
Das grüne Laub doch auch
Dem ausgerißnen Stamme!

PAUSANIAS

Noch stehst du ja, und frisch Gewässer spielt
Um deine Wurzel dir, es athmet mild
Die Luft um deine Gipfel, nicht von Vergänglichem
Gedeiht dein Herz; es walten über dir
Unsterblichere Kräfte.

EMPEDOKLES

Du mahnest mich der Jugendtage, lieber!

PAUSANIAS

Noch schöner dünkt des Lebens Mitte mir.

EMPEDOKLES

Und gerne sehen, wenn es nun
Hinab sich neigen will, die Augen
Der Schnellhinschwindenden noch Einmal
Zurük, der Dankenden. O jene Zeit!
Ihr Liebeswonnen, da die Seele mir
Von Göttern, wie Endymion, gewekt,

Nor I know you, the glorious, as I did?
Can you be so transformed, your noble face
Now an enigma to me, and remote?
And so to earth may suffering bow down
Heaven's own favourite? Are you not he?
And yet we thank you for it, all of us,
And never, amid golden joy, a man
Wielded such power as yours upon his people.

EMPEDOCLES

They honour me? Go quickly, then, and tell them
They are to cease. That ornament
Not well befits me now.
And does not the green foliage
Wilt, too, on trunks uprooted?

PAUSANIAS

But you still stand, and the cool brooklets play
About your roots, and mildly round your crest
The sweet air wafts, and that which is not transient
Sustains your core; the more immortal powers
Shape and watch over you.

EMPEDOCLES

It is my youth you call to mind, dear friend.

PAUSANIAS

The noon of life seems lovelier still to me.

EMPEDOCLES

And gladly, now that noon declines,
Once more the eyes of those look back
Who still more swiftly, and for ever, fade,
Look back, but to give thanks. O time of youth!
Delights of love, you ecstasies when my soul,
Awakened like Endymion by the gods,

295

Die kindlich schlummernde, sich öffnete,
Lebendig sie, die Immerjugendlichen,
Des Lebens große Genien
Erkannte – schöne Sonne! Menschen hatten mich
Es nicht gelehrt, mich trieb mein eigen Herz
Unsterblich liebend zu Unsterblichen,
Zu dir, zu dir, ich konnte Göttlichers
Nicht finden, stilles Licht! und so wie du
Das Leben nicht an deinem Tage sparst
Und sorgenfrei der goldnen Fülle dich
Entledigest, so gönnt' auch ich, der Deine,
Den Sterblichen die beste Seele gern
Und furchtlosoffen gab
Mein Herz, wie du, der ernsten E r d e sich,
Der schiksaalvollen; ihr in Jünglingsfreude
Das Leben so zu eignen bis zulezt,
Ich sagt' ihrs oft in trauter Stunde zu,
Band so den theuern Todesbund mit ihr.
Da rauscht' es anders, denn zuvor, im Hain,
Und zärtlich tönten ihrer Berge Quellen –
All deine Freuden, E r d e! wahr, wie sie,
Und warm und voll, aus Müh' und Liebe reifen,
Sie alle gabst du mir. Und wenn ich oft
Auf stiller Bergeshöhe saß und staunend
Der Menschen wechselnd Irrsaal übersann,
Zu tief von deinen Wandlungen ergriffen,
Und nah mein eignes Welken ahndete,
Dann athmete der A e t h e r, so wie dir,
Mir heilend um die liebeswunde Brust,
Und, wie Gewölk der Flamme, löseten
Im hohen Blau die Sorgen mir sich auf.

PAUSANIAS

O Sohn des Himmels!

Out of its childish drowsiness opened wide,
And, thrilled alive, it knew the ever-youthful
Spirits of life in their magnificence,
The genii—great *Sun*! No man had taught me
To name, to know them; it was my own heart,
Immortally loving, drove me to immortals,
To you, to you, for nothing more divine
Than you, still light, I found here; and as you
Never stint life in your day's daily fulness
And lavishly, taking no care, expend
Your golden wealth, so I, being yours, was glad
To give away to mortals my best soul
And, fearlessly candid, so
My heart to serious *Earth* I dedicated,
The many-destined; to her in youthful joy
As now, so lifelong, to devote my life
I promised her at many a solemn hour,
Pledging a firm, dear pact with her till death.
Then through the grove a different rustle ran,
And tenderly her mountains' wellsprings murmured—
Yes, all your pleasures, *Earth*, which true as she,
And warm and full, with love and labour ripen,
All these you gave me. Often, when I sat
High up, on some calm peak, and marvelling
Pondered the tangled, mutable ways of men,
Too deeply gripped by your vicissitudes,
And felt the nearness of my own decline,
Suddenly *Aether*, as on you, would waft
On me his breath, balm to the wounds of love,
And like the clouds of fire, my care and grief
Up in the cerulean heights were lost.

PAUSANIAS

You son of Heaven!

Ich war es! ja! und möcht es nun erzählen,
Ich Armer! möcht es Einmal noch
Mir in die Seele rufen,
Das Wirken deiner Geniuskräfte
Der Herrlichen deren Genoß ich war, o Natur,
Daß mir die stumme todesöde Brust
Von deinen Tönen allen wiederklänge,
Bin ich es noch? o Leben! und rauschten sie mir
All deine geflügelten Melodien und hört
Ich deinen alten Einklang, große Natur?
Ach! ich der Einsame, lebt ich nicht
Mit dieser heilgen Erd und diesem Licht
Und dir, von dem die Seele nimmer läßt,
O Vater Aether, und mit allen Lebenden
Der Götter Freund im gegenwärtigen
Olymp? ich bin heraus geworfen, bin
Ganz einsam, und das Weh ist nun
Mein Tagsgefährt' und Schlafgenosse mir.
Bei mir ist nicht der Seegen, geh!
Geh! frage nicht! denkst du, ich träum'?
O sieh mich an! und wundre deß dich nicht,
Du Guter, daß ich daherab
Gekommen bin; des Himmels Söhnen ist,
Wenn überglüklich sie geworden sind,
Ein eigner Fluch beschieden.

PAUSANIAS

Ich duld' es nicht,
Weh! solche Reden! du? ich duld es nicht.
Du solltest so die Seele dir und mir
Nicht ängstigen. Ein böses Zeichen dünkt
Es mir, wenn so der Geist, der immerfrohe, sich
Der Mächtigen umwölket.

EMPEDOCLES

Yes, that I was, and now will tell the story,
Wretch that I am, once more, and only once
Recall to my own soul
The working of those spirit powers,
Nature, your glorious powers whose companion I was,
So that my silent, desolate heart once more
With all your various music may resound.
Am I myself, O life, and did they once
Ring out to me, all your winged melodies, and did
I hear your ancient harmony, great Nature?
Oh, did I not, the lonely, live with her
This holy Earth, and live with you, this light,
And you from whom no soul can bear to part,
You, Father Aether, and with all that lives,
The friend of gods at home on real Olympus?
And now they've cast me out, and now they've left me
Utterly lonely, and now anguish is
My workmate, playmate, bedfellow, all in one.
No, do not come to me for blessings, friend!
Ask me no questions. Do you think I'm dreaming?
Just look at me! Nor is there any need,

Kind as you are, to wonder how it can be
That I have come to this; for sons of Heaven,
When too much joy, good fortune has been theirs,
A downfall like no other is reserved.

PAUSANIAS

I'll not allow it!
Such words from you! From you? I'll not allow it.
You should not frighten your own soul and mine
With blasphemous talk. It seems an evil omen
To see the ever clear and radiant minds
Of mighty men beclouded.

Fühlst dus? Es deutet, daß er bald
Zur Erd' hinab im Ungewitter muß.

PAUSANIAS

O laß den Unmuth, lieber!
O dieser, was that er euch, dieser Reine,
Daß ihm die Seele so verfinstert ist,
Ihr Todesgötter! haben die Sterblichen denn
Kein Eigenes nirgendswo, und reicht
Das Furchtbare denn ihnen bis ans Herz,
Und herrscht es in der Brust den Stärkeren noch
Das ewige Schiksaal? Bändige den Gram
Und übe deine Macht, bist du es doch
Der mehr vermag, denn andere, o sieh
An meiner Liebe, wer du bist,
Und denke dein, und lebe!

EMPEDOKLES

Du kennest mich und dich und Tod und Leben nicht.

PAUSANIAS

Den Tod, ich kenn' ihn wenig nur,
Denn wenig dacht' ich seiner.

EMPEDOKLES

Allein zu seyn,
Und ohne Götter, ist der Tod.

PAUSANIAS

Laß ihn, ich kenne dich, an deinen Thaten
Erkannt' ich dich, in seiner Macht
Erfuhr ich deinen Geist, und seine Welt,
Wenn oft ein Wort von dir
Im heilgen Augenblik
Das Leben vieler Jahre mir erschuff,

EMPEDOCLES

You sense it, then? It means that soon
They must come down to earth in a thunderstorm.

PAUSANIAS

Enough of this ill-humour, friend.
What has he done to you, you gods of death,
This pure one, to deserve the darkness fallen
Upon his soul? Is it that mortals have
Nothing that is their own, not anywhere,
But the dark powers reach to their very hearts,
And even in the stronger men's bosoms is it
Eternal Fate that governs? Tame your grief
And use your strength, for still you are the one
Who can do more than others. Let my love
Remind you of the man you were and are,
Think of yourself, and live!

EMPEDOCLES

You do not know me, nor yourself, nor life, nor death.

PAUSANIAS

Death I know little, true,
For I have given it little thought.

EMPEDOCLES

To be alone
And without gods is death.

PAUSANIAS

Forget it, I know *you*, and by your deeds
I came to know you, when death held me
First felt your spirit's force in a dead world,
Within one holy moment often
A single word from you
Made real for me the life of many years,

Daß eine neue große Zeit von da
Dem Jünglinge begann. Wie zahmen Hirschen,
Wenn ferne rauscht der Wald und sie
Der Heimath denken, schlug das Herz mir oft,
Wenn du vom Glük der alten Urwelt sprachst,
Der reinen Tage kundig und dir lag
Das ganze Schiksaal offen, zeichnetest
Du nicht der Zukunft große Linien
Mir vor das Auge, sichern Bliks, wie Künstler
Ein fehlend Glied zum ganzen Bilde reihn?
Und kennst du nicht die Kräfte der Natur,
Daß du vertraulich wie kein Sterblicher
Sie, wie du willst, in stiller Herrschaft lenkest?

EMPEDOKLES

Recht! alles weiß ich, alles kann ich meistern.
Wie meiner Hände Werk, erkenn ich es
Durchaus, und lenke, wie ich will
Ein Herr der Geister, das Lebendige.
Mein ist die Welt, und unterthan und dienstbar
Sind alle Kräfte mir,

       zur Magd ist mir
Die herrnbedürftige Natur geworden.
Und hat sie Ehre noch, so ists von mir.
Was wäre denn der Himmel und das Meer
Und Inseln und Gestirn, und was vor Augen
Den Menschen alles liegt, was wär es,
Diß todte Saitenspiel, gäb' ich ihm Ton
Und Sprach' und Seele nicht? was sind
Die Götter und ihr Geist, wenn ich sie nicht
Verkündige? nun! sage, wer bin ich?

PAUSANIAS

Verhöhne nur im Unmuth dich und alles

So that at once a whole great age began
For your disciple; and like the hearts of stags
When far away the forest roars, recalling
Their natural home to them, my heart would beat
When you evoked primeval worlds of bliss,
Versed in those pure days' lore, and all Fate's ways
Lay open to you. Did you not trace for me,
With mighty strokes, the very future's lines,
Your hand, your eye as sure as any painter's
Who adds the missing detail to the whole?
Are you not intimate with the powers of Nature,
And like no other mortal easily
Do you not rule them as you please in silence?

EMPEDOCLES

Quite true, I know all things, can master all.
Like my own handiwork thoroughly I control it
And as I please, a lord of spirits, rule,
Manipulate, make use of all that lives.
Mine is the world, submissive and subservient
To me are all its powers,
                          Nature herself,
Unfit, as well you know, to have her way,
Is now my servant girl; such honour
As men accord her still, she owes to me.
And what indeed would Heaven be and Ocean
And islands and the stars, and all that meets
The eyes of men, what would it mean or be,
This dead stringed instrument, did I not lend it
A resonance, a language and a soul?
What are the gods, and what their spirit, if I
Do not proclaim them? Tell me now, who am I?

PAUSANIAS

Out of mere bitterness mock yourself and all

303

Was Menschen herrlich macht,
Ihr Wirken und ihr Wort, verlaide mir
Den Muth im Busen, schröke mich zum Kinde
Zurük. O sprich es nur heraus! du hassest dich
Und was dich liebt und was dir gleichen möcht';
Ein anders willst du, denn du bist, genügst dir
In deiner Ehre nicht und opferst dich an Fremdes.
Du willst nicht bleiben, willst
Zu Grunde gehen. Ach! in deiner Brust
Ist minder Ruhe, denn in mir.

EMPEDOKLES

Unschuldiger!

PAUSANIAS

Und dich verklagst du?
Was ist es denn? o mache mir dein Leiden
Zum Räthsel länger nicht! mich peinigets!

EMPEDOKLES

Mit Ruhe wirken soll der Mensch,
Der sinnende, soll entfaltend
Das Leben um ihn fördern und heitern
                    denn hoher Bedeutung voll,
Voll schweigender Kraft umfängt
Den ahnenden, daß er bilde die Welt,
Die große Natur,
Daß ihren Geist hervor er rufe, strebt
Tief wurzelnd
Das gewaltige Sehnen ihm auf.
Und viel vermag er und herrlich ist
Sein Wort, es wandelt die Welt
Und unter den Händen

That makes men glorious,
Their workings and their word; make me ashamed
Of my own courage, cow me and drive me back
Into my childhood. Freely admit: You hate
Yourself and those who love and follow you;
Your will is bent on what you are not, your fame,
Grown strange to you, to strangers will betray you.
Not to remain on earth
Is your desire, you long to perish. Oh,
Your heart at last is less serene than mine.

EMPEDOCLES

You innocent!

PAUSANIAS

And you accuse yourself?
What is it, then? O cease to make a riddle
Of your affliction. You are tormenting me.

EMPEDOCLES

Serenely, true, should men,
The pondering, act upon
The life around them, to further and make bright
for full of lofty purpose,
Of power contained, unexpressed,
Great Nature surrounds their
Foreknowing minds, to bid them fashion a world,
Deep-rooted
Within them a mighty longing leaps up
So that her spirit will come to light.
And much he can do, and glorious is
Man's word, it transforms the world
And where his hands have

PANTHEA

Hast du doch, menschlich Irrsaal!
Ihm nicht das Herz verwöhnt,
Du Unbedeutendes! was gabst
Du Armes ihm? nun da der Mann
Zu seinen Göttern fort sich sehnt,
Wundern sie sich, als hätten sie
Die Thörigen ihm, die hohe Seele, geschaffen.
Umsonst nicht sind, o, die du alles ihm
Gegeben, Natur!
Vergänglicher deine Liebsten, denn andre!
Ich weiß es wohl!
Sie kommen und werden groß, und keiner sagt,
Wie sie's geworden, so entschwinden sie auch,
Die Glüklichen! wieder, ach! laßt sie doch.

DELIA

Ists denn nicht schön,
Bei Menschen wohnen; es weiß
Mein Herz von andrem nicht, es ruht
In diesem Einen, aber traurig dunkel droht
Vor meinem Auge das Ende
Des Unbegreiflichen, und du heißest ihn auch
Hinweggehn, Panthea?

ACT TWO (*CONCLUSION*)

PANTHEA

Surely not you it was,
The human labyrinth,
The insignificant, that spoiled
His heart? What could you give him,
Poor as you are? Now that the man
Longs to be gone and join his gods
They wonder at it, as if it were they, the foolish,
Who had endowed him with a lofty soul.
Nature, who gave him all, not without reason
Those you love best more briefly linger here!
Too well I know it.
They come and grow, and none of us can say
How they grew great, and so again they vanish,
Those happy ones. O leave them, let them go!

DELIA

Is it not good
To live among mortals? My heart
Knows of no other joy, it rests
Upon this *one* man, but sadly, darkly before
My eyes now threatens the end
Of him, the inscrutable, yet even you,
Panthea, bid him go?

307

PANTHEA

Ich muß. Wer will ihn binden?
Ihm sagen, mein bist du,
Ist doch sein eigen der Lebendige,
Und nur sein Geist ihm Gesez,
Und soll er die Ehre der Sterblichen
Zu retten, die ihn geschmäht,
Verweilen, wenn ihm
Der Vater die Arme
Der Aether öffnet?

DELIA

Sieh! herrlich auch
Und freundlich ist die Erde.

PANTHEA

Ja herrlich, und herrlicher izt.
Es darf nicht unbeschenkt
Von ihr ein Kühner scheiden.
Noch weilt er wohl
Auf deiner grünen Höhen einer, o Erde
Du Wechselnde!
Und siehet über die woogenden Hügel
Hinab ins freie Meer! und nimmt
Die lezte Freude sich. Vieleicht sehn wir
Ihn nimmer. Gutes Kind!
Mich trift es freilich auch und gerne möcht'
Ichs anders, doch ich schäme dessen mich.
Thut er es ja! Ists so nicht heilig?

DELIA

Wer ist der Jüngling, der
Vom Berge dort herabkömt?

PANTHEA

Pausanias. Ach! müssen wir so
Uns wiederfinden, Vaterloser?

I must. For who could bind him,
Say to him, you are mine,
When to himself that living one belongs,
For him no law but his own mind is valid?
And should he stay here to save
The honour of mortals
Who have reviled him, when now
The Father himself,
When Aether opens
His arms to him?

DELIA

Look! Glorious too
And kindly our Earth is.

PANTHEA

Glorious, true, and more glorious now.
Not without presents may
A bold man part from her.
Still he must be delaying
On one of your verdant summits, O Earth,
The for ever changing,
And gazes now across the billowing hills
Down to the open sea, and snatches
A joy from you, the last. Perhaps we shall
Not see him again. Dear child,
Me too, believe me, it hurts, and gladly I
Would have it otherwise, but feel ashamed of the wish.
His choice it is! That, surely, hallows the deed?

DELIA

What young man is that
Coming down from the mountain there?

PANTHEA.

Pausanias; poor fatherless boy!
Like this we must meet again?

PAUSANIAS. PANTHEA. DELIA

PAUSANIAS

Wo ist er? o Panthea!
Du ehrst ihn, suchest ihn auch,
Willst Einmal noch ihn sehn,
Den furchtbarn Wanderer, ihn, dem allein
Beschieden ist, den Pfad zu gehen mit Ruhm,
Den ohne Fluch betritt kein anderer.

PANTHEA

Ists from von ihm und groß
Das Allgefürchtete?
Wo ist er?

PAUSANIAS

Er sandte mich hinweg, indessen sah
Ich ihn nicht wieder. Droben rief
Ich im Gebürg' ihn, doch ich fand ihn nicht.
Er kehrt gewiß. Bis in die Nacht
Versprach er freundlich mir zu bleiben.
O käm er! Es flieht, geschwinder, wie Pfeile
Die liebste Stunde vorüber.
Denn freuen werden wir uns noch mit ihm,
Du wirst es, Panthea, und sie,
Die edle Fremdlingin, die ihn
Nur Einmal sieht, ein herrlich Meteor.
Von seinem Tode, ihr Weinenden
Habt ihr gehört?
Ihr Trauernden! o sehet ihn

LAST SCENE OF ACT TWO

PAUSANIAS, PANTHEA, DELIA

PAUSANIAS

Where is he? O Panthea,
You respect him, look for him too,
And long to see him once more,
That frightening wanderer who alone is fated
With glory to walk that path
Which to all other men a curse forbids.

PANTHEA

Is it godly for him, and great,
This way that all men fear?
Where is he?

PAUSANIAS

He sent me away, and I have not seen
Him since. Up in the mountains
I called his name, but did not find him.
He will surely return, having kindly promised me
That until nightfall he would stay.
If only he'd come! More swiftly
Than arrows the loveliest hour goes by.
For we shall yet enjoy his presence,
You, Panthea, and she as well,
The noble stranger who only once
Will see him, bright and brief, a meteor.
But you are weeping. Of his death
You've heard, then?
You grieve for him. O in his prime

311

In seiner Blüthe, den Hohen,
Ob trauriges nicht
Und was den Sterblichen schröklich dünkt,
Sich sänftige vor seeligem Auge.

DELIA

Wie liebst du ihn! und batest umsonst
Den Ernsten? mächtger ist, denn er
Die Bitte, Jüngling! und ein schöner Sieg
Wärs dir gewesen!

PAUSANIAS

Wie konnt' ich? trift
Er doch die Seele mir, wenn er
Antwortet, was sein Will ist.
Denn Freude nur giebt sein Versagen.
Diß ists und es tönt, je mehr auf seinem
Der Wunderbare besteht,
Nur tiefer das Herz ihm wieder. Es ist
Nicht eitel Überredung, glaub es mir,
Wenn er des Lebens sich
Bemächtiget.
Oft wenn er stille war
In seiner Welt,
Der Hochgenügsame, sah' ich ihn
Nur dunkel ahnend, rege war,
Und voll die Seele mir, doch konnt' ich nicht
Sie fühlen, und es ängstigte mich fast
Die Gegenwart des Unberührbaren.
Doch kam entscheidend von seiner Lippe das Wort,
Dann tönt' ein Freudenhimmel nach in ihm
Und mir und ohne Widerred
Ergriff es mich, doch fühlt' ich nur mich freier.
Ach, könnt' er irren, inniger
Erkennt' ich daran den unerschöpflich Wahren

Envisage that exalted man.
And that which grieves you,
That which to mortals seems most terrible,
May well look milder to eyes that are blessed.

DELIA

How you love him! And yet in vain
Implored the earnest man? The plea
Is mightier than himself, and you deserved
To win him over.

PAUSANIAS

How could I, when
In answering he speaks his will
And overwhelms my soul?
For his refusal even gladdens us.
What could I do? The more that marvellous man
Insists on his own way,
The deeper is the resonance in our hearts.
Nor is it mere persuasiveness, believe me,
When over life itself
He gains such power.
When he was quiet
In his own world,
Uniquely self-sufficient,
Often I watched him in his vague divining,
My own soul active, full of vigour, yet
I could not feel it, and almost I was awed
By his impalpable presence.
Yet when the decisive word came from his lips
A heaven of joy re-echoed both in him
And me, and without contradiction
I yielded to it, relieved and liberated.
If he could err, why, all the more deeply
By that I should know the inexhaustible truth of him.

Und stirbt er, so flammt aus seiner Asche nur heller
Der Genius mir empor.

Dich entzündet, große Seele! der Tod
Des Großen, aber es sonnen
Die Herzen der Sterblichen auch
An mildem Lichte sich gern, und heften
Die Augen an Bleibendes. O sage, was soll
Noch leben und dauern? Die Stillsten reißt
Das Schiksaal doch hinaus und haben
Sie ahnend sich gewagt, verstößt
Es bald die Trauten wieder, und es stirbt
An ihren Hofnungen die Jugend.
In seiner Blüthe bleibt
Kein Lebendes – ach! und die Besten,
Noch treten zur Seite der tilgenden,
Der Todesgötter, auch sie und gehen dahin
Mit Lust und machen zur Schmach es uns
Bei Sterblichen zu weilen!

PAUSANIAS

Verdammest du

DELIA

O warum lässest du
Zu sterben deinen Helden
So leicht es werden, Natur?
Zu gern nur, Empedokles,
Zu gerne opferst du dich,

And if he died, all the more brightly his genius
From his ashes would rise for me.

DELIA

Being great, your soul is kindled
By a great man's death, but the hearts
Of mortals too like to bask
In milder light, and attach
Their eyes to that which is lasting. O tell us,
What now shall live and last? The most quiet
Fate uproots and sweeps away,
And if, prophetic, they ventured out,
Soon it repels those brave ones; the young
Die of the hopes that sustained them.
Nothing that lives remains
In its flower and prime—and the best,
Even they seek out their destroyers,
The gods of death, and with pleasure
They perish, and make it our shame
To linger, to dwell among mortals.

PAUSANIAS

Do you condemn

DELIA

O Nature, why do you
Make it so easy
For your hero to die?
Empedocles, all too eagerly
You sacrifice yourself.

315

Die Schwachen wirft das Schiksaal um, und die andern
Die Starken achten es gleich, zu fallen, zu stehn,
Und werden, wie die Gebrechlichen.
Du Herrlicher! was du littest,
Das leidet kein Knecht
Und ärmer denn die andern Bettler
Durchwandertest du das Land,
Ja! freilich wahr ists,
Nicht die Verworfensten
Sind elend, wie eure Lieben, wenn einmal
Schmähliches sie berührt, ihr Götter.
Schön hat ers genommen.

PANTHEA

O nicht wahr?
Wie sollt er auch nicht?
Muß immer und immer doch
Was übermächtig ist
Der Genius überleben – gedachtet ihr,
Es halte der Stachel ihn auf? es beschleunigen ihm
Die Schmerzen den Flug und wie der Wagenlenker,
Wenn ihm das Rad in der Bahn
Zu rauchen beginnt, eilt
Der Gefährdete nur schneller zum Kranze!

DELIA

So freudig bist du, Panthea?

PANTHEA

Nicht in der Blüth' und Purpurtraub'
Ist heilge Kraft allein, es nährt
Das Leben vom Laide sich, Schwester!
Und trinkt, wie mein Held, doch auch
Am Todeskelche sich glüklich!

The weak by Fate are hurled down, and those others,
The strong, care little whether they fall or stand
And so become like the frail.
You glorious man, what you suffered
No slave could suffer,
And poorer than the poorest beggar
You roam across the land.
Yes, indeed it's true,
Not the utterly damned and rejected
Are wretched as are your loved ones, you gods,
Once disgrace has touched them.
And well he took it.

PANTHEA

Yes, well he took it
And how could he not?
When always and always the genius
Must outlive
That which is stronger than he—did you think
The goad would check him? The pain makes faster
His flight, and like the charioteer
When wheels begin to smoke on the track,
All the more swiftly
He, the endangered, rushes towards his garland.

DELIA

It's joy you feel, then, Panthea?

PANTHEA

Not in the blossom and purple grape
Alone is holy energy, but life
By suffering too is nourished, sister;
And, like my hero, even from
The deadly cup draws gladness.

317

Weh! must du so
Dich trösten, Kind?

PANTHEA

O nicht! es freuet mich nur,
Daß heilig, wenn es geschehn muß,
Das Gefürchtete, daß es herrlich geschieht.
Sind nicht, wie er, auch
Der Heroen einige zu den Göttern gegangen?
Erschroken kam, lautweinend
Vom Berge, das Volk, ich sah
Nicht einen, ders ihm hätte gelästert,
Denn nicht, wie die Verzweifelnden
Entfliehet er heimlich, sie hörten es all,
Und ihnen glänzt' im Laide das Angesicht
Vom Worte, das er gesprochen –

PAUSANIAS

So gehet festlich hinab
Das Gestirn und trunken
Von seinem Lichte glänzen die Thäler?

PANTHEA

Wohl geht er festlich hinab –
Der Ernste, dein Liebster, Natur!
Dein treuer, dein Opfer!
O die Todesfürchtigen lieben dich nicht,
Täuschend fesselt ihnen die Sorge
Das Aug', an deinem Herzen
Schlägt dann nicht mehr ihr Herz, sie verdorren
Geschieden von dir – o heilig All!
Lebendiges! inniges! dir zum Dank
Und daß er zeuge von dir, du Todesloses!
Wirft lächelnd seine Perlen ins Meer,

Dear child, is that
Your only comfort?

PANTHEA

By no means! And yet it cheers me
That when it must be, must come about,
The dreaded thing, with glory it comes about.
Like him, in the past
Did not more than one of the heroes go to the gods?
Though startled, weeping aloud,
The people came from the mountain,
Not one I saw who reproached him,
For not like despairing men
In secret he flees, but all of them heard it,
And in their sorrow their faces shone
With the word that he had spoken.

PAUSANIAS

Festively, then, the planet
Goes down, and drunken
With its effulgence the valleys gleam?

PANTHEA

Festively, yes, he goes down—
The grave man, your favourite, Nature,
Your loyal one, sacrificed.
O they who fear death do not love you,
But care, the deluding obstructs
Their eyes, and against your heart
No longer do their hearts beat, and they wither,
Divided from you—from the holy All.
And to bear witness to you, that are deathless,
Smiling into the sea, whence they came,

Aus dem sie kamen, der Kühne.
So mußt es geschehn.
So will es der Geist
Und die reifende Zeit,
Denn Einmal bedurften
Wir Blinden des Wunders.

He throws his pearls now, the bold.
So it had to be.
So the spirit would have it
And ripening Time;
For we who are blind
Needed a miracle once

PERSONEN

EMPEDOKLES

PAUSANIAS, sein Freund

MANES, ein Aegyptier

STRATO, Herr von Agrigent, Bruder des Empedokles

PANTHEA, seine Schwester

GEFOLGE

CHOR der Agrigentiner

CHARACTERS

EMPEDOCLES

PAUSANIAS, his friend

MANES, an Egyptian

STRATO, Ruler of Agrigentum, brother of Empedocles

PANTHEA, his sister

ATTENDANTS

CHORUS of Agrigentines

ERSTER ACT

ERSTER AUFTRITT

EMPEDOKLES
(vom Schlaf erwachend)

Euch ruf ich über das Gefild herein
Vom langsamen Gewölk, ihr heißen Stralen
Des Mittags, ihr Gereiftesten, daß ich
An euch den neuen Lebenstag erkenne.
Denn anders ists wie sonst! vorbei, vorbei
Das menschliche Bekümmerniß! als wüchsen
Mir Schwingen an, so ist mir wohl und leicht
Hier oben, hier, und reich genug und froh
Und herrlich wohn' ich, wo den Feuerkelch
Mit Geist gefüllt bis an den Rand, bekränzt
Mit Blumen, die er selber sich erzog,
Gastfreundlich mir der Vater Aetna beut.
Und wenn das unterirrdische Gewitter
Izt festlich auferwacht zum Wolkensiz
Des nahverwandten Donnerers hinauf
Zur Freude fliegt, da wächst das Herz mir auch.
Mit Adlern sing ich hier Naturgesang.
Das dacht er nicht, daß in der Fremde mir
Ein anders Leben blühte, da er mich
Mit Schmach hinweg aus unsrer Stadt verwies,
Mein königlicher Bruder. Ach! er wußt es nicht,
Der kluge, welchen Seegen er bereitete,
Da er vom Menschenbande los, da er mich frei
Erklärte, frei, wie Fittige des Himmels.
Drum galt es auch! drum ward es auch erfüllt!
Mit Hohn und Fluch drum waffnete das Volk,

SCENE ONE

ACT ONE

EMPEDOCLES

(awakening from sleep)

You now I call upon across the fields,
Call down and in from the slow clouds, hot sun rays
Of noontide, you the most matured, so that
In you I'll recognize my new life's day.
For all is different now; and gone, dispelled,
My human grief! as though grown birdlike, graced
With pinions overnight, I feel so light
Up here, so well, and rich enough and glad
And glorious here I dwell where Father Etna
Tenders hospitably the fiery chalice
Filled to the brim with spirit, garlanded
With flowers that for himself he has reared up.
Whenever, too, the subterranean thunder
Festively roused now to the cloudy seat
Of his close relative, the Thunderer,
To joy flies up, then my heart also grows
Here with the eagles I sing natural songs.
Of that he never thought, my royal brother,
When ignominiously he made me leave
Our city, that in exile, in the wilds
A different life would blossom out for me.
He never knew, that clever one, what blessing
He was bestowing on me when he severed
My human bonds, when he declared me free,
Free as the birds are, winged for heavenly flight.
And that was why! for that it was fulfilled!

Das mein war, gegen meine Seele sich
Und stieß mich aus und nicht vergebens gellt
Im Ohre mir das hundertstimmige,
Das nüchterne Gelächter, da der Träumer,
Der närrische, des Weges weinend gieng.
Beim Todtenrichter! wohl hab ichs verdient!
Und heilsam wars; die Kranken heilt das Gift
Und eine Sünde straft die andere.
Denn viel gesündiget hab ich von Jugend auf,
Die Menschen menschlich nie geliebt, gedient,
Wie Wasser nur und Feuer blinder dient,
Darum begegneten auch menschlich mir
Sie nicht, o darum schändeten sie mir
Mein Angesicht, und hielten mich, wie dich
Allduldende Natur! du hast mich auch,
Du hast mich, und es dämmert zwischen dir
Und mir die alte Liebe wieder auf,
Du rufst, du ziehst mich nah und näher an.
Vergessenheit – o wie ein glüklich Seegel
Bin ich vom Ufer los, des Lebens Welle
                            mich von selbst
Und wenn die Wooge wächst, und ihren Arm
Die Mutter um mich breitet, o was möcht'
Ich auch, was möcht' ich fürchten. Andre mag
Es freilich schröken. Denn es ist ihr Tod.
O du mir wohlbekant, du zauberische
Furchtbare Flamme! wie so stille wohnst
Du da und dort, wie scheuest du dich selbst
Und fliehest dich, du Seele des Lebendigen!
Lebendig wirst du mir und offenbar,
Mir birgst du dich, gebundner Geist, nicht länger,
Mir wirst du helle, denn ich fürcht es nicht.
Denn sterben will ja ich. Mein Recht ist diß.
Ha! Götter, schon, wie Morgenroth, ringsum

And they, the people once my own, could arm
Themselves with curses, taunts against my soul
And drive me out, and not for nothing still
My ears reverberate with the hundred-voiced,
Their hard, cold laughter when the fantast turned,
The silly dreamer, and weeping went his way.
By Hades! amply I deserved it all.
And it was good for me; poison heals the sick,
And we are purged of one sin by another.
For sinned I have, and greatly, from my youth,
Never have loved men humanly, but served
Only as fire or water blindly serves them.
And therefore too not humanly towards me
They acted, but defiled my face and used me
Like you, all-suffering Nature! And it is you
That hold me now, I'm yours, and between you
And me once more the old love rises up,
You call, you draw me close and ever closer.
Oblivion—O like a happy sail
I've left the shore behind, the wave of life
                              with its own force
And when the breaker swells and when the Mother
With her own arms enfolds me, O what could I,
What could I fear. Though other men, it's true,
Might well be frightened. For it is their death.
O you well known to me, enchanting one,
Terrible flame! How quietly you dwell
Now here, now there, how you avoid yourself,
Flee from yourself, you soul of all that lives!
You grow alive to me, and manifest,
No longer hide, bound spirit, from my sight,
For me grow bright, because I do not fear it.
For death is what I seek. It is my right.
Already, gods, like sunrise all round me

Und drunten tost der alte Zorn vorüber!
Hinab hinab ihr klagenden Gedanken!
Sorgfältig Herz! ich brauche nun dich nimmer.
Und hier ist kein Bedenken mehr. Es ruft
Der Gott –

(da er den Pausanias gewahr wird)

      und diesen Allzutreuen muß
Ich auch befrein, mein Pfad ist seiner nicht.

ZWEITER AUFTRITT

PAUSANIAS. EMPEDOKLES

PAUSANIAS

Du scheinest freudig auferwacht, mein Wanderer.

EMPEDOKLES

Schon hab ich, lieber, und vergebens nicht
Mich in der neuen Heimath umgesehn.
Die Wildniß ist mir hold, auch dir gefällt,
      die edle Burg,
          unser Aetna.

PAUSANIAS

Sie haben uns verbannt, sie haben dich,
Du Gütiger! geschmäht und glaub' es mir,
Unleidlich warst du ihnen längst und innig
In ihre Trümmer schien, in ihre Nacht
Zu helle den Verzweifelten das Licht.
Nun mögen sie vollenden, ungestört
Im uferlosen Sturm, indeß den Stern
Die Wolke birgt, ihr Schiff im Kreise treiben.
Das wußt ich wohl, du Göttlicher, an dir
Entweicht der Pfeil, der andre trift und wirft.
Und ohne Schaden, wie am Zauberstab

And underneath, the ancient wrath roars by.
Down with you, down, my poor complaining thoughts!
Painstaking heart, my need for you is over.
And no more scruples, wavering now. The god
It is who calls—

          (becoming aware of Pausanias)
               and this too loyal one

Shall have his freedom; my way is not his.

SCENE TWO

PAUSANIAS. EMPEDOCLES

PAUSANIAS

It seems you had a glad awakening,
My exiled master.

EMPEDOCLES

               For some time, dear friend,
And not in vain, I have been up, surveying
The prospect and the site of this new home.
The wilderness delights me, and you also
Take pleasure in   this noble fortress
our Etna.

PAUSANIAS

They've banished us, reviled you, kindly man,
And, friend, believe me, long before that time
Found you insufferable; tenderly
Into their rubble and their night it shone,
Too bright for those despairing ones, your light.
Now let them end the business, undisturbed
Through shoreless squalls, while clouds conceal the star,
In circles let them now propel their ship.
This I knew well, divine one, that from you
That dart rebounds which wounds and fells another.
And harmlessly, as on a magic wand

Die zahme Schlange, spielt' um dich von je
Die ungetreue Menge, die du zogst,
Die du am Herzen hegtest, liebender!
Nun! laß sie nur! sie mögen ungestalt
Lichtscheu am Boden taumeln der sie trägt,
Und allbegehrend, allgeängstiget
Sich müde rennen, brennen mag der Brand,
Bis er erlischt – wir wohnen ruhig hier!

EMPEDOKLES

Ja! ruhig wohnen wir; es öffnen groß
Sich hier vor uns die heilgen Elemente.
Die Mühelosen regen immergleich
In ihrer Kraft sich freudig hier um uns.
An seinen vesten Ufern wallt und ruht
Das alte Meer, und das Gebirge steigt
Mit seiner Ströme Klang, es woogt und rauscht
Sein grüner Wald von Thal zu Thal hinunter.
Und oben weilt das Licht, der Aether stillt
Den Geist und das geheimere Verlangen.
Hier wohnen ruhig wir!

PAUSANIAS

                        So bleibst du wohl
Auf diesen Höhn, und lebst in deiner Welt,
Ich diene dir und sehe, was uns noth ist.

EMPEDOKLES

Nur weniges ist noth, und selber mag
Ich gerne diß von jezt an mir besorgen.

PAUSANIAS

Doch lieber! hab ich schon für einiges,
Was du zuerst bedarfst, zuvorgesorgt.

EMPEDOKLES

Weist du, was ich bedarf?

Tame serpents will, around you ever played
The faithless mob that you yourself reared up,
Lovingly tended, warmed against your heart.
Well, let them be. Misshapen let them reel
Close to the soil that bears them, shunning light,
And all-desiring, all-intimidated,
Run themselves weary; let their slow fire burn
Till it goes out—peacefully we live here.

EMPEDOCLES

Yes, we live peacefully; and vastly here
The holy elements reveal themselves.
Ever the same, the untoiling joyously,
Surely and powerfully stir around us.
On its firm shores advances and reposes
The ancient sea, and the great mountains rise
With music of their springs, the green woods flow
And roar and rustle down from vale to vale.
And at the top light lingers, Aether stills
Our minds and the more secret of our longings.
Here we live peacefully.

PAUSANIAS

So you will stay
Here on these heights, and live in your own world,
And I shall serve you, see to what we need.

EMPEDOCLES

Little is needed, and that willingly
From now on I will see to and provide.

PAUSANIAS

Nevertheless, already, my dear teacher,
I've made provision for your urgent needs.

EMPEDOCLES

And do you know them?

PAUSANIAS

　　　　　　　Als wüßt ich nicht,
Womit genügt dem Hochgenügsamen.
Und wie das Leben, das zu lieber Noth
Der innigen Natur geworden ist,
Das kleinste dem Vertrauten viel bedeutet.
Indeß du gut auf kahler Erde hier
In heißer Sonne schliefst, gedacht' ich doch,
Ein waicher Boden, und die kühle Nacht
In einer sichern Halle wäre besser.
Auch sind wir hier, die Allverdächtigen,
Den Wohnungen der andern fast zu nah.
Nicht lange wollt ich ferne seyn von dir
Und eilt hinauf und glüklich fand ich bald,
Für dich und mich gebaut, ein ruhig Haus.
Ein tiefer Fels, von Eichen dicht umschirmt,
Dort in der dunkeln Mitte des Gebirgs,
Und nah entspringt ein Quell, es grünt umher
Die Fülle guter Pflanzen, und zum Bett
Ist Überfluß von Laub und Gras bereitet.
Da lassen sie dich ungeschmäht, und tief und still
Ists wenn du sinnst, und wenn du schläfst, um dich,
Ein Heiligtum ist mir mit dir die Grotte.
Komm, siehe selbst, und sage nicht, ich tauge
Dir künftig nicht, wem taugt' ich anders denn?

EMPEDOKLES

Du taugst zu gut.

PAUSANIAS

　　　Wie könt ich diß?

EMPEDOKLES

　　　　　　　　　Auch du
Bist allzutreu, du bist ein thöricht Kind.

PAUSANIAS

How could I not know
What would suffice the highly self-sufficient;
How in that life which now is the dear care
Of tender Nature, even smallest things
Mean much to one long grown familiar to me.
While you slept well here on the bare, hard ground
In blazing sunshine, yet it seemed to me,
A softer bed to lie on and cool night
Within firm walls, in safety, would be better.
Besides, all-suspect even in these wilds
Almost we are too near to other men's homes.
Not wishing to be far from you for long,
I hurried to these parts and quickly found
A quiet house, fitting for you and me.
Dense oak-trees there surround a sheer great rock
Up in the mountain-range's gloomy midst,
A spring wells up nearby, and all around
There's plenty of good plants, and more than plenty
Of leaves and grass for bedding. There they'll leave
You unmolested, and when you meditate,
And when you sleep, all's deep and still for you,
A holy place that grotto, shared with you.
See for yourself now, come, and never say
You've no more use for me—who else should use me?

EMPEDOCLES

You are too useful.

PAUSANIAS

Could I be?

EMPEDOCLES

You too
Are all too loyal; you're a foolish child.

353

PAUSANIAS

Das sagst du wohl, doch klügers weiß ich nicht,
Wie deß zu seyn, dem ich geboren bin.

EMPEDOKLES

Wie bist du sicher?

PAUSANIAS

        Warum denn nicht?
Wofür denn hättest du auch einst, da ich,
Der Waise gleich, am heldenarmen Ufer
Mir einen Schuzgott sucht und traurig irrte,
Du Gütiger, die Hände mir gereicht?
Wofür mit irrelosem Auge wärst du
Auf deiner stillen Bahn, du edles Licht
In meiner Dämmerung mir aufgegangen?
Seitdem bin ich ein anderer, und dein
Und näher dir und einsamer mit dir,
Wächst froher nur die Seele mir und freier.

EMPEDOKLES

O still davon!

PAUSANIAS

        Warum? Was ists? wie kan
Ein freundlich Wort dich irren, theurer Mann?

EMPEDOKLES

Geh! folge mir, und schweig und schone mich
Und rege du nicht auch das Herz mir auf. –
Habt ihr zum Dolche die Erinnerung
Nicht mir gemacht? nun wundern sie sich noch
Und treten vor das Auge mir und fragen.
Nein! du bist ohne Schuld – nur kann ich, Sohn!
Was mir zu nahe kömmt, nicht wohl ertragen.

PAUSANIAS

Well you may say so, but I can be no wiser
Than to belong to him whose child I am.

EMPEDOCLES

Are you so sure of that?

PAUSANIAS

               How can I help it?
Why else, when like an orphan on a shore
That breeds few heroes, sadly I strayed about
Seeking a tutelary god, did you,
Most kind one, offer me your hand? Why else
With your unstraying eyes, in your sure orbit,
Did you, most noble light, rise in my dawn?
Since then I have been different, and am yours,
And closer to you, lonelier with you,
My soul grows all the gladder and more free.

EMPEDOCLES

No, please—not that.

PAUSANIAS

               Why not? What is it? Can
A friendly word distress you, then, my teacher?

EMPEDOCLES

Come, follow me, keep silent, friend, and spare me,
Unlike those others, do not stir my heart.
Did they not turn my memories into daggers?
And after that they wonder at it all,
And seek me out, and ask me this and that.
No, you are not to blame—only, my son,
I cannot bear too deep, too close a probing.

PAUSANIAS

Und mich, mich stößest du von dir? o denk an dich,
Sei, der du bist, und siehe mich, und gieb,
Was ich nun weniger entbehren kann,
Ein gutes Wort aus reicher Brust mir wieder.

EMPEDOKLES

Erzähle, was dir wohlgefällt, dir selbst,
Für mich ist, was vorüber ist, nicht mehr.

PAUSANIAS

Ich weiß es wohl, was dir vorüber ist,
Doch du und ich, wir sind uns ja geblieben.

EMPEDOKLES

Sprich lieber mir von anderem, mein Sohn!

PAUSANIAS

Was hab ich sonst?

EMPEDOKLES

       Verstehest du mich auch?
Hinweg! ich hab es dir gesagt und sag
Es dir, es ist nicht schön, daß du dich
So ungefragt mir an die Seele dringest,
An meine Seite stets, als wüßtest du
Nichts anders mehr, mit armer Angst dich hängst.
Du must es wissen, dir gehör ich nicht
Und du nicht mir, und deine Pfade sind
Die meinen nicht; mir blüht es anderswo.
Und was ich mein', es ist von heute nicht,
Da ich geboren wurde, wars beschlossen.
Sieh auf und wags! was Eines ist, zerbricht,
Die Liebe stirbt in ihrer Knospe nicht
Und überall in freier Freude theilt
Des Lebens luftger Baum sich auseinander.

PAUSANIAS

And so you cast me off! Think of yourself,
Be what you are and look at me and give me
What now less easily I can do without,
A token of your former self and friendship.

EMPEDOCLES

Tell any tales you please—but to yourself;
For me what's past is done with once for all.

PAUSANIAS

O, I know well enough what's past for you,
But you and I, must our good bonds be broken?

EMPEDOCLES

I beg you, speak of other things, my son.

PAUSANIAS

What else is there?

EMPEDOCLES

                 But do you understand me?
Away! I've told you once and say again,
It is not right that uninvited here
You prod my soul, as though incapable
Of other movement now, in pitiable fear
Always you cling to me. But you must know,
I am not yours, no more than you are mine,
Where you walk, I do not; my blossoming
Elsewhere awaits me. And that of which I speak
Not now has come about, not on this day,
But at my birth already was decided.
Look up and dare to know it: what is One
Breaks up, yet in its bud love does not die,
And everywhere in bold, untrammelled joy,
Unforced, the airy tree of life divides.

337

Kein zeitlich Bündniß bleibet, wie es ist,
Wir müssen scheiden, Kind! und halte nur
Mein Schiksaal mir nicht auf und zaudre nicht.

O sieh! es glänzt der Erde trunknes Bild,
Das göttliche, dir gegenwärtig, Jüngling,
Es rauscht und regt durch alle Lande sich
Und wechselt, jung und leicht, mit frommem Ernst
Der geschäfftge Reigentanz, womit den Geist
Die Sterblichen, den alten Vater, feiern.
Da gehe du und wandle taumellos
Und menschlich mit und denk am Abend mein.
Mir aber ziemt die stille Halle, mir
Die hochgelegene, geräumige,
Denn Ruhe brauch' ich wohl, zu träge sind,
Zum schnellgeschäftigen Spiel der Sterblichen,
Die Glieder mir und hab ich sonst dabei
Ein feiernd Lied in Jugendlust gesungen,
Zerschlagen ist das zarte Saitenspiel.
O Melodien über mir! es war ein Scherz!
Und kindisch wagt' ich sonst euch nachzuahmen,
Ein fühllos leichtes Echo tönt' in mir,
Und unverständlich nach –
Nun hör ich ernster euch, ihr Götterstimmen.

PAUSANIAS

Ich kenne nimmer dich, nur traurig ist
Mir, was du sagst, doch alles ist ein Räthsel.
Was hab ich auch, was hab ich dir gethan,
Daß du mich so, wie dirs gefällt, bekümmerst
Und nahmenlos dein Herz, des Einen noch,
Des Lezten los zu seyn, sich freut und müht.
Das hofft' ich nicht, da wir Geächtete
Den Wohnungen der Menschen scheu vorüber

No temporal tie remains what it has been;
Child, we must part; and, please, do not obstruct
My destiny, and do not hesitate.

But, look! Earth's drunken image gleams,
Holy, divine, and present to you, friend;
Through every land it roars, it teems and rushes,
And youthful, light, yet serious too and pious,
It changes, that perpetual round dance
Wherewith we mortals celebrate the Spirit,
The ancient Father. There now go, join in,
There move ungiddied, humanly, and think
Of me at evening. But as for me,
It is the quiet hall that's fitting, one
More spacious, higher up, remote, aloof,
For rest is what I need, too heavy now
My limbs have grown for the quick, busy dance
Of mortals, and if in it once I sang
A canticle of praise with youthful zest,
The delicate instrument, my lyre, is shattered.
O melodies above me! It was all a jest!
And childlike then I dared to imitate you,
A light unfeeling echo rang in me,
Incomprehensibly reverberated—
More gravely now I hear you, voices of the gods.

PAUSANIAS

I do not recognize you, only sad
To me is what you say, but all a riddle.
What have I done, what have I done to you
That now, as the mood takes you, you offend me
And namelessly your heart strives and rejoices
To rid itself of this one friend, the last.
I never dreamed of that when after exile,
Shyly avoiding human habitations,

Zusammen wandelten in wilder Nacht,
Und darum, lieber! war ich nicht dabei,
Wenn mit den Thränen dir des Himmels Reegen
Vom Angesichte trof, und sah es an,
Wenn lächelnd du das rauhe Sclavenkleid
Mittags an heißer Sonne troknetest
Auf schattenlosem Sand, wenn du die Spuren
Wohl manche Stunde wie ein wundes Wild
Mit deinem Blute zeichnetest, das auf
Den Felsenpfad von nakter Sohle rann.
Ach! darum lies ich nicht mein Haus und lud
Des Volkes und des Vaters Fluch mir auf,
Daß du mich, wo du wohnen willst und ruhn,
Wie ein verbraucht Gefäß, bei Seite werfest.
Und willst du weit hinweg? wohin? wohin?
Ich wandre mit, zwar steh ich nicht wie du
Mit Kräften der Natur in trautem Bunde,
Mir steht wie dir Zukünftiges nicht offen,
Doch freudig in der Götter Nacht hinaus
Schwingt seine Fittige mein Sinn, und fürchtet
Noch immer nicht die mächtigeren Blike.
Ja! wär ich auch ein Schwacher, dennoch wär
Ich, weil ich so dich liebe, stark, wie du.
Beim göttlichen Herakles! stiegst du auch,
Um die Gewaltigen, die drunten sind,
Versöhnend die Titanen heimzusuchen,
Ins bodenlose Thal, vom Gipfel dort,
Und wagtest dich ins Heiligtum des Abgrunds,
Wo duldend vor dem Tage sich das Herz
Der Erde birgt und ihre Schmerzen dir
Die dunkle Mutter sagt, o du der Nacht
Des Aethers Sohn! ich folgte dir hinunter.

EMPEDOKLES

So bleib!

Together through the desolate night we trudged,
And not for that I was beside you, dear one,
When mixed with tears the rain of heaven poured
Down from your face, nor yet for that looked on
When smiling in the noonday sun you dried
Your rough slave's tunic on the shadowless sand,
When like a wounded animal's, hour after hour
The trail you left was one of blood that trickled
From your bare heels on to the rocky path.
Oh, not for that I left my house and bore
The curse both of my father and my people,
That now, because you wish to rest and settle,
You'd cast me off like a discarded vessel.
And is it far you're going? Where? O where?
I'll stay with you, for though no secret pact,
Such as you formed, binds me to powers of Nature,
The future things you see are closed to me,
Yet bravely out into the night of gods
My mind directs its flight, and even now
Goes in no fear of those more mighty glances.
Indeed, if I were feeble in myself,
My love for you would make me strong as you are.
By Hercules, the divine! though you resolved
To visit and appease those violent ones
Who dwell below, the Titans, and climbed down
Into the bottomless valley from that summit there,
Daring to tread the sanctum of the abyss
Where, patient, Earth conceals her heart from day
And the dark Mother will confide to you
Her sufferings, her griefs, O son of Night,
Of Aether, even then I'd follow you down.

EMPEDOCLES

Then stay!

PAUSANIAS

Wie meinst du diß?

EMPEDOKLES

Du gabst
Dich mir, bist mein; so frage nicht!

PAUSANIAS

Es sei!

EMPEDOKLES

Und sagst du mirs noch einmal, Sohn, und giebst
Dein Blut und deine Seele mir für immer?

PAUSANIAS

Als hätt ich so ein loses Wort gesagt
Und zwischen Schlaf und Wachen dirs versprochen?
Unglaubiger! ich sags und wiederhohl' es:
Auch diß, auch diß, es ist von heute nicht,
Da ich geboren wurde, wars beschlossen.

EMPEDOKLES

Ich bin nicht, der ich bin, Pausanias,
Und meines Bleibens ist auf Jahre nicht,
Ein Schimmer nur, der bald vorüber muß,
Im Saitenspiel ein Ton –

PAUSANIAS

So tönen sie,
So schwinden sie zusammen in die Luft!
Und freundlich spricht der Wiederhall davon.
Versuche nun mich länger nicht und laß
Und gönne du die Ehre mir, die mein ist!
Hab ich nicht Laid genug, wie du, in mir?
Wie möchtest du mich noch belaidigen!

PAUSANIAS

How do you mean that?

EMPEDOCLES

You have given
Yourself to me, are mine; now ask no questions!

PAUSANIAS

So be it!

EMPEDOCLES

Will you say that once again,
And pledge your blood and soul to me for ever?

PAUSANIAS

As though I'd only blabbed an idle word
And made a promise between sleep and waking?
You doubting man! I say it and repeat it:
This too, this too was not determined now,
But at my birth already was decided.

EMPEDOCLES

I am not what I am. Pausanias,
And not for years may sojourn here, become
Only a gleam, a glint that soon must pass,
One note the lyre-strings hold—

PAUSANIAS

Then let them sound
Together let them vanish in the air!
And kindly will the echo of them speak.
No longer tempt me, try me now, but grant me
Such honour as deservedly is mine.
Am I not filled with grief enough, as you are?
How can you add the sting of your disdain!

343

O allesopfernd Herz! und dieser giebt
Schon mir zu lieb die goldne Jugend weg!
Und ich! o Erd und Himmel! siehe! noch,
Noch bist du nah, indeß die Stunde flieht,
Und blühest mir, du Freude meiner Augen.
Noch ists, wie sonst, ich halt im Arme,
Als wärst du mein, wie meine Beute dich,
Und mich bethört der holde Traum noch einmal.
Ja! herrlich wärs, wenn in die Grabesflamme
So Arm in Arm statt Eines Einsamen
Ein festlich Paar am Tagesende gieng',
Und gerne nähm' ich, was ich hier geliebt,
Wie seine Quellen all ein edler Strom,
Der heilgen Nacht zum Opfertrank, hinunter.
Doch besser ists, wir gehen unsern Pfad
Ein jeder, wie der Gott es ihm beschied.
Unschuldiger ist diß, und schadet nicht.
Und billig ists und recht, daß überall
Des Menschen Sinn sich eigen angehört.
Und dann – es trägt auch leichter seine Bürde
Und sicherer der Mann, wenn er allein ist.
So wachsen ja des Waldes Eichen auch
Und keines kennt, so alt sie sind, das andre.

PAUSANIAS

Wie du es willst! Ich widerstrebe nicht.
Du sagst es mir und wahr ists wohl und lieb
Ist billig mir diß lezte Wort von dir.
So geh ich denn! und störe deine Ruhe
Dir künftig nicht, auch meinest du es gut,
Daß meinem Sinne nicht die Stille tauge.

EMPEDOKLES

Doch, lieber, zürnst du nicht?

EMPEDOCLES

All-sacrificing heart! So this one gives
His golden youth away, all for my sake!
And I! O Earth and Heaven, look, even now,
Still you are near, though now the hour runs out,
And blossom for me, and delight my eyes.
Still, as before, I hold you in my arms
As though you were mine, as though you were my booty,
And the dear dream beclouds me once again.
Yes, glorious it would be if to the pyre
Instead of one, a lonely man, arm in arm
Like this a festive pair towards nightfall went,
And gladly I would take what here I loved,
As might a noble river all its sources,
Down for libation into holy Night.
Yet it is better that each go his own way
And walk the path that God ordained for him.
More innocent it is, and does no harm;
And it is meet and right that everywhere
Men's minds should be self-governed and self-owned.
Besides—more safely and more easily
A man will bear his burden when alone.
So too the oak-trees of the forest grow
And, ancient though it be, none knows the other.

PAUSANIAS

Have your own will! I'll not oppose my own.
You say so, and no doubt it's true, and precious
To me, and apt, this parting word from you.
I'll go, then, and in future shall not trouble
Your peace of mind; and for my own good surely
You hint that stillness ill becomes my kind.

EMPEDOCLES

But you're not angry, friend?

PAUSANIAS

       Mit dir? Mit dir?

EMPEDOKLES

Was ist es denn? ja! weist du nun, wohin?

PAUSANIAS

Gebiet es mir.

EMPEDOKLES

       Es war mein lezt Gebot,
Pausanias! die Herrschaft ist am Ende.

PAUSANIAS

Mein Vater! rathe mir!

EMPEDOKLES

       Wohl manches sollt
Ich sagen, doch verschweig ich dirs,
Es will zum sterblichen Gespräche fast
Und eitlem Wort die Zunge nimmer dienen.
Sieh! liebster! anders ists und leichter bald
Und freier athm' ich auf, und wie der Schnee
Des hohen Aetna dort am Sonnenlichte
Erwarmt und schimmert und zerrinnt, und los
Vom Berge woogt und Iris froher Bogen sich
Der blühende beim Fall der Woogen schwingt,
So rinnt und woogt vom Herzen mir es los,
So hallt es weg, was mir die Zeit gehäuft,
Die Schwere fällt, und fällt, und helle blüht
Das Leben das ätherische, darüber.
Nun wandre muthig, Sohn, ich geb und küsse
Verheißungen auf deine Stirne dir,
Es dämmert dort Italiens Gebirg,
Das Römerland, das thatenreiche, winkt,
Dort wirst du wohlgedeihn, dort, wo sich froh

PAUSANIAS

       With you? With you?

EMPEDOCLES

What is it, then? Oh, where to go? What now?

PAUSANIAS

Tell me, direct me!

EMPEDOCLES

           That was my last command,
Pausanias. My government is ended.

PAUSANIAS

My father, counsel me!

EMPEDOCLES

              No doubt there's much
That I should say, yet I withhold it from you,
For almost now for mortal conversation
And idle words my tongue will serve no more.
Look, dearest one, it's different now, and soon
More lightly and more freely I shall breathe,
And as that snow up there on Etna's peak
Grows warm in sunlight, gleams and melts away,
And loosened from the mountain billows down
And the glad bow of Iris, the bright-blossoming,
Flexed, rises up where those quick billows fall,
So from my heart it billows and pours down,
And dies away, what time heaped up for me,
The heaviness falls and falls, and brightly blooms
That other life, aetherial life, above me.
Now bravely travel, son; upon your brow
With heart and soul and lips I lay good wishes,
There in the distance glimmer Italy's hills,
The Roman land, the rich in deeds, is beckoning,
There you will prosper, there, where gladly bold

Die Männer in der Kämpferbahn begegnen,
O Heldenstädte dort! und du, Tarent!
Ihr brüderlichen Hallen, wo ich oft
Lichttrunken einst mit meinem Plato gieng
Und immerneu uns Jünglingen das Jahr
Und jeder Tag erschien in heilger Schule.
Besuch ihn auch, o Sohn, und grüß ihn mir,
Den alten Freund an seiner Heimath Strom,
Am blumigen Ilissus, wo er wohnt.
Und will die Seele dir nicht ruhn, so geh
Und frage sie, die Brüder in Aegyptos.
Dort hörest du das ernste Saitenspiel
Uraniens und seiner Töne Wandel.
Dort öffnen sie das Buch des Schiksaals dir.
Geh! fürchte nichts! es kehret alles wieder.
Und was geschehen soll, ist schon vollendet.

(Pausanias geht ab)

DRITTER AUFTRITT

MANES. EMPEDOKLES

MANES

Nun! säume nicht! bedenke dich nicht länger.
Vergeh! vergeh! damit es ruhig bald
Und helle werde, Trugbild!

EMPEDOKLES

    Was? woher?
Wer bist du, Mann!

MANES

   Der Armen Einer auch
Von diesem Stamm, ein Sterblicher, wie du.
Zu rechter Zeit gesandt, dir, der du dich

In the arena men compete with men,
Cities of heroes there! And you, Tarentum,
You brotherly mansions where so often once
Drunken with light I walked at Plato's side
And to us youths for ever new the year,
And every day seemed, in our holy school.
Visit him too, my son, and take my greetings
To my old friend by his own homeland's river,
By flowery Ilissus where he dwells.
And if your spirit will not rest, then go
And question them, my brothers in Egyptos.
There you will hear the lilt of serious lyres,
Urania's, and modulated music.
There they will open destiny's book for you.
Go, and fear nothing. Everything recurs.
And what's to come already is completed.

SCENE THREE

MANES. EMPEDOCLES

(Exit Pausanias)

MANES

Well, long enough you've pondered and delayed.
Now perish, perish! so that soon it will
Grow bright and quiet, phantom!

EMPEDOCLES

                              What? Where from?
Who are you, man!

MANES

                    One of the wretched, too,
And of this race, a mortal, as you are.
Sent at the right time, sent to you who think

Des Himmels Liebling dünkst, des Himmels Zorn,
Des Gottes, der nicht müßig ist, zu nennen.

EMPEDOKLES

Ha! kennst du den?

MANES

       Ich habe manches dir
Am fernen Nil gesagt.

EMPEDOKLES

       Und du? du hier?
Kein Wunder ists! Seit ich den Lebenden
Gestorben bin, erstehen mir die Todten.

MANES

Die Todten reden nicht, wo du sie fragst.
Doch wenn du eines Worts bedarfst, vernimm.

EMPEDOKLES

Die Stimme, die mich ruft, vernehm ich schon.

MANES

So redet es mit dir?

EMPEDOKLES

       Was soll die Rede, Fremder!

MANES

Ja! fremde bin ich hier und unter Kindern.
Das seid ihr Griechen all. Ich hab es oft
Vormals gesagt. Doch wolltest du mir nicht,
Wie dirs ergieng bei deinem Volke, sagen?

EMPEDOKLES

Was mahnst du mich? Was rufst du mir noch einmal?
Mir gieng es, wie es soll.

350

Yourself the favourite of Heaven, to name
The wrath of Heaven, that God's who never rests.

EMPEDOCLES

Ha, so you know him?

MANES

This and that I told you
Once by the distant Nile.

EMPEDOCLES

And you? You here?
No wonder. Now that to the living I
Have died, it is the dead who rise for me.

MANES

The dead refuse to speak, where you consult them.
Yet if you need a word from me, then hear.

EMPEDOCLES

The voice that calls to me I hear already.

MANES

And that is how it talks?

EMPEDOCLES

What does your talk mean, stranger?

MANES

Yes, I'm a stranger here, and among children.
For all you Greeks are that—as before now
I've often said. But was it not your will
To tell me how you fared among your people?

EMPEDOCLES

Why do you raise the past? And call to me again?
I fared as fare I must.

351

MANES

Ich wußt es auch
Schon längst voraus, ich hab es dir geweissagt.

EMPEDOKLES

Nun denn! was hältst du es noch auf? was drohst
Du mit der Flamme mir des Gottes, den
Ich kenne, dem ich gern zum Spiele dien',
Und richtest mir mein heilig Recht, du Blinder!

MANES

Was dir begegnen muß, ich ändr' es nicht.

EMPEDOKLES

So kamst du her, zu sehen, wie es wird?

MANES

O scherze nicht, und ehre doch dein Fest,
Umkränze dir dein Haupt, und schmük es aus,
Das Opferthier, das nicht vergebens fällt.
Der Tod, der jähe, er ist ja von Anbeginn,
Das weist du wohl, den Unverständigen
Die deinesgleichen sind, zuvorbeschieden.
Du willst es und so seis! Doch sollst du mir
Nicht unbesonnen, wie du bist, hinab,
Ich hab ein Wort, und diß bedenke, Trunkner!
Nur Einem ist es Recht, in dieser Zeit,
Nur Einen adelt deine schwarze Sünde.
Ein größrer ists, denn ich! denn wie die Rebe
Von Erd und Himmel zeugt, wenn sie getränkt
Von hoher Sonn aus dunklem Boden steigt,
So wächst er auf, aus Licht und Nacht geboren.
Es gährt um ihn die Welt, was irgend nur
Beweglich und verderbend ist im Busen
Der Sterblichen, ist aufgeregt von Grund aus.

352

MANES

And I foreknew it
All long ago, and prophesied it to you.

EMPEDOCLES

Well, then, why do you now detain it? Threaten
Me with the flame of that God whom I know,
Whom as a plaything willingly I serve,
And make to judge my sacred right, you blind man!

MANES

That which awaits you now I shall not alter.

EMPEDOCLES

So you came here to see how it turns out?

MANES

O do not jest, but honour your festive day,
Garland your head, and solemnly array it,
The votive beast that not in vain will fall.
Death, sudden death, as well you know, for those
Who do not comprehend, for such as you,
From the beginning has been preordained.
You wish it, and so be it! Yet not unthinking
As now you are, would I have you go down,
I have a word, and, drunken man, that consider:
One only has the privilege, at this time,
One only your black sin serves to ennoble.
Greater he is than I. For as the vine
To Earth and Heaven bears witness, when transfused
By the high sun it rises from dark soil,
So he grows up, born of both light and darkness.
Round him the world ferments, whatever is
Movable and pernicious in the hearts
Of mortals, from its depth and centre is stirred up.

353

Der Herr der Zeit, um seine Herrschaft bang,
Thront finster blikend über der Empörung.
Sein Tag erlischt, und seine Blize leuchten,
Doch was von oben flammt, entzündet nur,
Und was von unten strebt, die wilde Zwietracht.
Der Eine doch, der neue Retter faßt
Des Himmels Stralen ruhig auf, und liebend
Nimmt er, was sterblich ist, an seinen Busen,
Und milde wird in ihm der Streit der Welt.
Die Menschen und die Götter söhnt er aus
Und nahe wieder leben sie, wie vormals.
Und daß, wenn er erschienen ist, der Sohn
Nicht größer, denn die Eltern sei, und nicht
Der heilge Lebensgeist gefesselt bleibe
Vergessen über ihm, dem Einzigen,
So lenkt er aus, der Abgott seiner Zeit,
Zerbricht, er selbst, damit durch reine Hand
Dem Reinen das Nothwendige geschehe,
Sein eigen Glük, das ihm zu glüklich ist,
Und giebt, was er besaß, dem Element,
Das ihn verherrlichte, geläutert wieder.
Bist du der Mann? derselbe? bist du diß?

EMPEDOKLES

Ich kenne dich im finstern Wort, und du,
Du Alleswissender, erkennst mich auch.

MANES

O sage, wer du bist! und wer bin ich?

EMPEDOKLES

Versuchst du noch, noch immer mich, und kömst,
Mein böser Geist, zu mir in solcher Stunde?
Was lässest du mich nicht stille gehen, Mann?
Und wagst dich hier an mich und reizest mich,

The Lord of Time, afraid for his dominion,
Glowering on his throne surveys revolt.
His day extinguishes, his lightning shines,
Yet that which flames above, and that which presses
Up from below, further ignite contention.
The One, however, the new saviour calmly
Seizes the rays of Heaven, and lovingly
Takes to his bosom those of mortal mould,
And in him the world's conflict is allayed.
Between the gods and men he mediates,
The gods live near again, as in the past,
And so that, having once appeared, the Son
Shall not be greater than his parents, nor
The holy Spirit of life remain in bondage,
Forgotten because of him, the Only One,
He turns aside, the idol of his time.
And, that a pure hand for the Pure may do
What must be done, by his own choice he breaks
His own good fortune, grown too great for him,
And to the element that gave him glory
Gives back all his possessions, purified.
Are you that man? The same? That very man?

EMPEDOCLES

I know you in the darkening word, and you,
Omniscient one, me too have recognized.

MANES

O tell me who you are! And who am I?

EMPEDOCLES

Still do you tempt me, even now, and come,
My evil spirit, to me at this hour?
And will not let me go in peace now. Why?
And dare accost me here and bait and rouse me

Daß ich im Zorn die heilgen Pfade wandle?
Ein Knabe war ich, wußte nicht, was mir
Ums Auge fremd am Tage sich bewegt',
Und wunderbar umfiengen mir die großen
Gestalten dieser Welt, die freudigen,
Mein unerfahren schlummernd Herz im Busen.
Und staunend hört ich oft die Wasser gehn
Und sah die Sonne blühn, und sich an ihr
Den Jugendtag der stillen Erd entzünden.
Da ward in mir Gesang und helle ward
Mein dämmernd Herz im dichtenden Gebete,
Wenn ich die Fremdlinge, die gegenwärt'gen,
Die Götter der Natur mit Nahmen nannt'
Und mir der Geist im Wort, im Bilde sich,
Im seeligen, des Lebens Räthsel löste.
So wuchs ich still herauf, und anderes
War schon bereitet. Denn gewaltsamer,
Wie Wasser, schlug die wilde Menschenwelle
Mir an die Brust, und aus dem Irrsaal kam
Des armen Volkes Stimme mir zum Ohre.
Und wenn, indeß ich in der Halle schwieg,
Um Mitternacht der Aufruhr weheklagt,
Und durchs Gefilde stürzt, und lebensmüd
Mit eigner Hand sein eignes Haus zerbrach,
Und die verlaideten verlaßnen Tempel,
Wenn sich die Brüder flohn, und sich die Liebsten
Vorübereilten, und der Vater nicht
Den Sohn erkannt, und Menschenwort nicht mehr
Verständlich war, und menschliches Gesez,
Da faßte mich die Deutung schaudernd an:
Es war der scheidende Gott meines Volks!
Den hört ich, und zum schweigenden Gestirn
Sah ich hinauf, wo er herabgekommen.
Und ihn zu sühnen, gieng ich hin. Noch wurden uns

So that in anger I walk the holy paths?
I was a boy and did not know what things
They were that stirred about my eyes in daylight,
And marvellously the world's powers and shapes,
The great and joyous, wrapped themselves around
My slumbering, my inexperienced heart.
And wondering often I heard the waters flow
And saw the sun in flower, and by that flame
Kindled the youthful day of quiet Earth.
Then song arose in me, my darkling heart,
Illumined, warmed by poetry that was prayer,
When by their names I called those alien ones,
Those closely present ones, the gods of Nature,
And spirit in the word, life's mystery
In the found image blissfully was resolved.
So quietly I grew up, and other things
Already were prepared. More forcefully yet,
Like water, did the savage human wave
Beat on my breast, and the poor people's voice,
Humming in blind confusion, reach my ear.
And when, while silent in my room I sat,
At midnight tumult and revolt cry out,
And through the fields they rush, and weary of life
With their own hands break up their own good houses
And temples, long made odious, and forsaken,
When brothers fled each other, men hurried past
Those they loved most, and fathers no longer knew
Their sons, and human language had become
Incomprehensible, and human law,
The meaning of it, shivering me, struck home:
It was the departure of my people's god!
Him I could hear, and up to the silent planet
Whence he had come to us, I turned my gaze.
And to propitiate him I set out.

Der schönen Tage viel. Noch schien es sich
Am Ende zu verjüngen; und es wich,
Der goldnen Zeit, der allvertrauenden,
Des hellen kräftgen Morgens eingedenk,
Der Unmuth mir, der furchtbare vom Volk,
Und freie veste Bande knüpften wir,
Und riefen die lebendgen Götter an.
Doch oft, wenn mich des Volkes Dank bekränzte,
Wenn näher immer mir, und mir allein,
Des Volkes Seele kam, befiel es mich,
Denn wo ein Land ersterben soll, da wählt
Der Geist noch Einen sich zulezt, durch den
Sein Schwanensang, das lezte Leben tönet.
Wohl ahndet ichs, doch dient' ich willig ihm.
Es ist geschehn. Den Sterblichen gehör ich
Nun nimmer an. O Ende meiner Zeit!
O Geist, der uns erzog, der du geheim
Am hellen Tag und in der Wolke waltest,
Und du o Licht! und du, du Mutter Erde!
Hier bin ich, ruhig, denn es wartet mein
Die längstbereitete, die neue Stunde.
Nun nicht im Bilde mehr, und nicht, wie sonst,
Bei Sterblichen, im kurzen Glük, ich find'
Im Tode find ich den Lebendigen
Und heute noch begegn' ich ihm, denn heute
Bereitet er, der Herr der Zeit, zur Feier
Zum Zeichen ein Gewitter mir und sich.
Kennst du die Stille rings? kennst du das Schweigen
Des schlummerlosen Gotts? erwart' ihn hier!
Um Mitternacht wird er es uns vollenden.
Und wenn du, wie du sagst, des Donnerers
Vertrauter bist, und Eines Sinns mit ihm
Dein Geist mit ihm, der Pfade kundig, wandelt.
So komm mit mir, wenn izt, zu einsam sich,

Still many a happy day was granted us.
Still, in the end, renewal seemed at hand;
And, my mind fixed upon the golden age,
When trust was general, that bright, strong morning,
My gloom, the people's terrible gloom, dispersed
And we made pacts as firm as they were free,
And once again invoked the living gods.
Yet often, when the people's gratitude
Crowned me with wreaths, and ever closer to me,
To me alone, the people's soul drew, quickly
It dawned on me: that where a land must die
The Spirit at the last elects one more
Through whom the swansong, the last life, shall sound.
Well I divined it, yet I served him gladly.
Now it is done. And nevermore shall I
Belong to mortals. O my evening time!
O Spirit, you that reared us, secretly
Both in the cloud and in the bright noon govern,
And you, O light, and you, O Mother Earth,
See, I am here, and calm, for now awaits me
The hour long since matured, the turning-point.
No longer in the image now, nor yet
As formerly, with mortals, in brief joy,
No, but in death I find the Living One
And this day shall confront him, for this day
It is that he, the Lord of Time, in token,
In celebration of it, ushers in
A thunderstorm prepared for him and me.
Is it intelligible, known to you,
The stillness all around us here, the silence
Of the unslumbering god? Await him here!
At midnight he will consummate it for us.
If, as you say, you are the Thunderer's
Familiar, and unanimous with him,
Acquainted with the paths, your spirit journeys,
Then come with me when now, too much alone,

Das Herz der Erde klagt, und eingedenk
Der alten Einigkeit die dunkle Mutter
Zum Aether aus die Feuerarme breitet
Und izt der Herrscher kömt in seinem Stral,
Dann folgen wir, zum Zeichen, daß wir ihm
Verwandte sind, hinab in heil'ge Flammen.
Doch wenn du lieber ferne bleibst, für dich,
Was gönnst du mir es nicht? wenn dir es nicht
Beschieden ist zum Eigentum, was nimmst
Und störst du mirs! O euch, ihr Genien,
Die ihr, da ich begann, mir nahe waret,
Ihr Fernentwerfenden! euch dank ich, daß ihr mirs
Gegeben habt, die lange Zahl der Leiden
Zu enden hier, befreit von andrer Pflicht
In freiem Tod, nach göttlichem Geseze!
Dir ists verbotne Frucht! drum laß und geh,
Und kannst du mir nicht nach, so richte nicht!

MANES

Dir hat der Schmerz den Geist entzündet, Armer.

EMPEDOKLES

Was heilst du denn, Unmächtiger, ihn nicht?

MANES

Wie ists mit uns? siehst du es so gewiß?

EMPEDOKLES

Das sage du mir, der du alles siehst!

MANES

Laß still uns seyn, o Sohn! und immer lernen.

EMPEDOKLES

Du lehrtest mich, heut lerne du von mir.

MANES

Hast du nicht alles mir gesagt?

The heart of Earth laments, and mindful of
The ancient unity, now the dark Mother
Up towards Aether extends her fiery arms,
And now the Ruler comes within his beam,
And thereupon, to prove ourselves his kin,
We follow him down amid the holy flames.
But if you'd rather stand aside, aloof,
Why grudge it, then, to me? If as your own
To you it was not granted, why deprive
And trouble me? You rather, heavenly spirits,
Who when I started out were near to me,
You far-designing ones, to you I owe it
That here I may cut off and put an end
To the long chain of suffering, liberated
From other duties, in self-chosen death
And in accordance with god-given laws!
Forbidden fruit for you, man! Therefore leave me,
And if you cannot follow me, do not judge!

MANES

Pain has inflamed your mind. I pity you.

EMPEDOCLES

Sage that you are, then why do *you* not heal it?

MANES

How is it with us? Do you see so clearly?

EMPEDOCLES

You ask me that? You that can see all things?

MANES

Let us be silent, son, and always learn.

EMPEDOCLES

You taught me once; now this day learn from me.

MANES

Have you not told me everything?

361

EMPEDOKLES

O nein!

MANES

So gehst du nun?

EMPEDOKLES

Noch geh ich nicht, o Alter!
Von dieser grünen guten Erde soll
Mein Auge mir nicht ohne Freude gehen.
Und denken möcht' ich noch vergangner Zeit,
Der Freunde meiner Jugend noch, der Theuern,
Die fern in Hellas frohen Städten sind,
Des Bruders auch, der mir geflucht, so mußt'
Es werden; laß mich izt, wenn dort der Tag
Hinunter ist, so siehest du mich wieder.

EMPEDOCLES

Far from it!

MANES

And now you're going?

EMPEDOCLES

No, not yet, old seer!
No, from this good green earth my eye shall not
Depart without a tribute of late gladness.
And still I wish to dwell upon things past,
Recall once more the dear friends of my youth
Remote now in the happy towns of Hellas,
My brother too, who cursed me—so it had
To be. Now leave me. When over there the light
Of day goes down, you'll see me once again.

SCHLUSSCHOR

DES ERSTEN AKTES

(Entwurf)

Neue Welt

                und es hängt, ein ehern Gewölbe
der Himmel über uns, es lähmt Fluch
die Glieder den Menschen, und die stärkenden, die erfreuenden
Gaaben der Erde sind, wie Spreu, es
spottet unser, mit ihren Geschenken, die Mutter
und alles ist Schein –
O wann, wann
        schon öffnet sie sich
        die Fluth über die Dürre.

Aber wo ist er?

    Daß er beschwöre den lebendigen Geist

DRAFT FOR THE CONCLUDING CHORUS OF ACT ONE

New world

       and a brazen vault
Heaven hangs over us, a curse
freezes the limbs of mortals, and the strengthening,
joy-giving presents of Earth are like chaff, the
Mother mocks us with her gifts
and all is mere semblance—
O when, when
      will it break at last,
      the flood, over the parched land.

But where is he?

    That he might adjure the living spirit

† Chorus   Future

SECOND ACT

Scene I.

Pausanias, Panthea.

Scene II.

Strato, Attendants.

Scene III.

Strato alone.

Chorus ?

THIRD ACT

Empedocles, Pausanias, Panthea, Strato.

Manes.

Attendants of Strato.

Agrigentines.

Chorus ?

FOURTH ACT

Scene I.

Lyric or

epic?   Empedocles, Pausanias, Panthea.

Scene II.

Elegiac heroic

Heroic eleg.   Empedocles.

Scene III.

Lyric heroic   Manes, Empedocles.

Scene IV.

Heroic lyric   Empedocles.

FIFTH ACT

Manes, Pausanias, Panthea, Strato.

† Agrigentines, Attendants of Strato.

† Manes, the all-experienced, the seer, astonished by Empedocles' speeches, and by his mind, says that he is the one who was called, who kills and gives life, in whom and through whom a world was being at once destroyed and renewed. And that man who felt his country's decline with such deadly force could have a presentiment of such a new life. The following day, the day of the Saturnalia, he will proclaim to them what was the last will of Empedocles.

THE HYMNS

(1799-1803)

LEBENSALTER

Ihr Städte des Euphrats!
Ihr Gassen von Palmyra!
Ihr Säulenwälder in der Eb'ne der Wüste,
Was seid ihr?
Euch hat die Kronen,
Dieweil ihr über die Gränze
Der Othmenden seid gegangen,
Von Himmlischen der Rauchdampf und
Hinweg das Feuer genommen;
Jezt aber siz' ich unter Wolken (deren
Ein jedes eine Ruh' hat eigen) unter
Wohleingerichteten Eichen, auf
Der Heide des Rehs, und fremd
Erscheinen und gestorben mir
Der Seeligen Geister.

THE AGES OF LIFE

You cities of Euphrates,
You streets at Palmyra,
You forests of pillars in the desert plain,
What are you?
Your crests, as you passed beyond
The bounds of those who breathe,
By smoke of heavenly powers and
By fire were taken away;
But now I sit beneath clouds (each one
With a quietness all of its own) beneath
A pleasing order of oak-trees, on
The heath where the roe-deer feed, and strange
To me, remote and dead seem
The souls of the blessèd.

HÄLFTE DES LEBENS

Mit gelben Birnen hänget
Und voll mit wilden Rosen
Das Land in den See,
Ihr holden Schwäne,
Und trunken von Küssen
Tunkt ihr das Haupt
Ins heilignüchterne Wasser.

Weh mir, wo nehm' ich, wenn
Es Winter ist, die Blumen, und wo
Den Sonnenschein,
Und Schatten der Erde?
Die Mauern stehn
Sprachlos und kalt, im Winde
Klirren die Fahnen.

THE MIDDLE OF LIFE

With yellow pears the land
And full of wild roses
Hangs down into the lake,
You lovely swans,
And drunk with kisses
You dip your heads
Into the hallowed, the sober water.

But oh, where shall I find
When winter comes, the flowers, and where
The sunshine
And shade of the earth?
The walls loom
Speechless and cold, in the wind
Weathercocks clatter.

WIE WENN AM FEIERTAGE...

Wie wenn am Feiertage, das Feld zu sehn
Ein Landmann geht, des Morgens, wenn
Aus heißer Nacht die kühlenden Blize fielen
Die ganze Zeit und fern noch tönet der Donner,
In sein Gestade wieder tritt der Strom,
Und frisch der Boden grünt
Und von des Himmels erfreuendem Reegen
Der Weinstok trauft und glänzend
In stiller Sonne stehn die Bäume des Haines:

So stehn sie unter günstiger Witterung
Sie die kein Meister allein, die wunderbar
Allgegenwärtig erzieht in leichtem Umfangen
Die mächtige, die göttlichschöne Natur.
Drum wenn zu schlafen sie scheint zu Zeiten des Jahrs
Am Himmel oder unter den Pflanzen oder den Völkern
So trauert der Dichter Angesicht auch,
Sie scheinen allein zu seyn, doch ahnen sie immer.
Denn ahnend ruhet sie selbst auch.

Jezt aber tagts! Ich harrt und sah es kommen,
Und was ich sah, das Heilige sei mein Wort.
Denn sie, sie selbst, die älter denn die Zeiten
Und über die Götter des Abends und Orients ist,
Die Natur ist jezt mit Waffenklang erwacht,
Und hoch vom Aether bis zum Abgrund nieder
Nach vestem Geseze, wie einst, aus heiligem Chaos gezeugt,
Fühlt neu die Begeisterung sich,
Die Allerschaffende wieder.

AS ON A HOLIDAY...

As on a holiday, to see the field
A countryman goes out, at morning, when
Out of hot night the cooling flashes had fallen
For hours on end, and thunder still rumbles afar,
The river enters its banks once more,
New verdure sprouts from the soil,
And with the gladdening rain of heaven
The grapevine drips, and gleaming
In tranquil sunlight stand the trees of the grove:

So now in favourable weather they stand
Whom no mere master teaches, but in
A light embrace, miraculously omnipresent,
God-like in power and beauty, Nature brings up.
So when she seems to be sleeping at times of the year
Up in the sky or among plants or the peoples,
The poets' faces likewise are sad,
They seem to be alone, but are always divining,
For divining too she herself is at rest.

But now day breaks! I waited and saw it come,
And what I saw, the hallowed, my word shall convey,
For she, she herself, who is older than the ages
And higher than the gods of Orient and Occident,
Nature has now awoken amid the clang of arms,
And from high Aether down to the low abyss,
According to fixed law, begotten, as in the past, on holy Chaos,
Delight, the all-creative,
Delights in self-renewal.

373

Und wie im Aug' ein Feuer dem Manne glänzt,
Wenn hohes er entwarf; so ist
Von neuem an den Zeichen, den Thaten der Welt jezt
Ein Feuer angezündet in Seelen der Dichter.
Und was zuvor geschah, doch kaum gefühlt,
Ist offenbar erst jezt,
Und die uns lächelnd den Aker gebauet,
In Knechtsgestalt, sie sind erkannt,
Die Allebendigen, die Kräfte der Götter.

Erfrägst du sie? im Liede wehet ihr Geist
Wenn es der Sonne des Tags und warmer Erd
Entwächst, und Wettern, die in der Luft, und andern
Die vorbereiteter in Tiefen der Zeit,
Und deutungsvoller, und vernehmlicher uns
Hinwandeln zwischen Himmel und Erd und unter den Völkern.
Des gemeinsamen Geistes Gedanken sind,
Still endend in der Seele des Dichters,

Daß schnellbetroffen sie, Unendlichem
Bekannt seit langer Zeit, von Erinnerung
Erbebt, und ihr, von heilgem Stral entzündet,
Die Frucht in Liebe geboren, der Götter und Menschen Werk
Der Gesang, damit er beiden zeuge, glükt.
So fiel, wie Dichter sagen, da sie sichtbar
Den Gott zu sehen begehrte, sein Bliz auf Semeles Haus
Und die göttlichgetroffne gebahr,
Die Frucht des Gewitters, den heiligen Bacchus.

Und daher trinken himmlisches Feuer jezt
Die Erdensöhne ohne Gefahr.
Doch uns gebührt es, unter Gottes Gewittern,
Ihr Dichter! mit entblößtem Haupte zu stehen
Des Vaters Stral, ihn selbst, mit eigner Hand

And as a fire gleams in the eye of that man
Who has conceived a lofty design,
Once more by the tokens, the deeds of the world now
A fire has been lit in the souls of the poets.
And that which happened before, but hardly was felt,
Only now is manifest,
And they who smiling worked our fields for us,
Assuming the shape of labourers, now are known,
The all-alive, all-animating powers of the gods.

Do you ask where they are? In song their spirit wafts
When from the sun of day and from warm soil
It grows, and storms that are in the air, and others
That, more prepared in the depths of time,
More full of meaning and more audible to us,
Drift on between Heaven and Earth and amid the peoples.
The thoughts of the communal spirit they are,
And quietly come to rest in the poet's soul,

So that quickly struck and long familiar
To infinite powers, it shakes
With recollection and kindled by
The holy ray, that fruit conceived in love, the work of gods and men,
To bear witness to both, the song succeeds.
So once, the poets tell, when she desired to see
The god in person, visible, did his lightning fall
On Semele's house, and the divinely struck gave birth to
The thunderstorm's fruit, to holy Bacchus.

And hence it is that without danger now
The sons of Earth drink heavenly fire.
Yet, fellow poets, us it behoves to stand
Bare-headed beneath God's thunderstorms,
To grasp the Father's ray, no less, with our own two hands

Zu fassen und dem Volk ins Lied
Gehüllt die himmlische Gaabe zu reichen.
Denn sind nur reinen Herzens,
Wie Kinder, wir, sind schuldlos unsere Hände,

Des Vaters Stral, der reine versengt es nicht
Und tieferschüttert, die Leiden des Stärkeren
Mitleidend, bleibt in den hochherstürzenden Stürmen
Des Gottes, wenn er nahet, das Herz doch fest.
Doch weh mir! wenn von

Weh mir!

Und sag ich gleich,

Ich sei genaht, die Himmlischen zu schauen,
Sie selbst, sie werfen mich tief unter die Lebenden
Den falschen Priester, ins Dunkel, daß ich
Das warnende Lied den Gelehrigen singe.
Dort

And, wrapping in song the heavenly gift,
To offer it to the people.
For if only we are pure in heart,
Like children, and our hands are guiltless,

   The Father's ray, the pure, will not sear our hearts
And, deeply convulsed, and sharing his sufferings
Who is stronger than we are, yet in the far-flung down-rushing storms of
The God, when he draws near, will the heart stand fast.
But, oh, my shame! when of

My shame!

   And let me say at once

That I approached to see the Heavenly,
And they themselves cast me down, deep down
Below the living, into the dark cast down
The false priest that I am, to sing,
For those who have ears to hear, the warning song.
There

DER MUTTER ERDE

GESANG DER BRÜDER

OTTMAR HOM TELLO

OTTMAR

Statt offner Gemeine sing' ich Gesang.
So spielt von erfreulichen Händen
Wie zum Versuche berühret, eine Saite
Von Anfang. Aber freudig ernster neigt
Bald über die Harfe
Der Meister das Haupt und die Töne
Bereiten sich ihm, und werden geflügelt
So viele sie sind und zusammen tönt es unter dem Schlage
Des Wekenden und voll, wie aus Meeren schwingt
Unendlich sich in die Lüfte die Wolke des Wohllauts.

Doch wird ein anderes noch
Wie der Harfe Klang
Der Gesang seyn
Der Chor des Volks.
Denn wenn er schon der Zeichen genug
Und Fluthen in seiner Macht und Wetterflammen
Wie Gedanken hat der heilige Vater,
    unaussprechlich wär er wohl
Und nirgend fänd er wahr sich unter den Lebenden wieder
Wenn zum Gesange nicht hätt ein Herz die Gemeinde.

Noch aber

Doch wie der Fels erst ward,

FOR MOTHER EARTH

SONG OF THE BROTHERS

OTTMAR HOM TELLO

OTTMAR

Instead of open community, song I sing.
So, touched by pleasing hands
As though to try it out only, a string
Plays from the start. But more happily serious
Soon the master bows
His head over the harp, and the tones
Respond to him, and grow winged
However many of them, and they sound in unison, plucked
By him who awakened them, full, as though out of oceans
Infinite up into winds the cloud of euphony soars.

Yet other even than
The sound of the harp
Will the song be,
The people's choir.
For though he has tokens enough
And floods in his power and thunder-flames
Like thoughts, the holy Father,
       yet, it seems, he would be unutterable
And nowhere he would find himself truly again among the living
If the community had no heart for singing.

But as yet

But as the rock was first shaped

Und geschmiedet wurden in schattiger Werkstatt,
  die ehernen Vesten der Erde,
Noch ehe Bäche rauschten von den Bergen
Und Hain' und Städte blüheten an den Strömen,
So hat er donnernd schon
Geschaffen ein reines Gesez,
Und reine Laute gegründet.

HOM

 Indessen schon', o Mächtiger deß
Der einsam singt, und gieb uns Lieder genug,
Bis ausgesprochen ist, wie wir
Es meinen unserer Seele Geheimniß.
Denn öfters hört' ich
Des alten Priesters Gesänge

    und so
Zu danken bereite die Seele mir auch.

 Doch wandeln im Waffensaale
Mit gebundener Hand in müßigen Zeiten
Die Männer und schauen die Rüstungen an,
Voll Ernstes stehen sie und einer erzählt,
Wie die Väter sonst den Bogen gespannet
Fernhin des Zieles gewiß,
Und alle glauben es ihm
Doch keiner darf es versuchen
Wie ein Gott sinken die Arme
Der Menschen,
Auch ziemt ein Feiergewand an jedem Tage sich nicht.

 Die Tempelsäulen stehn
Verlassen in Tagen der Noth,

And in the shadowy workshop were forged
      the brazen fortresses of Earth,
Even before any stream roared down from the mountains
Or groves and cities flowered by the rivers,
So already thundering He
Has created a law that is pure
And established pure sounds.

HOM

Meanwhile, O mighty one, spare
Him who lonely sings, and give us tunes enough
Until uttered as we intend it
Is the mystery of our souls.
For at times I have heard
The hymns of the ancient priest

      and now
Likewise to offer thanks prepare my soul also.

  Yet with tied hands in the armoury
Men wander about in idle ages,
Gazing up at the coats of mail,
Full of gravity stand, and one of them tells
How the forefathers once had flexed the bow,
Sure of their aim from afar,
And all believe what he says
Yet none may try it
Like a god   the arms of men
Hang loose,
Nor is a festive garment fitting for every day.

  The temple columns stand
Forsaken in days of need,

Wohl tönet des Nordsturms Echo
            tief in den Hallen,
Und der Reegen machet sie rein,
Und Moos wächst und es kehren die Schwalben,
In Tagen des Frühlings, nahmlos aber ist
In ihnen der Gott, und die Schaale des Danks
Und Opfergefäß und alle Heiligtümer
Begraben dem Feind in verschwiegener Erde.

TELLO

Wer will auch danken, eh' er empfängt,
Und Antwort geben, eh' er gehört hat?
Ni   indeß ein Höherer spricht,
Zu fallen in die tönende Rede.
Viel hat er zu sagen und anders Recht,
Und Einer ist, der endet in Stunden nicht,
Und die Zeiten des Schaffenden sind,
Wie Gebirg,
Das hochaufwoogend von Meer zu Meer
Hinziehet über die Erde,

Es sagen der Wanderer viele davon,
Und das Wild irrt in den Klüften,
Und die Horde schweifet über die Höhen,
In heiligem Schatten aber,
Am grünen Abhang wohnet
Der Hirt und schauet die Gipfel.
So

And though the northern gale's echo
Resounds   deep in the halls
And rain washes them clean
And moss grows, and the swallows return
In the spring season, yet nameless in them
Is the God, and the cup of thanks
And the vessel of sacrifice and all the holy things
Buried against the foe in a place kept secret.

TELLO

And who would give thanks before he receives,
And give an answer before he has heard?
Not   while a higher one speaks
To interrupt the resounding speech.
He has much to say and a different law,
And One there is who does not end within hours
And the ages of him who creates
Are like a mountain range
Which billowing high from sea to sea
Stretches over the Earth,

Many travellers tell of it,
And the wild animals roam in ravines,
And the horde sweeps on over the high passes,
But in holy shade
On the green slope dwells
The shepherd and looks up at the peaks.
So

AM QUELL DER DONAU

Denn, wie wenn hoch von der herrlichgestimmten, der Orgel
Im heiligen Saal,
Reinquillend aus den unerschöpflichen Röhren,
Das Vorspiel, wekend, des Morgens beginnt
Und weitumher, von Halle zu Halle,
Der erfrischende nun, der melodische Strom rinnt,
Bis in den kalten Schatten das Haus
Von Begeisterungen erfüllt,
Nun aber erwacht ist, nun, aufsteigend ihr,
Der Sonne des Fests, antwortet
Der Chor der Gemeinde; so kam
Das Wort aus Osten zu uns,
Und an Parnassos Felsen und am Kithäron hör' ich
O Asia, das Echo von dir und es bricht sich
Am Kapitol und jählings herab von den Alpen

Kommt eine Fremdlingin sie
Zu uns, die Erwekerin,
Die menschenbildende Stimme.

AT THE SOURCE OF THE DANUBE

For as when high from the gloriously voiced, the organ
Within a holy hall
Untainted welling from inexhaustible pipes,
The prelude, awakening men, rings out in the morning
And far and wide, from mansion to mansion,
Now pours the refreshing, the melodious current,
Down to the chilly shadows even filling
The house with inspirations,
But now awake and rising to it, to
The sun of celebration, responds the
Community's choir—so the word
Came down to us from the East,
And by the rocks of Parnassus and by Cithaeron,
O Asia, I hear the echo of you, and it breaks
Upon the Capitol and sudden down from the Alps

A stranger it comes
To us, that quickening word,
The voice that moulds and makes human.

385

Da faßt' ein Staunen die Seele
Der Getroffenen all und Nacht
War über den Augen der Besten.
Denn vieles vermag
Und die Fluth und den Fels und Feuersgewalt auch
Bezwinget mit Kunst der Mensch
Und achtet, der Hochgesinnte, das Schwerdt
Nicht, aber es steht
Vor Göttlichem der Starke niedergeschlagen,

  Und gleichet dem Wild fast; das,
Von süßer Jugend getrieben,
Schweift rastlos über die Berg'
Und fühlet die eigene Kraft
In der Mittagshizze. Wenn aber
Herabgeführt, in spielenden Lüften,
Das heilige Licht, und mit dem kühleren Stral
Der freudige Geist kommt zu
Der seeligen Erde, dann erliegt es, ungewohnt
Des Schönsten und schlummert wachenden Schlaf,
Noch ehe Gestirn naht. So auch wir. Denn manchen erlosch
Das Augenlicht schon vor den göttlichgesendeten Gaben,

  Den freundlichen, die aus Ionien uns,
Auch aus Arabia kamen, und froh ward
Der theuern Lehr' und auch der holden Gesänge
Die Seele jener Entschlafenen nie,
Doch einige wachten. Und sie wandelten oft
Zufrieden unter euch, ihr Bürger schöner Städte,
Beim Kampfspiel, wo sonst unsichtbar der Heros
Geheim bei Dichtern saß, die Ringer schaut und lächelnd
Pries, der gepriesene, die müßigernsten Kinder.
Ein unaufhörlich Lieben wars und ists.
Und wohlgeschieden, aber darum denken

Amazement then took hold of
The souls of all who were struck, and night
Obscured the eyes of the best men.
For much can our kind
Accomplish, and flood and rock and even the might of fire
With art can subdue,
Nor, noble in mind, recoils from
The sword-blade, but faced with powers divine
The strong will stand abashed

   And almost are like the beast of the wilds; which
Impelled by sweet youth
Roams restless over the hills
And feels its own strength in
The noonday heat. But when,
Led down, in frolicking breezes,
The holy light, and with its cool beam
The joyful spirit descend
To blessèd Earth, it succumbs, unfamiliar
With utmost beauty, and drowses in waking sleep,
Though stars are not rising yet. So it is with us. For many's
The man whose vision went out in face of those god-sent gifts,

   The kindly, that from Ionia came
To us, from Arabia too, and never
The souls of these now gone to their rest were glad
Of precious doctrine nor yet of the lovely songs,
Yet some kept awake. And often, you citizens
Of beautiful towns, they walked among you contented,
At Games, where once in secret the hero
Invisible sat with poets, watched the wrestlers and smiling
Praised—he, the recipient of praise—those idly serious children.
An endless loving it was, and is.
And rightly severed; yet nonetheless we think

Wir aneinander doch, ihr Fröhlichen am Isthmos,
Und am Cephyß und am Taygetos,
Auch eurer denken wir, ihr Thale des Kaukasos,
So alt ihr seid, ihr Paradiese dort
Und deiner Patriarchen und deiner Propheten,

O Asia, deiner Starken, o Mutter!
Die furchtlos vor den Zeichen der Welt,
Und den Himmel auf Schultern und alles Schiksaal,
Taglang auf Bergen gewurzelt,
Zuerst es verstanden,
Allein zu reden
Zu Gott. Die ruhn nun. Aber wenn ihr
Und diß ist zu sagen,
Ihr Alten all, nicht sagtet, woher?
Wir nennen dich, heiliggenöthiget, nennen,
Natur! dich wir, und neu, wie dem Bad entsteigt
Dir alles Göttlichgeborne.

Zwar gehn wir fast, wie die Waisen;
Wohl ists, wie sonst, nur jene Pflege nicht wieder;
Doch Jünglinge, der Kindheit gedenk,
Im Haußе sind auch diese nicht fremde.
Sie leben dreifach, eben wie auch
Die ersten Söhne des Himmels.
Und nicht umsonst ward uns
In die Seele die Treue gegeben.
Nicht uns; auch Eures bewahrt sie,
Und bei den Heiligtümern, den Waffen des Worts
Die scheidend ihr den Ungeschikteren uns
Ihr Schiksaalssöhne, zurükgelassen

Ihr guten Geister, da seid ihr auch,
Oftmals, wenn einen dann die heilige Wolk umschwebt,

Of one another still, you happy ones at the Isthmus,
And by Cephissus and by Taygetus,
And you we think of, vales of the Caucasus,
However ancient, you paradises there,
And of your patriarchs and of your prophets,

O Asia, of all your mighty ones, Mother,
Who fearless in face of the signs of the world,
The heavens heaped upon shoulders and all manner of fate,
For days were rooted on mountains
And were the first who knew
How to speak alone
To God. These now are at rest. But if,
And this must be said, you ancients
Would never tell us whence it is that
We name you, under a holy compulsion we
Now name you Nature, and new, as from a bath
From you emerges all that's divinely born.

True, like orphans almost we walk;
Though much is what it was, that tutelage now is lacking;
But youths who are mindful of childhood,
These are not strangers now in the house.
Threefold they live, as did
The very first-born of Heaven.
And not for nothing in
Our souls was loyalty fixed.
Not us alone, but that which is yours it preserves
And in those holy relics, the weapons of the word
Which, parting, you sons of Fate,
You left behind for us the less fated,
The less endowed with rightness,

You kindly spirits, in them you are present too,
And often, when the holy cloud is hovering round a man,

Da staunen wir und wissens nicht zu deuten.
Ihr aber würzt mit Nectar uns den Othem
Und dann frohloken wir oft oder es befällt uns
Ein Sinnen, wenn ihr aber einen zu sehr liebt
Er ruht nicht, bis er euer einer geworden.
Darum, ihr Gütigen! umgebet mich leicht,
Damit ich bleiben möge, denn noch ist manches zu singen,
Jezt aber endiget, seeligweinend,
Wie eine Sage der Liebe,
Mir der Gesang, und so auch ist er
Mir, mit Erröthen, Erblassen,
Von Anfang her gegangen. Doch Alles geht so.

We are amazed and do not know the meaning.
But you with nectar spice our breath, and then
We may exult or else a pondering befalls us,
But when too greatly you love a man
He finds no rest till he is one of you.
Therefore, benign ones, surround me lightly,
And let me stay a while, for much remains to be sung;
But now, like a legend of love,
Blissfully weeping, my song
Comes to its end, and so too,
Amid blushing and blanching, it's gone
With me from the start. But that is now all things go.

DIE WANDERUNG

Glükseelig Suevien, meine Mutter,
Auch du, der glänzenderen, der Schwester
Lombarda drüben gleich,
Von hundert Bächen durchflossen!
Und Bäume genug, weißblühend und röthlich,
Und dunklere, wild, tiefgrünenden Laubs voll
Und Alpengebirg der Schweiz auch überschattet
Benachbartes dich; denn nah dem Heerde des Haußes
Wohnst du, und hörst, wie drinnen
Aus silbernen Opferschaalen
Der Quell rauscht, ausgeschüttet
Von reinen Händen, wenn berührt

Von warmen Stralen
Krystallenes Eis und umgestürzt
Vom leichtanregenden Lichte
Der schneeige Gipfel übergießt die Erde
Mit reinestem Wasser. Darum ist
Dir angeboren die Treue. Schwer verläßt,
Was nahe dem Ursprung wohnet, den Ort.
Und deine Kinder, die Städte,
Am weithindämmernden See,
An Nekars Weiden, am Rheine,
Sie alle meinen, es wäre
Sonst nirgend besser zu wohnen.

Ich aber will dem Kaukasos zu!
Denn sagen hört' ich
Noch heut in den Lüften:

THE JOURNEY

Most happy Swabia, my mother,
Whom like the more shining, your sister
Lombarda over there
A hundred rivulets thread!
And trees enough, white-flowering and reddish
And darker ones, wild, full of deeply greening foliage,
And alpine ranges of Switzerland cast their shade
On you, the neighbouring, too; for close to the hearth of
The house you dwell, and hear how within
From silver votive vessels
The wellspring purls, poured out
By hands that are pure, when touched

By warming beams
The crystalline ice and, tumbled
By gently quickening light
The snowy summit drenches the earth
With purest water. Therefore
Innate in you is loyalty. For whatever dwells
Close to its origin is loathe to leave the place.
And so your children, the towns by
The distantly glimmering lake,
By Neckar's willows and by the Rhine,
All these affirm that
No dwelling-place could be better.

But I am bound for the Caucasus!
For only today
I heard it said in the breezes

Frei sei'n, wie Schwalben, die Dichter.
Auch hat mir ohnediß
In jüngeren Tagen Eines vertraut,
Es seien vor alter Zeit
Die Eltern einst, das deutsche Geschlecht,
Still fortgezogen von Wellen der Donau
Am Sommertage, da diese
Sich Schatten suchten, zusammen
Mit Kindern der Sonn'
Am schwarzen Meere gekommen;
Und nicht umsonst sei diß
Das gastfreundliche genennet.

    Denn, als sie erst sich angesehen,
Da nahten die Anderen erst; dann sazten auch
Die Unseren sich neugierig unter den Ölbaum.
Doch als sich ihre Gewande berührt,
Und keiner vernehmen konnte
Die eigene Rede des andern, wäre wohl
Entstanden ein Zwist, wenn nicht aus Zweigen herunter
Gekommen wäre die Kühlung,
Die Lächeln über das Angesicht
Der Streitenden öfters breitet, und eine Weile
Sahn still sie auf, dann reichten sie sich
Die Hände liebend einander. Und bald

    Vertauschten sie Waffen und all
Die lieben Güter des Haußes,
Vertauschten das Wort auch und es wünschten
Die freundlichen Väter umsonst nichts
Beim Hochzeitjubel den Kindern.
Denn aus den heiligvermählten
Wuchs schöner, denn Alles,
Was vor und nàch

That free as swallows the poets are.
Besides, when I was younger
Someone confided to me
That time out of mind our parents,
The German people, had quietly
Departed from the waves of the Danube
One summer day, and when those
Were looking for shade, had met
With children of the Sun
Not far from the Black Sea's beaches;
And not for nothing that sea
Was called the hospitable.

   For when they first exchanged glances
It was the others who first approached; only then did
Our people too, inquisitive, seat themselves under the olive tree.
But when their garments had touched
And none could comprehend
The other's peculiar speech, a quarrel
Might well have begun, if coolness had not fallen
Upon them from the boughs,
Eliciting a smile, as it often does,
From faces that frowned with anger; and for a while
They raised their eyes in silence, then
They lovingly held out their hands. And soon

   They bartered weapons and all
The precious goods of the house,
And bartered the word, and not in vain
Did kindly fathers bless there with any wish
Their children's jubilant nuptials.
For from the sacredly married
There sprang a people more beautiful
Than all who before or since

Von Menschen sich nannt', ein Geschlecht auf. Wo,
Wo aber wohnt ihr, liebe Verwandten,
Daß wir das Bündniß wiederbegehn
Und der theuern Ahnen gedenken?

   Dort an den Ufern, unter den Bäumen
Ionias, in Ebenen des Kaisters,
Wo Kraniche, des Aethers froh,
Umschlossen sind von fernhindämmernden Bergen;
Dort wart auch ihr, ihr Schönsten! oder pflegtet
Der Inseln, die mit Wein bekränzt,
Voll tönten von Gesang; noch andere wohnten
Am Tayget, am vielgepriesnen Himettos,
Die blühten zulezt; doch von
Parnassos Quell bis zu des Tmolos
Goldglänzenden Bächen erklang
Ein ewiges Lied; so rauschten
Damals die Wälder und all
Die Saitenspiele zusamt
Von himmlischer Milde gerühret.

   O Land des Homer!
Am purpurnen Kirschbaum oder wenn
Von dir gesandt im Weinberg mir
Die jungen Pfirsiche grünen,
Und die Schwalbe fernher kommt und vieles erzählend
An meinen Wänden ihr Haus baut, in
Den Tagen des Mais, auch unter den Sternen
Gédenk' ich, o Ionia, dein! doch Menschen
Ist Gegenwärtiges lieb. Drum bin ich
Gekommen, euch, ihr Inseln, zu sehn, und euch,
Ihr Mündungen der Ströme, o ihr Hallen der Thetis,
Ihr Wälder, euch, und euch, ihr Wolken des Ida!

Have called themselves human. But where,
O where do you dwell, dear kin,
So that we may renew the pact
And remember those worthy forbears?

There on the shores, beneath the trees of
Ionia, on plains of the Cayster
Where, gladdened by Aether, cranes
Are surrounded by mountains distantly glimmering,
There you were also, loveliest ones, or haunted
The islands garlanded with vines
And filled with resonant song; or others dwelled
Beside Taygetus, by widely praised Hymettus,
These were the last to thrive; but from
Parnassus' wellspring down to the brooks,
Gold-glittering, of Tmolus rang
An everlasting melody; so then did all
The holy woods and all
The lyres in unison resound
By heaven's own mercy plucked.

O land of Homer!
Beside the crimson cherry-tree, or when,
Your emissaries, in the vineyard for me
The young green peaches cling
And the swallow comes from afar and, telling many a tale,
Builds on my walls her house,
In May-time days, and also under the stars,
Ionia, I think of you! And that is why
I've come to see you, you islands, and you,
The river estuaries, halls of Thetis,
You woods, and you, the clouds over Ida!

Doch nicht zu bleiben gedenk ich.
Unfreundlich ist und schwer zu gewinnen
Die Verschlossene, der ich entkommen, die Mutter.
Von ihren Söhnen einer, der Rhein,
Mit Gewalt wollt' er ans Herz ihr stürzen und schwand
Der Zurükgestoßene, niemand weiß, wohin, in die Ferne.
Doch so nicht wünscht' ich gegangen zu seyn,
Von ihr und nur, euch einzuladen,
Bin ich zu euch, ihr Gratien Griechenlands,
Ihr Himmelstöchter, gegangen,
Daß, wenn die Reise zu weit nicht ist,
Zu uns ihr kommet, ihr Holden!

Wenn milder athmen die Lüfte,
Und liebende Pfeile der Morgen
Uns Allzugedultigen schikt,
Und leichte Gewölke blühn
Uns über den schüchternen Augen,
Dann werden wir sagen, wie kommt
Ihr, Charitinnen, zu Wilden?
Die Dienerinnen des Himmels
Sind aber wunderbar,
Wie alles Göttlichgeborne.
Zum Traume wirds ihm, will es Einer
Beschleichen und straft den, der
Ihm gleichen will mit Gewalt;
Oft überraschet es einen,
Der eben kaum es gedacht hat.

Yet not to stay I am minded,
Ungracious and intractable is
The taciturn whom I fled from, my mother.
One of her sons, the Rhine,
By force once tried to rush to her heart and vanished,
Repulsed, no one knows where, in the distance;
Not so, however, would I depart
From her and only to invite you here,
You Graces of Hellas, you daughters
Of Heaven, I went to you,
So that, if the journey is not too far,
You may come to us, beloved ones.

When milder the breezes blow
And morning sends loving arrows
To us the all too patient,
And downy clouds like blossom
Drift over our diffident eyes,
Then we shall say, how did
You Charities come to barbarians?
But like all that's divinely born,
The servant girls of Heaven
Are strange, miraculous.
If someone tries to grasp it by stealth, he holds
A dream in his hand, and him who uses force
To make himself its peer, it punishes.
Yet often it takes by surprise
A man whose mind it has hardly entered.

GERMANIEN

Nicht sie, die Seeligen, die erschienen sind,
Die Götterbilder in dem alten Lande,
Sie darf ich ja nicht rufen mehr, wenn aber
Ihr heimatlichen Wasser! jezt mit euch
Des Herzens Liebe klagt, was will es anders,
Das Heiligtrauernde? Denn voll Erwartung liegt
Das Land und als in heißen Tagen
Herabgesenkt, umschattet heut
Ihr Sehnenden! uns ahnungsvoll ein Himmel.
Voll ist er von Verheißungen und scheint
Mir drohend auch, doch will ich bei ihm bleiben,
Und rükwärts soll die Seele mir nicht fliehn
Zu euch, Vergangene! die zu lieb mir sind.
Denn euer schönes Angesicht zu sehn,
Als wärs, wie sonst, ich fürcht' es, tödtlich ists,
Und kaum erlaubt, Gestorbene zu weken.

Entflohene Götter! auch ihr, ihr gegenwärtigen, damals
Wahrhaftiger, ihr hattet eure Zeiten!
Nichts läugnen will ich hier und nichts erbitten.
Denn wenn es aus ist, und der Tag erloschen
Wohl trifts den Priester erst, doch liebend folgt
Der Tempel und das Bild ihm auch und seine Sitte
Zum dunkeln Land und keines mag noch scheinen.
Nur als von Grabesflammen, ziehet dann
Ein goldner Rauch, die Sage drob hinüber,
Und dämmert jezt uns Zweifelnden um das Haupt,
Und keiner weiß, wie ihm geschieht. Er fühlt
Die Schatten derer, so gewesen sind,

GERMANIA

Not them, the blessed, who once appeared,
Those images of gods in the ancient land,
Them, it is true, I may not now invoke, but if,
You waters of my homeland, now with you
The love of my heart laments, what else does it want, in
Its hallowed sadness? For full of expectation lies
The country, and as though it had been lowered
In sultry dog-days, on us a heaven today,
You yearning rivers, casts prophetic shade.
With promises it is fraught, and to me
Seems threatening too, yet I will stay with it,
And backward now my soul shall not escape
To you, the vanished, whom I love too much.
To look upon your beautiful brows, as though
They were unchanged, I am afraid, for deadly
And scarcely permitted it is to awaken the dead.

Gods who are fled! And you also, present still,
But once more real, you had your time, your ages!
No, nothing here I'll deny and ask no favours.
For when it's over, and Day's light gone out,
The priest is the first to be struck, but lovingly
The temple and the image and the cult
Follow him down into darkness, and none of them now may shine.
Only as from a funeral pyre henceforth
A golden smoke, the legend of it, drifts
And glimmers on around our doubting heads
And no one knows what's happening to him. He feels
The shadowy shapes of those who once were here,

Die Alten, so die Erde neubesuchen.
Denn die da kommen sollen, drängen uns,
Und länger säumt von Göttermenschen
Die heilige Schaar nicht mehr im blauen Himmel.

Schon grünet ja, im Vorspiel rauherer Zeit
Für sie erzogen das Feld, bereitet ist die Gaabe
Zum Opfermahl und Thal und Ströme sind
Weitoffen um prophetische Berge,
Daß schauen mag bis in den Orient
Der Mann und ihn von dort der Wandlungen viele bewegen.
Vom Aether aber fällt
Das treue Bild und Göttersprüche reegnen
Unzählbare von ihm, und es tönt im innersten Haine.
Und der Adler, der vom Indus kömmt,
Und über des Parnassos
Beschneite Gipfel fliegt, hoch über den Opferhügeln
Italias, und frohe Beute sucht
Dem Vater, nicht wie sonst, geübter im Fluge
Der Alte, jauchzend überschwingt er
Zulezt die Alpen und sieht die vielgearteten Länder.

Die Priesterin, die stillste Tochter Gottes,
Sie, die zu gern in tiefer Einfalt schweigt,
Sie suchet er, die offnen Auges schaute,
Als wüßte sie es nicht, jüngst, da ein Sturm
Todtdrohend über ihrem Haupt ertönte;
Es ahnete das Kind ein Besseres,
Und endlich ward ein Staunen weit im Himmel
Weil Eines groß an Glauben, wie sie selbst,
Die seegnende, die Macht der Höhe sei;
Drum sandten sie den Boten, der, sie schnell erkennend,
Denkt lächelnd so: Dich, unzerbrechliche, muß
Ein ander Wort erprüfen und ruft es laut,

The ancients, newly visiting the earth.
For those who are to come now jostle us,
Nor longer will that holy host of beings
Divinely human linger in azure Heaven.

   Already, in the prelude of a rougher age
Raised up for them, the field grows green, prepared
Are offerings for the votive feast and valley
And rivers lie wide open round prophetic mountains,
So that into the very Orient
A man may look and thence be moved by many transformations.
But down from Aether falls
The faithful image, and words of gods rain down
Innumerable from it, and the innermost grove resounds.
And the eagle that comes from the Indus
And flies over the snow-covered peaks of
Parnassus, high above the votive hills
Of Italy, and seeks glad booty for
The Father, not as he used to, more practised in flight,
That ancient one, exultant, over the Alps
Wings on at last and sees the diverse countries.

   The priestess, her, the quietest daughter of God,
Too fond of keeping silent in deep ingenuousness,
Her now he seeks, who open-eyed looked up
As though she did not know it, lately when a storm,
Threatening death, rang out above her head;
A better destiny the child divined,
And in the end amazement spread in heaven
Because one being was as great in faith
As they themselves, the blessing powers on high;
Therefore they sent the messenger, who, quick to recognize her,
Smilingly thus reflects: you the unbreakable
A different word must try, and then proclaims,

403

Der Jugendliche, nach Germania schauend:

»Du bist es, auserwählt,

»Allliebend und ein schweres Glük

»Bist du zu tragen stark geworden,

Seit damals, da im Walde verstekt und blühendem Mohn

Voll süßen Schlummers, trunkene, meiner du

Nicht achtetest, lang, ehe noch auch geringere fühlten

Der Jungfrau Stolz und staunten weß du wärst und woher,

Doch du es selbst nicht wußtest. Ich miskannte dich nicht,

Und heimlich, da du träumtest, ließ ich

Am Mittag scheidend dir ein Freundeszeichen,

Die Blume des Mundes zurük und du redetest einsam.

Doch Fülle der goldenen Worte sandtest du auch

Glükseelige! mit den Strömen und sie quillen unerschöpflich

In die Gegenden all. Denn fast, wie der heiligen,

Die Mutter ist von allem,

Die Verborgene sonst genannt von Menschen,

So ist von Lieben und Leiden

Und voll von Ahnungen dir

Und voll von Frieden der Busen.

O trinke Morgenlüfte,

Biß daß du offen bist,

Und nenne, was vor Augen dir ist,

Nicht länger darf Geheimniß mehr

Das Ungesprochene bleiben,

Nachdem es lange verhüllt ist;

Denn Sterblichen geziemet die Schaam,

Und so zu reden die meiste Zeit,

Ist weise auch von Göttern.

Wo aber überflüssiger, denn lautere Quellen

Das Gold und ernst geworden ist der Zorn an dem Himmel,

Muß zwischen Tag und Nacht

The youthful, looking towards Germania:
'Yes, it is you, elected
All-loving and to bear
A burdensome good fortune have grown strong,

Since, hidden in the woods and flowering poppies
Filled with sweet drowsiness, you, drunken, did not heed
Me for a long time, before lesser ones even felt
The virgin's pride, and marvelled whose you are and where from,
But you yourself did not know. Yet I did not misjudge you
And secretly, while you dreamed, at noon,
Departing I left a token of friendship,
The flower of the mouth behind, and lonely you spoke.
Yet you, the greatly blessed, with the rivers too
Dispatched a wealth of golden words, and they well unceasing
Into all regions now. For almost as is the holy
The Mother of all things, upholder of the abyss,
Whom men at other times call the Concealed,
Now full of loves and sorrows
And full of presentiments
And full of peace is your bosom.

O drink the morning breezes
Until you are opened up
And name what you see before you;
No longer now the unspoken
May remain a mystery
Though long it has been veiled;
For shame behoves us mortals
And most of the time to speak thus
Of gods indeed is wise.
But where more superabundant than purest wellsprings
The gold has become and the anger in Heaven earnest,
For once between Day and Night must

Einsmals ein Wahres erscheinen.
Dreifach umschreibe du es,
Doch ungesprochen auch, wie es da ist,
Unschuldige, muß es bleiben.

O nenne Tochter du der heiligen Erd’
Einmal die Mutter. Es rauschen die Wasser am Fels
Und Wetter im Wald und bei dem Nahmen derselben
Tönt auf aus alter Zeit Vergangengöttliches wieder.
Wie anders ists! und rechthin glänzt und spricht
Zukünftiges auch erfreulich aus den Fernen.
Doch in der Mitte der Zeit
Lebt ruhig mit geweihter
Jungfräulicher Erde der Aether
Und gerne, zur Erinnerung, sind
Die unbedürftigen sie
Gastfreundlich bei den unbedürftgen
Bei deinen Feiertagen
Germania, wo du Priesterin bist
Und wehrlos Rath giebst rings
Den Königen und den Völkern.

A truth be made manifest.
Now threefold circumscribe it,
Yet unuttered also, just as you found it,
Innocent virgin, let it remain.

Once only, daughter of holy Earth,
Pronounce your Mother's name. The waters roar on the rock
And thunderstorms in the wood, and at their name
Divine things past ring out from time immemorial.
How all is changed! And to the right there gleam
And speak things yet to come, joy-giving, from the distance.
Yet at the centre of Time
In peace with hallowed,
With virginal Earth lives Aether
And gladly, for remembrance, they
The never-needy dwell
Hospitably amid the never-needy,
Amid your holidays,
Germania, where you are priestess and
Defenceless proffer all round
Advice to the kings and the peoples.'

DER RHEIN

AN ISAAK VON SINCLAIR

Im dunkeln Epheu saß ich, an der Pforte
Des Waldes, eben, da der goldene Mittag,
Den Quell besuchend, herunterkam
Von Treppen des Alpengebirgs,
Das mir die göttlichgebaute,
Die Burg der Himmlischen heißt
Nach alter Meinung, wo aber
Geheim noch manches entschieden
Zu Menschen gelanget; von da
Vernahm ich ohne Vermuthen
Ein Schiksaal, denn noch kaum
War mir im warmen Schatten
Sich manches beredend, die Seele
Italia zu geschweift
Und fernhin an die Küsten Moreas.

Jezt aber, drinn im Gebirg,
Tief unter den silbernen Gipfeln
Und unter fröhlichem Grün,
Wo die Wälder schauernd zu ihm,
Und der Felsen Häupter übereinander
Hinabschaun, taglang, dort
Im kältesten Abgrund hört'
Ich um Erlösung jammern
Den Jüngling, es hörten ihn, wie er tobt',
Und die Mutter Erd' anklagt',
Und den Donnerer, der ihn gezeuget,
Erbarmend die Eltern, doch
Die Sterblichen flohn von dem Ort,

THE RHINE

TO ISAAK VON SINCLAIR

Amid dark ivy I was sitting, at
The forest's gate, just as a golden noon,
To visit the wellspring there, came down
From steps of the Alpine ranges
Which, following ancient lore,
I call the divinely built,
The fortress of the Heavenly,
But where, determined in secret
Much even now reaches men; from there
Without surmise I heard
A destiny, for, debating
Now this, now that in the warm shade,
My soul had hardly begun
To make for Italy
And far away for the shores of Morea.

But now, within the mountains,
Deep down below the silvery summits
And in the midst of gay verdure,
Where shuddering the forests
And the heads of rocks overlapping
Look down at him, all day
There in the coldest chasm
I heard the youth implore
Release; and full of pity his parents heard
Him rage there and accuse
His Mother Earth and the Thunderer
Who fathered him, but mortals
Fled from the place, for dreadful,

Denn furchtbar war, da lichtlos er
In den Fesseln sich wälzte,
Das Rasen des Halbgotts.

Die Stimme wars des edelsten der Ströme,
Des freigeborenen Rheins,
Und anderes hoffte der, als droben von den Brüdern,
Dem Tessin und dem Rhodanus,
Er schied und wandern wollt', und ungeduldig ihn
Nach Asia trieb die königliche Seele.
Doch unverständig ist
Das Wünschen vor dem Schiksaal.
Die Blindesten aber
Sind Göttersöhne. Denn es kennet der Mensch
Sein Haus und dem Thier ward, wo
Es bauen solle, doch jenen ist
Der Fehl, daß sie nicht wissen wohin?
In die unerfahrne Seele gegeben.

Ein Räthsel ist Reinentsprungenes. Auch
Der Gesang kaum darf es enthüllen. Denn
Wie du anfiengst, wirst du bleiben,
So viel auch wirket die Noth,
Und die Zucht, das meiste nemlich
Vermag die Geburt,
Und der Lichtstral, der
Dem Neugebornen begegnet.
Wo aber ist einer,
Um frei zu bleiben
Sein Leben lang, und des Herzens Wunsch
Allein zu erfüllen, so
Aus günstigen Höhn, wie der Rhein,
Und so aus heiligem Schoose
Glüklich geboren, wie jener?

As without light he writhed
Within his fetters, was
The demigod's raving.

   The voice it was of the noblest of rivers,
Of free-born Rhine,
And different were his hopes when up there from his brothers
Ticino and Rhodanus
He parted and longed to roam, and impatiently
His regal soul drove him on towards Asia.
Yet in the face of fate
Imprudent it is to wish.
The sons of gods, though,
Are blindest of all. For human beings know
Their house, and the animals
Where they must build, but in
Their inexperienced souls the defect
Of not knowing where was implanted.

   A mystery are those of pure origin.
Even song may hardly unveil it.
For as you began, so you will remain,
And much as need can effect,
And breeding, still greater power
Adheres to your birth
And the ray of light
That meets the new-born infant.
But where is anyone
So happily born as the Rhine
From such propitious heights
And from so holy a womb,
To remain free
His whole life long and alone fulfil
His heart's desire, like him?

Drum ist ein Jauchzen sein Wort.
Nicht liebt er, wie andere Kinder,
In Wikelbanden zu weinen;
Denn wo die Ufer zuerst
An die Seit ihm schleichen, die krummen,
Und durstig umwindend ihn,
Den Unbedachten, zu ziehn
Und wohl zu behüten begehren
Im eigenen Zahne, lachend
Zerreißt er die Schlangen und stürzt
Mit der Beut und wenn in der Eil'
Ein Größerer ihn nicht zähmt,
Ihn wachsen läßt, wie der Bliz, muß er
Die Erde spalten, und wie Bezauberte fliehn
Die Wälder ihm nach und zusammensinkend die Berge.

Ein Gott will aber sparen den Söhnen
Das eilende Leben und lächelt,
Wenn unenthaltsam, aber gehemmt
Von heiligen Alpen, ihm
In der Tiefe, wie jener, zürnen die Ströme.
In solcher Esse wird dann
Auch alles Lautre geschmiedet,
Und schön ists, wie er drauf,
Nachdem er die Berge verlassen,
Stillwandelnd sich im deutschen Lande
Begnüget und das Sehnen stillt
Im guten Geschäffte, wenn er das Land baut
Der Vater Rhein und liebe Kinder nährt
In Städten, die er gegründet.

Doch nimmer, nimmer vergißt ers.
Denn eher muß die Wohnung vergehn,
Und die Sazung und zum Unbild werden

And that is why his word is a jubilant roar,
Nor is he fond, like other children,
Of weeping in swaddling bands;
For where the banks at first
Slink to his side, the crooked,
And greedily entwining him,
Desire to educate
And carefully tend the feckless
Within their teeth, he laughs,
Tears up the serpents and rushes
Off with his prey, and if in haste
A greater one does not tame him,
But lets him grow, like lightning he
Must rend the earth and like things enchanted
The forests join his flight and, collapsing, the mountains.

A god, however, wishes to spare his sons
A life so fleeting and smiles
When, thus intemperate but restrained
By holy Alps, the rivers
Like this one rage at him in the depth.
In such a forge, then, all
That's pure is given shape
And it is good to see
How then, after leaving the mountains,
Content with German lands he calmly
Moves on and stills his longing
In useful industry, when he tills the land,
Now Father Rhine, and supports dear children
In cities which he has founded.

Yet never, never does he forget.
For sooner the dwelling shall be destroyed,
And all the laws, and the day of men

Der Tag der Menschen, ehe vergessen
Ein solcher dürfte den Ursprung
Und die reine Stimme der Jugend.
Wer war es, der zuerst
Die Liebesbande verderbt
Und Strike von ihnen gemacht hat?
Dann haben des eigenen Rechts
Und gewiß des himmlischen Feuers
Gespottet die Trozigen, dann erst
Die sterblichen Pfade verachtend
Verwegnes erwählt
Und den Göttern gleich zu werden getrachtet.

Es haben aber an eigner
Unsterblichkeit die Götter genug, und bedürfen
Die Himmlischen eines Dings,
So sinds Heroën und Menschen
Und Sterbliche sonst. Denn weil
Die Seeligsten nichts fühlen von selbst,
Muß wohl, wenn solches zu sagen
Erlaubt ist, in der Götter Nahmen
Theilnehmend fühlen ein Andrer,
Den brauchen sie; jedoch ihr Gericht
Ist, daß sein eigenes Haus
Zerbreche der und das Liebste
Wie den Feind schelt' und sich Vater und Kind
Begrabe unter den Trümmern,
Wenn einer, wie sie, seyn will und nicht
Ungleiches dulden, der Schwärmer.

Drum wohl ihm, welcher fand
Ein wohlbeschiedenes Schiksaal,
Wo noch der Wanderungen
Und süß der Leiden Erinnerung

Become iniquitous, than such as he
Forget his origin
And the pure voice of his youth.
Who was the first to coarsen,
Corrupt the bonds of love
And turn them into ropes?
Then, sure of their own rights
And of the heavenly fire
Defiant rebels mocked, not till then
Despising mortal ways,
Chose foolhardy arrogance
And strove to become the equals of gods.

But their own immortality
Suffices the gods, and if
The Heavenly have need of one thing,
It is of heroes and human beings
And other mortals. For since
The most Blessed in themselves feel nothing
Another, if to say such a thing is
Permitted, must, I suppose,
Vicariously feel in the name of the gods,
And him they need; but their rule is that
He shall demolish his
Own house and curse like an enemy
Those dearest to him and under the rubble
Shall bury his father and child,
When one aspires to be like them, refusing
To bear with inequality, the fantast.

So happy he who has found
A well-allotted fate
Where still of his wanderings
And sweetly of his afflictions

Aufrauscht am sichern Gestade,
Daß da und dorthin gern
Er sehn mag bis an die Grenzen
Die bei der Geburt ihm Gott
Zum Aufenthalte gezeichnet.
Dann ruht er, seeligbescheiden,
Denn alles, was er gewollt,
Das Himmlische, von selber umfängt
Es unbezwungen, lächelnd
Jezt, da er ruhet, den Kühnen.

    Halbgötter denk' ich jezt
Und kennen muß ich die Theuern,
Weil oft ihr Leben so
Die sehnende Brust mir beweget.
Wem aber, wie, Rousseau, dir,
Unüberwindlich die Seele
Die starkausdauernde ward,
Und sicherer Sinn
Und süße Gaabe zu hören,
Zu reden so, daß er aus heiliger Fülle
Wie der Weingott, thörig göttlich
Und gesezlos sie die Sprache der Reinesten giebt
Verständlich den Guten, aber mit Recht
Die Achtungslosen mit Blindheit schlägt
Die entweihenden Knechte, wie nenn ich den Fremden?

    Die Söhne der Erde sind, wie die Mutter,
Allliebend, so empfangen sie auch
Mühlos, die Glüklichen, Alles.
Drum überraschet es auch
Und schrökt den sterblichen Mann,
Wenn er den Himmel, den
Er mit den liebenden Armen

The memory murmurs on banks that are sure,
So that this way, that way with pleasure
He looks as far as the bounds
Which God at birth assigned
To him for his term and site.
Then, blissfully humble, he rests,
For all that he has wanted,
Though heavenly, of itself surrounds
Him uncompelled, and smiles
Upon the bold one now that he's quiet.

Of demigods now I think
And I must know these dear ones
Because so often their lives
Move me and fill me with longing.
But he whose soul, like yours,
Rousseau, ever strong and patient,
Became invincible,
Endowed with steadfast purpose
And a sweet gift of hearing,
Of speaking, so that from holy profusion
Like the wine-god foolishly, divinely
And lawlessly he gives it away,
The language of the purest, comprehensible to the good,
But rightly strikes with blindness the irreverent,
The profaning rabble, what shall I call that stranger?

The sons of Earth, like their mother are
All-loving, so without effort too
All things those blessèd ones receive.
And therefore it surprises
And startles the mortal man
When he considers the heaven
Which with loving arms he himself

Sich auf die Schultern gehäufft,
Und die Last der Freude bedenket;
Dann scheint ihm oft das Beste,
Fast ganz vergessen da,
Wo der Stral nicht brennt,
Im Schatten des Walds
Am Bielersee in frischer Grüne zu seyn,
Und sorglosarm an Tönen,
Anfängern gleich, bei Nachtigallen zu lernen.

Und herrlich ists, aus heiligem Schlafe dann
Erstehen und aus Waldes Kühle
Erwachend, Abends nun
Dem milderen Licht entgegenzugehn,
Wenn, der die Berge gebaut
Und den Pfad der Ströme gezeichnet,
Nachdem er lächelnd auch
Der Menschen geschäfftiges Leben
Das othemarme, wie Seegel
Mit seinen Lüften gelenkt hat,
Auch ruht und zu der Schülerin jezt,
Der Bildner, Gutes mehr
Denn Böses findend,
Zur heutigen Erde der Tag sich neiget. —

Dann feiern das Brautfest Menschen und Götter,
Es feiern die Lebenden all,
Und ausgeglichen
Ist eine Weile das Schiksaal.
Und die Flüchtlinge suchen die Heerberg,
Und süßen Schlummer die Tapfern,
Die Liebenden aber
Sind, was sie waren, sie sind
Zu Hauße, wo die Blume sich freuet

Has heaped upon his shoulders,
And feels the burden of joy;
Then often to him it seems best
Almost wholly forgotten to be
Where the beam does not sear,
In the forest's shade
By Lake Bienne amid foliage newly green,
And blithely poor in tones,
Like beginners, to learn from nightingales.

And glorious then it is to arise once more
From holy sleep and awakening
From coolness of the woods, at evening
Walk now toward the softer light
When he who built the mountains
And drafted the paths of the rivers,
Having also smiling directed
The busy lives of men,
So short of breath, like sails,
And filled them with his breezes,
Reposes also, and down to his pupil
The master craftsmen, finding
More good than evil,
Day now inclines to the present Earth.

Then gods and mortals celebrate their nuptials,
All the living celebrate,
And Fate for a while
Is levelled out, suspended.
And fugitives look for asylum,
For sweet slumber the brave,
But lovers are
What always they were, at home
Wherever flowers are glad

Unschädlicher Gluth und die finsteren Bäume
Der Geist umsäuselt, aber die Unversöhnten
Sind umgewandelt und eilen
Die Hände sich ehe zu reichen,
Bevor das freundliche Licht
Hinuntergeht und die Nacht kommt.

　　Doch einigen eilt
Diß schnell vorüber, andere
Behalten es länger.
Die ewigen Götter sind
Voll Lebens allzeit; bis in den Tod
Kann aber ein Mensch auch
Im Gedächtniß doch das Beste behalten,
Und dann erlebt er das Höchste.
Nur hat ein jeder sein Maas.
Denn schwer ist zu tragen
Das Unglük, aber schwerer das Glük.
Ein Weiser aber vermocht es
Vom Mittag bis in die Mitternacht,
Und bis der Morgen erglänzte,
Beim Gastmahl helle zu bleiben.

　　Dir mag auf heißem Pfade unter Tannen oder
Im Dunkel des Eichwalds gehüllt
In Stahl, mein Sinklair! Gott erscheinen oder
In Wolken, du kennst ihn, da du kennest, jugendlich,
Des Guten Kraft, und nimmer ist dir
Verborgen das Lächeln des Herrschers
Bei Tage, wenn
Es fieberhaft und angekettet das
Lebendige scheinet oder auch
Bei Nacht, wenn alles gemischt
Ist ordnungslos und wiederkehrt
Uralte Verwirrung.

Of harmless fervour and the spirit wafts
Around the darkling trees, but those unreconciled
Are changed and hurry now
To hold out their hands to the other
Before the benevolent light
Goes down, and night comes.

    For some, however,
This quickly passes, others
Retain it longer.
The eternal gods are full
Of life at all times; but until death
A mortal too can retain
And bear in mind what is best
And then is supremely favoured.
Yet each of us has his measure.
For hard to bear
Is misfortune, but good fortune harder.
A wise man, though, was able
From noon to midnight, and on
Till morning lit up the sky
To keep wide awake at the banquet.

    To you in the heat of a path under fir-trees or
Within the oak forest's half-light, wrapped
In steel, my Sinclair, God may appear, or
In clouds, you'll know him, since, youthfully, you know
The good God's power, and never from you
The smile of the Ruler is hidden
By day, when all
That lives seems febrile
And fettered, or also
By night, when all is mingled
Chaotically and back again comes
Primaeval confusion.

VERSÖHNENDER DER DU NIMMERGEGLAUBT...

Vorstufen zur FRIEDENSFEIER

Versöhnender der du nimmergeglaubt
Nun da bist,   Freundesgestalt mir
Annimmst Unsterblicher, aber wohl
Erkenn ich   das Hohe
Das mir die Knie beugt,
Und fast wie ein Blinder muß ich
Dich, himmlischer fragen wozu du mir,
Woher du seiest, seeliger Friede!
Diß Eine weiß ich, sterbliches bist du nichts,
Denn manches mag ein Weiser oder
Der treuanblikenden Freunde einer erhellen, wenn aber
Ein Gott erscheint, auf Himmel und Erd und Meer
Kömt allerneuende Klarheit.

(Einst freueten wir uns auch,
Zur Morgenstunde wo stille die Werkstatt war
Am Feiertag, und die Blumen in der Stille,
Wohl blühten schöner auch sie und helle quillten lebendige Brunnen.
Fern rauschte der Gemeinde schauerlicher Gesang,
Wo heiligem Wein gleich, die geheimeren Sprüche
Gealtert aber gewaltiger einst, aus Gottes
Gewittern im Sommer gewachsen,
Die Sorgen doch mir stillten
Und die Zweifel aber nimmer wußt ich, wie mir geschah,
Denn kaum geboren, warum breitetet
Ihr mir schon über die Augen eine Nacht,
Daß ich die Erde nicht sah und mühsam
Euch athmen mußt, ihr himmlischen Lüfte.

CONCILIATOR, YOU THAT NO LONGER BELIEVED IN . . .

Preliminary drafts for CELEBRATION OF PEACE

Conciliator, you that no longer believed in
Are here now, assuming the shape of
A friend, immortal, yet indeed
I recognize   what exalted power
It is that bends my knees,
And almost like a blind man I
Must ask you, the heavenly, for what
And whence you have come to me, blessèd Peace!
This one thing I do know, a mortal you are not,
For much a wise man or one of
The loyally gazing friends may elucidate, but when
A god appears, on heaven and earth and ocean
An all-renewing clarity shines.

(Once, it is true, we rejoiced, at
The morning hour when the workshop was quiet on
A holiday, and indeed in that stillness the flowers
More beautifully blossomed and brightly the living fountains welled,
Far off, but awe-inspiring, droned the community's singing
Where like a holy wine, the more mysterious responses,
Aged now but once more mighty, grown up
In summer from the thunderstorms of God,
Could yet allay my cares
And doubts, but never I knew what was happening to me,
For why, when I had hardly been born,
Already did you cover my eyes with a night,
So that I could not see the earth and with
An effort must inhale you, heavenly breezes.

Zuvorbestimmt wars. Und es lächelt Gott,
Wenn unaufhaltsam aber von seinen Bergen gehemmt
Ihm zürnend in den ehernen Ufern brausen die Ströme,
Tief wo kein Tag die begrabenen nennt.
Und o, daß immer allerhaltender, du auch mich
So haltest, und leichtentfliehende Seele mir sparest,)
Drum hab ich heute das Fest, und abendlich in der Stille
Blüht rings der Geist und wär auch silbergrau mir die Loke,
Doch würd ich rathen, daß wir sorgten ihr Freunde
Für Gastmahl und Gesang, und Kränze genug und Töne
Bei solcher Zeit unsterblichen Jünglingen gleich.

Und manchen möcht' ich laden, aber o du,
Der freundlich ernst den Menschen zugethan
Dort unter syrischer Palme
Wo nahe lag die Stadt am Brunnen gerne weiltest,
Das Kornfeld rauschte rings   still athmete die Kühlung
Vom Dunkel des geweiheten Gebirgs,
Und die lieben Freunde, das treue Gewölk
Umschätteten dich auch, damit der reine, kühne
Durch Wildniß mild der Stral von oben kam o Jüngling!
Ach! aber dunkler umschattete, mitten im Wort dich
Furchtbar entscheidend ein tödtlich Verhängniß. So ist schnell
Vergänglich alles Himmlische; aber umsonst nicht.

Denn schonend rührt, des Maases allzeit kundig
Nur einen Augenblik die Wohnungen der Menschen
Ein Gott an, unversehn, und keiner weiß es, wer?
Und drüber hin darf alles Freche gehn,
Und kommen muß zum heilgen Ort das Wilde
Von Enden fern, und blindbetastend übt den Wahn
Am Göttlichen, und trift ein Schiksaal darin. Dank
Folgt niemals auf dem Fuße solchem Geschenke.
Zu schwer ist jenes zu fassen,

Pre-ordained it was. And God smiles
When not to be stopped but restrained by his mountains
The rivers, raging, roar at him in their brazen banks,
Deep down where no day calls the buried by their names.
And O that ever, Upholder of All, me too you shall
Hold thus and spare my soul that all too readily flees,)
Today I celebrate, and vespertine now in the stillness
All round the spirit blossoms and though my hair
Were silver-grey, yet, my friends, I'd advise that
We see to banquet and song and garlands enough and music
At such a time like men immortally young.

And there are many I would invite, but you,
O you that benignly, gravely disposed to men
Down there beneath the Syrian palm-tree, where
The town lay near, by the well were fond of lingering,
Round you the cornfield rustled, quietly coolness breathed
From darkness of the hallowed mountainsides
And your dear friends, the faithful cloud
Cast shade upon you too, so that the pure, the bold,
The beam through wilderness gently should fall from above, O youth.
But, oh, more darkly, even as you spoke
And dreadfully determining, a deadly doom overshadowed you there. So all
That's heavenly fleets on; but not for nothing.

For sparingly, at all times knowing the measure,
A god for a moment only will touch the dwellings
Of men, by none foreseen, and no one knows who it was,
And over it all insolence may pass,
And to the holy place must come the savage
From ends remote, and blindly fingering, works out his
Delusion upon the divine, and fulfils a fate. But thanks
Will never follow at once upon such a gift.
Too hard this is to grasp, for

Denn wäre der es giebt, nicht sparsam
Längst wäre vom Seegen des Heerds
Uns Gipfel und Boden entzündet.

   Des Göttlichen aber empfiengen wir
Doch viel. Es ward die Flamm uns
In die Hände gegeben, und Boden und Meersfluth.
Denn nur auf menschliche Weise, nimmermehr
Sind jene mit uns, die fremden Kräfte vertraut
Und es lehret das Gestirn dich, das
Vor Augen dir ist, denn nimmer kannst du ihm gleichen
Dem Alllebendigen von dem
Viel Freuden sind und Gesänge,

   Ist einer ein Sohn, ein Ruhigmächtiger ist er,
Denn nun erkennen wir ihn,
Jezt da wir kennen den Vater,
Und Feiertage zu halten
Der Hohe sich der Geist
Sich froh zu Menschen geneigt hat.

   Zur Herrschaft war der immer zu groß
Und geringer denn er, so weit es auch gereichet sein Feld.
Es mag ein Gott auch, Sterblichen gleich
Erwählen ein Tagewerk und theilen alles Schiksaal
Daß alle sich einander erfahren, und wenn
Die Stille wiederkehret, eine Sprache unter Lebenden
Sei. Wie der Meister tritt er dann, aus der
Werkstatt, und andres Gewand nicht denn ein festliches ziehet er an.
Die Geseze aber, die unter Liebenden gelten
Die schönausgleichenden sie sind dann allgeltend
Von der Erde bis hoch in den Himmel.

If he who gives it were not sparing,
The wealth of our hearth long ago would
Have fired both the roof and the floor.

    Yet much that's divine nonetheless we
Received. The flame was entrusted
To us, and the ground we walk on and ocean flood,
Much more than humanly only, never again
Are these, the alien powers, familiar with us,
And you are taught by the stars
In front of your eyes, but never you can be like them.
Yet to the All-Living from whom
Many joys and songs have sprung

    There's one who is a son, and quietly powerful is he,
For now we recognize him
Now that we know the Father,
And to keep holidays
The Exalted, the Spirit of the World
Has gladly inclined towards men.

    For dominion he has always been too great
And smaller than he, far though it stretches, his field.
A god, like mortals, too may choose
Mere daily tasks and share all manner of fate,
That all might have knowledge of all, and when
The silence returns, there might be a language among
The living. Like the master then he steps out of
His workshop, and none but a festive garment he puts on.
The laws, however, that count for lovers
And gently resolve their discords, then are all-prevailing
From Earth to high up in Heaven.

Denn siehe es ist der Abend der Zeit
Und der Vater thront nun nimmer oben allein.
Und andere sind noch bei ihm.
Viel hat erfahren der Mensch. Der Himmlischen viele genannt,
Seit ein Gespräch wir sind
Und hören können voneinander.

Sei gegenwärtig Jüngling, jezt erst, denn noch ehe du ausgeredet
Rief es herab, und schnell verhüllt war jenes Freudige, das
Du reichtest, und weit umschattend breitete sich über dir
Und furchtbar ein Verhängniß,
So ist schnellvergänglich alles Himmlische, aber umsonst nicht.
Des Maases allzeit kundig rührt mit schönender Hand
Die Wohnungen der Menschen
Ein Gott an, einen Augenblik nur
Und sie wissen es nicht, doch lange
Gedenken sie deß, und fragen, wer es gewesen.
Wenn aber eine Zeit vorbei ist, kennen sie es.

Und menschlicher Wohlthat folget der Dank,
Auf göttliche Gaabe aber jahrlang
Die Mühn erst und das Irrsaal,
Daß milder auf die folgende Zeit
Der hohe Stral
Durch heilige Wildniß scheine.
Darum, o Göttlicher! sei gegenwärtig,
Und schöner, wie sonst, o sei
Versöhnender nun versöhnt daß wir des Abends
Mit den Freunden dich nennen, und singen
Von den Hohen, und neben dir noch andere sein.

Denn versiegt fast, all in Opferflammen
War ausgeathmet das heilige Feuer
Da schikte schnellentzündend der Vater
Das liebendste, was er hatte, herab
Damit entbrennend,

For, look, it is the Evening of Time, and
No longer alone the Father sits enthroned above.
And others now are with him.
Much men have learnt. Have called by their names many of those in Heaven
Since we have been a discourse
And able to hear from each other.

Be present youth, only now, for before you had finished speaking
The voice cried, away, and quickly that joy was obscured which
You proffered, and widely overshadowing and terrible
A doom descended upon you;
So all that's heavenly fleets on, but not for nothing.
At all times knowing the measure, with a sparing hand
A god will touch the dwellings
Of men, for a moment only
And they do not know it, yet long they
Remember it and ask who it was.
Yet when a certain time has gone by, they know it.

And human beneficence is followed by thanks,
But god-sent gifts for years at first
By suffering and confusion
So that more mildly in the years that follow
The lofty beam
Through holy wilderness shall shine.
Therefore, divine one, be present now
And O more beautifully than before,
Conciliator, now be reconciled, so that at Evening
Together with your friends we may name you, and sing
Of them, the celestial, and there shall be others beside you.

For almost exhausted, all breathed out
In sacrificial flames was the holy fire
When swiftly kindling, the Father sent down the
Most loving of all that are his
To start a stronger blaze;

Und wenn fortzehrend von Geschlecht zu Geschlecht,
Die Menschen wären des Seegens zu voll,
Daß jeder sich genügt und übermüthig vergäße des Himmels,
Dann   sprach er   soll ein neues beginnen,
Und siehe! was du verschwiegest,
Der Zeiten Vollendung hat es gebracht.
Wohl wußtest du es, aber nicht zu leben, zu sterben warst du gesandt,
Und immer größer, denn sein Feld, wie der Götter Gott
Er selbst, muß einer der anderen auch seyn.

    Wenn aber die Stunde schlägt
Wie der Meister tritt er, aus der Werkstatt,
Und ander Gewand nicht, denn
Ein festliches ziehet er an
Zum Zeichen, daß noch anderes auch
Im Werk ihm übrig gewesen.
Geringer und größer erscheint er.
Und so auch du
Und gönnest uns, den Söhnen der liebenden Erde,
Daß wir, so viel herangewachsen
Der Feste sind, sie alle feiern und nicht
Die Götter zählen, Einer ist immer für alle.
Mir gleich dem Sonnenlichte! göttlicher sei
Am Abend deiner Tage gegrüßet.
Und mögen bleiben wir nun.

And if, consuming it generation after generation,
Mankind should be too full of blessings,
Each man becoming self-sufficient and arrogantly oblivious of Heaven,
Then, so he said, a new age shall begin
And, look, what you kept unspoken
The end of the ages has brought to light.
And well you knew it, but not to live, to die you were sent,
And always greater than his field, like the God of gods
Himself, must one of the others be also.

 But when the hour strikes
Like the master he steps from his workshop
And none but a festive garment
He now puts on, as a sign
That he remained aware
Of things left undone in his work.
Both smaller and greater he seems now
And likewise you,
Who grant us, the sons of this loving Earth,
That, many as are the holidays that have
Grown up, we may celebrate them all, and need
Not count the gods; one always stands for them all.
To me like the sunlight! divine one, let
Us greet you at the Evening of your days.
And may we now abide.

FRIEDENSFEIER

Ich bitte dieses Blatt nur gutmüthig zu lesen. So wird es sicher nicht unfaßlich, noch weniger anstößig seyn. Sollten aber dennoch einige eine solche Sprache zu wenig konventionell finden, so muß ich ihnen gestehen: ich kann nicht anders. An einem schönen Tage läßt sich ja fast jede Sangart hören, und die Natur, wovon es her ist, nimmts auch wieder.

Der Verfasser gedenkt dem Publikum eine ganze Sammlung von dergleichen Blättern vorzulegen, und dieses soll irgend eine Probe seyn davon.

    Der himmlischen, still wiederklingenden,
Der ruhigwandelnden Töne voll,
Und gelüftet ist der altgebaute,
Seeliggewohnte Saal; um grüne Teppiche duftet
Die Freudenwolk' und weithinglänzend stehn,
Gereiftester Früchte voll und goldbekränzter Kelche,
Wohlangeordnet, eine prächtige Reihe,
Zur Seite da und dort aufsteigend über dem
Geebneten Boden die Tische.
Denn ferne kommend haben
Hieher, zur Abendstunde,
Sich liebende Gäste beschieden.

    Und dämmernden Auges denk' ich schon,
Vom ernsten Tagwerk lächelnd,
Ihn selbst zu sehn, den Fürsten des Fests.
Doch wenn du schon dein Ausland gern verläugnest,
Und als vom langen Heldenzuge müd,
Dein Auge senkst, vergessen, leichtbeschattet,
Und Freundesgestalt annimmst, du Allbekannter, doch
Beugt fast die Knie das Hohe. Nichts vor dir,
Nur Eines weiß ich, Sterbliches bist du nicht.

CELEBRATION OF PEACE

All I ask is that the reader be kindly disposed towards these pages. In that case he will certainly not find them incomprehensible, far less objectionable. But if, nonetheless, some should think such a language too unconventional, I must confess to them: I cannot help it. On a fine day—they should consider—almost every mode of song makes itself heard; and Nature, whence it originates, also receives it again.

The author intends to offer the public an entire collection of such pieces, and this one should be regarded as a kind of sample.

With heavenly, quietly echoing,
With calmly modulating music filled,
And aired is the anciently built,
The sweetly familiar hall; upon green carpets wafts
The fragrant cloud of joy and, casting their brightness far,
Full of most mellow fruit and chalices wreathed with gold,
Arranged in seemly order, a splendid row,
Erected here and there on either side above
The levelled floor, stand the tables.
For, come from distant places,
Here, at the evening hour,
Loving guests have forgathered.

And already with eyes dusk-dim,
With solemn day-labour smiling,
I think that I see him in person, the prince of the feast-day.
But though you like to disavow your foreign land,
And weary, it seems, with long heroic war,
Cast down your eyes, oblivious, lightly shaded,
Assuming the shape of a friend, you known to all men, yet
Almost it bends our knees, such loftiness. Nothing in
Your presence I know; but one thing: mortal you are not.

Ein Weiser mag mir manches erhellen; wo aber
Ein Gott noch auch erscheint,
Da ist doch andere Klarheit.

Von heute aber nicht, nicht unverkündet ist er;
Und einer, der nicht Fluth noch Flamme gescheuet,
Erstaunet, da es stille worden, umsonst nicht, jezt,
Da Herrschaft nirgend ist zu sehn bei Geistern und Menschen.
Das ist, sie hören das Werk,
Längst vorbereitend, von Morgen nach Abend, jezt erst,
Denn unermeßlich braußt, in der Tiefe verhallend,
Des Donnerers Echo, das tausendjährige Wetter,
Zu schlafen, übertönt von Friedenslauten, hinunter.
Ihr aber, theuergewordne, o ihr Tage der Unschuld,
Ihr bringt auch heute das Fest, ihr Lieben! und es blüht
Rings abendlich der Geist in dieser Stille;
Und rathen muß ich, und wäre silbergrau
Die Loke, o ihr Freunde!
Für Kränze zu sorgen und Mahl, jezt ewigen Jünglingen ähnlich.

Und manchen möcht' ich laden, aber o du,
Der freundlichernst den Menschen zugethan,
Dort unter syrischer Palme,
Wo nahe lag die Stadt, am Brunnen gerne war;
Das Kornfeld rauschte rings, still athmete die Kühlung
Vom Schatten des geweiheten Gebirges,
Und die lieben Freunde, das treue Gewölk,
Umschatteten dich auch, damit der heiligkühne

A wise man could elucidate much for me; but where
A God as well appears,
A different clarity shines.

Yet not sprung up today, nor unproclaimed he comes;
And one who did not balk at either flood or flame
Not without reason astonishes us, now that all is quiet,
Dominion nowhere to be seen among spirits or mortals.
That is, only now do they hear
The work that long has prepared them, from Orient to Occident,
For now immeasurably, fading away in the deeps,
The Thunderer's echo, the millennial storm
Rolls down to sleep, intermingled with peaceful music.
But you, grown dear to us, O days of innocence,
It's you, beloved, that bring this feast-day too, and round us
The spirit flowers, vespertine in this quiet;
And, friends, I must advise you, though
Our hair had turned silver-grey,
To see to garlands and banquet, now like men immortally young.

And many there are I would invite, but you,
O you that benignly, gravely disposed to men
Down there beneath the Syrian palm-tree, where
The town lay near, by the well were glad to be;
Round you the cornfield rustled, quietly coolness breathed
From shadows of the hallowed mountainsides,
And your dear friends, the faithful cloud
Cast shade upon you too, so that the holy, the bold,

Durch Wildniß mild dein Stral zu Menschen kam, o Jüngling!
Ach! aber dunkler umschattete, mitten im Wort, dich
Furchtbarentscheidend ein tödtlich Verhängniß. So ist schnell
Vergänglich alles Himmlische; aber umsonst nicht;

Denn schonend rührt des Maases allzeit kundig
Nur einen Augenblick die Wohnungen der Menschen
Ein Gott an, unversehn, und keiner weiß es, wenn?
Auch darf alsdann das Freche drüber gehn,
Und kommen muß zum heilgen Ort das Wilde
Von Enden fern, übt rauhbetastend den Wahn,
Und trift daran ein Schiksaal, aber Dank,
Nie folgt der gleich hernach dem gottgegebnen Geschenke;
Tiefprüfend ist es zu fassen.
Auch wär' uns, sparte der Gebende nicht
Schon längst vom Seegen des Heerds
Uns Gipfel und Boden entzündet.

Des Göttlichen aber empfiengen wir
Doch viel. Es ward die Flamm' uns
In die Hände gegeben, und Ufer und Meersfluth.
Viel mehr, denn menschlicher Weise
Sind jene mit uns, die fremden Kräfte, vertrauet.
Und es lehret Gestirn dich, das
Vor Augen dir ist, doch nimmer kannst du ihm gleichen.
Vom Alllebendigen aber, von dem
Viel Freuden sind und Gesänge,
Ist einer ein Sohn, ein Ruhigmächtiger ist er,
Und nun erkennen wir ihn,

The beam through wilderness gently should fall on men, O youth.
But oh, more darkly, even as you spoke,
And dreadfully determining a deadly doom overshadowed you there.
                                        So all
That's heavenly fleets on; but not for nothing;

    For sparingly, at all times knowing the measure,
A God for a moment only will touch the dwellings
Of men, by none foreseen, and no one knows when.
And over it then all insolence may pass,
And to the holy place must come the savage
From ends remote, and roughly fingering works out his
Delusion, so fulfilling a fate, but thanks
Will never follow at once upon the god-sent gift;
Probed deeply, this can be grasped.
And were not the giver sparing
The wealth of our hearth long ago would
Have fired both the roof and the floor.

    Yet much that's divine nonetheless we
Received. The flame was entrusted
To us, and shore and ocean flood.
Much more than humanly only
Are these, the alien powers, familiar with us.
And you are taught by the stars
In front of your eyes, but never you can be like them.
Yet to the All-Living from whom
Many joys and songs have sprung
There's one who is a son, and quietly powerful is he,
And now we recognize him,

Nun, da wir kennen den Vater
Und Feiertage zu halten
Der hohe, der Geist
Der Welt sich zu Menschen geneigt hat.

Denn längst war der zum Herrn der Zeit zu groß
Und weit aus reichte sein Feld, wann hats ihn aber erschöpfet?
Einmal mag aber ein Gott auch Tagewerk erwählen,
Gleich Sterblichen und theilen alles Schiksaal.
Schiksaalgesez ist diß, daß Alle sich erfahren,
Daß, wenn die Stille kehrt, auch eine Sprache sei.
Wo aber wirkt der Geist, sind wir auch mit, und streiten,
Was wohl das Beste sei. So dünkt mir jezt das Beste,
Wenn nun vollendet sein Bild und fertig ist der Meister,
Und selbst verklärt davon aus seiner Werkstatt tritt,
Der stille Gott der Zeit und nur der Liebe Gesez,
Das schönausgleichende gilt von hier an bis zum Himmel.

Viel hat von Morgen an,
Seit ein Gespräch wir sind und hören voneinander,
Erfahren der Mensch; bald sind wir aber Gesang.
Und das Zeitbild, das der große Geist entfaltet,
Ein Zeichen liegts vor uns, daß zwischen ihm und andern
Ein Bündniß zwischen ihm und andern Mächten ist.
Nicht er allein, die Unerzeugten, Ew'gen
Sind kennbar alle daran, gleichwie auch an den Pflanzen
Die Mutter Erde sich und Licht und Luft sich kennet.
Zulezt ist aber doch, ihr heiligen Mächte, für euch

Now that we know the Father
And to keep holidays
The exalted, the Spirit of
The World has inclined towards men.

For long now he had been too great to rule
As Lord of Time, and wide his field extended, but when did it exhaust him?
For once, however, even a God may choose
Mere daily tasks, like mortals, and share all manner of fate.
This is a law of fate, that each shall know all others,
That when the silence returns there shall be a language too.
Yet where the Spirit is active, we too will stir and debate
What course might be the best. So now it seems best to me
If now the Master completes his image and, finished,
Himself transfigured by it, steps out of his workshop,
The quiet God of Time, and only the law of love,
That gently resolves all difference, prevails from here up to Heaven.

Much, from the morning onwards,
Since we have been a discourse and have heard from one another,
Has human kind learnt; but soon we shall be song.
That temporal image too, which the great Spirit reveals,
As a token lies before us that between him and others,
Himself and other powers, there is a pact of peace.
Not he alone, the Unconceived, Eternal
Can all be known by this, as likewise by the plants
Our Mother Earth and light and air are known.
Yet ultimately, you holy powers, our token

Das Liebeszeichen, das Zeugniß
Daß ihrs noch seiet, der Festtag,

   Der Allversammelnde, wo Himmlische nicht
Im Wunder offenbar, noch ungesehn im Wetter,
Wo aber bei Gesang gastfreundlich untereinander
In Chören gegenwärtig, eine heilige Zahl
Die Seeligen in jeglicher Weise
Beisammen sind, und ihr Geliebtestes auch,
An dem sie hängen, nicht fehlt; denn darum rief ich
Zum Gastmahl, das bereitet ist,
Dich, Unvergeßlicher, dich, zum Abend der Zeit,
O Jüngling, dich zum Fürsten des Festes; und eher legt
Sich schlafen unser Geschlecht nicht,
Bis ihr Verheißenen all,
All ihr Unsterblichen, uns
Von eurem Himmel zu sagen,
Da seid in unserem Hauße.

   Leichtathmende Lüfte
Verkünden euch schon,
Euch kündet das rauchende Thal
Und der Boden, der vom Wetter noch dröhnet,
Doch Hoffnung röthet die Wangen,
Und vor der Thüre des Haußes
Sizt Mutter und Kind,
Und schauet den Frieden
Und wenige scheinen zu sterben

Of love for you, and the proof
That still you are holy to us, is the feast-day,

   The all-assembling, where heavenly beings are
Not manifest in miracles, nor unseen in thunderstorms,
But where in hymns hospitably conjoined
And present in choirs, a holy number,
The blessèd in every way
Meet and forgather, and their best-beloved,
To whom they are attached, is not missing; for that is why
You to the banquet now prepared I called,
The unforgettable, you, at the Evening of Time,
O youth, called you to the prince of the feast-day; nor shall
Our nation ever lie down to sleep until
All you that were prophesied,
Every one of you Immortals,
To tell us about your Heaven
Are here with us in our house.

   Winds lightly breathing
Already announce you,
The vapour that drifts from the valley
And the ground still resounding with thunder,
But hope now flushes our cheeks,
In front of the door of their house
Sit mother and child,
And look upon peace,
And few now seem to be dying;

Es hält ein Ahnen die Seele,
Vom goldnen Lichte gesendet,
Hält ein Versprechen die Ältesten auf.

Wohl sind die Würze des Lebens,
Von oben bereitet und auch
Hinausgeführet, die Mühen.
Denn Alles gefällt jezt,
Einfältiges aber
Am meisten, denn die langgesuchte,
Die goldne Frucht,
Uraltem Stamm
In schütternden Stürmen entfallen,
Dann aber, als liebstes Gut, vom heiligen Schiksaal selbst,
Mit zärtlichen Waffen umschüzt,
Die Gestalt der Himmlischen ist es.

Wie die Löwin, hast du geklagt,
O Mutter, da du sie,
Natur, die Kinder verloren.
Denn es stahl sie, Allzuliebende, dir
Dein Feind, da du ihn fast
Wie die eigenen Söhne genommen,
Und Satyren die Götter gesellt hast.
So hast du manches gebaut,
Und manches begraben,
Denn es haßt dich, was
Du, vor der Zeit
Allkräftige, zum Lichte gezogen.

The souls of the oldest even
Held back by a hint, a promise
Conveyed by the golden light.

Indeed it is travails, designed from
Above and there carried out,
That are the spice of life.
For now all things are pleasing
But most of all the
Ingenuous, because the long-sought,
The golden fruit,
In shattering gales fallen down from
An age-old bough
But then, as the dearest possession, by Fate herself
Protected with tender weapons,
The shape of the Heavenly it is.

Like the lioness you lamented,
O Mother, when you lost
Your children, Nature,
For they were stolen from you, the all too loving, by
Your enemy, when almost
Like your own sons you had nursed him
And with satyrs made gods consort.
So there is much you built
And much you buried,
For you are hated by
That which too soon
All-powerful, you raised to the light.

Nun kennest, nun lässest du diß;

Denn gerne fühllos ruht,

Bis daß es reift, furchtsamgeschäfftiges drunten.

Now you know the fault, and desist;
For, till grown ripe, unfeeling
What's timidly busy likes to rest down below.

DER EINZIGE

Erste Fassung

Was ist es, das
An die alten seeligen Küsten
Mich fesselt, daß ich mehr noch
Sie liebe, als mein Vaterland?
Denn wie in himmlische
Gefangenschaft verkaufft
Dort bin ich, wo Apollo gieng
In Königsgestalt,
Und zu unschuldigen Jünglingen sich
Herablies Zevs und Söhn' in heiliger Art
Und Töchter zeugte
Der Hohe unter den Menschen?

Der hohen Gedanken
Sind nemlich viel
Entsprungen des Vaters Haupt
Und große Seelen
Von ihm zu Menschen gekommen.
Gehöret hab' ich
Von Elis und Olympia, bin
Gestanden oben auf dem Parnaß,
Und über Bergen des Isthmus,
Und drüben auch
Bei Smyrna und hinab
Bei Ephesos bin ich gegangen;

Viel hab' ich schönes gesehn,
Und gesungen Gottes Bild,

THE ONLY ONE

First Version

What is it that
To the ancient, the happy shores
Binds me, so that I love them
Still more than my own homeland?
For as though into heavenly
Captivity sold,
I am where Apollo walked
In the guise of a king,
And Zeus condescended
To innocent youths, and sons in a holy fashion
Begot, and daughters,
The exalted, amid mankind.

For many a thought
Sublime and great
Has sprung from the Father's head
And lofty souls
Come down from him to mortals.
Of Elis and
Olympia I have heard, and stood
High up on the top of Parnassus
And up above hills of the Isthmus
And over there
By Smyrna too, and down
By Ephesus I have walked;

Have looked upon much that is lovely
And sung the image of God

Hab' ich, das lebet unter
Den Menschen, aber dennoch
Ihr alten Götter und all
Ihr tapfern Söhne der Götter
Noch Einen such ich, den
Ich liebe unter euch,
Wo ihr den lezten eures Geschlechts
Des Haußes Kleinod mir
Dem fremden Gaste verberget.

Mein Meister und Herr!
O du, mein Lehrer!
Was bist du ferne
Geblieben? und da
Ich fragte unter den Alten,
Die Helden und
Die Götter, warum bliebest
Du aus? Und jezt ist voll
Von Trauern meine Seele
Als eifertet, ihr Himmlischen, selbst
Daß, dien' ich einem, mir
Das andere fehlet.

Ich weiß es aber, eigene Schuld
Ists! Denn zu sehr,
O Christus! häng' ich an dir,
Wiewohl Herakles Bruder
Und kühn bekenn' ich, du
Bist Bruder auch des Eviers, der
An den Wagen spannte
Die Tyger und hinab
Bis an den Indus
Gebietend freudigen Dienst
Den Weinberg stiftet und
Den Grimm bezähmte der Völker.

As here among human kind
It lives, and yet, and yet,
You ancient gods and all
You valiant sons of the gods,
One other I look for whom
Within your ranks I love,
Where hidden from the alien guest, from me,
You keep the last of your kind,
The treasured gem of the house.

My Master and Lord!
O you, my teacher!
Why did you keep
Away? And when
I asked among the ancients,
The heroes and
The gods, then why were you
Not there? And now my soul
Is full of sadness as though
You Heavenly yourselves excitedly cried
That if I serve one I
Must lack the other.

And yet I know, it is my
Own fault! For too greatly,
O Christ, I'm attached to you,
Although Heracles' brother.
And boldly I confess,
You are the brother also of Evius
Who to his chariot harnessed
The tigers and right down
As far as the Indus
Commanding joyful service,
First planted the vineyard and tamed
The fierceness and rage of the peoples.

Es hindert aber eine Schaam
Mich dir zu vergleichen
Die weltlichen Männer. Und freilich weiß
Ich, der dich zeugte, dein Vater,
Derselbe der,

Denn nimmer herrscht er allein.

Es hänget aber an Einem
Die Liebe. Diesesmal
Ist nemlich vom eigenen Herzen
Zu sehr gegangen der Gesang,
Gut machen will ich den Fehl
Wenn ich noch andere singe.
Nie treff ich, wie ich wünsche,
Das Maas. Ein Gott weiß aber
Wenn kommet, was ich wünsche das Beste.

And yet a shame forbids me
To associate with you
The worldly men. And indeed I know
That he who begot you, your Father,
The same who

For never he reigns alone.

To One alone, however,
Love clings. For this time too much
From my own heart the song
Has come; if other songs follow
I'll make amends for the fault.
Much though I wish to, never
I strike the right measure. But
A god knows when it comes, what I wish for, the best.

451

Denn wie der Meister
Gewandelt auf Erden
Ein gefangener Aar,

   Und viele, die
Ihn sahen, fürchteten sich,
Dieweil sein Äußerstes that
Der Vater und sein Bestes unter
Den Menschen wirkete wirklich,
Und sehr betrübt war auch
Der Sohn so lange, bis er
Gen Himmel fuhr in den Lüften,
Dem gleich ist gefangen die Seele der Helden.
Die Dichter müssen auch
Die geistigen weltlich seyn.

For as the Master
Once moved on earth,
A captive eagle,

And many who
Looked on him were afraid,
While the Father did
His utmost, effectively bringing
The best to bear upon men,
And sorely troubled in mind
The Son was also until
To Heaven he rose in the winds,
So too, the souls of the heroes are captive.
The poets, and those no less who
Are spiritual, must be worldly.

DER EINZIGE

Zweite Fassung

Was ist es, das
An die alten seeligen Küsten
Mich fesselt, daß ich mehr noch
Sie liebe, als mein Vaterland?
Denn wie in himmlischer
Gefangenschaft gebükt, in flammender Luft
Dort bin ich, wo, wie Steine sagen Apollo gieng
In Königsgestalt,
Und zu unschuldigen Jünglingen sich
Herạblies Zevs und Söhn in heiliger Art
Und Töchter zeugte
Der Hohe unter den Menschen?

Der hohen Gedanken
Sind nemlich viel
Entsprungen des Vaters Haupt
Und große Seelen
Von ihm zu Menschen gekommen.
Gehöret hab' ich
Von Elis und Olympia, bin
Gestanden oben auf dem Parnaß,
Und über Bergen des Isthmus,
Und drüben auch
Bei Smyrna und hinab
Bei Ephesos bin ich gegangen;

Viel hab' ich schönes gesehn,
Und gesungen Gottes Bild

THE ONLY ONE

Second Version

What is it that
To the ancient, the happy shores
Binds me, so that I love them
Still more than my own homeland?
For as though in heavenly
Captivity cowering, in flaming air
I am where the stones tell Apollo walked
In the guise of a king
And Zeus condescended
To innocent youths, and sons in a holy fashion
Begot, and daughters,
The exalted, amid mankind.

For many a thought
Sublime and great
Has sprung from the Father's head
And lofty souls
Come down from him to mortals
Of Elis and
Olympia I have heard, and stood
High up on the top of Parnassus
And up above hills of the Isthmus
And over there
By Smyrna too, and down
By Ephesus I have walked;

Have looked upon much that is lovely
And sung the image of God

Hab' ich, das lebet unter
Den Menschen, denn sehr dem Raum gleich ist
Das Himmlische reichlich in
Der Jugend zählbar, aber dennoch
O du der Sterne Leben und all
Ihr tapfern Söhne des Lebens
Noch Einen such ich, den
Ich liebe unter euch,
Wo ihr den lezten eures Geschlechts
Des Haußes Kleinod mir
Dem fremden Gaste verberget.

    Mein Meister und Herr!
O du, mein Lehrer!
Was bist du ferne
Geblieben? und da
Ich fragte unter den Alten,
Die Helden und
Die Götter, warum bliebest
Du aus? Und jezt ist voll
Von Trauern meine Seele
Als eifertet, ihr Himmlischen, selbst
Daß, dien' ich einem, mir
Das andere fehlet.

    Ich weiß es aber, eigene Schuld ists! Denn zu sehr
O Christus! häng' ich an dir, wiewohl Herakles Bruder
Und kühn bekenn' ich, du bist Bruder auch des Eviers, der
Die Todeslust der Völker aufhält und zerreißet den Fallstrik,
Fein sehen die Menschen, daß sie
Nicht gehn den Weg des Todes und hüten das Maas, daß einer
Etwas für sich ist, den Augenblik
Das Geschik der großen Zeit auch
Ihr Feuer fürchtend, treffen sie, und wo

As here among human kind
It lives, for very much like space
In youth the Heavenly in plenty
Is numerable, and yet, and yet
O you the life of the stars and all
You valiant sons of life,
One other I look for whom
Within your ranks I love,
Where hidden from the alien guest, from me
You keep the last of your kind,
The treasured gem of the house.

    My Master and Lord!
O you, my teacher,
Why did you keep
Away? And when
I asked among the ancients
The heroes and
The gods, why were you
Not there? And now my soul
Is full of sadness as though
You Heavenly yourselves excitedly cried
That if I serve one I
Must lack the other.

    And yet I know, it is my own fault. For too greatly
O Christ, I'm attached to you, although Heracles' brother,
And boldly I confess, you are the brother also of Evius, who
Restrains the death-wish of the peoples and breaks up the snare,
Well men can see now, so that
They do not go the way of death and keep the measure, so that
A man shall be something in himself and fear
The moment, the destiny of great eras and
Their fires no less, they strike, and where

Des Wegs ein anderes geht, da sehen sie
Auch, wo ein Geschik sei, machen aber
Das sicher, Menschen gleichend oder Gesezen.

Es entbrennet aber sein Zorn; daß nemlich
Das Zeichen die Erde berührt, allmälich
Aus Augen gekommen, als an einer Leiter.
Dißmal. Eigenwillig sonst, unmäßig
Gränzlos, daß der Menschen Hand
Anficht das Lebende, mehr auch, als sich schiket
Für einen Halbgott, heiliggeseztes übergeht
Der Entwurf. Seit nemlich böser Geist sich
Bemächtiget des glüklichen Altertums, unendlich,
Langher währt Eines, gesangsfeind, klanglos, das
In Maasen vergeht, des Sinnes gewaltsames. Ungebundenes aber
Hasset Gott. Fürbittend aber

Hält ihn der Tag von dieser Zeit, stillschaffend,
Des Weges gehend, die Blüthe der Jahre.
Und Kriegsgetön, und Geschichte der Helden unterhält,
                                        hartnäkig Geschik,
Die Sonne Christi, Gärten der Büßenden, und
Der Pilgrime Wandern und der Völker ihn, und des Wächters
Gesang und die Schrift
Des Barden oder Afrikaners. Ruhmloser auch
Geschik hält ihn, die an den Tag
Jezt erst recht kommen, das sind väterliche Fürsten. Denn
                                        viel ist der Stand
Gottgleicher, denn sonst. Denn Männern mehr
Gehöret das Licht. Nicht Jünglingen.
Das Vaterland auch. Nemlich frisch

Noch unerschöpfet und voll mit Loken.
Der Vater der Erde freuet nemlich sich deß

Another goes that way, they also see
Where there's a destiny, but make
It safe, resembling human beings or laws.

   His fury flares up, however; that is, so that
The sign shall touch the earth, gradually
Released from eyes, as though by a ladder.
This time. Wilful at other times, immoderately
Boundless, so that the hands of men
Impugn whatever is living, more than is fitting for
A demigod, the design transgresses beyond
What's divinely ordained. For since evil spirit
Has taken possession of happy antiquity, unendingly'
Long now one power has prevailed, hostile to song, without resonance,
That perishes in masses, the violence of the mind. But God hates
The unbound. Yet interceding

   The day of this age holds him back, creating in silence,
Proceeding on its way, the blossom of the years.
And uproar of war and history of heroes holds him,
                          stiff-necked destiny,
The sun of Christ, gardens of the penitent, and
The wandering of pilgrims and of the peoples, and the song
Of the watchman and the writings
Of the bard or the African. And the destiny
Of those unfamous holds him, who only now
Are really having their day, paternal princes, that is. For
                        now that rank
Is much more godlike than before. For more to men
Now light belongs, not to youths.
Our homeland also. For fresh

   Still unexhausted and full of curls.
For the Father of Earth is glad of this too,

Auch, daß Kinder sind, so bleibet eine Gewißheit
Des Guten. So auch freuet
Das ihn, daß eines bleibet.
Auch einige sind, gerettet, als
Auf schönen Inseln. Gelehrt sind die.
Versuchungen sind nemlich
Gränzlos an die gegangen.
Zahllose gefallen. Also gieng es, als
Der Erde Vater bereitet ständiges
In Stürmen der Zeit. Ist aber geendet.

That there are children, so that a certainty
Of goodness remains. So too
He is glad that one remains.
And some there are, saved, as though
On beautiful islands. Learnèd are these,
For they have been subject to
Temptations without end.
Countless fallen. So it went when
The Father of Earth prepared what is constant
In storms of the age. But that is ended.

PATMOS

DEM LANDGRAFEN VON HOMBURG

Nah ist
Und schwer zu fassen der Gott.
Wo aber Gefahr ist, wächst
Das Rettende auch.
Im Finstern wohnen
Die Adler und furchtlos gehn
Die Söhne der Alpen über den Abgrund weg
Auf leichtgebaueten Brüken.
Drum, da gehäuft sind rings
Die Gipfel der Zeit, und die Liebsten
Nah wohnen, ermattend auf
Getrenntesten Bergen,
So gieb unschuldig Wasser,
O Fittige gieb uns, treuesten Sinns
Hinüberzugehn und wiederzukehren.

So sprach ich, da entführte
Mich schneller, denn ich vermuthet
Und weit, wohin ich nimmer
Zu kommen gedacht, ein Genius mich
Vom eigenen Hauß'. Es dämmerten
Im Zwielicht, da ich gieng
Der schattige Wald
Und die sehnsüchtigen Bäche
Der Heimath; nimmer kannt' ich die Länder;
Doch bald, in frischem Glanze,
Geheimnißvoll
Im goldenen Rauche, blühte

PATMOS

FOR THE LANDGRAVE OF HOMBURG

Near is
And difficult to grasp, the God.
But where danger threatens
That which saves from it also grows.
In gloomy places dwell
The eagles, and fearless over
The chasm walk the sons of the Alps
On bridges lightly built.
Therefore, since round about
Are heaped the summits of Time
And the most loved live near, growing faint
On mountains most separate,
Give us innocent water,
O pinions give us, with minds most faithful
To cross over and to return.

So I spoke, when more swiftly
Than ever I had expected,
And far as I never thought
I should come, a Genius carried me
From my own house. There glimmered
In twilight, as I went,
The shadowy wood
And the yearning streams of
My homeland; no longer I knew those regions;
But soon, in a radiance fresh,
Mysteriously,
In the golden haze,

Schnellaufgewachsen,
Mit Schritten der Sonne,
Mit tausend Gipfeln duftend,

Mir Asia auf, und geblendet sucht'
Ich eines, das ich kennete, denn ungewohnt
War ich der breiten Gassen, wo herab
Vom Tmolus fährt
Der goldgeschmükte Pactol
Und Taurus stehet und Messogis,
Und voll von Blumen der Garten,
Ein stilles Feuer; aber im Lichte
Blüht hoch der silberne Schnee;
Und Zeug unsterblichen Lebens
An unzugangbaren Wänden
Uralt der Epheu wächst und getragen sind
Von lebenden Säulen, Cedern und Lorbeern
Die feierlichen,
Die göttlichgebauten Palläste.

Es rauschen aber um Asias Thore
Hinziehend da und dort
In ungewisser Meeresebene
Der schattenlosen Straßen genug,
Doch kennt die Inseln der Schiffer.
Und da ich hörte
Der nahegelegenen eine
Sei Patmos,
Verlangte mich sehr,
Dort einzukehren und dort
Der dunkeln Grotte zu nahn.
Denn nicht, wie Cypros,
Die quellenreiche, oder
Der anderen eine
Wohnt herrlich Patmos,

Quickly grown up,
With strides of the sun,
And fragrant with a thousand peaks,

Now Asia burst into flower for me, and dazzled
I looked for one thing there I might know, being unaccustomed
To those wide streets where down
From Tmolus drives
The golden-bedded Pactolus,
And Taurus stands, and Messogis,
And full of flowers the garden,
A quiet fire; but in the light, high up
There blossoms the silver snow;
And, witness to life immortal,
On inaccessible walls
Pristine the ivy grows, and supported
On living pillars, cedars and laurels,
There stand the festive,
The palaces built by gods.

But around Asia's gates there murmur,
Extending this way and that
In the uncertain plain of the sea,
Shadowless roads enough;
Yet the boatman knows the islands.
And when I heard
That of the near islands one
Was Patmos,
I greatly desired
There to be lodged, and there
To approach the dark grotto.
For not like Cyprus,
The rich in wellsprings,
Nor any of the others
Magnificently does Patmos dwell,

Gastfreundlich aber ist
Im ärmeren Haußе
Sie dennoch
Und wenn vom Schiffbruch oder klagend
Um die Heimath oder
Den abgeschiedenen Freund
Ihr nahet einer
Der Fremden, hört sie es gern, und ihre Kinder
Die Stimmen des heißen Hains,
Und wo der Sand fällt, und sich spaltet
Des Feldes Fläche, die Laute
Sie hören ihn und liebend tönt
Es wieder von den Klagen des Manns. So pflegte
Sie einst des gottgeliebten,
Des Sehers, der in seeliger Jugend war

   Gegangen mit
Dem Sohne des Höchsten, unzertrennlich, denn
Es liebte der Gewittertragende die Einfalt
Des Jüngers und es sahe der achtsame Mann
Das Angesicht des Gottes genau,
Da, beim Geheimnisse des Weinstoks, sie
Zusammensaßen, zu der Stunde des Gastmals,
Und in der großen Seele, ruhigahnend den Tod
Aussprach der Herr und die lezte Liebe, denn nie genug
Hatt' er von Güte zu sagen
Der Worte, damals, und zu erheitern, da
Ers sahe, das Zürnen der Welt.
Denn alles ist gut. Drauf starb er. Vieles wäre
Zu sagen davon. Und es sahn ihn, wie er siegend blikte
Den Freudigsten die Freunde noch zulezt,

   Doch trauerten sie, da nun
Es Abend worden, erstaunt,

Hospitable nonetheless
In her poorer house
She is,
And when, after shipwreck or lamenting for
His homeland or else for
The friend departed from him,
A stranger draws near
To her, she is glad to hear it, and her children,
The voices of the hot noonday copse,
And where the sand falls, and the field's
Flat surface cracks, the sounds—
These hear him, and lovingly all is loud
With the man's re-echoed lament. So once
She tended the God-beloved,
The seer who in blessèd youth

Had walked with
The son of the Highest, inseparable, for
The bearer of thunder loved the disciple's
Ingenuousness, and the attentive man
Saw the face of the God exactly
When over the mystery of the vine
They sat together at the banqueting hour
And in his great soul, calmly foreknowing,
The Lord pronounced death and the ultimate love, for never
He could find words enough
To say about kindness, then, and to soothe, when
He saw it, the wrath of the world.
For all things are good. After that he died. Much could
Be said of it. And the friends at the very last
Saw him, the gladdest, looking up triumphant,

Yet they were sad, now that
The evening had come, amazed,

Denn Großentschiedenes hatten in der Seele
Die Männer, aber sie liebten unter der Sonne
Das Leben und lassen wollten sie nicht
Vom Angesichte des Herrn
Und der Heimath. Eingetrieben war,
Wie Feuer im Eisen, das, und ihnen gieng
Zur Seite der Schatte des Lieben.
Drum sandt' er ihnen
Den Geist, und freilich bebte
Das Haus und die Wetter Gottes rollten
Ferndonnernd über
Die ahnenden Häupter, da, schwersinnend
Versammelt waren die Todeshelden,

    Izt, da er scheidend
Noch einmal ihnen erschien.
Denn izt erlosch der Sonne Tag
Der Königliche und zerbrach
Den geradestralenden,
Den Zepter, göttlichleidend, von selbst,
Denn wiederkommen sollt es
Zu rechter Zeit. Nicht wär es gut
Gewesen, später, und schroffabbrechend, untreu,
Der Menschen Werk, und Freude war es
Von nun an,
Zu wohnen in liebender Nacht, und bewahren
In einfältigen Augen, unverwandt
Abgründe der Weisheit. Und es grünen
Tief an den Bergen auch lebendige Bilder,

    Doch furchtbar ist, wie da und dort
Unendlich hin zerstreut das Lebende Gott.
Denn schon das Angesicht
Der theuern Freunde zu lassen

For the souls of these men contained
Things greatly predetermined, but under the sun they loved
This life and were loath to part from
The visible face of the Lord
And their homeland. Driven in,
Like fire into iron, was this, and beside them
The loved one's shadow walked.
Therefore he sent them
The Spirit, and mightily trembled
The house, and God's thunderstorms rolled
Distantly rumbling above
Their heads foreknowledge bowed, when deep in thought
Assembled were the heroes of death,

Now that, departing,
Once more he appeared to them.
For now the kingly one extinguished
The day of the sun and broke
The straightly beaming, the sceptre,
Divinely suffering, yet of his own free will,
For it was to come back when
The time was due. To have done so later
Would not have been good, and the work of men
Abruptly broken off, disloyally, and from now on
A joy it was
To dwell in loving Night and in fixed,
Ingenuous eyes to preserve
Abysses of wisdom. And low down at
The foot of mountains, too, will living images thrive,

Yet dreadful it is how here and there
Unendingly God disperses whatever lives.
For only to part from the sight
Of their dear friends

Und fernhin über die Berge zu gehn
Allein, wo zweifach
Erkannt, einstimmig
War himmlischer Geist; und nicht geweissagt war es, sondern
Die Loken ergriff es, gegenwärtig,
Wenn ihnen plözlich
Ferneilend zurük blikte
Der Gott und schwörend,
Damit er halte, wie an Seilen golden
Gebunden hinfort
Das Böse nennend, sie die Hände sich reichten —

Wenn aber stirbt alsdenn
An dem am meisten
Die Schönheit hieng, daß an der Gestalt
Ein Wunder war und die Himmlischen gedeutet
Auf ihn, und wenn, ein Räthsel ewig füreinander
Sie sich nicht fassen können
Einander, die zusammenlebten
Im Gedächtniß, und nicht den Sand nur oder
Die Weiden es hinwegnimmt und die Tempel
Ergreifft, wenn die Ehre
Des Halbgotts und der Seinen
Verweht und selber sein Angesicht
Der Höchste wendet
Darob, daß nirgend ein
Unsterbliches mehr am Himmel zu sehn ist oder
Auf grüner Erde, was ist diß?

Es ist der Wurf des Säemanns, wenn er faßt
Mit der Schaufel den Waizen,
Und wirft, dem Klaren zu, ihn schwingend über die Tenne.
Ihm fällt die Schaale vor den Füßen, aber
Ans Ende kommet das Korn,

And far across the mountains to go
Alone, when doubly
Perceived, heavenly spirit before had been
Unanimous; and not predicted was this,
But seized them by the hair, on the instant,
When suddenly the God
Far off in haste looked back
At them, and vowing,
So that he would stay, from now on goldenly
Bound fast as to ropes,
Calling the evil by name, they linked hands—

But when thereupon he dies
To whom beauty most adhered, so that
A miracle was wrought in his person and
The Heavenly had pointed at him,
And when, an enigma to one another
For ever, they cannot understand
One another who lived together
Conjoined by remembrance, and not only
The sand or the willows it takes away,
And seizes the temples, when even
The demigod's honour and that of his friends
Is blown away by the wind, and the Highest
Himself averts his face
Because nowhere now
An immortal is to be seen in the skies or
On our green earth, what is this?

It is the sower's cast when he scoops up
The wheat in his shovel
And throws it, towards clear space, swinging it over the thrashing-floor.
The husk falls at his feet, but
The grain reaches its end,

Und nicht ein Übel ists, wenn einiges
Verloren gehet und von der Rede
Verhallet der lebendige Laut,
Denn göttliches Werk auch gleichet dem unsern,
Nicht alles will der Höchste zumal.
Zwar Eisen träget der Schacht,
Und glühende Harze der Aetna,
So hätt' ich Reichtum,
Ein Bild zu bilden, und ähnlich
Zu schaun, wie er gewesen, den Christ,

Wenn aber einer spornte sich selbst,
Und traurig redend, unterweges, da ich wehrlos wäre
Mich überfiele, daß ich staunt' und von dem Gotte
Das Bild nachahmen möcht' ein Knecht —
Im Zorne sichtbar sah' ich einmal
Des Himmels Herrn, nicht, daß ich seyn sollt etwas, sondern
Zu lernen. Gütig sind sie, ihr Verhaßtestes aber ist,
So lange sie herrschen, das Falsche, und es gilt
Dann Menschliches unter Menschen nicht mehr.
Denn sie nicht walten, es waltet aber
Unsterblicher Schiksaal und es wandelt ihr Werk
Von selbst, und eilend geht es zu Ende.
Wenn nemlich höher gehet himmlischer
Triumphgang, wird genennet, der Sonne gleich
Von Starken der frohlokende Sohn des Höchsten,

Ein Loosungszeichen, und hier ist der Stab
Des Gesanges, niederwinkend,
Denn nichts ist gemein. Die Todten weket
Er auf, die noch gefangen nicht
Vom Rohen sind. Es warten aber
Der scheuen Augen viele
Zu schauen das Licht. Nicht wollen

And there's no harm if some of it
Is lost, and of the speech
The living sound dies away,
For the work of gods, too, is like our own,
Not all things at once does the Highest intend.
The pit bears iron, though,
And glowing resins Etna,
And so I should have wealth
With which to form an image and see
The Christ as he truly was,

    But if someone spurred himself on
And, talking sadly, on the road, when I was
Defenceless, attacked me, so that amazed I tried
To copy the God's own image, I, a servant—
In anger visible once I saw
The Lord of Heaven, not that I should be something, but
To learn. Benign they are, but what they most abhor,
While their reign lasts, is falsehood, and then
What's human no longer counts among human kind.
For they do not govern, the fate
It is of immortals that governs, and their work
Proceeds by its own force and hurrying seeks its end.
For when heavenly triumph goes higher
The jubilant son of the Highest
Is called like the sun by the strong,

    A secret token, and here is the wand
Of song, signalling downward,
For nothing is common. The dead
He reawakens whom coarseness has not
Made captive yet. But many timid eyes
Are waiting to see the light.
They are reluctant to flower

Am scharfen Strale sie blühn,
Wiewohl den Muth der goldene Zaum hält.
Wenn aber, als
Von schwellenden Augenbraunen
Der Welt vergessen
Stillleuchtende Kraft aus heiliger Schrift fällt, mögen
Der Gnade sich freuend, sie
Am stillen Blike sich üben.

Und wenn die Himmlischen jezt
So, wie ich glaube, mich lieben
Wie viel mehr Dich,
Denn Eines weiß ich,
Daß nemlich der Wille
Des ewigen Vaters viel
Dir gilt. Still ist sein Zeichen
Am donnernden Himmel. Und Einer stehet darunter
Sein Leben lang. Denn noch lebt Christus.
Es sind aber die Helden, seine Söhne
Gekommen all und heilige Schriften
Von ihm und den Bliz erklären
Die Thaten der Erde bis izt,
Ein Wettlauf unaufhaltsam. Er ist aber dabei. Denn seine
Werke sind
Ihm alle bewußt von jeher.

Zu lang, zu lang schon ist
Die Ehre der Himmlischen unsichtbar.
Denn fast die Finger müssen sie
Uns führen und schmählich
Entreißt das Herz uns eine Gewalt.
Denn Opfer will der Himmlischen jedes,
Wenn aber eines versäumt ward,
Nie hat es Gutes gebracht.

Beneath the searing beam, though it is
The golden bridle that curbs their courage.
But when, as if
By swelling eyebrows made
Oblivious of the world
A quietly shining strength falls from holy scripture,
Rejoicing in grace, they
May practise upon the quiet gaze.

    And if the Heavenly now
Love me as I believe,
How much more you
They surely love,
For one thing I know:
The eternal Father's will
Means much to you. Now silent is
His sign on thundering heaven. And there is one who stands
Beneath it his whole life long. For Christ lives yet.
But all the heroes, his sons,
Have come, and holy scriptures
About him, and lightning is explained by
The deeds of the world until now,
A race that cannot be stopped. But he is present in it. For known
To him are all his works from the beginning.

    Too long, too long now
The honour of the Heavenly has been invisible.
For almost they must guide
Our fingers, and shamefully
A power is wresting our hearts from us.
For every one of the Heavenly wants sacrifices, and
When one of these was omitted
No good ever came of it.

Wir haben gedienet der Mutter Erd'
Und haben jüngst dem Sonnenlichte gedient,
Unwissend, der Vater aber liebt,
Der über allen waltet,
Am meisten, daß gepfleget werde
Der veste Buchstab, und bestehendes gut
Gedeutet. Dem folgt deutscher Gesang.

We have served Mother Earth
And lately have served the sunlight,
Unwittingly, but what the Father
Who reigns over all loves most
Is that the solid letter
Be given scrupulous care, and the existing
Be well interpreted. This German song observes.

PATMOS

DEM LANDGRAFEN VON HOMBURG

Bruchstücke der späteren Fassung

Voll Güt' ist; keiner aber fasset
Allein Gott.
Wo aber Gefahr ist, wächst
Das Rettende auch.
Im Finstern wohnen
Die Adler, und furchtlos gehn
Die Söhne der Alpen über den Abgrund weg
Auf leichtgebaueten Brüken.
Drum, da gehäuft sind rings, um Klarheit,
Die Gipfel der Zeit,
Und die Liebsten nahe wohnen, ermattend auf
Getrenntesten Bergen,
So gieb unschuldig Wasser,
O Fittige gieb uns, treuesten Sinns
Hinüberzugehn und wiederzukehren.

So sprach ich, da entführte
Mich künstlicher, denn ich vermuthet
Und weit, wohin ich nimmer
Zu kommen gedacht, ein Genius mich
Vom eigenen Hauß'. Es kleideten sich
Im Zwielicht, Menschen ähnlich, da ich gieng
Der schattige Wald
Und die sehnsüchtigen Bäche
Der Heimath; nimmer kannt' ich die Länder.
Viel aber mitgelitten haben wir, viel Maale. So
In frischem Glanze, geheimnißvoll,

PATMOS

Fragments of the Later Version

   Most kind is; but no one by himself
Can grasp God.
But where danger threatens
That which saves from it also grows.
In gloomy places dwell
The eagles, and fearless over
The chasm walk the sons of the Alps
On bridges lightly built.
Therefore, since round about are heaped, around clearness,
The summits of Time,
And the most loved live near, growing faint
On mountains most separate,
Give us innocent water,
O pinions give us, with minds most faithful
To cross over and to return.

   So I spoke when more ingeniously
Than ever I had expected
And far as I never thought
I should come, a Genius carried me
From my own house. There clothed themselves,
Like men, in the twilight, as I went,
The shadowy wood
And the yearning streams of
My homeland; no longer I knew those regions.
Yet much we have suffered with them, many times.
So, in a radiance fresh, mysteriously,

In goldenem Rauche blühte
Schnellaufgewachsen,
Mit Schritten der Sonne,
Von tausend Tischen duftend, jezt,

Mir Asia auf und geblendet ganz
Sucht' eins ich, das ich kennete, denn ungewohnt
War ich der breiten Gassen, wo herab
Vom Tmolus fährt
Der goldgeschmükte Pactol
Und Taurus stehet und Messogis,
Und schläfrig fast von Blumen der Garten,

O Insel des Lichts!
Denn wenn erloschen ist der Ruhm die Augenlust und gehalten nicht mehr
Von Menschen, schattenlos, die Pfade zweifeln und die Bäume,
Und Reiche, das Jugendland der Augen sind vergangen
Athletischer,
Im Ruin,   und Unschuld angeborne
Zerrissen ist. Von Gott aus nemlich kommt gediegen
Und gehet das Gewissen, Offenbarung, die Hand des Herrn
Reich winkt aus richtendem Himmel, dann und eine Zeit ist
Untheilbar Gesez, und Amt, und die Hände
Zu erheben, das, und das Niederfallen
Böser Gedanken, los, zu ordnen. Grausam nemlich hasset
Allwissende Stirnen Gott. Rein aber bestand

In the golden haze
Quickly grown up,
With strides of the sun,
And fragrant with a thousand tables,

   Now, Asia burst into flower for me, and wholly dazzled
I looked for one thing there I might know, being unaccustomed
To those wide streets where down
From Tmolus drives
The golden-bedded Pactolus,
And Taurus stands, and Messogis,
And drowsy almost with flowers the garden,

   O island of light!
For when extinguished is fame, the delight in seeing, and no longer maintained
By human kind, shadowless, the paths succumb to doubt, and the trees,
And kingdoms, the youthful land of eyes, are perished,
More athletic
In ruin,   and inborn innocence
Is torn to shreds. For from God unalloyed
Does conscience come and go, revelation, the hand of the Lord
Richly beckons from judging Heaven, then and for a time there
Is indivisible law, and office, and hands to
Be raised, both this and to control
The falling of evil thoughts, loose. For cruelly
God hates omniscient brows. But pure

Auf ungebundnem Boden Johannes. Wenn einer
Für irrdisches prophetisches Wort erklärt

Vom Jordan und von Nazareth
Und fern vom See, an Capernaum,
Und Galiläa die Lüfte, und von Cana.
Eine Weile bleib ich, sprach er. Also mit Tropfen
Stillt er das Seufzen des Lichts, das durstigem Wild
War ähnlich in den Tagen, als um Syrien
Jammert der getödteten Kindlein heimatliche
Anmuth im Sterben, und das Haupt
Des Täuffers gepflükt, war unverwelklicher Schrift gleich
Sichtbar auf weilender Schüssel. Wie Feuer
Sind Stimmen Gottes. Schwer ists aber
Im Großen zu behalten das Große.
Nicht eine Waide. Daß einer
Bleibet im Anfang. Jezt aber
Geht dieses wieder, wie sonst.

Johannes. Christus. Diesen möcht'
Ich singen, gleich dem Herkules, oder
Der Insel, welche vestgehalten und gerettet, erfrischend
Die benachbarte mit kühlen Meereswassern aus der Wüste
Der Fluth, der weiten, Peleus. Das geht aber
Nicht. Anders ists ein Schiksaal. Wundervoller.
Reicher, zu singen. Unabsehlich
Seit jenem die Fabel. Und jezt

On a site unbound did John remain. When someone
Declares that a prophetic word is earthly

From Jordan and from Nazareth
And far from the lake, at Capernaum,
And Galilee the breezes, and from Canaan.
A little while I shall stay, he said. So with drops
He quenched the sighing of the light that was
Like thirsty wild beasts in those days, when for Syria
Lamented the native grace in dying of
Small children killed, and the Baptist's head,
Just picked, was visible like an unwithering script
On the abiding platter. Like fire
Are voices of God. Yet it is hard
In great events to preserve what is great.
Not a pasture. So that one shall
Abide in the beginning. But now
This goes on again, as before.

John. Christ. This latter now I wish
To sing, like Hercules or the island which
Was held and saved, refreshing
The neighbouring one with cool sea waters drawn
From ocean's desert, the vast, Peleus. But that's
Impossible. A fate is different. More marvellous.
More rich to sing. Immeasurable
The fable ever since. And now

Möcht' ich die Fahrt der Edelleute nach
Jerusalem, und das Leiden irrend in Canossa,
Und den Heinrich singen. Daß aber
Der Muth nicht selber mich aussezze. Begreiffen müssen
Diß wir zuvor. Wie Morgenluft sind nemlich die Nahmen
Seit Christus. Werden Träume. Fallen, wie Irrtum
Auf das Herz und tödtend, wenn nicht einer

   Erwäget, was sie sind und begreift.
Es sah aber der achtsame Mann
Das Angesicht des Gottes,
Damals, da, beim Geheimnisse des Weinstoks sie
Zusammensaßen, zu der Stunde des Gastmals,
Und in der großen Seele, wohlauswählend, den Tod
Aussprach der Herr, und die lezte Liebe, denn nie genug
Hatt er, von Güte, zu sagen
Der Worte, damals, und zu bejahn bejahendes. Aber sein Licht war
Tod. Denn karg ist das Zürnen der Welt.
Das aber erkannt' er. Alles ist gut. Drauf starb er.
Es sahen aber, gebükt, deß ungeachtet, vor Gott die Gestalt
Des Verläugnenden, wie wenn
Ein Jahrhundert sich biegt, nachdenklich, in der Freude der Wahrheit
Noch zulezt die Freunde,

   Doch trauerten sie, da nun
Es Abend worden. Nemlich rein
Zu seyn, ist Geschik, ein Leben, das ein Herz hat,
Vor solchem Angesicht', und dauert über die Hälfte.
Zu meiden aber ist viel. Zu viel aber
Der Liebe, wo Anbetung ist,
Ist gefahrreich, triffet am meisten. Jene wollten aber
Vom Angesichte des Herrn
Nicht lassen und der Heimath. Eingeboren
Wie Feuer war in dem Eisen das, und ihnen

I wish to sing the journey of the nobles to
Jerusalem, and anguish wandering at Canossa,
And Heinrich himself. If only
My very courage does not expose me. This first we
Must understand. For like morning air are the names
Since Christ. Become dreams. Fall on the heart
Like error, and killing, if one does not

   Consider what they are and understand.
But the attentive man saw
The face of God,
At that time, when over the mystery of the vine
They sat together, at the banqueting hour,
And in his great soul, carefully choosing, the Lord
Pronounced death, and the ultimate love, for never
He could find words enough
To say about kindness, then, and to affirm the affirmative. But his light was
Death. For niggardly is the wrath of the world.
Yet this he recognized. All is good. Thereupon he died.
But nevertheless, bowed down, the friends at the very last
Before God saw the denier's presence, as when
A century bends, thoughtfully, in
The joy of truth,

   Yet they were sad, now that
The evening had come. For to
Be pure is a skill, a life that has a heart, in
The presence of such a face, and outlasts the middle.
But much is to be avoided. Too much
Of love, though, where there is idolatry,
Is dangerous, strikes home most. But those men were loath
To part from the face of the Lord
And from their homeland. Inborn
Like fire in iron was this, and beside them

Zur Seite gieng, wie eine Seuche, der Schatte des Lieben.
Drum sandt er ihnen
Den Geist, und freilich bebte
Das Haus und die Wetter Gottes rollten
Ferndonnernd, Männer schaffend, wie wenn Drachenzähne,
                              prächtigen Schiksaals,

Walked, like a plague, the loved one's shadow.
Therefore he sent them
The Spirit, and mightily trembled
The house and God's thunderstorms rolled
Distantly rumbling, creating men, as when dragons' teeth,
                                        of glorious fate,

ANDENKEN

Der Nordost wehet,
Der liebste unter den Winden
Mir, weil er feurigen Geist
Und gute Fahrt verheißet den Schiffern.
Geh aber nun und grüße
Die schöne Garonne,
Und die Gärten von Bourdeaux
Dort, wo am scharfen Ufer
Hingehet der Steg und in den Strom
Tief fällt der Bach, darüber aber
Hinschauet ein edel Paar
Von Eichen und Silberpappeln;

Noch denket das mir wohl und wie
Die breiten Gipfel neiget
Der Ulmwald, über die Mühl',
Im Hofe aber wächset ein Feigenbaum.
An Feiertagen gehn
Die braunen Frauen daselbst
Auf seidnen Boden,
Zur Märzenzeit,
Wenn gleich ist Nacht und Tag,
Und über langsamen Stegen,
Von goldenen Träumen schwer,
Einwiegende Lüfte ziehen.

Es reiche aber,
Des dunkeln Lichtes voll,
Mir einer den duftenden Becher,

REMEMBRANCE

The north-easterly blows,
Of winds the dearest to me
Because a fiery spirit
And happy voyage it promises mariners.
But go now, go and greet
The beautiful Garonne
And the gardens of Bordeaux,
To where on the rugged bank
The path runs and into the river
Deep falls the brook, but above them
A noble pair of oaks
And white poplars looks out;

Still well I remember this, and how
The elm wood with its great leafy tops
Inclines, towards the mill,
But in the courtyard a fig-tree grows.
On holidays there too
The brown women walk
On silken ground,
In the month of March,
When night and day are equal
And over slow footpaths,
Heavy with golden dreams,
Lulling breezes drift.

But someone pass me
The fragrant cup
Full of the dark light,

Damit ich ruhen möge; denn süß
Wär' unter Schatten der Schlummer.
Nicht ist es gut,
Seellos von sterblichen
Gedanken zu seyn. Doch gut
Ist ein Gespräch und zu sagen
Des Herzens Meinung, zu hören viel
Von Tagen der Lieb',
Und Thaten, welche geschehen.

Wo aber sind die Freunde? Bellarmin
Mit dem Gefährten? Mancher
Trägt Scheue, an die Quelle zu gehn;
Es beginnet nemlich der Reichtum
Im Meere. Sie,
Wie Mahler, bringen zusammen
Das Schöne der Erd' und verschmähn
Den geflügelten Krieg nicht, und
Zu wohnen einsam, jahrlang, unter
Dem entlaubten Mast, wo nicht die Nacht durchglänzen
Die Feiertage der Stadt,
Und Saitenspiel und eingeborener Tanz nicht.

Nun aber sind zu Indiern
Die Männer gegangen,
Dort an der luftigen Spiz'
An Traubenbergen, wo herab
Die Dordogne kommt,
Und zusammen mit der prächt'gen
Garonne meerbreit
Ausgehet der Strom. Es nehmet aber
Und giebt Gedächtniß die See,
Und die Lieb' auch heftet fleißig die Augen,
Was bleibet aber, stiften die Dichter.

So that I may rest now; for sweet
It would be to drowse amid shadows.
It is not good
To be soulless
With mortal thoughts. But good
Is converse, and to speak
The heart's opinion, to hear many tales
About the days of love
And deeds that have occurred.

But where are the friends? Where Bellarmine
And his companions? Many a man
Is shy of going to the source;
For wealth begins in
The sea. And they,
Like painters, bring together
The beautiful things of the earth
And do not disdain winged war, and
To live in solitude, for years, beneath the
Defoliate mast, where through the night do not gleam
The city's holidays
Nor music of strings, nor indigenous dancing.

But now to Indians
Those men have gone,
There on the airy peak
On grape-covered hills, where down
The Dordogne comes
And together with the glorious
Garonne as wide as the sea
The current sweeps out. But it is the sea
That takes and gives remembrance,
And love no less keeps eyes attentively fixed,
But what is lasting the poets provide.

DER ISTER

Jezt komme, Feuer!
Begierig sind wir
Zu schauen den Tag,
Und wenn die Prüfung
Ist durch die Knie gegangen,
Mag einer spüren das Waldgeschrei.
Wir singen aber vom Indus her
Fernangekommen und
Vom Alpheus, lange haben
Das Schikliche wir gesucht,
Nicht ohne Schwingen mag
Zum Nächsten einer greifen
Geradezu
Und kommen auf die andere Seite.
Hier aber wollen wir bauen.
Denn Ströme machen urbar
Das Land. Wenn nemlich Kräuter wachsen
Und an denselben gehn
Im Sommer zu trinken die Thiere,
So gehn auch Menschen daran.

Man nennet aber diesen den Ister.
Schön wohnt er. Es brennet der Säulen Laub,
Und reget sich. Wild stehn
Sie aufgerichtet, untereinander; darob
Ein zweites Maas, springt vor
Von Felsen das Dach. So wundert
Mich nicht, daß er
Den Herkules zu Gaste geladen,

THE ISTER

Now come, fire!
We are impatient
To look upon Day,
And when the trial
Has passed through the knees
One may perceive the cries in the wood.
But, as for us, we sing from the Indus,
Arrived from afar, and
From the Alpheus, long we
Have sought what is fitting,
Not without wings may one
Reach out for that which is nearest
Directly
And get to the other side.
But here we wish to build.
For rivers make arable
The land. For when herbs are growing
And to the same in summer
The animals go to drink,
There too will human kind go.

This one, however, is called the Ister.
Beautifully he dwells. The pillars' foliage burns,
And stirs. Wildly they stand
Supporting one another; above,
A second measure, juts out
The roof of rocks. No wonder, therefore,
I say, this river
Invited Hercules,

Fernglänzend, am Olympos drunten,
Da der, sich Schatten zu suchen
Vom heißen Isthmos kam,
Denn voll des Muthes waren
Daselbst sie, es bedarf aber, der Geister wegen,
Der Kühlung auch. Darum zog jener lieber
An die Wasserquellen hieher und gelben Ufer,
Hoch duftend oben, und schwarz
Vom Fichtenwald, wo in den Tiefen
Ein Jäger gern lustwandelt
Mittags, und Wachstum hörbar ist
An harzigen Bäumen des Isters,

　　Der scheinet aber fast
Rükwärts zu gehen und
Ich mein, er müsse kommen
Von Osten.
Vieles wäre
Zu sagen davon. Und warum hängt er
An den Bergen gerad? Der andre
Der Rhein ist seitwärts
Hinweggegangen. Umsonst nicht gehn
Im Troknen die Ströme. Aber wie? Ein Zeichen braucht es
Nichts anderes, schlecht und recht, damit es Sonn
Und Mond trag' im Gemüth', untrennbar,
Und fortgeh, Tag und Nacht auch, und
Die Himmlischen warm sich fühlen aneinander.
Darum sind jene auch
Die Freude des Höchsten. Denn wie käm er
Herunter? Und wie Hertha grün,
Sind sie die Kinder des Himmels. Aber allzugedultig
Scheint der mir, nicht
Freier, und fast zu spotten. Nemlich wenn

Distantly gleaming, down by Olympus,
When he, to look for shadows,
Came up from the sultry isthmus,
For full of courage they were
In that place, but, because of the spirits,
There's need of coolness too. That is why that hero
Preferred to come here to the wellsprings and yellow banks,
Highly fragrant on top, and black
With fir woods, in whose depths
A huntsman loves to amble
At noon, and growth is audible
In resinous trees of the Ister,

    Yet almost this river seems
To travel backwards and
I think it must come from
The East.
Much could
Be said about this. And why does
It cling to the mountains, straight? The other,
The Rhine, has gone away
Sideways. Not for nothing rivers flow
Through dry land. But how? A sign is needed,
Nothing else, plain and honest, so that
Sun and moon it may bear in mind, inseparable,
And go away, day and night no less, and
The Heavenly feel warm one beside the other.
That also is why these are
The joy of the Highest. For how
Would he get down? And like Hertha green
They are the children of Heaven. But all too patient
He seems to me, not
More free, and nearly derisive. For when

Angehen soll der Tag
In der Jugend, wo er zu wachsen
Anfängt, es treibet ein anderer da
Hoch schon die Pracht, und Füllen gleich
In den Zaum knirscht er, und weithin hören
Das Treiben die Lüfte,
Ist der zufrieden;
Es brauchet aber Stiche der Fels
Und Furchen die Erd',
Unwirthbar wär es, ohne Weile;
Was aber jener thuet der Strom,
Weis niemand.

Day is due to begin
In youth, where it starts
To grow, another already there
Drives high the splendour, and like foals
He grinds the bit, and far off the breezes
Can hear the commotion,
If he is contented;
But the rock needs incisions
And the earth needs furrows,
Would be desolate else, unabiding;
Yet what that one does, the river,
Nobody knows.

MNEMOSYNE

Dritte Fassung

Reif sind, in Feuer getaucht, gekochet
Die Frücht und auf der Erde geprüfet und ein Gesez ist
Daß alles hineingeht, Schlangen gleich,
Prophetisch, träumend auf
Den Hügeln des Himmels. Und vieles
Wie auf den Schultern eine
Last von Scheitern ist
Zu behalten. Aber bös sind
Die Pfade. Nemlich unrecht,
Wie Rosse, gehn die gefangenen
Element' und alten
Geseze der Erd. Und immer
Ins Ungebundene gehet eine Sehnsucht. Vieles aber ist
Zu behalten. Und Noth die Treue.
Vorwärts aber und rükwärts wollen wir
Nicht sehn. Uns wiegen lassen, wie
Auf schwankem Kahne der See.

Wie aber liebes? Sonnenschein
Am Boden sehen wir und trokenen Staub
Und heimatlich die Schatten der Wälder und es blühet
An Dächern der Rauch, bei alter Krone
Der Thürme, friedsam; gut sind nemlich
Hat gegenredend die Seele
Ein Himmlisches verwundet, die Tageszeichen.
Denn Schnee, wie Majenblumen
Das Edelmüthige, wo
Es seie, bedeutend, glänzet auf

498

MNEMOSYNE

Third Version

Ripe are, dipped in fire, cooked
The fruits and tried on the earth, and it is law,
Prophetic, that all must enter in
Like serpents, dreaming on
The mounds of heaven. And much
As on the shoulders a
Load of logs must be
Retained. But evil are
The paths, for crookedly
Like horses go the imprisoned
Elements and ancient laws
Of the earth. And always
There is a yearning that seeks the unbound. But much
Must be retained. And loyalty is needed.
Forward, however, and back we will
Not look. Be lulled and rocked as
On a swaying skiff of the sea.

But how, my dear one? On the ground
Sunshine we see and the dry dust
And, a native sight, the shadows of forests, and on rooftops
There blossoms smoke, near ancient crests
Of the turrets, peaceable; for good indeed
When, contradicting, the soul
Has wounded one of the Heavenly, are the signs of day.
For snow, like lilies of the valley
By indicating where
The noble-minded is, shines brightly

Der grünen Wiese
Der Alpen, hälftig, da, vom Kreuze redend, das
Gesezt ist unterwegs einmal
Gestorbenen, auf hoher Straß
Ein Wandersmann geht zornig,
Fern ahnend mit
Dem andern, aber was ist diß?

  Am Feigenbaum ist mein
Achilles mir gestorben,
Und Ajax liegt
An den Grotten der See,
An Bächen, benachbart dem Skamandros.
An Schläfen Sausen einst, nach
Der unbewegten Salamis steter
Gewohnheit, in der Fremd', ist groß
Ajax gestorben
Patroklos aber in des Königes Harnisch. Und es starben
Noch andere viel. Am Kithäron aber lag
Elevtherä, der Mnemosyne Stadt. Der auch als
Ablegte den Mantel Gott, das abendliche nachher löste
Die Loken. Himmlische nemlich sind
Unwillig, wenn einer nicht die Seele schonend sich
Zusammengenommen, aber er muß doch; dem
Gleich fehlet die Trauer.

On the green meadow
Of the Alps, half melted, where
Discoursing of the cross which once was placed
There on the wayside for the dead,
High up, in anger, distantly divining
A traveller walks
With the other, but what is this?

 Beside the fig-tree
My Achilles has died and is lost to me,
And Ajax lies
Beside the grottoes of the sea,
Beside brooks that neighbour Scamandros.
Of a rushing noise in his temples once,
According to the changeless custom of
Unmoved Salamis, in foreign parts
Great Ajax died,
Not so Patroclus, dead in the King's own armour.
And many others died. But by Cithaeron there stood
Eleutherae, Mnemosyne's town. From her also
When God laid down his festive cloak, soon after did
The powers of Evening sever a lock of hair. For the Heavenly, when
Someone has failed to collect his soul, to spare it,
Are angry, for still he must; like him
Here mourning is at fault.

FRAGMENTS OF OTHER HYMNS

(1800-1805)

DEUTSCHER GESANG

Wenn der Morgen trunken begeisternd heraufgeht
Und der Vogel sein Lied beginnt,
Und Stralen der Strom wirft, und rascher hinab
Die rauhe Bahn geht über den Fels,
Weil ihn die Sonne gewärmet.

Und der
Verlangend in anders Land
Die Jünglinge

Und das Thor erwacht und der Marktplaz,
Und von heiligen Flammen des Heerds
Der röthliche Duft steigt, dann schweigt er allein,
Dann hält er still im Busen das Herz,
Und sinnt in einsamer Halle.

Doch wenn

       dann sizt im tiefen Schatten,
Wenn über dem Haupt die Ulme säuselt,
Am kühlathmenden Bache der deutsche Dichter
Und singt, wenn er des heiligen nüchternen Wassers
Genug getrunken, fernhin lauschend in die Stille,
Den Seelengesang.
Und noch, noch ist er des Geistes zu voll,
Und die reine Seele

Bis zürnend er

GERMAN SONG

When drunkenly inspiring the morning rises
And the bird begins his tune,
And the river flashes beams and more quickly takes
Its rough course over the rock,
Because the sun has warmed it.

And the
Longing to go to another land
The youths

And the gate awakens and the market-place,
And from holy flames of the hearth
The reddish odour rises, then he alone is silent,
Then quiet in his bosom he keeps his heart
And ponders in the solitary hall.

But when

        then in the deep shade, when
Above his head the elm-tree rustles,
By the stream that breathes out coolness the German poet sits
And sings, when of the hallowed sober water
Enough he has drunk, listening far out into silence,
The song of the soul.
And still, still his mind is too full of thought,
And his pure soul

Until in anger he

Und es glühet ihm die Wange vor Schaam,
Unheilig jeder Laut des Gesangs.

Doch lächeln über des Mannes Einfalt
Die Gestirne, wenn vom Orient her
Weissagend über den Bergen unseres Volks
Sie verweilen
Und wie des Vaters Hand ihm über den Loken geruht,
In Tagen der Kindheit,
So krönet, daß er schaudernd es fühlt
Ein Seegen das Haupt des Sängers,
Wenn dich, der du
Um deiner Schöne willen, bis heute,
Nahmlos geblieben o göttlichster!
O guter Geist des Vaterlands
Sein Wort im Liede dich nennet.

And his cheeks are flushed with shame,
Unholy every note of his song.

   Yet the planets smile at the man's
Simplicity when, come from the East,
They linger prophesying above
Our people's mountains
And as his father's hand had rested upon his locks
In childhood days,
A blessing, so that he feels a shiver,
Now crowns the singer's head,
When you that for
Your beauty's sake, till today, have been
Kept nameless, O most divine,
Good spirit of our homeland,
When you his word names in song.

WIE VÖGEL LANGSAM ZIEHN...

Wie Vögel langsam ziehn
Es bliket voraus
Der Fürst und kühl wehn
An die Brust ihm die Begegnisse wenn
Es um ihn schweiget, hoch
In der Luft, reich glänzend aber hinab
Das Gut ihm liegt der Länder, und mit ihm sind
Das erstemal siegforschend die Jungen.
Er aber mäßiget mit
Der Fittige Schlag.

AS SLOWLY BIRDS MIGRATE...

As slowly birds migrate
He looks ahead,
The prince, and coolly blows
Against his breast all that he meets with when
There's silence round about him, high
Up in the air, but richly shining below him
Lies his estate of regions, and with him, for
The first time seeking victory, are the young.
But with his wingbeats
He moderates.

HEIMATH

Und niemand weiß

Indessen laß mich wandeln
Und wilde Beeren pflüken
Zu löschen die Liebe zu dir
An deinen Pfaden, o Erd'

Hier wo — — —
　　　　　und Rosendornen
Und süße Linden duften neben
Den Buchen, des Mittags, wenn im falben Kornfeld
Das Wachstum rauscht, an geradem Halm,
Und den Naken die Ähre seitwärts beugt
Dem Herbste gleich, jezt aber unter hohem
Gewölbe der Eichen, da ich sinn
Und aufwärts frage, der Glokenschlag
Mir wohlbekannt
Fernher tönt, goldenklingend, um die Stunde, wenn
Der Vogel wieder wacht. So gehet es wohl.

HOME

And no one knows

But meanwhile let me walk
And pick wild berries
To quench my love for you
Upon your paths, O Earth

Here where
                    and thorns of roses
And sweet lime-trees give out their fragrance
Beside the beeches, at noon, when in the yellowish cornfield
There is a whisper of growth, by the straight stalk,
And the ear inclines its neck to one side
Like autumn, but now beneath
The oaks' high vault, where I ponder
And question heavenward, the stroke of the bell,
Familiar to me,
Rings out from afar, with a golden ring, at the hour when
The bird's awake once more. Then all is well.

WENN NEMLICH DER REBE SAFT...

Wenn nemlich der Rebe Saft,
Das milde Gewächs suchet Schatten
Und die Traube wächset unter dem kühlen
Gewölbe der Blätter,
Den Männern eine Stärke,
Wohl aber duftend den Jungfraun,
Und Bienen,
Wenn sie, vom Wohlgeruche
Des Frühlings trunken, der Geist
Der Sonne rühret, irren ihr nach
Die Getriebenen, wenn aber
Ein Stral brennt, kehren sie
Mit Gesumm, vielahnend
            darob
        die Eiche rauschet,

FOR WHEN THE GRAPE-VINE'S SAP . . .

For when the grape-vine's sap,
That gentle plant, looks for shade
And the grape grows beneath the cool
Involutions of the leaves,
To men a source of strength,
But to young women pleasantly fragrant,
And bees
When, drunken with the fragrance
Of Spring, they are stirred
By the spirit of the sun,
Driven on, they fumble for it,
But when a ray burns,
Buzzing, they turn back,
Divining much
                    above it
        the oak-tree rustles,

AUF FALBEM LAUBE...

Auf falbem Laube ruhet
Die Traube, des Weines Hoffnung, also ruhet auf der Wange
Der Schatten von dem goldenen Schmuk, der hängt
Am Ohre der Jungfrau.

Und ledig soll ich bleiben
Leicht fanget aber sich
In der Kette, die
Es abgerissen, das Kälblein.

Fleißig

Es liebet aber der Sämann
Zu sehen eine,
Des Tages schlafend über
Dem Strikstrumpf.

Nicht will wohllauten
Der deutsche Mund
Aber lieblich
Am stechenden Bart rauschen
Die Küsse.

ON FALLOW FOLIAGE...

On fallow foliage rests
The grape, the hope of wine, and so on the cheek rests
The shadow of the gold ornament that hangs
On the young woman's ear.

And I must not get married
Yet easily in the chain
It has torn off, the little
Calf entangles itself.

Busy

But the sower
Loves to see a woman
Fallen asleep in the daytime
Over a half-knitted stocking.

The German mouth
Will yield no euphony
But brushing the prickly beard
Charmingly patter
The kisses.

WAS IST DER MENSCHEN LEBEN...

Was ist der Menschen Leben   ein Bild der Gottheit.
Wie unter dem Himmel wandeln die Irrdischen alle, sehen
Sie diesen. Lesend aber gleichsam, wie
In einer Schrift, die Unendlichkeit nachahmen und den Reichtum
Menschen. Ist der einfältige Himmel
Denn reich? Wie Blüthen sind ja
Silberne Wolken. Es regnet aber von daher
Der Thau und das Feuchte. Wenn aber
Das Blau ist ausgelöschet, das Einfältige, scheint
Das Matte, das dem Marmelstein gleichet, wie Erz,
Anzeige des Reichtums.

WHAT IS THE LIFE OF MEN . . .

What is the life of men   an image of the godhead.
As all the earthly move under heaven they see
This heaven. But reading, so to speak,
As though in a script, men imitate
Infinity and riches. Is simple heaven
Rich, then? Surely like blossoms are
Silvery clouds. Yet from there it is that dew and
Moisture rain down. But when
The blueness is extinguished, the simpleness,
Then shines the pale hue that resembles marble, like ore,
An indication of riches.

AN DIE MADONNA

Viel hab' ich dein
Und deines Sohnes wegen
Gelitten, o Madonna,
Seit ich gehöret von ihm
In süßer Jugend;
Denn nicht der Seher allein,
Es stehen unter einem Schiksaal
Die Dienenden auch. Denn weil ich

Und manchen Gesang, den ich
Dem höchsten zu singen, dem Vater
Gesonnen war, den hat
Mir weggezehret die Schwermuth.

Doch Himmlische, doch will ich
Dich feiern und nicht soll einer
Der Rede Schönheit mir
Die heimatliche, vorwerfen,
Dieweil ich allein
Zum Felde gehe, wo wild
Die Lilie wächst, furchtlos,
Zum unzugänglichen,
Uralten Gewölbe
Des Waldes,
         das Abendland,

              und gewaltet über
Den Menschen hat, statt anderer Gottheit sie
Die allvergessende Liebe.

TO THE VIRGIN MARY

Much I have suffered
On your account
And on your son's, Our Lady,
Since first in my sweet youth
I heard of him;
For not the seer alone,
But even those who serve
A destiny rules. Because I

And many a song which to
The Highest, the Father, I once was
Disposed to sing, was lost
To me, devoured by sadness.

Yet, heavenly one, yet you
I'll celebrate and let no one
Reproach me with
The beauty of native speech,
Now that alone
I go to the field where wild
The lily grows, fearless,
To the inaccessible
Primordial vault
Of the forest,
          the Occident,

          and over mankind
In place of other deities there reigned
The all-oblivious, Love.

Denn damals sollt es beginnen
Als

Geboren dir im Schoose
Der göttliche Knabe und um ihn
Der Freundin Sohn, Johannes genannt
Vom stummen Vater, der kühne
Dem war gegeben
Der Zunge Gewalt,
Zu deuten

Und die Furcht der Völker und
Die Donner und
Die stürzenden Wasser des Herrn.

Denn gut sind Sazungen, aber
Wie Drachenzähne, schneiden sie
Und tödten das Leben, wenn im Zorne sie schärft
Ein Geringer oder ein König.
Gleichmuth ist aber gegeben
Den Liebsten Gottes. So dann starben jene.
Die Beiden,   so auch sahst
Du göttlichtrauernd in der starken Seele sie sterben.
Und wohnst deswegen

                    und wenn in heiliger Nacht
Der Zukunft einer gedenkt und Sorge für
Die sorglosschlafenden trägt
Die frischaufblühenden Kinder
Kömmst lächelnd du, und fragst, was er, wo du
Die Königin seiest, befürchte.

Denn nimmer vermagst du es

For then it was to begin
When

Born from within you the boy
Divine and when about him
The son of your friend, named John
By his dumb father, he the bold one
To whom was given
The power of the tongue
To interpret

And the fear of the peoples and
The thunder and
The rushing waters of the Lord.

For good are statutes, but
Like dragons' teeth, they cut
And kill the living, when in anger whetted
By a lowly man or a king.
But equanimity is given
To those most loved by God. So then they died
Those two,   so you also saw
Them die, divinely mourning in your mighty soul.
And for that reason dwell

          and when in holy Night
Of coming ages someone remembers and
Is troubled for their sake who untroubled sleep
The freshly unfolding children,
Then smiling you come and ask him what,
Where you are Queen, he could fear.

For never you could be moved

Die keimenden Tage zu neiden,
Denn lieb ist dirs, von je,
Wenn größer die Söhne sind,
Denn ihre Mutter. Und nimmer gefällt es dir
Wenn rükwärtsblikend
Ein Älteres spottet des Jüngern.
Wer denkt der theuern Väter
Nicht gern und erzählet
Von ihren Thaten,

                  wenn aber Verwegnes geschah,
Und Undankbare haben
Das Ärgerniß   gegeben
Zu gerne blikt
Dann   zum
Und thatenscheu
Unendliche Reue und es haßt das Alte die Kinder.

Darum beschüze
Du Himmlische sie
Die jungen Pflanzen und wenn
Der Nord kömmt oder giftiger Thau weht oder
Zu lange dauert die Dürre
Und wenn sie üppigblühend
Versinken unter der Sense
Der allzuscharfen, gieb erneuertes Wachstum.
Und daß nur niemals nicht
Vielfältig, in schwachem Gezweige
Die Kraft mir vielversuchend
Zerstreue das frische Geschlecht, stark aber sei
Zu wählen aus Vielem das beste.

Nichts ists, das Böse. Das soll
Wie der Adler den Raub

To envy the days that are burgeoning,
But always have been pleased
When the sons are greater
Than their mother. And never you approve
When looking backwards
An older one mocks at the younger.
Who does not like to think
Of the dear fathers and tell
About their deeds,

        but when reckless deeds were done,
And ungrateful men gave cause
For   annoyance
Too gladly then
Looks   to
And shy of action
Unending remorse and the old will hate the children.

Therefore protect them,
O heavenly one,
Those tender plants, and when
The North Wind comes or poisonous dew wafts
Or too long a drought has lasted
And when in copious flower
They sink beneath the sickle,
The all too sharp, then grant them renewal of growth.
And never, above all,
Attempting much and multifarious
In feeble branches let a power
Disperse the new generation, but strong let it be
Out of many to choose the best.

A mere nothing is Evil. This
As an eagle his prey

Mir Eines begreifen.

Die Andern dabei. Damit sie nicht

Die Amme, die

Den Tag gebieret

Verwirren, falsch anklebend

Der Heimath und der Schwere spottend

Der Mutter ewig sizen

Im Schoose. Denn groß ist

Von dem sie erben den Reichtum.

Der

Vor allem, daß man schone

Der Wildniß göttlichgebaut

Im reinen Geseze, woher

Es haben die Kinder

Des Gotts, lustwandelnd unter

Den Felsen und Haiden purpurn blühn

Und dunkle Quellen

Dir, o Madonna und

Dem Sohne, aber den anderen auch

Damit nicht, als von Knechten,

Mit Gewalt das ihre nehmen

Die Götter.

An den Gränzen aber, wo stehet

Der Knochenberg, so nennet man ihn

Heut, aber in alter Sprache heißet

Er Ossa, Teutoburg ist

Daselbst auch und voll geistigen Wassers

Umher das Land, da

Die Himmlischen all

Sich Tempel

Let someone grasp.
The others no less. So that they
Do
Not perplex the nurse
Who gives birth to day,
Wrongly sticking to home and mocking
At hardship, endlessly sit
On their mother's lap. For great
Is he whose wealth they inherit.
He

Above all, let them spare
The wilderness divinely built
In the spirit of pure law,
Whence the God's children have it,
Pleasantly strolling under
The rocks; and heaths are in purple flower
And dark the sources
For you, our Lady, and
For the son, but for the others also,
Lest as from slaves by force
The gods
Should take what is theirs.

But near the frontiers, where lies
The Knochenberg, so now it is called,
But in ancient speech its name
Was Ossa, Teutoburg also
Is there and full of spiritual waters
The country round about, where
The heavenly all
(Built) themselves temples

Ein Handwerksmann.

Uns aber die wir
Daß

Und zu sehr zu fürchten die Furcht nicht!
Denn du nicht, holde

aber es giebt
Ein finster Geschlecht, das weder einen Halbgott
Gern hört, oder wenn mit Menschen ein Himmlisches oder
In Woogen erscheint, gestaltlos, oder das Angesicht
Des reinen ehrt, des nahen
Allgegenwärtigen Gottes.

Doch wenn unheilige schon
in Menge
und frech

Was kümmern sie dich
O Gesang den Reinen, ich zwar
Ich sterbe, doch du
Gehest andere Bahn, umsonst
Mag dich ein Neidisches hindern.

Wenn dann in kommender Zeit
Du einem Guten begegnest
So grüß ihn, und er denkt,
Wie unsere Tage wohl

An artisan.

But to us who
That

Nor be too greatly afraid of fear!
For, gracious one, not you

        but there is
A gloomy race which does not like to hear
Either a demi-god or when with mortals a heavenly being
Appears or in waves, amorphous, nor will honour
The face of him, the pure,
The near and omnipresent God.

But even if the unholy
      in masses
          and insolent

What do they matter to you
O Song, that are pure; indeed
I die, but you
Follow a different course, in vain
Shall the envious try to impede you.

And if in a coming age
You should meet with a good man,
Then greet him and he will think
How once our days were full

Voll Glüks, voll Leidens gewesen.
Von einem gehet zum andern

Noch Eins ist aber
Zu sagen. Denn es wäre
Mir fast zu plözlich
Das Glük gekommen,
Das Einsame, daß ich unverständig
Im Eigentum
Mich an die Schatten gewandt,
Denn weil du gabst
Den Sterblichen
Versuchend Göttergestalt,
Wofür ein Wort? so meint' ich, denn es hasset die Rede, wer
Das Lebenslicht das herzernährende sparet.
Es deuteten vor Alters
Die Himmlischen sich, von selbst, wie sie
Die Kraft der Götter hinweggenommen.

Wir aber zwingen
Dem Unglük ab und hängen die Fahnen
Dem Siegsgott, dem befreienden auf, darum auch
Hast du Räthsel gesendet. Heilig sind sie
Die Glänzenden, wenn aber alltäglich
Die Himmlischen und gemein
Das Wunder scheinen will, wenn nemlich
Wie Raub Titanenfürsten die Gaaben
Der Mutter greifen, hilft ein Höherer ihr.

Of joy, of suffering.
From one will go to another

Yet one thing remains
To be said. For almost
Too suddenly
This happiness would have been granted,
This lonely happiness: that, lacking knowledge
Of what is mine
To the shadows I would have turned,
For because you gave
To mortals
The tentative shape of gods,
Why waste a word? So then I thought, for he hates speech
Who husbands the light of life that nourishes the heart.
In ancient times
The heavenly beings themselves interpreted
How they had taken away the strength of the gods.

But we
Wrest from misfortune and hang the flags
Upon the god of victory, the liberator, and that is why
You sent enigmas. Holy are they,
The shining, but when the heavenly
Would seem quotidian and vulgar
The miracle and when, indeed,
Like stolen booty Titanic princes seize
The Mother's gifts, then One who is higher comes to her aid.

DIE TITANEN

Nicht ist es aber
Die Zeit. Noch sind sie
Unangebunden. Göttliches trift untheilnehmende nicht.
Dann mögen sie rechnen
Mit Delphi. Indessen, gieb in Feierstunden
Und daß ich ruhen möge, der Todten
Zu denken. Viele sind gestorben
Feldherrn in alter Zeit
Und schöne Frauen und Dichter
Und in neuer
Der Männer viel
Ich aber bin allein.

       und in den Ocean schiffend
Die duftenden Inseln fragen
Wohin sie sind.

Denn manches von ihnen ist
In treuen Schriften überblieben
Und manches in Sagen der Zeit.
Viel offenbaret der Gott.
Denn lang schon wirken
Die Wolken hinab
Und es wurzelt vielesbereitend heilige Wildniß.
Heiß ist der Reichtum. Denn es fehlet
An Gesang, der löset den Geist.
Verzehren würd' er
Und wäre gegen sich selbst

THE TITANS

Not yet, however,
The time has come. They still are
Untethered. What's divine does not strike the unconcerned.
Then let them reckon
With Delphi. Meanwhile in festive hours,
And so that I may rest, allow me
To think of the dead. In olden days
Died many generals
And lovely women and poets,
In modern times
A host of men.
But I am on my own.

        and sailing into the ocean
The fragrant islands ask
Where they have gone.

For something of them has been
Preserved in faithful writings
And something in lore of the age.
Much does the God reveal.
For long already the clouds
Have worked upon what's below them,
And holy wilderness, pregnant with much, has grown roots.
Hot is wealth. For we lack
Song that loosens the mind.
It would devour
And would make war on itself

Denn nimmer duldet
Die Gefangenschaft das himmlische Feuer.

Es erfreuet aber
Das Gastmahl oder wenn am Feste
Das Auge glänzet und von Perlen
Der Jungfrau Hals.
Auch Kriegesspiel

        und durch die Gänge
Der Gärten schmettert
Das Gedächtniß der Schlacht und besänftiget
An schlanker Brust
Die tönenden Wehre ruhn
Von Heldenvätern den Kindern.
Mich aber umsummet
Die Bien und wo der Akersmann
Die Furchen machet singen gegen
Dem Lichte die Vögel. Manche helfen
Dem Himmel. Diese siehet
Der Dichter. Gut ist es, an andern sich
Zu halten. Denn keiner trägt das Leben allein.

Wenn aber ist entzündet
Der geschäfftige Tag
Und an der Kette, die
Den Bliz ableitet
Von der Stunde des Aufgangs
Himmlischer Thau glänzt,
Muß unter Sterblichen auch
Das Hohe sich fühlen.
Drum bauen sie Häußer
Und die Werkstatt gehet
Und über Strömen das Schiff.

For never they who are captive
Can bear the heavenly fire.

Yet men are gladdened by
The banquet, and when in celebration
Our eyes are bright, and with pearls
The virgin's neck.
Martial games no less

       and through the walks
Of gardens blares
The memory of battle and, soothed
Upon the slender breasts
Of children quiet lie
Loud weapons of their heroic ancestors.
But around me hums
The bee, and where the ploughman draws
His furrows, birds are singing
Against the light. Many give help
To Heaven. And them
The poet sees. It is good to rely
Upon others. For no one can bear this life on his own.

But when the busy day
Has been kindled
And on the chain that
Conducts the lightning
From the hour of sunrise
Glistens heavenly dew,
Among mortals also
What is high must feel at home.
That is why they build houses
And the workshop's astir
And over currents the ship.

Und es bieten tauschend die Menschen
Die Händ' einander, sinnig ist es
Auf Erden und es sind nicht umsonst
Die Augen an den Boden geheftet.

Ihr fühlet aber
Auch andere Art.
Denn unter dem Maaße
Des Rohen brauchet es auch
Damit das Reine sich kenne.
Wenn aber

Und in die Tiefe greifet
Daß es lebendig werde
Der Allerschütterer, meinen die
Es komme der Himmlische
Zu Todten herab und gewaltig dämmerts
Im ungebundenen Abgrund
Im allesmerkenden auf.
Nicht möcht ich aber sagen
Es werden die Himmlischen schwach
Wenn schon es aufgährt.
Wenn aber
          und es gehet

An die Scheitel dem Vater, daß

          und der Vogel des Himmels ihm
Es anzeigt. Wunderbar
Im Zorne kommet er drauf.

And, bartering, men hold out
Their hands to one another; pensive it is
On earth, and not for nothing
Are eyes fixed on the ground.

Yet you also sense
A different kind.
For measure demands that
Crudity, coarseness exist, so that
What is pure shall know itself.
But when

And down into the depth
To make it come to life,
Reaches he who shakes all things,
They believe the Heavenly comes
Down to the dead, and mightily
In the unfettered abyss,
The all-perceiving, light breaks.
But I do not wish to say
That the Heavenly are growing weak
Though now it erupts.
But when
        and it rises

Up to the partings of the Father's hair, so that

       and the bird of Heaven
Makes it known to him. Then
Marvellous in anger he comes.

EINST HAB ICH DIE MUSE GEFRAGT...

Einst hab ich die Muse gefragt, und sie
Antwortete mir
Am Ende wirst du es finden.
Kein Sterblicher kann es fassen.
Vom Höchsten will ich schweigen.
Verbotene Frucht, wie der Lorbeer, aber ist
Am meisten das Vaterland. Die aber kost'
Ein jeder zulezt,

Viel täuschet Anfang
Und Ende.
Das lezte aber ist
Das Himmelszeichen, das reißt
       und   Menschen
Hinweg. Wohl hat Herkules das
Gefürchtet. Aber da wir träge
Geboren sind, bedarf es des Falken, dem
Befolgt' ein Reuter, wenn
Er jaget, den Flug.

Im   wenn
Und der Fürst

      und Feuer und Rauchdampf blüht
Auf dürrem Rasen
Doch ungemischet darunter
Aus guter Brust, das Labsaal

AT ONE TIME I QUESTIONED THE MUSE...

At one time I questioned the Muse, and she
Replied to me,
In the end you will find it.
No mortal can grasp it.
About the Highest I will not speak.
But, like the laurel, forbidden fruit
Your country is, above all. To be tasted last
By any man,

Beginning and end
Greatly deceive us.
The last thing, however, is
The heavenly sign; it sweeps
                and   men
Away. Of this even Hercules
Was doubtless afraid. But since we are
Born lazy, the hawk is needed,
Whose flight, when he hunts,
A horseman follows.

In the   when
And the prince

        and fire and smoke are in flower
On a dry lawn
Yet unmingled on to it wells,
From a good breast, the battle's

Der Schlacht, die Stimme quillet des Fürsten.

Gefäße machet ein Künstler.
Und es kauffet

                wenn es aber
Zum Urteil kommt
Und keusch hat es die Lippe
Von einem Halbgott berührt

Und schenket das Liebste
Den Unfruchtbaren
Denn nimmer, von nun an
Taugt zum Gebrauche das Heilge.

Refreshment, the voice of the prince.

An artist makes vessels.
And they are bought

        but when
It comes to the judgement
And chastely it has been touched
By the lip of a demigod

And never now will he
Give away what's dearest to him
To those unfruitful, from now on
The holy is fit for use.

DER ADLER

Mein Vater ist gewandert, auf dem Gotthard,
Da wo die Flüsse, hinab,
Wohl nach Hetruria seitwärts,
Und des geraden Weges
Auch über den Schnee,
Zu dem Olympos und Hämos
Wo den Schatten der Athos wirft,
Nach Höhlen in Lemnos.
Anfänglich aber sind
Aus Wäldern des Indus
Starkduftenden
Die Eltern gekommen.
Der Urahn aber
Ist geflogen über der See
Scharfsinnend, und es wunderte sich
Des Königes goldnes Haupt
Ob dem Geheimniß der Wasser,
Als roth die Wolken dampften
Über dem Schiff und die Thiere stumm
Einander schauend
Der Speise gedachten, aber
Es stehen die Berge doch still,
Wo wollen wir bleiben?

Der Fels ist zu Waide gut,
Das Trokne zu Trank.

THE EAGLE

My father roamed, up on the Gotthard,
Where the rivers are, downward,
Perhaps to Etruria, sideways,
And by the straight way too
Over the snow,
To Olympus and Haemus
Where Athos casts its shadow,
To caves in Lemnos.
In the beginning, though,
My parents came
Out of the forests of the Indus,
The strongly fragrant.
But the first forefather
Flew across the sea,
Pondering sharply, and the golden head
Of the king was full of wonder
At the mystery of the waters,
When red the clouds were steaming
Above the ship, and the animals,
Dumbly gazing at one another,
Gave thought to food, but
Nonetheless the mountains stand still,
Where shall we settle?

The rock is good for pasture,
What is dry, for drink,

Das Nasse aber zu Speise.
Will einer wohnen,
So sei es an Treppen,
Und wo ein Häuslein hinabhängt
Am Wasser halte dich auf.
Und was du hast, ist
Athem zu hohlen.
Hat einer ihn nemlich hinauf
Am Tage gebracht,
Er findet im Schlaf ihn wieder.
Denn wo die Augen zugedekt,
Und gebunden die Füße sind,
Da wirst du es finden.
Denn wo erkennest,

But what is wet, for food.
If someone wishes to dwell,
Let it be on steps
And where a small house hangs down
Near water, there spend your days.
And what is yours
Is to draw breath.
For if someone has brought it
Up to the top by day,
In sleep he finds it again.
For where the eyes are covered
And the feet are bound,
There you will find it.
For where will you recognise,

DAS NÄCHSTE BESTE

Dritte Fassung

    offen die Fenster des Himmels
Und freigelassen der Nachtgeist
Der himmelstürmende, der hat unser Land
Beschwäzet, mit Sprachen viel, unbändigen, und
Den Schutt gewälzet
Bis diese Stunde.
Doch kommt das, was ich will,
Wenn
Drum wie die Staaren
Mit Freudengeschrei, wenn auf Gasgogne, Orten, wo viel Gärten sind,
Wenn im Olivenland, und
In liebenswürdiger Fremde,
Springbrunnen an grasbewachsnen Wegen
Die Bäum unwissend in der Wüste
Die Sonne sticht,
Und das Herz der Erde thuet
Sich auf, wo um
Den Hügel von Eichen
Aus brennendem Lande
Die Ströme und wo
Des Sonntags unter Tänzen
Gastfreundlich die Schwellen sind,
An blüthenbekränzten Straßen, stillegehend.
Sie spüren nemlich die Heimath,
Wenn grad   aus falbem Stein,
Die Wasser silbern rieseln
Und heilig Grün sich zeigt

WHATEVER IS NEAREST

Third Version

opened the windows of Heaven
And let loose the spirit of Night
Who takes Heaven by storm—he has talked over
Our country, with many languages, unrestrained, and
Has rolled his ball of rubble
Up to this hour.
Yet what I want shall come
When
Therefore like the starlings
With jubilant cries, when in Gascony, places with many gardens,
When in the olive country, and
In lovable foreign parts,
Fountains by pathways overgrown with grass
The trees ignorant in the desert
Are stung by the sun,
And the heart of Earth
Opens up, where round
The hill of oaks
From a burning land
The rivers and where
On Sundays amid dances
Hospitable are the thresholds
On streets all hung with garlands, quietly moving.
For it is home that they sense
When straight   from dun-coloured stone
The waters trickle silver
And holy green appears

Auf feuchter Wiese der Charente,

Die klugen Sinne pflegend.   wenn aber
Die Luft sich bahnt,
Und ihnen machet waker
Scharfwehend die Augen der Nordost, fliegen sie auf,
Und Ek um Eke
Das Liebere gewahrend
Denn immer halten die sich genau an das Nächste,
Sehn sie die heiligen Wälder und die Flamme, blühendduftend
Des Wachstums und die Wolken des Gesanges fern und athmen Othem
Der Gesänge. Menschlich ist
Das Erkentniß. Aber die Himmlischen
Auch haben solches mit sich, und des Morgens beobachten
Die Stunden und des Abends die Vögel. Himmlischen auch
Gehöret also solches. Wolan nun. Sonst in Zeiten
Des Geheimnisses hätt ich, als von Natur, gesagt,
Sie kommen, in Deutschland. Jezt aber, weil, wie die See
Die Erd ist und die Länder, Männern gleich, die nicht
Vorüber gehen können, einander, untereinander
Sich schelten fast, so sag ich. Abendlich wohlgeschmiedet
Vom Oberlande biegt sich das Gebirg, wo auf hoher Wiese die Wälder
                                                      sind wohl an
Der bairischen Ebne. Nemlich Gebirg
Geht weit und streket, hinter Amberg sich und
Fränkischen Hügeln. Berühmt ist dieses. Umsonst nicht hat
Seitwärts gebogen Einer von Bergen der Jugend
Das Gebirg, und gerichtet das Gebirg
Heimatlich. Wildniß nemlich sind ihm die Alpen und
Das Gebirg, das theilet die Tale und die Länge lang
Geht über die Erd. Dort aber

Gehn mags nun. Fast, unrein, hatt sehn lassen und das Eingeweid

On a sodden meadow of the Charente,

Cultivating the prudent senses.   but when
The air becomes passible
And the northeasterly, sharply blowing,
Makes bold their eyes, they fly off
And corner by corner
Perceiving that which is dearer to them,
For always they are guided by that which is nearest,
They see the holy woods and the flame, fragrantly blossoming,
Of growth and the clouds of song far away, and breathe the breath
Of songs. Human it is
To perceive, to seek knowledge. But the Heavenly too
Have something like it about them, and in the mornings observe
The hours, and at nightfall the birds. To the Heavenly, therefore, too
This appertains. Very well, then. Before, at times when
The secret was kept, as though by nature, I should have said,
They are coming, in Germany. But now, because the earth
Is like the sea and the countries are like men
Who cannot pass one another, but almost
Are scolding one another, I speak. Nocturnally, well forged
By highlands the mountain range bends, where on the alpine pasture the
                                              woods are
Near the Bavarian plain. For mountain ranges
Extend far off and stretch beyond Amberg and
Franconian hills. Famous these are. Not for nothing
Did someone bend sideways from mountains of youth
The range and turned it to face
Towards home. For wilderness are the alps to him and
The range that divides the valleys and sprawled full length
Runs across the earth. But there

Now let it run. Almost, impurely, it showed and the entrails

Der Erde.   Bei Ilion aber
War auch das Licht der Adler. Aber in der Mitte
Der Himmel der Gesänge. Neben aber
Am Ufer zornige Greise, der Entscheidung nemlich, die alle
Drei unser sind.

Of Earth.   Near Ilion, however,
The light of the eagles was too. But in the midst
The heaven of songs. But near by
Angry old men on the shore, of decision, that is,
Which all three are ours.

UND MITZUFÜHLEN DAS LEBEN...

Und mitzufühlen das Leben
Der Halbgötter oder Patriarchen, sizend
Zu Gericht. Nicht aber überall ists
Ihnen gleich um diese, sondern Leben, summendheißes auch von
                                                    Schatten Echo
Als in einen Brennpunct
Versammelt. Goldne Wüste. Oder wohlunterhalten dem Feuerstahl
                                                    des lebenswarmen
Heerds gleich schlägt dann die Nacht Funken, aus geschliffnem Gestein
Des Tages, und um die Dämmerung noch
Ein Saitenspiel tönt. Gegen das Meer zischt
Der Knall der Jagd. Die Aegypterin aber, offnen Busens sizt
Immer singend wegen Mühe gichtisch das Gelenk
Im Wald, am Feuer. Recht Gewissen bedeutend
Der Wolken und der Seen des Gestirns
Rauscht in Schottland wie an dem See
Lombardas dann ein Bach vorüber. Knaben spielen
Perlfrischen Lebens gewohnt so um Gestalten
Der Meister, oder der Leichen, oder es rauscht so um der Thürme Kronen
Sanfter Schwalben Geschrei.

Nein wahrhaftig der Tag
Bildet keine
Menschenformen. Aber erstlich
Ein alter Gedanke, Wissenschaft
Elysium.

                    und verlorne Liebe
Der Turniere   Rosse, scheu und feucht

AND TO FEEL WITH THE LIVES...

And to feel with the lives
Of demigods or the patriarchs, sitting
In judgement. Yet not everywhere are they
Impartial about these, but life, hummingly hot and the shadows' echo
As though in a focal point
Concentrated. Golden desert. Or, well maintained like the steel for
                                                    striking fire
Of the life-warm stove, then the night strikes sparks, out of polished stones
Of day, and around nightfall still
A lyre resounds. Towards the ocean hisses
The cracking shots of the hunt. But the Egyptian woman sits,
Her breast exposed, always singing because of toil her joints arthritic
In the wood, by the fire. Signifying clear conscience
Of the clouds and the lakes of the planet.
In Scotland a stream rushes on
As beside Lombardy's lake. So boys will play
Accustomed to pearl-fresh life around the figures
Of masters, or of corpses, or so round the crests of towers rushes
The crying of gentle swallows.

No indeed the day
Moulds no
Human shapes. But first
An ancient thought, erudition
Elysium.

          and lost love
Of the tournaments   horses, shy and moist

VOM ABGRUND NEMLICH...

Vom Abgrund nemlich haben
Wir angefangen und gegangen
Dem Leuen gleich, in Zweifel und Ärgerniß,
Denn sinnlicher sind Menschen
In dem Brand
Der Wüste
Lichttrunken und der Thiergeist ruhet
Mit ihnen. Bald aber wird, wie ein Hund, umgehn
In der Hizze meine Stimme auf den Gassen der Gärten
In denen wohnen Menschen
In Frankreich
Der Schöpfer
Frankfurt aber, nach der Gestalt, die
Abdruk ist der Natur zu reden
Des Menschen nemlich, ist der Nabel
Dieser Erde, diese Zeit auch
Ist Zeit, und deutschen Schmelzes.
Ein wilder Hügel aber stehet über dem Abhang
Meiner Gärten. Kirschenbäume. Scharfer Othem aber wehet
Um die Löcher des Felses. Allda bin ich
Alles miteinander. Wunderbar
Aber über Quellen beuget schlank
Ein Nußbaum und   sich. Beere, wie Korall
Hängen an dem Strauche über Röhren von Holz,
Aus denen
Ursprünglich aus Korn, nun aber zu gestehen, bevestigter Gesang von
                                             Blumen als
Neue Bildung aus der Stadt, wo
Bis zu Schmerzen aber der Nase steigt

FOR FROM THE ABYSS...

For from the abyss we
Began and have walked like
The lion, in doubt and annoyance,
For more sensual are men
In the blaze
Of deserts,
Drunk with light, and the spirit of animals
Joins in their rest. But soon like a dog my voice
Will walk in the heat through the alleys of gardens
In which men and women live
In France
The creator
Frankfurt, though to speak according to the shape
Of nature's imprint, human nature, I mean,
Is the navel of this earth, our time too
Is time, and of German mould.
But a wild hill looms above the slope of
My gardens. Cherry-trees. A sharp breath, however,
Blows around the holes of the rock. And there I am
All things at once. But wonderfully
Over wellsprings there slenderly bends
A nut tree and   Berries like coral
Hang on the shrub above wooden gutters
From which
Originally of corn, but now to be confessed, fortified song of flowers
As new education from town, where
To the point of pain in the nose

Citronengeruch auf und das Öl, aus der Provence, und es haben diese
Dankbarkeit mir die Gasgognischen Lande
Gegeben. Gezähmet aber, noch zu sehen, und genährt hat mich
Die Rappierlust und des Festtags gebraten Fleisch
Der Tisch und braune Trauben, braune
                        und mich leset o
Ihr Blüthen von Deutschland, o mein Herz wird
Untrügbarer Krystall an dem
Das Licht sich prüfet wenn   Deutschland

A smell of lemons rises and of oil, from Provence, and it is
The Gascon regions that have given me
This thankfulness. But what tamed me, still to be seen, and fed me
Is love of rapiers and the holiday's roast meat
The table and brown grapes, brown ones

                    and read me, gather me O
You flowers of Germany, O my heart is turning
To crystal that cannot lie, in which
The light is tested when   Germany

...DER VATIKAN...

der Vatikan,
Hier sind wir   in der Einsamkeit
Und drunten gehet der Bruder, ein Esel auch dem braunen Schleier nach
Wenn aber der Tag   , allbejahend von wegen des Spotts
Schiksaale macht, denn aus Zorn der Natur-
Göttin, wie ein Ritter gesagt von Rom, in derlei
Pallästen, gehet izt viel Irrsaal, und alle Schlüssel des Geheimnisses
                                                                                wissend

Fragt bös Gewissen
Und Julius Geist um derweil, welcher Calender
Gemachet, und dort drüben, in Westphalen,
Mein ehrlich Meister.
Gott rein und mit Unterscheidung
Bewahren, das ist uns vertrauet,
Damit nicht, weil an diesem
Viel hängt, über der Büßung, über einem Fehler
Des Zeichens
Gottes Gericht entstehet.
Ach! kennet ihr den nicht mehr
Den Meister des Forsts, und den Jüngling in der Wüste, der von Honig
Und Heuschreken sich nährt. Still Geists ists. Fraun
                              Oben wohl
Auf Monte   , wohl auch seitwärts,
Irr ich herabgekommen
Über Tyrol, Lombarda, Loretto, wo des Pilgrims Heimath
                    auf dem Gotthard, gezäunt, nachlässig, unter Gletschern
Karg wohnt jener, wo der Vogel
Mit Eiderdünnen, eine Perle des Meers
Und der Adler den Accent rufet, vor Gott, wo das Feuer läuft der
                                                            Menschen wegen

...THE VATICAN...

the Vatican,

Here we are   in the solitude

And down below walks the brother, a donkey too according to the

brown veil

But when the day   , all-affirming because of the mockery

Makes destinies, for out of wrath of the Nature-

Goddess, as a knight said of Rome, in suchlike

Palaces much confusion teems, and knowing all keys to the secret

Bad conscience asks

And the spirit of Julius meanwhile, who

Made calendars, and over there in Westphalia,

My honest master.

To preserve God pure and with discrimination

Is the task entrusted to us,

Lest, because much depends

On this, through a penitence, through a mistake

In the sign

God's day of judgement set in.

Oh, have you forgotten, then

The forest's master and the youth in the desert who feeds

On locusts and honey. Of the quiet spirit it is. Women

Up there perhaps

On Monte   , sideways too perhaps

I stray, come down

Across Tirol, Lombardy, Loretto, where the pilgrim's home is

on the Gotthard, fenced, carelessly, under glaciers

Poorly he lives, where the bird

With eiderdown, a pearl of the sea

And the eagle there calls the accent, before God, where the fire runs

because of men

Des Wächters Horn tönt aber über den Garden

Der Kranich hält die Gestalt aufrecht

Die Majestätische, keusche, drüben

In Patmos, Morea, in der Pestluft.

Türkisch. und die Eule, wohlbekannt der Schriften

Spricht, heischern Fraun gleich in zerstörten Städten. Aber

Die erhalten den Sinn. Oft aber wie ein Brand

Entstehet Sprachverwirrung. Aber wie ein Schiff,

Das lieget im Hafen, des Abends, wenn die Gloke lautet

Des Kirchthurms, und es nachhallt unten

Im Eingewaid des Tempels und der Mönch

Und Schäfer Abschied nehmet, vom Spaziergang

Und Apollon, ebenfalls

Aus Roma, derlei Pallästen, sagt

Ade! unreinlich bitter, darum!

Dann kommt das Brautlied des Himmels.

Vollendruhe. Goldroth. Und die Rippe tönet

Des sandigen Erdballs in Gottes Werk

Ausdrüklicher Bauart, grüner Nacht

Und Geist, der Säulenordnung, wirklich

Ganzem Verhältniß, samt der Mitt,

Und glänzenden

But the watchman's horn rings out over the guards
The crane holds his body erect
The majestic, the chaste, over there
In Patmos, Morea, the pestilent air.
Turkish, and the owl, well versed in writings,
Speaks like hoarse women in cities destroyed. But
They catch the meaning. Yet often like a fire
Confusion of tongues breaks out. But like a ship
That lies in the harbour, at evening, when the bell rings
Down from the church tower and reverberates in
The temple's entrails below and the monk
And shepherd take leave, from the walk
And Apollo, likewise
From Rome, suchlike palaces, say
Farewell! dirtily bitter, that's why!
Then comes the nuptial song of Heaven.
Rest of perfection. Reddish-golden. And loud sings the rib
Of the sandy globe in the work of God
A definite style of building, green night
And spirit, the pillars' order, true to
Total proportions, including the centre,
And to gleaming

GRIECHENLAND

Erste Fassung

Wege des Wanderers!

Denn   Schatten der Bäume
Und Hügel, sonnig, wo
Der Weg geht
Zur Kirche,

Reegen, wie Pfeilenregen
Und Bäume stehen, schlummernd, doch
Eintreffen Schritte der Sonne,
Denn eben so, wie sie heißer
Brennt über der Städte Dampf
So gehet über des Reegens
Behangene Mauren die Sonne

Wie Epheu nemlich hänget
Astlos der Reegen herunter. Schöner aber
Blühn Reisenden die Wege
        im Freien   wechselt wie Korn.
Avignon waldig über den Gotthardt
Tastet das Roß, Lorbeern
Rauschen um Virgilius und daß
Die Sonne nicht
Unmänlich suchet, das Grab. Moosrosen
Wachsen
Auf den Alpen. Blumen fangen
Vor Thoren der Stadt an, auf geebneten Wegen unbegünstiget
Gleich Krystallen in der Wüste wachsend des Meers.
Gärten wachsen um Windsor. Hoch
Ziehet, aus London,

GREECE

First Version

                    ways of the wanderer!
For   shadows of trees
And hills, sunny where
The path runs
Up to the church,
                    rain like showers of arrows,
And trees loom, drowsing, yet
Strides of the sun arrive.
For just as more hotly
It burns above the vapour of cities
So does the sun move above
The draped walls of the rain

For like ivy
Branchless the rain hangs down. But
More beautifully to travellers blossom the roads
          out in the open   changes like corn.
Avignon woody over the Gotthart
The horse gropes its way, laurels
Rustle around Vergil and, so that
Not unmanly the sun
Shall search, the grave. Moss roses
Grow
On the Alps. Flowers begin
Before the city gates, on levelled roads, unfavoured
Like crystals growing in the desert of the sea.
Gardens grow around Windsor. High up,
From London,

Der Wagen des Königs.
Schöne Gärten sparen die Jahrzeit.
Am Canal. Tief aber liegt
Das ebene Weltmeer, glühend.

The King's coach drives on.
Fine gardens save up the season.
By the canal. But deep down lies
The level ocean, glowing.

GRIECHENLAND

Zweite Fassung

O ihr Stimmen des Geschiks, ihr Wege des Wanderers
Denn an dem Himmel
Tönt wie der Amsel Gesang
Der Wolken sichere Stimmung gut
Gestimmt vom Daseyn Gottes, dem Gewitter.
Und Rufe, wie hinausschauen, zur
Unsterblichkeit und Helden;
Viel sind Erinnerungen.
Und wo die Erde, von Verwüstungen her, Versuchungen der Heiligen
Großen Gesezen nachgeht, die Einigkeit
Und Zärtlichkeit und den ganzen Himmel nachher
Erscheinend singen
Gesangeswolken. Denn immer lebt
Die Natur. Wo aber allzusehr sich
Das Ungebundene zum Tode sehnet
Himmlisches einschläft, und die Treue Gottes,
Das Verständige fehlt.
Aber wie der Reigen
Zur Hochzeit,
Zu Geringem auch kann kommen
Großer Anfang.
Alltag aber wunderbar
Gott an hat ein Gewand.
Und Erkentnissen verberget sich sein Angesicht
Und deket die Lüfte mit Kunst.
Und Luft und Zeit dekt
Den Schröklichen, wenn zu sehr ihn
Eins liebet mit Gebeten oder
Die Seele.

GREECE

Second Version

O you voices of fate, you ways of the wanderer
For on the heavens
Rings out like the blackbird's song
The clouds' even mood, well
Tempered by the existence of God, the thunderstorm.
And calls, like looking out, for
Immortality and heroes;
Memories are many.
And where the Earth, proceeding from devastations, temptations of the saints,
Pursues great laws, afterwards
Song-clouds, becoming visible, sing
Concord and tenderness
And the whole of Heaven. For always
Nature lives. But where all too greatly
The unbound longs for death,
The Heavenly, and God's faithfulness, go to sleep,
Reason is lacking.
But like the dance
To a wedding
A great beginning can come
Even to humble things.
Everyday but marvellous
God has put on a garment.
And his face is withheld from the knowing
And covers the winds with art.
And air and time cover
The terrible one, when too much
Someone loves him with prayers, or
Else the soul.

GRIECHENLAND

Dritte Fassung

O ihr Stimmen des Geschiks, ihr Wege des Wanderers
Denn an der Schule Blau,
Fernher, am Tosen des Himmels
Tönt wie der Amsel Gesang
Der Wolken heitere Stimmung gut
Gestimmt vom Daseyn Gottes, dem Gewitter.
Und Rufe, wie hinausschauen, zur
Unsterblichkeit und Helden;
Viel sind Erinnerungen. Wo darauf
Tönend, wie des Kalbs Haut
Die Erde, von Verwüstungen her, Versuchungen der Heiligen
Denn anfangs bildet das Werk sich
Großen Gesezen nachgehet, die Wissenschaft
Und Zärtlichkeit und den Himmel breit lauter Hülle nachher
Erscheinend singen Gesangeswolken.
Denn fest ist der Erde
Nabel. Gefangen nemlich in Ufern von Gras sind
Die Flammen und die allgemeinen
Elemente. Lauter Besinnung aber oben lebt der Aether. Aber silbern
An reinen Tagen
Ist das Licht. Als Zeichen der Liebe
Veilchenblau die Erde.
Zu Geringem auch kann kommen
Großer Anfang.
Alltag aber wunderbar zu lieb den Menschen
Gott an hat ein Gewand.
Und Erkentnissen verberget sich sein Angesicht
Und deket die Lüfte mit Kunst.

GREECE

Third Version

O you voices of fate, you ways of the wanderer!
For amid the blue of the school,
From afar, amid the uproar of heaven
Rings out like the blackbird's song
The clouds' happy mood, well
Tempered by the existence of God, the thunderstorm.
And calls, like looking out, for
Immortality and heroes;
Memories are many. Where ringing out
On it, as on the calf's hide,
The earth, proceeding from devastations, temptations of the saints,
For at the beginning the work is shaped,
Pursues great laws, and knowledge
And tenderness and the width of heaven, all wrapping, later becoming
Visible, sing clouds of song.
For firmly fixed is the navel
Of Earth. For captive in banks of grass are
The flames and the common
Elements. But above, all reflection, lives Aether. But silver
On pure days
Is light. As a sign of love
Violet-blue the earth.
A great beginning can come
Even to humble things.
Everyday but marvellous, for the sake of men,
God has put on a garment.
And his face is withheld from the knowing
And covers the winds with art.

Und Luft und Zeit dekt
Den Schröklichen, daß zu sehr nicht eins
Ihn liebet mit Gebeten oder
Die Seele. Denn lange schon steht offen
Wie Blätter, zu lernen, oder Linien und Winkel
Die Natur
Und gelber die Sonnen und die Monde,
Zu Zeiten aber
Wenn ausgehn will die alte Bildung
Der Erde, bei Geschichten nemlich
Gewordnen, muthig fechtenden, wie auf Höhen führet
Die Erde Gott. Ungemessene Schritte
Begränzt er aber, aber wie Blüthen golden thun
Der Seele Kräfte dann der Seele Verwandtschaften sich zusammen,
Daß lieber auf Erden
Die Schönheit wohnt und irgend ein Geist
Gemeinschaftlicher sich zu Menschen gesellet.

Süß ists, dann unter hohen Schatten von Bäumen
Und Hügeln zu wohnen, sonnig, wo der Weg ist
Gepflastert zur Kirche. Reisenden aber, wem,
Aus Lebensliebe, messend immerhin,
Die Füße gehorchen, blühn
Schöner die Wege, wo das Land

And air and time cover
The terrible one, so that not too much a man
With prayers shall love him.
Or else the soul. For long already like leaves,
To learn, or like lines and angles,
Nature lies open
And more yellow the suns and the moons,
But at times
When the ancient knowledge of earth is in danger
Of going out, amid histories, that is, grown, come to pass
And boldly fencing, as on high places God
Leads on the Earth. Unmeasured paces, though,
He limits, but like blossoms golden then
The faculties, affinities of the soul consort
So that more willingly
Beauty dwells on earth and one or the other spirit
More communally joins in human affairs.

Sweet it is then to dwell under the high shade
Of trees and hills, sunny, where the road
Is paved to church. To travellers, though,
To him whose feet, from love of life,
Measuring all along, obey him,
More beautifully blossom the roads, where the land

POEMS OF HIS MADNESS

(1805-1843)

WENN AUS DER FERNE...

Wenn aus der Ferne, da wir geschieden sind,
  Ich dir noch kennbar bin, die Vergangenheit
    O du Theilhaber meiner Leiden!
      Einiges Gute bezeichnen dir kann,

So sage, wie erwartet die Freundin dich?
  In jenen Gärten, da nach entsezlicher
    Und dunkler Zeit wir uns gefunden?
      Hier an den Strömen der heilgen Urwelt.

Das muß ich sagen, einiges Gutes war
  In deinen Bliken, als in den Fernen du
    Dich einmal fröhlich umgesehen
      Immer verschlossener Mensch, mit finstrem

Aussehn. Wie flossen Stunden dahin, wie still
  War meine Seele über der Wahrheit daß
    Ich so getrennt gewesen wäre?
      Ja! ich gestand es, ich war die deine.

Wahrhafftig! wie du alles Bekannte mir
  In mein Gedächtniß bringen und schreiben willst,
    Mit Briefen, so ergeht es mir auch
      Daß ich Vergangenes alles sage.

Wars Frühling? war es Sommer? die Nachtigall
  Mit süßem Liede lebte mit Vögeln, die
    Nicht ferne waren im Gebüsche
      Und mit Gerüchen umgaben Bäum' uns.

IF FROM THE DISTANCE...

If from the distance where we went separate ways
  I'm recognizable to you still, the past,
    O you the sharer of my sufferings,
      Still can convey to you something pleasant,

Then tell me how your girl friend awaits you now?
  In those same gardens where after horrible
    And darkened years once more we're meeting,
      Here by the holy primaevum's rivers.

This much I'm bound to say, something good there was
  About your glances when in the distances
    For once you cheerfully looked round, you
      Man always shut like a clam, of gloomy

Appearance. How the hours slipped away, how calm
  My soul was at the thought of the truth that I
    Had been so long and wholly parted?
      Yes, I confessed, I was yours entirely.

Indeed! As you are trying to bring and write
  These well-known things all back to my memory,
    With letters, so it is with me, and
      All that is past I now freely speak of.

Was it in spring? In summer? The nightingale
  Lived sweetly singing with other birds that were
    Not far away within the thicket,
      And there was fragrance of trees around us.

573

Die klaren Gänge, niedres Gesträuch und Sand
   Auf dem wir traten, machten erfreulicher
     Und lieblicher die Hyacinthe
       Oder die Tulpe, Viole, Nelke.

Um Wänd und Mauern grünte der Epheu, grünt'
   Ein seelig Dunkel hoher Alleeen. Offt
     Des Abends, Morgens waren dort wir
       Redeten manches und sahn uns froh an.

In meinen Armen lebte der Jüngling auf,
   Der, noch verlassen, aus den Gefilden kam,
     Die er mir wies, mit einer Schwermuth,
       Aber die Nahmen der seltnen Orte

Und alles Schöne hatt' er behalten, das
   An seeligen Gestaden, auch mir sehr werth
     Im heimatlichen Lande blühet
       Oder verborgen, aus hoher Aussicht,

Allwo das Meer auch einer beschauen kann,
   Doch keiner seyn will. Nehme vorlieb, und denk
     An die, die noch vergnügt ist, darum,
       Weil der entzükende Tag uns anschien,

Der mit Geständniß oder der Hände Druk
   Anhub, der uns vereinet. Ach! wehe mir!
     Es waren schöne Tage. Aber
       Traurige Dämmerung folgte nachher.

Du seiest so allein in der schönen Welt
   Behauptest du mir immer, Geliebter! das
     Weist aber du nicht,

The clear-cut pathways, shrubs rather low and sand
   On which we walked were made more agreeable,
      More charming by the hyacinth or
         Tulip, the violet or carnation.

On walls and housefront ivy grew green, green too
   A blissful darkness made by tall avenues.
      There we spent many mornings, evenings,
         Said this and that and exchanged glad glances.

In my embrace it was that the youth revived
   Who, still forsaken, came from the very fields
      He showed to me, with such deep sadness,
         But all the names of those curious places

And all the lovely things, he remembers still
   Which, very dear to me also, are in bloom
      On blessèd shores, our native country,
         Or else concealed, from a high perspective,

Wherever men can look at the ocean too,
   But no one wants to be. Now excuse me, think
      Of her who still is glad because that
         Day so enchanting shone down upon us

Which started with confessions or holding hands
   And which united us. But ah, woe is me.
      Those days were beautiful. However,
         Sad was the twilight that followed after.

That you're so much alone in this lovely world,
   You always claim, my darling, but as for that,
      You cannot know . . .

DER SPAZIERGANG

Ihr Wälder schön an der Seite,
Am grünen Abhang gemahlt,
Wo ich umher mich leite,
Durch süße Ruhe bezahlt
Für jeden Stachel im Herzen,
Wenn dunkel mir ist der Sinn,
Den Kunst und Sinnen hat Schmerzen
Gekostet von Anbeginn.
Ihr lieblichen Bilder im Thale,
Zum Beispiel Gärten und Baum,
Und dann der Steg der schmale,
Der Bach zu sehen kaum,
Wie schön aus heiterer Ferne
Glänzt Einem das herrliche Bild
Der Landschaft, die ich gerne
Besuch' in Witterung mild.
Die Gottheit freundlich geleitet
Uns erstlich mit Blau,
Hernach mit Wolken bereitet,
Gebildet wölbig und grau,
Mit sengenden Blizen und Rollen
Des Donners, mit Reiz des Gefilds,
Mit Schönheit, die gequollen
Vom Quell ursprünglichen Bilds.

THE WALK

You wayside woods, well painted
On the green and sloping glade
Where I conduct my footsteps
With lovely quiet repaid
For every thorn in my bosom,
When dark are my mind and heart
Which paid from the beginning
In grief for thought and art.
You graceful views in the valley,
For instance garden and tree
And then the footbridge, the narrow,
The stream one can hardly see,
How beautiful, clear from the distance
These glorious pictures shine
Of the landscape I like to visit
When the weather is mild and fine.
The deity kindly escorts us,
At first with unblemished blue,
Later with clouds provided,
Well rounded and grey in hue,
With scorching flashes and rolling
Of thunder, and charm of the fields,
With beauty the bubbling source of
The primal image yields.

WENN AUS DEM HIMMEL...

Wenn aus dem Himmel hellere Wonne sich
   Herabgießt, eine Freude den Menschen kommt,
     Daß sie sich wundern über manches
      Sichtbares, Höheres, Angenehmes:

Wie tönet lieblich heilger Gesang dazu!
   Wie lacht das Herz in Liedern die Wahrheit an,
     Daß Freudigkeit an einem Bildniß —
      Über dem Stege beginnen Schaafe

Den Zug, der fast in dämmernde Wälder geht.
   Die Wiesen aber, welche mit lautrem Grün
     Bedekt sind, sind wie jene Haide,
      Welche gewöhnlicher Weise nah ist

Dem dunkeln Walde. Da, auf den Wiesen auch
   Verweilen diese Schaafe. Die Gipfel, die
     Umher sind, nakte Höhen sind mit
      Eichen bedeket und seltnen Tannen.

Da, wo des Stromes regsame Wellen sind,
   Daß einer, der vorüber des Weges kommt,
     Froh hinschaut, da erhebt der Berge
      Sanfte Gestalt und der Weinberg hoch sich.

Zwar gehn die Treppen unter den Reben hoch
   Herunter, wo der Obstbaum blühend darüber steht
     Und Duft an wilden Heken weilet,
      Wo die verborgenen Veilchen sprossen;

WHEN DOWN FROM HEAVEN...

When down from heaven there gushes a brighter bliss,
  A human joy approaches for human kind
    So that they feel amazed by much that's
      Visible, lofty and pleasing to them—

How lovely, blended with it, sound holy hymns!
  How the heart laughs in canticles at the truth
    That to one image clings rejoicing!
      Over the footbridge now sheep begin their

Long track that almost takes them to glimmering woods.
  The meadows, though, all covered with flawless green,
    Are like that heath which, in a fashion
      Usual enough, is not far away from

The gloomy wood. And there, in the meadows, too
  These sheep remain. The hilltops around those parts,
    Bare, arid heights they seem, are covered
      Sparsely with oaks and uncommon pine-trees.

There, where the river's frolicsome ripples are,
  So that a man who passes them on his way
    Is glad to see them, there the gentle
      Shape of the hills and the vineyard rises.

Although amid the grape-vines quite steeply steps
  Descend, where high the blossoming fruit-tree looms
    And on wild hedges fragrance lingers,
      Hidden the violets grow and flower,

Gewässer aber rieseln herab, und sanft
　Ist hörbar dort ein Rauschen den ganzen Tag;
　　Die Orte aber in der Gegend
　　　Ruhen und schweigen den Nachmittag durch.

Yet waters trickle down, and though quiet, faint,
A murmur there is audible all day long;
The places in those parts, however,
Rest after noon and for hours keep silence.

AN ZIMMERN

Von einem Menschen sag ich, wenn der ist gut
Und weise, was bedarf er? Ist irgend eins
    Das einer Seele gnüget? ist ein Halm, ist
        Eine gereifteste Reb' auf Erden

Gewachsen, die ihn nähre? Der Sinn ist deß
Also. Ein Freund ist oft die Geliebte, viel
    Die Kunst. O Theurer, dir sag ich die Wahrheit.
        Dädalus Geist und des Walds ist deiner.

TO ZIMMER

About a man I say, if he's virtuous
  And wise, what can he lack? Is there anything
    Could satisfy a soul? Is there a blade of corn, one
      Vine grown on earth with a fruit so mellow

That it could nourish him? What I mean is this:
  A friend quite often is the beloved, and art
    Is much. Dear fellow, I'll tell you the truth now:
      Daedalus' spirit is yours, the forest's.

ÜBERZEUGUNG

Als wie der Tag die Menschen hell umscheinet,
Und mit dem Lichte, das den Höh'n entspringet,
Die dämmernden Erscheinungen vereinet,
Ist Wissen, welches tief der Geistigkeit gelinget.

CONVICTION

Like the bright day that shines on human kind
And with a light of heavenly origin
All things obscure and various gathers in,
Is knowledge, deeply granted to the mind.

DAS ANGENEHME DIESER WELT...

Das Angenehme dieser Welt hab' ich genossen,
Die Jugendstunden sind, wie lang! wie lang! verflossen,
April und Mai und Julius sind ferne,
Ich bin nichts mehr, ich lebe nicht mehr gerne!

THE WORLD'S AGREEABLE THINGS...

The world's agreeable things were mine to enjoy,
The hours of youth, how long they have been gone!
Remote is April, May, remote, July;
I'm nothing now, and listless I live on.

AN ZIMMERN

Die Linien des Lebens sind verschieden
Wie Wege sind, und wie der Berge Gränzen.
Was hier wir sind, kan dort ein Gott ergänzen
Mit Harmonien und ewigem Lohn und Frieden.

TO ZIMMER

The lines of life are various; they diverge and cease
Like footpaths and the mountains' utmost ends.
What here we are, elsewhere a God amends
With harmonies, eternal recompense and peace.

DER RUHM

Es knüpft an Gott der Wohllaut, der geleitet
Ein sehr berühmtes Ohr, denn wunderbar
Ist ein berühmtes Leben groß und klar,
Es geht der Mensch zu Fuße oder reitet.

Der Erde Freuden, Freundlichkeit und Güter,
Der Garten, Baum, der Weinberg mit dem Hüter,
Sie scheinen mir ein Wiederglanz des Himmels,
Gewähret von dem Geist den Söhnen des Gewimmels. —

Wenn Einer ist mit Gütern reich beglüket,
Wenn Obst den Garten ihm, und Gold ausschmüket
Die Wohnung und das Haus, was mag er haben
Noch mehr in dieser Welt, sein Herz zu laben?

FAME

With God links up the euphony that attends
A very famous ear; for great indeed
A famous life is, wonderfully clear.
On foot or else on horseback men proceed.

The pleasures of this earth, its gifts, indulgence,
The garden, tree, the vineyard with its keeper,
These seem to me a heavenly refulgence
The Spirit grants our teeming multitude's sons.

If goods in plenty blessed a man who had
Fruits to adorn his orchard, and had gold
To adorn his house and dwelling, then what more
In this world could he have to make him glad?

DER SOMMER

Noch ist die Zeit des Jahrs zu sehn, und die Gefilde
Des Sommers stehn in ihrem Glanz, in ihrer Milde;
Des Feldes Grün ist prächtig ausgebreitet,
Allwo der Bach hinab mit Wellen gleitet.

So zieht der Tag hinaus durch Berg und Thale,
Mit seiner Unaufhaltsamkeit und seinem Strale,
Und Wolken ziehn in Ruh', in hohen Räumen,
Es scheint das Jahr mit Herrlichkeit zu säumen.

                                        Mit Unterthänigkeit
        d. 9 ten Merz   Scardanelli
            1940.

SUMMER

Still you can see the season, and the field
Of summer shows its mildness and its pride.
The meadow's green is splendidly outspread
Where down the brook and all its wavelets glide.

So now the day moves on through hill and valley,
Not to be stopped and in its beam arrayed,
And clouds move calmly on through lofty space
As though the year in majesty delayed.

                Your humble and obedient servant

March 9th   Scardanelli
  1940.

DER HERBST

Die Sagen, die der Erde sich entfernen,
Vom Geiste, der gewesen ist und wiederkehret,
Sie kehren zu der Menschheit sich, und vieles lernen
Wir aus der Zeit, die eilends sich verzehret.

Die Bilder der Vergangenheit sind nicht verlassen
Von der Natur, als wie die Tag' verblassen
Im hohen Sommer, kehrt der Herbst zur Erde nieder,
Der Geist der Schauer findet sich am Himmel wieder.

In kurzer Zeit hat vieles sich geendet,
Der Landmann, der am Pfluge sich gezeiget,
Er siehet, wie das Jahr sich frohem Ende neiget,
In solchen Bildern ist des Menschen Tag vollendet.

Der Erde Rund mit Felsen ausgezieret
Ist wie die Wolke nicht, die Abends sich verlieret,
Es zeigt sich mit einem goldnen Tage,
Und die Vollkommenheit ist ohne Klage.

AUTUMN

The legends that depart from land and sea,
Of spirit that once was here and will return,
These turn to men, and there is much we learn
From time that, self-devoured, moves speedily.

No image of the past is quite mislaid
By Nature; summer's dog-days fade,
But back to earth at once will autumn fly;
The ghost of showers gathers in the sky.

In a short time how much has passed away!
'The countryman observed behind his plough
Sees how the year meets a glad ending now;
Such images complete the human day.

The sphere of earth adorned with rocks revolves
Not like a cloud, which after dusk dissolves;
Within a golden day the earth appears,
And to perfection no complaint adheres.

DER WINTER

Wenn ungesehn und nun vorüber sind die Bilder
Der Jahreszeit, so kommt des Winters Dauer,
Das Feld ist leer, die Ansicht scheinet milder,
Und Stürme wehn umher und Reegenschauer.

Als wie ein Ruhetag, so ist des Jahres Ende,
Wie einer Frage Ton, daß dieser sich vollende,
Alsdann erscheint des Frühlings neues Werden,
So glänzet die Natur mit ihrer Pracht auf Erden.

                        Mit Unterthänigkeit
d. 24 April   Scardanelli.
   1849

WINTER

When past, unseen the season's images are,
Winter's duration comes to us again;
The field is bare, the view seems milder far,
And gales blow round about and showers of rain.

A day of rest, such is the year's conclusion,
A question's tone that seeks a complement
Then to our eyes the Spring's new growth is lent—
So Nature shines on earth in her profusion.

                    Your humble and obedient servant
April 24th   Scardanelli
    1849.

DER FRÜHLING

Wenn aus der Tiefe kommt der Frühling in das Leben,
Es wundert sich der Mensch, und neue Worte streben
Aus Geistigkeit, die Freude kehret wieder
Und festlich machen sich Gesang und Lieder.

Das Leben findet sich aus Harmonie der Zeiten,
Daß immerdar den Sinn Natur und Geist geleiten,
Und die Vollkommenheit ist Eines in dem Geiste,
So findet vieles sich, und aus Natur das Meiste.

Mit Unterthänigkeit

d. 24 Mai   Scardanelli.
  1758.

SPRING

When springtime from the depth returns to life,
Men are amazed, and from their minds aspire
New words, and happiness once more is rife,
And festive music rings from house and choir.

Life finds itself in seasonal harmonies,
That ever Nature, Spirit might attend our thought,
And *one* within our minds perfection is;
So, most of all from Nature, much to itself is brought.

Your humble and obedient servant

May 24th   Scardanelli
   1758.

IN LIEBLICHER BLÄUE...

In lieblicher Bläue blühet mit dem metallenen Dache der Kirchthurm. Den umschwebet Geschrei der Schwalben, den umgiebt die rührendste Bläue. Die Sonne gehet hoch darüber und färbet das Blech, im Winde aber oben stille krähet die Fahne. Wenn einer unter der Gloke dann herabgeht, jene Treppen, ein stilles Leben ist es, weil, wenn abgesondert so sehr die Gestalt ist, die Bildsamkeit herauskommt dann des Menschen. Die Fenster, daraus die Gloken tönen, sind wie Thore an Schönheit. Nemlich, weil noch der Natur nach sind die Thore, haben diese die Ähnlichkeit von Bäumen des Walds. Reinheit aber ist auch Schönheit. Innen aus Verschiedenem entsteht ein ernster Geist. So sehr einfältig aber die Bilder, so sehr heilig sind die, daß man wirklich oft fürchtet, die zu beschreiben. Die Himmlischen aber, die immer gut sind, alles zumal, wie Reiche, haben diese, Tugend und Freude. Der Mensch darf das nachahmen. Darf, wenn lauter Mühe das Leben, ein Mensch aufschauen und sagen: so will ich auch seyn? Ja. So lange die Freundlichkeit noch am Herzen, die Reine, dauert, misset nicht unglüklich der Mensch sich mit der Gottheit. Ist unbekannt Gott? Ist er offenbar wie der Himmel? dieses glaub' ich eher. Des Menschen Maaß ist's. Voll Verdienst, doch dichterisch, wohnet der Mensch auf dieser Erde. Doch reiner ist nicht der Schatten der Nacht mit den Sternen, wenn ich so sagen könnte, als der Mensch, der heißet ein Bild der Gottheit.

Giebt es auf Erden ein Maaß? Es giebt keines. Nemlich es hemmen den Donnergang nie die Welten des Schöpfers. Auch eine Blume ist schön, weil sie blühet unter der Sonne. Es findet das Aug' oft im Leben Wesen, die viel schöner noch zu nennen wären als die Blumen. O! ich weiß das wohl! Denn zu bluten an Gestalt und Herz, und ganz

IN LOVELY BLUENESS...

In lovely blueness with its metal roof the steeple blossoms.

Around it the crying of swallows hovers, most moving blueness surrounds it. The sun hangs high above it and colours the sheets of tin, but up above in the wind silently crows the weathercock. If now someone comes down beneath the bell, comes down those steps, a still life it is, because, when the figure is so detached, the man's plasticity is brought out. The windows from which the bells are ringing are like gates in beauty. That is, because gates still conform to nature, these have a likeness to trees of the wood. But purity too is beauty. Within, out of diversity a serious mind is formed. Yet these images are so simple, so very holy are these, that really often one is afraid to describe them. But the Heavenly, who are always good, all things at once, like the rich, have these, virtue and pleasure. This men may imitate. May, when life is all hardship, may a man look up and say: I too would like to resemble these? Yes. As long as kindliness, which is pure, remains in his heart not unhappily a man may compare himself with the divinity. Is God unknown? Is He manifest as the sky? This rather I believe. It is the measure of man. Full of acquirements, but poetically, man dwells on this earth. But the darkness of night with all the stars is not purer, if I could put it like that, than man, who is called the image of God.

Is there a measure on earth? There is none. For never the Creator's worlds constrict the progress of thunder. A flower too is beautiful, because it blooms under the sun. Often in life the eye discovers beings that could be called much more beautiful still than flowers. Oh, well I know it! For to bleed both in body and heart, and wholly to be no

601

nicht mehr zu seyn, gefällt das Gott? Die Seele aber, wie ich glaube, muß rein bleiben, sonst reicht an das Mächtige auf Fittigen der Adler mit lobendem Gesange und der Stimme so vieler Vögel. Es ist die Wesenheit, die Gestalt ist's. Du schönes Bächlein, du scheinest rührend, indem du rollest so klar, wie das Auge der Gottheit, durch die Milchstraße. Ich kenne dich wohl, aber Thränen quillen aus dem Auge. Ein heiteres Leben seh' ich in den Gestalten mich umblühen der Schöpfung, weil ich es nicht unbillig vergleiche den einsamen Tauben auf dem Kirchhof. Das Lachen aber scheint mich zu grämen der Menschen, nemlich ich hab' ein Herz. Möcht' ich ein Komet seyn? Ich glaube. Denn sie haben die Schnelligkeit der Vögel; sie blühen an Feuer, und sind wie Kinder an Reinheit. Größeres zu wünschen, kann nicht des Menschen Natur sich vermessen. Der Tugend Heiterkeit verdient auch gelobt zu werden vom ernsten Geiste, der zwischen den drei Säulen wehet des Gartens. Eine schöne Jungfrau muß das Haupt umkränzen mit Myrthenblumen, weil sie einfach ist ihrem Wesen nach und ihrem Gefühl. Myrthen aber giebt es in Griechenland.

———————

Wenn einer in den Spiegel siehet, ein Mann, und siehet darinn sein Bild, wie abgemahlt; es gleicht dem Manne. Augen hat des Menschen Bild, hingegen Licht der Mond. Der König Oedipus hat ein Auge zuviel vieleicht. Diese Leiden dieses Mannes, sie scheinen unbeschreiblich, unaussprechlich, unausdrüklich. Wenn das Schauspiel ein solches darstellt, kommt's daher. Wie ist mir's aber, gedenk' ich deiner jezt? Wie Bäche reißt das Ende von Etwas mich dahin, welches sich wie Asien ausdehnet. Natürlich dieses Leiden, das hat Oedipus. Natürlich ist's darum. Hat auch Herkules gelitten? Wohl. Die Dioskuren in ihrer Freundschaft haben die nicht Leiden auch getragen? Nemlich wie Herkules mit Gott zu streiten, das ist Leiden. Und die Unsterblichkeit im Neide dieses Lebens, diese zu theilen, ist ein Leiden auch. Doch das ist auch ein Leiden, wenn mit Sommerfleken ist bedekt ein Mensch, mit manchen Fleken ganz überdekt zu seyn! Das thut die schöne Sonne: nemlich die ziehet alles auf. Die more, does that please God? Yet the soul, it is my belief, must remain pure, else on pinions the eagle reaches far as the Mighty with songs of praise and the voice of so many birds. It is the essence, the form it is. You beautiful little stream, you seem touching, as you flow so clear, clear as the eye of divinity, through the Milky Way. I know you well, but tears gush out of my eyes. A serene life I see blossom around me in the shapes of creation, because not unfittingly I compare it to the solitary doves of the churchyard. But the laughter of men seems to grieve me, for I have a heart. Would I like to be a comet? I think so. For they possess the swiftness of birds; they blossom with fire and are like children in purity. To desire more than that, human nature cannot presume. The serenity of virtue also deserves to be praised by the serious spirit which wafts between the garden's three columns. A beautiful virgin must wreathe her head with myrtle, because she is simple both in her nature and in her feelings. But myrtles are to be found in Greece.

If someone looks into the mirror, a man, and in it sees his image, as though it were a painted likeness; it resembles the man. The image of man has eyes, whereas the moon has light. King Oedipus has an eye too many perhaps. The sufferings of this man, they seem indescribable, unspeakable, inexpressible. If the drama represents something like this, that is why. But what comes over me if I think of you now? Like brooks the end of something sweeps me away, which expands like Asia. Of course, this affliction, Oedipus has it too. Of course, that is why. Did Hercules suffer too? Indeed. The Dioscuri in their friendship, did not they bear afflictions too? For to fight with God, like Hercules, that is an affliction. And immortality amidst the envy of this life, to share in that, is an affliction too. But this also is an affliction, when a man is covered with freckles, to be wholly covered with many a spot! The beautiful sun does that: for it rears up all things. It leads young men along their course with the

Jünglinge führt die Bahn sie mit Reizen ihrer Stralen wie mit Rosen. Die Leiden scheinen so, die Oedipus getragen, als wie ein armer Mann klagt, daß ihm etwas fehle. Sohn Laios, armer Fremdling in Griechenland! Leben ist Tod, und Tod ist auch ein Leben.

---

allurements of its beams as though with roses. The afflictions that Oedipus bore seem like this, as when a poor man complains that there is something he lacks. Son of Laios, poor stranger in Greece! Life is death, and death is a kind of life.

———

P. 23 *The Excellent*   In November 1794 Hölderlin wrote to his friend Christian Ludwig Neuffer from Jena: '. . . a sentence which I happened to see today in the announcement of Wieland's collected works still burns in my heart. It says that Wieland's Muse began with the beginning of German poetry and will end with its decline. Wonderful! Call me a childish fool, but a thing like that can spoil a whole week for me. . . .'

P. 73 *Vanini*   Lucilio Vanini (1585-1619) was an Italian philosopher burnt at the stake for atheism and for dabbling in magic and astrology. Hölderlin sees him as the inspired philosopher-prophet at odds with the 'nexus of rulers and clerics', and thus as a figure akin both to Empedocles and himself.

P. 105 *To a Princess of Dessau*   Alcaic ode, probably written in November 1799, after the renewed outbreak of war, to which there are several allusions in the poem. The reference to Italy suggests that the ode was addressed to the Duchess Luise of Anhalt-Dessau, rather than to her daughter-in-law Amalie, a sister of Hölderlin's patron Princess Augusta of Homburg. The Duchess had travelled in Italy from 1795 to 1796. Luisium is the name of a palace near Dessau, the grounds of which Hölderlin had seen in 1795 while walking from Jena to Halle.

P. 109 *To Princess Augusta of Homburg*   Alcaic ode, written for her twenty-third birthday. The Princess was not only devoted to Hölderlin's novel *Hyperion*—the only work of his available in book form at this time—but made copies of several of his poems that might otherwise have been lost. The middle sections of the ode refer to the withdrawal of the French revolutionary troops from Homburg in March 1799. The 'hero' of the fifth stanza is most probably Napoleon, whose recent *coup d'état* was welcomed in many quarters as a promise of lasting peace in Europe. Princess Augusta's mother, Caroline, is known to have admired Napoleon.

P. 129 *Rousseau*   This attempt to recast his Asclepiadean ode *To the*

Germans shows how much better the Alcaic form lent itself to the peculiar flow of Hölderlin's later odes. The change in subject is not so significant, since the Rousseau of this ode is a figure deeply akin to the solitary poet of the other ode.

P. 165 *Nature and Art*   The eighteenth-century preoccupation with the antinomy between Nature and Art is touched upon in the Introduction. Hölderlin identifies the triumph of Art over Nature with the triumph of Jupiter over Saturn, drawing on ancient poetic tradition, yet giving it a personal twist. Jupiter becomes closely identified with the *Zeitgeist* of his earlier ode; he is called 'Kronion' because Hölderlin identifies Kronos (Saturn) with Chronos (Time), so that Jupiter becomes both 'the son of Kronos' and a 'son of Time'. This anticipates the curious theology of the hymns, with their two parallel orders of divinity—one temporal and temporary (the gods), the other timeless and eternal (God). Compare Hölderlin's letter on the one quarrel in the world (Introduction, p. 11).

P. 169 *Sung Beneath the Alps*   The one completed ode by Hölderlin written in a modified Sapphic metre. Hölderlin saw the Swiss Alps in 1801.

P. 173 *The Poet's Vocation*   The last line has puzzled many commentators. Hölderlin's disgust with the exploitation and debasement of religion, science and art is such that the allusion to God's absence has been construed as irony. Yet Hölderlin is quite serious in stating that the dominant trends in our civilization will never be reversed until there is a general recognition of God's absence in our lives. Only this awareness of God's absence can bring about a general *metanoia*—and so release the poet and prophet from his irreligious solitude.

P. 179 *Voice of the People*   Cf. S. T. Coleridge: 'I never said that the *vox populi* was of course the *vox Dei*. It may be, but it may be and with equal probability, *a priori*, *vox Diaboli*. That the voice of ten millions of men calling for the same thing, is a spirit, I believe; but whether that be a spirit of Heaven or Hell, I can only know by trying the thing called for by the prescript of reason and God's will' (*Table Talk*, 1888, p. 160). It is such rational and moral doubts as Coleridge's that the peculiar reticence and impersonality of this ode imply from the opening lines onward; but Hölderlin's vision here is tragic rather than moral, and what the Christian moralist would see as wickedness and unreason he must affirm as a tragic sacrifice. There is no need to point out that Hölderlin's recognition of a communal 'death-wish' anticipates some of the discoveries of Freud and other psychologists.

P. 185 *The Blind Singer*   The quotation is from the *Ajax* of Sophocles, line 706, and means 'Cruel woe has Ares lifted from our eyes'.

P. 205 *Timidness*   In the last strophe Hölderlin plays on various derivations from the verb *schicken* (to send). 'Geschickt', literally 'sent', also means 'skilful'—so that there is an etymological connection between the artist's skill and his mission or his fitness to serve, for fitness is implied in the German word 'Geschicklichkeit'. Yet the nouns 'Geschick' and 'Schicksal' also mean fate or destiny—and again Hölderlin takes up the etymological link. These multiple meanings could be rendered only by adding alternative words in English.

P. 209 *Ganymede*   This last ode renders what Hölderlin meant by saying (in his letter to Böhlendorff) that Apollo had struck him. His madness, among other things, was a release from tremendous mental and spiritual exertions, and a removal from the entire sphere of human relations, human converse ('Gespräch') and human conflict. In the last versions of these late odes Hölderlin translates personal experiences into myth, identifying himself with a centaur (Chiron) and a spirit or demigod (Ganymede)

P. 243 *Bread and Wine*   In this elegy Hölderlin develops his notion of alternating eras or cycles of Day and Night, epiphany and retraction. The conception, though new, owes something to the thought of Empedocles and his predecessors, and is pantheistic in its likening of history to natural processes. Hölderlin's purpose here is to 'justify the ways of God to Men', yet in a way consonant with his own tragic sense of life and his experience of God's absence in his own time. His notion of the 'searing beam', the unbearable brightness of God, on the other hand, is firmly rooted in Biblical, esoteric and poetic tradition. *Paradise Lost* presents parallels; and so does the poetry of William Blake, who wrote in *The Little Black Boy*:

And we are put on earth a little space

That we may learn to bear the beams of love.

P. 379 *For Mother Earth*   Probably written late in 1800, and left unfinished like the Pindaric 'hymn' *As on a holiday* . . . An extant prose
draft suggests that, as in the case of the earlier hymn, Hölderlin could
not fit all he had to say into the form he had chosen—a choric form in
both cases, demanding a strict balance between each group of three
strophes.

The names of the three brothers have a mythical aura, but seem
to be Hölderlin's own invention—a rare analogy with William Blake's
names in his prophetic poems. A number of poems by Klopstock
provided a precedent for the three persons of his poem.

P. 409 *The Rhine*   St. 14, lines 12-15. The 'wise man' is Socrates in
Plato's *Symposium*.

P. 423 *Conciliator, you that no longer believed in* . . . St. 4, line 7 'The
faithful cloud' is the disciples, the 'cloud of witness'.

P. 433 *Celebration of Peace*   Whole books have been devoted to specu-
lations about the identity of the 'prince of the feast-day', who has been
interpreted historically (as Napoleon, because the poem was
occasioned by the Treaty of Lunéville in February 1801), ideologically
(as the 'genius of the German people'), allegorically (as Peace) and
even, untenably, as Christ, though at one point in the poem Christ is
entreated to join the prince of the feast-day. What is certain is that
Hölderlin did not want to establish his identity, as we see by com-
paring the preliminary drafts, in which Peace is unequivocally
addressed. The introduction to the prince, in the second strophe, contains a characteristic syntactical ambiguity; strictly speaking, the
opening two lines should be taken to describe the 'I' of the poem, not
the prince, but throughout the poem Hölderlin uses syntax for his
own poetic ends, not least for the creation of suspense and mystery.
The opening strophe is a striking example of Hölderlin's poetic
'architecture'. The syntactic suspension of the word 'tables', for
instance, serves to give this word exactly the right place in a design at
once pictorial and mythical. By the time we read the word it has been

610

invested with all the functions and associations which Hölderlin attributes to the phenomenon.

P. 479 *Patmos* (Fragments of the later Version)   'More athletic in ruin' (St. 3): compare Hölderlin's letter to Böhlendorff, *Introduction*, pp. 12-14.

P. 493 *The Ister*   'Ister' was the classical name of the Danube. 'Hertha' (St. 3), according to Tacitus, was the 'terra mater' of the ancient Germans.

P. 501 *Mnemosyne*   'Mnemosyne' means 'memory', and she was the mother of the Muses. Mourning for the past—as the earlier hymns had already stated, is not permitted to the poet, who must 'collect his soul' for a different task, that of interpreting 'the signs of day', all that is present and actual. (Cf. the conclusion of *Patmos*.) Cooking in the opening line, denotes the natural process of ripening, as distinct from roasting or burning—a distinction observed in ancient sacrificial rites. Paracelsus wrote: 'The ripening of fruit is natural cookery: therefore what nature has in her, she cooks, and when it is cooked, then nature is whole.' Serpents traditionally are prophetic creatures. Since they slough their skins, they are also symbols of renewal or (in oriental and Gnostic lore) of eternity. To 'sever a lock of hair', in Greek mythology, is to mark a person out for death.

P. 519 *To the Virgin Mary*   'By a lowly man or king.' Hölderlin is thinking of Herod, who had John the Baptist decapitated, and those responsible for the death of Christ; but also of Creon whose laws (in the *Antigone*) are contrasted with the 'unwritten unalterable laws of Heaven'.

'Spiritual water.' This is ambiguous, since in eighteenth-century German usage 'geistiges Wasser' denoted 'mineral water'. Hölderlin is referring to the mineral springs at Bad Driburg in Westphalia, where he spent part of the year 1796, not far from the *Knochenberg* (literally: mountain of bones), which he associates with the Thessalian mountain Ossa. This region was also the site of the battle between the Romans and the ancient Germans under Arminius; hence the allusion to Teutoburg.

'To the shadows I would have turned.' Once again Hölderlin

611

alludes to the forbidden pleasure of communing with the dead and with the past. Instead, he praises the Virgin, God's representative in the present transitional age of Night or 'wilderness'. It is she who desires that the coming era, 'the germinating days', shall be greater than the era of her reign. There are allusions to traditional symbols associated with the Virgin Mary, such as lilies and the enclosed garden.

P. 557 *The Vatican*   'and over there in Westphalia, my honest master'. Probably a reference to Wilhelm Heinse ('Cf. Introduction, p. 5).

P. 573 *If from the Distance* . . .   The only poem of Hölderlin's madness which directly alludes to events in his past life. Susette Gontard, of course, had been dead for some years by the time this fragmentary Alcaic ode was written. Strangely enough, the poem is addressed to the poet by the woman, not vice versa, as would be more usual. The French poet Philippe Jacottet has quoted the fifth and sixth strophes of this ode as an instance of 'the moment when poetry, without seeming to do so, since it is divested of all brilliancy, attains what for me is the highest point, (which) seems at first to be simpler than anything else. In reality, however, it is the most difficult and rarest of all.'

P. 577 *The Walk*   Here Hölderlin seems to interpret the 'philosophic calm' of his madness as a kind of compensation for the stresses of his earlier life. The tone of this poem, and some of the reflections on the seasons, is not unlike that of certain poems written by John Clare in his madness.

P. 585 *Conviction*   Inscribed in Christopher Schwab's copy of Hölderlin's first collection of poems, *Gedichte* (1826), edited by Ludwig Uhland and Gustav Schwab; the lines were written and entered there at Christopher Schwab's request, preceded by four lines of prose.

P. 593 *Summer*   The fictitious date and the signature 'Scardanelli' are typical of Hölderlin's escape both from time and identity in his madness. He would also call himself 'Buonarotti' or 'Scaliger Rosa'.

P. 601 *In Lovely Blueness* . . .   This poem is printed last because its authenticity is doubtful. It is taken from the novel *Phaeton* (1823), by Wilhelm Waiblinger, a Swabian poet who saw a great deal of Hölderlin in his madness and drew on his knowledge of him for the character of Phaeton, a sculptor. In 1822 Waiblinger mentioned in his diary that he had access to Hölderlin's unpublished work, and the prose poem in the novel is introduced as follows: 'At that time he covered with writing all the paper he could lay his hands on. Here are a few pages from his papers, which at the same time give us a deep insight into his terribly confused state of mind. In the original they are divided into lines like verses in the Pindaric manner.' The most likely hypothesis is that Waiblinger adapted the piece from one or more poems given to him by Hölderlin and now lost, possibly adding and omitting passages in the process. In 1827 Waiblinger wrote an early account of Hölderlin's 'Life, Work and Madness'.

INDEX OF FIRST LINES (ENGLISH)

About a man I say, if he's virtuous, 583

Always you trifle and joke?, 71

Amid dark ivy I was sitting, at, 409

And no one knows, 511

And to feel with the lives, 551

Are the cranes returning to you, and the mercantile vessels, 213

As on a holiday, to see the field, 373

As slowly birds migrate, 509

As though the old flood waters, which, 117

At one time I questioned the Muse, and she, 537

At peace the ploughman sits in the shade outside, 91

At rest in fulness, calm lies the autumn day, 99

Beautiful being, you live as do delicate blossoms in winter, 25

Being at one is god-like and good, 71

Bliss of the heavenly muse who on elements once imposed order, 27

Cold hypocrites, of gods do not dare to speak!, 61

Conciliator, you that no longer believed in, 423

Content the boatman turns to the river's calm, 49, 143

Daily I search, now here, now there my wandering takes me, 233

Dearest brothers, whatever you do, 23

Dearest one, you lie sick, so that with weeping my, 51

Deep in my heart I abhor the nexus of rulers and clerics, 23

Do not laugh at the child when with his whip and spurs, 59

Do you hear the frenzied crowd?, 267

Echo of Heaven, heart that is hallowed, why, 161

For as when high from the gloriously voiced, the organ, 385

For from the abyss we, 553

For when the grape-vine's sap, 513

From afar let me hear music of strings or song, 87

Go down, then, lovely sun, for but little they, 115

God's enemy, despiser, they called you, heaped, 73

Has not love hallowed, filled with new life my heart, 47

High my spirit aspired, truly, however, love, 43

High up in day you govern, your law prevails, 165

Holy being, I know, often I've troubled your, 39

Holy Socrates, why always with deference, 67

How narrowly confined is our day-time here, 129

If from the distance where we went separate ways, 573

If you drop an old friend, if, O you grateful ones, 145

If you drop an old friend, laugh at the artist and, 55

If to those warning ones now I listened, they'd smile at me, thinking, 85

In lovely blueness with its metal roof the steeple blossoms, 601

In my boyhood days, 81

In younger days each morning rose with joy, 41

Innocence, you the holy, dearest and nearest, 169

Instead of open community, song I sing, 379

Is not all that's alive close and akin to you, 201

Latest news: Apollo's become the god of journalists, 23

Like the bright day that shines on human kind, 585

Living in life, learn your art, 71

Long I have loved you and wish, for my own delight, 133

Many have tried, but in vain, with joy to express the most joyful, 71

More you also desired, but every one of us, 149

Most happy Swabia, my mother, 393

Most kind is; but no one by himself, 479

Much I have suffered, 519

My father roamed up on the Gotthard, 541

Nature, look, your most loved drowses and ails, and you, 151

Nature, she who's your friend drowses and ails, and you, 53

Near is, 462

Never fear the poet when nobly he rages, 71

Never laugh at the child, seeing the silly one, 123

Not them, the blessed, who once appeared, 401

Not yet, however, 531

Now come, fire!, 493

O heavenly love, the tender, if you I should, 193

O hope, benignly active one, dear to men, 195

O the worldly wise man!, 23

O you voices of fate, you ways of the wanderer!, 565, 567

Of the living are not many well-known to you?, 205

On fallow foliage rests, 515

One summer only grant me, you powerful fates, 33

opened the windows of Heaven, 545

Poets are holy vessels, 29

Quite soon, dear brothers, perhaps our art, 57

Ripe are, dipped in fire, cooked, 499

Round us the town is at rest; the street, in pale lamplight, grows quiet, 243

Send her flowers and fruit from inexhaustible fulness, 37

So we wanted to part? Thought it both good and wise?, 153

Still kindly lingering the year from your eye departs, 109

Still you can see the season, and the field, 593

The banks of the Ganges heard how the god of joy, 69, 173

The gods will often send from a quiet house, 105

The legends that depart from land and sea, 595

The lines of life are various; they diverge and cease, 589

The north-easterly blows, 489

the Vatican, 557

The voice of God I called you and thought you once, 179

The world's agreeable things were mine to enjoy, 587

There in the Alps a gleaming night still delays and, composing, 255

Though every day I follow a different path, 113

Too long above my head you have governed there, 89

True, on this living earth there are many lands, 95

ways of the wanderer, 561

What is it that, 447, 455

What is the life of men an image of the godhead, 517

When down from heaven there gushes a brighter bliss, 579

When drunkenly inspiring the morning rises, 505

When past, unseen the season's images are, 597

When scarcely from the waters, O Earth, for you, 75,

When springtime from the depth returns to life, 599

Where are you? Dazzled, drunken my soul grows faint, 63, 65

Where are you, thought-infusing, which at this time, 189

Where are you, youthful herald who always once, 185

Why do you sleep and dream, in yourself wrapped up, 207

Why do you sleep, lie crooked, ill-humoured here, 209

Why Earth, around me glimmer your friendly leaves? 103

'Why so brief now, so curt?, Do you no longer, then, 45

With dew the lawn is glistening; more nimbly now, 93

With God links up the euphony that attends, 591

With heavenly, quietly echoing, 433

With yellow pears the land, 371

You cities of Euphrates, 369

You come now, friendly spirit of fire, and wrap, 197

You gentle breezes, heralds of Italy, 159

You look for life, you look and from deeps of Earth, 31

You now I call upon across the fields, 325

You silent Aether, always in pain or grief, 137

You suffer and keep silent and, strange to them, 35

You suffer and keep silent, unknown to them, 157

You walk above in the light, 79

You wayside woods, well painted, 577

Your banks and dells awakened my heart to life, 139

You've a head *and* a heart? 23

INDEX OF FIRST LINES (GERMAN)

Auf falbem Laube ruhet, 514
Aus stillem Hauße senden die Götter oft, 104

Da ich ein Knabe war, 80
Das Angenehme dieser Welt hab' ich genossen, 586
Das Leben suchst du, suchst, und es quillt und glänzt, 30
Deine Freundin, Natur! leidet und schläft und du, 52
Den Gottverächter schalten sie dich? mit Fluch, 72
Denn, wie wenn hoch von der herrlichgestimmten, der Orgel, 384
Der himmlischen, still wiederklingenden, 432
Der Nordost wehet, 488
der Vatican, 556
Des Ganges Ufer hörten des Freudengotts, 68, 172
Die Linien des Lebens sind verschieden, 588
Die Sagen, die der Erde sich entfernen, 594
Die Schönheit ist den Kindern eigen, 584
Drinn in den Alpen ists noch helle Nacht und die Wolke, 254
Du schweigst und duldest, denn sie verstehn dich nicht, 156
Du schweigst und duldest, und sie versteh'n dich nicht, 34
Du seiest Gottes Stimme, so glaubt' ich sonst, 178
Du stiller Aether! immer bewahrst du schön, 136
Du waltest hoch am Tag' und es blühet dein, 164

Echo des Himmels! heiliges Herz! warum, 160

Einig zu seyn, ist göttlich und gut, 70
Einst hab ich die Muse gefragt, und sie, 536
Es knüpft an Gott der Wohllaut, der geleitet, 590
Euch ruf ich über das Gefild herein, 324

Froh kehrt der Schiffer an den stillen Strom, 48
Froh kehrt der Schiffer heim an den stillen Strom, 142
Fürchtet den Dichter nicht, wenn er edel zürnet, 70

Geh unter, schöne Sonne, sie achteten, 114
Glückseelig Suevien, meine Mutter, 392
Größers wolltest auch du, aber die Liebe zwingt, 148

Hast du Verstand und ein Herz, 22
Heilig Wesen! gestört hab' ich die goldene, 38
Heilige Gefäße sind die Dichter, 28
Heilige Unschuld, du der Menschen und der, 168
Himmlische Liebe! zärtliche! wenn ich dein, 192
Hoch auf strebte mein Geist, aber die Liebe zog, 42
Hör' ich ferne nur her, wenn ich für mich geklagt, 86
Hörst du das trunkne Volk?, 266
Hört' ich die Warnenden izt, sie lächelten meiner und dächten, 84

Ihr kalten Heuchler, sprecht von den Göttern nicht!, 60
Ihr milden Lüfte! Boten Italiens!, 158

Ihr Städte des Euphrats!, 368
Ihr Wälder schön an der Seite, 576
Ihr wandelt droben im Licht, 78
Im dunkeln Epheu saß ich, an der Pforte, 408
Immer spielt ihr und scherzt?, 70
In deinen Thälern wachte mein Herz mir auf, 138
In jüngern Tagen war des Morgens froh, 40
In liebliche Bläue blühet mit den metallenen Dache, 600
In seiner Fülle ruhet der Herbsttag nun, 98
Ist nicht heilig mein Herz, schöneren Lebens voll, 46

Jezt komm und hülle, freundlicher Feuergeist, 196
Jezt komme, Feuer!, 492

Kaum sproßten aus den Wassern, o Erde, dir, 74
Kehren die Kraniche wieder zu dir, und suchen zu deinen, 212
Komm und besänftige mir, die du einst Elemente versöhntest, 26

Lange lieb' ich dich schon, möchte dich, mir zu Lust, 132
Lern im Leben die Kunst, 70
Lieben Brüder! es reift unsere Kunst vieleicht, 56
Lieben Brüder! versucht es nur nicht, 22

Mein Vater ist gewandert, auf dem Gotthard, 540
Mit gelben Birnen hänget, 370

Nah ist, 462
Nicht ist es aber, 530
Nicht sie, die Seeligen, die erschienen sind, 400
Noch freundlichzögernd scheidet vom Auge dir, 108
Noch ist die Zeit des Jahrs zu sehn, und die Gefilde, 592
Nur Einen Sommer gönnt, ihr Gewaltigen!, 32

O der Menschenkenner!, 22
O Hofnung! holde! gutiggeschäfftige!, 194
O ihr Stimmen des Geschiks, ihr Wege des Wanderers, 564, 566
offen die Fenster des Himmels, 544

Reif sind, in Feuer getaucht, gekochet, 498
Rings um ruht die Stadt; still wird die erleuchtete Gässe, 242

Schönes Leben! du lebst, wie die zarten Blüthen im Winter, 24
Schönes Leben! du liegst krank, und das Herz ist mir, 50
Send' ihr Blumen und Frücht' aus nieversiegender Fülle, 36
Sieh! dein Liebstes Natur, leidet und schläft und du, 150
Sind denn dir nicht bekannt viele Lebendigen?, 204
Sind denn dir nicht verwandt alle Lebendigen, 200
Spottet ja nicht des Kinds, wenn es mit Peitsch' und Sporn, 58
Spottet nimmer des Kinds, wenn noch das alberne, 122
Statt offner Gemeine sing' ich Gesang, 378

Täglich geh' ich heraus, und such' ein Anderes immer, 232
Tief im Herzen haß ich den Troß der Despoten und Pfaffen, 22
Trennen wollten wir uns? wähnten es gut und klug?, 152

Und mitzufühlen das Leben, 550
Und niemand weiß, 510

Versöhnender der du nimmergeglaubt, 422

Viel hab' ich dein, 518
Viele versuchten umsonst das Freudigste freudig zu sagen, 70
Voll Güt' ist; keiner aber fasset, 478
Vom Abgrund nemlich haben, 552
Vom Thaue glänzt der Rasen; beweglicher, 92
Von einem Menschen sag ich, wenn der ist gut, 582
Vor seiner Hütte ruhig im Schatten sizt, 90

Warum bist du so kurz? liebst du, wie vormals, denn, 44
Warum huldigest du, heiliger Sokrates, 66
Was dämmert um mich, Erde! dein freundlich Grün?, 102
Was ist der Menschen Leben ein Bild der Gottheit, 516
Was ist es, das, 446, 454
Was schläfst du, Bergsohn, liegest in Unmuth, schief, 208
Was schläfst und träumst du Jüngling, gehüllt in dich, 206
Wege des Wanderers!, 560
Wenn aus dem Himmel hellere Wonne sich, 578
Wenn aus der Ferne, da wird geschieden sind, 572
Wenn aus der Tiefe kommt der Frühling in das Leben, 598

Wenn der Morgen trunken begeisternd heraufgeht, 504
Wenn ihr Freunde vergeßt, wenn ihr den Künstler höhnt, 54
Wenn ihr Freunde vergeßt, wenn ihr die Euern all, 144
Wenn nemlich der Rebe Saft, 512
Wenn ungesehn und nun vorüber sind die Bilder, 596
Wie eng begränzt ist unsere Tageszeit, 128
Wie Vögel langsam ziehn, 508
Wie wenn am Feiertag, das Feld zu sehn, 372
Wie wenn die alten Wasser, die, 116
Wißt! Apoll ist der Gott der Zeitungsschreiber geworden, 22
Wo bist du, Jugendliches! das immer mich, 184
Wo bist du, Nachdenkliches! das immer muß, 188
Wo bist du? trunken dämmert die Seele mir, 62, 64
Wohl geh' ich täglich andere Pfade, bald, 112
Wohl manches Land der Lebenden Erde möcht', 94

Zu lang schon waltest über dem Haupte mir, 88

INDEX OF TITLES (ENGLISH)

Advocatus Diaboli, 23
Ages of Life, The, 369
And to feel with the lives . . ., 551
Angry Poet, The, 71
Archipelago, The, 213
As on a holiday . . ., 373
As slowly birds migrate . . ., 509
At one time I questioned the Muse . . ., 537
At the Source of the Danube, 385
Autumn, 595

Blind Singer, The, 185
Bonaparte, 29
Bread and Wine, 243
Brevity, 45

Capricious, The, 87
Celebration of Peace, 433
Chiron, 189
Conciliator, you that no longer believed in . . ., 423
Conviction, 585
Course of Life, The, 43, 149

Death of Empedocles, The (second version), 263; (third version), 323
Descriptive Poetry, 23
Diotima, 27, 35, 157

Eagle, The, 541
Empedocles, 31
Evening Fantasy, 91
Excellent, The, 23
Exhortation, 161

False Popularity, 23
Fame, 591
Farewell, The, 153
Fettered River, The, 207
For from the abyss . . ., 553
For Mother Earth, 379
For when the grape-vine's sap . . ., 513

Ganymede, 209
German Song, 505
Germania, 401
Gods, The, 137
Go down then, lovely sun . . ., 115
Good Advice, 23
Good Faith, 51
Greece (first version), 561; (second version), 565; (third version), 567

Heidelberg, 133
Her Recovery, 53, 151
Home, 49, 143, 511
Homecoming, 255
Human Applause, 47
Hyperion's Song of Fate, 79

If from the distance . . ., 573
If to those warning ones . . ., 85
In lovely blueness . . ., 601
In my boyhood days . . ., 81
In the Morning, 93
Ister, The, 493

Jokers, The, 71
Journey, The, 393

Love, 145

Man, 75
Menon's Lament for Diotima, 233
Middle of Life, The, 371
Mnemosyne, 499
My Possessions, 99

Nature and Art or Saturn and Jupiter, 165
Neckar, The, 139

On fallow foliage . . ., 515
Only One, The (first version), 447; (second version), 455

Palinode, 103

Patmos, 463; (fragments of the later version), 479
Peace, 117
Plea for Forgiveness, 39
Poet's Courage, The, 201
Poet's Vocation, The, 173
Προς Εαυτον (To Himself), 71

Remembrance, 489
Return to the Homeland, 159
Rhine, The, 409
River Main, The, 95
Root of All Evil, The, 71
Rousseau, 129

Sanctimonious Poets, The, 61
Socrates and Alcibiades, 67
Sophocles, 71
Spirit of the Age, The, 89
Spring, 599
Summer, 593
Sung beneath the Alps, 169
Sunset, 65

Tears, 193
Then and Now, 41
Though every day I follow . . ., 113
Timidness, 205

Titans, The, 531
To a Princess of Dessau, 105
To Diotima, 25
To her Genius, 37
To Hope, 195
To Our Great Poets, 69
To Princess Augusta of Homburg, 109
To the Fates, 33
To the Germans, 59, 123
To the Sun-God, 63
To the Virgin Mary, 519
To the Young Poets, 57
To Zimmer, 583, 589

Unpardonable, The, 55

Vanini, 73
Vatican, The, 557
Voice of the People, 179
Vulcan, 197

Walk, The, 577
What is the life of men . . ., 517
Whatever is Nearest, 545
When down from heaven . . ., 579
Winter, 597
World's agreeable Things, The, 587

INDEX OF TITLES (GERMAN)

Abbitte, 38
Abendphantasie, 90
Abschied, Der, 152
Adler, Der, 540
Advocatus Diaboli, 22
Am Quell der Donau, 384
An die Deutschen, 58, 122
An die Hofnung, 194
An die jungen Dichter, 56
An die Madonna, 518
An Diotima, 24
An eine Fürstin von Dessau, 104
An die Parzen, 32
An ihren Genius, 36
An unsre grossen Dichter, 68
An Zimmern, 582, 588
Andenken, 488
Angenehme dieser Welt . . ., Das,
    586
Archipelagus, Der, 212
Auf den Tod eines Kindes, 584
Auf falbem Laube . . ., 514

beschreibende Pöesie, Die, 22
blinde Sänger, Der, 184
Blödigkeit, 204
Brod und Wein, 242
Buonaparte, 28

Chiron, 188

Da ich ein Knabe war . . ., 80
Der Mutter Erde, 378
Der Prinzessin Auguste von Hom-
    burg, 108
Des Morgens, 92
Dem Sonnengott, 62
Deutscher Gesang, 504
Dichterberuf, 172
Dichtermuth, 200
Diotima, 26, 34, 156

Ehmals und Jezt, 40

Einst hab ich die Muse gefragt . . .,
    536
Einzige, Der (erste Fassung), 446;
    (zweite Fassung), 454
Empedokles, 30
Ermunterung, 160

Falsche Popularität, 22
Frieden, Der, 116
Friedensfeier, 432
Frühling, Der, 598

Ganymed, 208
gefesselte Strom, Der, 206
Geh unter, schöne Sonne . . ., 114
Germanien, 400
Götter, Die, 136
Griechenland (erste Fassung), 560;
    (zweite Fassung), 564; (dritte
    Fassung), 566
gute Glaube, Der, 50
Guter Rath, 22

Hälfte des Lebens, 370
Heidelberg, 132
Heimath, 510
Heimath, Die, 48, 142
Heimkunft, 254
Herbst, Der, 594
Hört' ich die Warnenden izt . . ., 84
Hyperions Schiksaalslied, 78

Ihre Genesung, 52, 150
In lieblicher Bläue . . ., 600
Ister, Der, 492

Kürze, Die, 44

Launischen, Die, 86
Lebensalter, 368
Lebenslauf, 42, 148
Liebe, Die, 144

Main, Der, 94
Mein Eigentum, 98
Menons Klagen um Diotima, 232
Mensch, Der, 74
Menschenbeifall, 46
Mnemosyne, 498

nächste Beste, Das, 544
Natur und Kunst oder Saturn und Jupiter, 164
Nekar, Der, 138

Palinodie, 102
Patmos, 462; (Bruchstücke der späteren Fassung), 478
Πρὸς Εαυτον, 70

Rhein, Der, 408
Rousseau, 128
Ruhm, Der, 590
Rükkehr in die Heimath, 158
scheinheiligen Dichter, Die, 60
Scherzhaften, Die, 70
Sokrates und Alcibiades, 66
Sommer, Der, 592
Sonnenuntergang, 64
Sophokles, 70
Spaziergang, Der, 576
Stimme des Volks, 178

Thränen, 192

Titanen, Die, 530
Tod des Empedokles, Der (zweite Fassung), 264; (dritte Fassung), 322
Und mitzufühlen das Leben . . ., 550
Unter den Alpen gesungen, 168
Unverzeihliche, Das, 54

Vanini, 72
Vatikan, Der, 556
Versöhnender der du nimmer geglaubt . . ., 422
Vom Abgrund nemlich . . ., 552
Vortreflichen, Die, 22
Vulkan, 196

Wanderung, Die, 392
Was ist der Menschen Leben . . ., 516
Wenn aus dem Himmel . . ., 578
Wenn aus der Ferne . . ., 572
Wenn nemlich der Rebe Saft . . ., 512
Wie Vögel langsam ziehn . . ., 508
Wie wenn am Feiertage . . ., 372
Winter, Der, 596
Wohl geh' ich täglich . . ., 112
Wurzel alles Übels, 70

Zeitgeist, Der, 88
zürnende Dichter, Der, 70